GETTING
AWAY WITH
MURDER:
The Canadian
Criminal Justice
System

GETTING
AWAY WITH
MURDER:
The Canadian
Criminal Justice
System

David M. Paciocco

Getting Away with Murder: The Canadian Criminal Justice System
© Publications for Professionals, 1999

Published in 1999 by
Irwin Law
325 Humber College Blvd.
Toronto, ON
M9W 7C3

ISBN: 1-55221-032-4

Canadian Cataloguing in Publication Data available
from the National Library of Canada.

Printed and bound in Canada

1 2 3 4   01 00 99 98

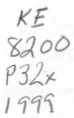

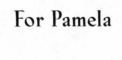

For Pamela

Contents

Preface

Many Canadians are losing faith in the criminal justice system. They believe that courts are letting too many people go and are being too soft on those who are punished. It is not too strong to suggest that some of these people are disgusted with what they see. This declining confidence in the Canadian criminal justice system is worrisome because the stock in trade of any criminal justice system is public confidence. Without it, the system is disabled. It loses the ability to give comfort to victims and to the public, and to maintain the respect for the law that is essential to the well-being of society. Public morale is damaged. People become dispirited, some even afraid. When the public demands that the system be made tougher, politicians respond, all too often making changes that undermine those basic principles that hold the system together. Declining confidence in a criminal justice system is dangerous for it can destroy it.

For this reason, when my friend and colleague William (Bill) Kaplan, who is affiliated with Irwin Law, approached me to write a book for the Canadian public on the Canadian criminal justice system, I was quick to accept. I saw it as an opportunity to help restore credibility to the criminal justice system by trying to persuade those who administer the system of justice to change things that anger the public but which are not indispensable to criminal justice, and by explaining to those who are not in the system why people get away with murder and other crimes. No matter what changes get made to the system, there will always be technicalities, and occasionally criminals will find shelter in them. If the Canadian public truly understands why this is so, I believe they may come, albeit grudgingly, to accept it.

Although I did not have the imagination to initiate this project, I managed, in short order, to convince myself that I was well situated to undertake it, primarily because my colleagues at the Ontario Crown Attorney's office, where I had the privilege to work as a prosecutor, believe that I am too liberal, while my colleagues in the defence bar, where I now toil part-time, maintain that I am too conservative. At the time I was approached to write this book, I interpreted this to mean that I had attained a fine balance that would permit me to undertake a credible examination of the system. I continued in this belief until my wife pointed out, in her characteristically gentle fashion, that it might signify nothing more than that no one agrees with me.

Because of this, I lodge no claim that my "balance" will make this book worthwhile. What I do rely on to give value to this project, however, is my love of the law. For me, the law is a vocation, a hobby, even a passion. I love the look and texture of law books, the older the better. I love walking through the courthouse. I love watching others perform the craft, and I love performing it myself. I love netting arguments together and marshalling evidence and digging for precedents. As sycophantic as it sounds, I even enjoy bowing for judges. And I love sharing the majesty of the law, particularly with my students. But mostly, I love what law is. A society crafts laws, especially laws about crime, to protect its most basic and essential norms and values. It is the primary tool a society uses in its quest for self-improvement. If you want to find the soul of a culture, look at its laws. If you want to find its history, look at its laws. If you want to find its future, look at its laws. Our laws tell us who we were, who we are, and what we are likely to become. Our law is the collected wisdom of generations of people, working in pursuit of justice, fairness, and equality, working to find a way to protect the inherent dignity of human beings.

To be sure, the law not only carries the wisdom of the past but also bears the stains of the prejudices, biases, and excesses of each generation and of the privilege of its judges and lawyers. For that reason, we can never rest content with how the law is, but, with appropriate respect and humility, must always work to improve it. Still, there is no denying it. The study of law is inspiring because it reveals the story of a quest for a better world, for a just society. Contrary to popular belief, it is not the product of old white men who are out of touch with reality. It is the legacy of the efforts of decent people who lived and worked and played in the very societies they tried to improve. I do not believe that it is possible to examine the origins and the current complexion of our criminal justice system without developing a sense of awe at the quality of our humanity as a people and a respect for our institutions. If my love of the law, its traditions, and its commitment to human decency has found its way, even in small measure, onto these pages, I believe this book will help to ameliorate some of the loss of faith we Canadians now have in our criminal justice system.

A great deal of pain is relived in this book. When criminal tragedy touches people, it robs them of their dignity. Because our system of justice must be a public one, it also robs them of their privacy. I bring much of that tragedy out of the law books and newspapers and into this volume, but I have taken no pleasure in doing so. I have done it because I believe it to be necessary. The story of our criminal justice system is far too real to be told in the abstract. It has to have context, and it must be personified to have meaning. Those of us who tamper with the law have to know that it affects real people, and I am confident that the only way to bring its implications to life is to use real people as the backdrop.

The stories I tell are based on reported case law, primarily appellate level cases, and on newspaper or magazine articles. In some cases I have developed dialogue, moods, and settings in an effort to bring the stories to life, but I have tried to remain true to what happened, based on the findings of courts and the evidence that has been presented. I know that some of this information will be inaccurate. Like all historians, those who make factual findings in courts of law can base their conclusions solely on the trace evidence and testimony they are brought. I have undoubtedly repeated those errors that courts have made in getting it right, and hope I have not injected any of my own.

I owe a debt of gratitude to many people. I am most indebted to Bill Kaplan for inspiring me to write this book and for providing valuable comments and criticisms. David Borges, who has been my research assistant for the past year, has been a dedicated and valuable colleague, and Tracy Ross helped out with some of the early research. Elaine Deluzio read much of the book and, because she is my cousin, told me it was good. My friend John Green read parts of it and suggested it needed pictures. It is to him that I therefore dedicate the feet on the cover of the book. Judge Lynn Ratushny was kind enough to review parts of the work, as was Professor Patrick Healy of the Faculty of Law at McGill University. None of these people agree with all I have to say, and they bear absolutely no responsibility for any errors or indiscretions the book may contain.

A number of lawyers provided me with information, including Lawrence Greenspon, Professor Allan Young of Osgoode Hall Law School, Gary Chayko, George Dzioba, Joel Pink, Colin Sweeney, William Ehrcke, Bart Rosborough, Clayton Ruby, Jeffrey Green, Mona Duckett, Sheldon Goldberg, Timothy Breen, and Gary Trotter. I am certain there are others I have missed, and I want to thank them all. I would also like to thank Carol Sparling, regional manager of the National Parole Board, for her courteous and prompt responses to my requests for information.

I would like to thank my associate, Michael Edelson, for agreeing to work with a defence lawyer who sometimes thinks like a crown attorney, and for supporting this project. I am grateful, also, to the Common Law Section of the Faculty of Law at the University of Ottawa for supporting both my research and my professional development, and to the Law Foundation of Ontario and QL Systems Limited for their generous support of legal research.

My publisher and I owe a debt of gratitude to my friend Vern Krishna, who suggested the title for this book. Although copies may still end up unsold in the bargain bins of department stores, they would most certainly have done so if I had gotten away with calling it "The Incredible Cost of Liberty." I would like to thank Jeffrey Miller of Irwin Law for his encouragement and support, and Rosemary Shipton and Maraya Raduha for their marvellous editorial work.

Of course, I owe more than gratitude to Pamela, Palma, Tony, and Nina for giving light to my life. As always, throughout this project they were a source of inspiration and comfort. Finally, I would like to thank Rocky and Whiskers for not chewing the manuscript.

FAITH AND
JUSTICE

CHAPTER 1

The Credibility Crisis

I knew it was coming. I had prepared the family for it and steeled myself for the moment. Still, those two words, "Not guilty," had more the impact of a rude assault than a reasoned verdict. For me, it was an assault only on my sensibilities; its sole physical trace was that dryness you get in your mouth that makes you think you might become ill. For the mother and sister of the dead man it was far worse. The verdict struck like the rude stomp of a boot-heel. It had as great an impact as the photos of his body, lying sprawled and lifeless on a cold floor. Those two words, transient sounds uttered with calm inflection by a kindly judge, forced air from their lungs as if they had been kicked in the gut. Along with their breath, any faith they may have had in the criminal justice system was driven from them as well. Slowly, they gathered themselves up. With dignity they dried the corners of their eyes and steadied each other as they made their way to the oak doors. They thanked me politely and shook hands with the investigators. It was the kind of salutation that occurs at the door of a funeral home, sincere but somehow detached, warm but somehow despairing, no one really knowing what to say. I could see in their faces that these women had accepted the inevitability of the result, but not the result itself. Theirs was the resigned and dispirited acceptance of people who had given up on the justice system. "Justice will have to be done by God," one of them said.

These words displayed an enviable faith, but the woman who spoke them was only partially right. If there is a God who extracts retribution, she was right that punishment would have to be done by God. But as for "justice," it was done that day — much as it pains me to say so. The evidence was simply not there to prove that the accused was guilty. The case I prosecuted had disintegrated. It would have been unjust for the judge to have convicted the accused on the evidence I managed to present. In part the proof was lost because of technicalities, but for the most part it was because the witnesses were afraid and would not tell the judge in front of the accused what they had told us in the safety of the police station and the prosecutor's office. That day I hated "justice," not because it had produced a wrong result, but because, given the evidence at trial, justice meant it was right for the judge to be wrong about what had happened.

◆   ◆   ◆

In Canada, people are getting away with murder. They are getting away, as well, with countless other atrocities. Every day in the courtrooms of this country, decent people, victims of crimes of brutality and wanton destruction, have to endure the spectacle of their tormentors swaggering out of court, acquitted of crimes they committed. Canadians thumb newspapers with disgust, reading yet again about another charge thrown out, or another sentence that does not reflect the suffering that the self-indulgent or pointless acts of the offender have caused. Public opinion polls and surveys confirm what anyone who lives in this society can sense and feel, simply by reading editorials, watching news magazines, listening to open-line talk shows, or bringing the criminal justice system up in casual conversation. Many Canadians believe that the criminal justice system is failing. They want it to make their homes safer, but that is not happening. They want it to protect them from the injuries, the brutality, and the sordid indignities that humans can inexplicably inflict on one another, but that is not happening. We are not being protected from crime. The criminal justice system is, in the eyes of many, a system in crisis.[1]

To be sure, the criminal justice system is far from perfect. Another crime victim, Ellen Green, the sister of euthanasia activist Bruce Hutchinson, who was found shot in the head in an easy chair in his own apartment, said when expressing her disbelief that the man she believed had murdered her brother was being set free: "I have to fall back on God . . . Human justice is flawed. Divine justice is not."[2] Without question, Green is right. Human justice is flawed. It does not mean, however, that the Canadian criminal justice system is failing. Even with all of its short-comings, we have one of the best criminal justice systems in the world. This is not just some platitudinous endorsement from an insider. It is a fact. There is no criminal justice crisis. What there is, however, is almost as serious. There is a crisis of confidence in the criminal justice system.

Those of us who administer criminal justice cannot ignore the pervasive lack of faith in the system. If the Canadian public, the proprietors of the criminal justice system, do not have confidence in it, the system cannot function properly. People will not come to it when they are injured, and crimes will continue to go unreported. If Canadians do not have faith in the system, it becomes ineffective at performing one of its main functions — to reflect and advance basic societal values and standards of behaviour. Indeed, if Canadians distrust their system, it fails in its primary mission, which is to give Canadians generally, and victims in particular, confidence that those who contravene society's most basic rules are being held accountable by society, whenever possible. Without that confidence, the public becomes dispirited. The very impression Canadians have of the quality of the society they live in is damaged, and this, in turn, damages the quality of their lives. It causes them to be angry, cynical, jaded, and needlessly afraid. A criminal justice system that has lost public confidence is a lost system.

A parallel problem that emerges when the public loses confidence in the criminal justice system is that people clamour for change. Politicians, anxious to cash in on the political dividends of being hard on crime, capitalize on this demand, as do the purveyors of sexual politics and victims rights advocates. Law reform comes to be inspired by "moral panic"[3] and political expedience, regardless of the damage it can do to the fragile structure of the criminal justice system and the cruelty it can produce. A system of criminal justice, without credibility, can destroy itself in a desperate grasp for acceptance. In the process, it can needlessly destroy, or disproportionately damage, the lives of those who come into contact with it.

Those of us who administer the criminal justice system have the responsibility to ask why this has happened. How is it that the Canadian public has such little faith in the administration of criminal justice? The short, glib answer is that it is run by lawyers, but that is, at best, only partly right. As with all social phenomena, there are many reasons — some that those of us within the system can control, and others that we cannot.

The most popular targets are the news media, which have earned the right to share some of the blame. Perhaps because of our feeling of vulnerability, or perhaps because of some deep, ugly fascination with the worst that humanity can offer, crime sells. It sells when it is fictional, and it sells, perhaps even better, when it is real. Crime sells newspapers, it sells news magazines, and it sells advertising. What kind of stories sell? Not the run-of-the-mill guilty pleas that form the staple in our criminal courts, but the sensational stories, the most shocking crimes. And they sell best when the system fails, or when the sentence seems inexplicably low. Looking in on the system of criminal justice from the outside, using the window of the popular press and the media, one cannot help but gain the impression that the system is failing and that we are not safe even in our own beds.

To be fair, there are many responsible journalists and many civic-minded newspapers. At least indirectly, they endorse the importance of the presumption of innocence. Many dutifully reported the proceedings of the

Guy Paul Morin inquiry so that Canadians, if they were interested, could share in the unspeakable tragedy of a young man who will forever be associated with an act of savagery against an innocent child, and who was punished and vilified despite having done nothing. The papers report dry statistics that show that the crime rates are actually falling rather than rising, and they try to explain why this decline is happening. But these kinds of stories fail to catch the imagination the way that travesties of justice involving the wrongful acquittal of the guilty do, or the way that horrendous crimes that the system has not prevented do. Why? Perhaps because none of us imagine we will ever be in Morin's place, and all of us fear being struck from behind when alone in the dark, or seeing the shadow of an intruder at the foot of our bed. On a daily basis we hear more about the failure of the system to protect the public than about its successes; those failures gain larger print, and they leave a greater impression.

What can be done about this imbalance? Probably little. It is as realistic to ask the media to write more about the successes of the system and less about its failures as it is to expect them to report more about those riverbanks that hold back the water and less about those that don't. News is news. It is not the banal and commonplace that gains notice. Given that, I am quite happy that the story "Killer freed on technicality" gains the front page of a paper. If the headline had screamed out in large print "A killer is finally convicted," then we would know we have a crisis. If the system was not working, travesties of justice would not be news. This subtlety is lost in the blood and gore the stories contain, and in the anger the headlines engender.

Those of us within the system who like to blame the media for our poor showing in public opinion polls have to appreciate that the news media are not the agents of the administration of justice. They are not some propaganda machine for those of us who believe in the system. While it is fair to identify "the media" as part of the cause for the problem, providing we apologize to those journalists who are indeed making the effort, it would simply be wrong for us to count on the media to provide the solution.

Although it is a less significant factor, the appearance of a crisis in the Canadian criminal justice system is also enhanced by the poor performance of some police officers. I say this with great reticence, not only because I do not want to be targeted for a lot of traffic tickets but because my experience is that most police officers are honest and committed professionals. But the sad fact is that either police training is woefully inadequate or the aptitude or ethos of a significant minority of police officers prevents them from performing their roles adequately. As a result, cases that should never be lost are lost, and the public is outraged. Anyone who spends time in the criminal courts knows, for example, even if they will not admit it, that the main cause for high acquittal rates in impaired driving cases is poor police performance. But it is not just in alcohol driving cases. Cases are lost sometimes because the officers on the street fail to understand the law, and therefore contravene it. Sometimes it is simply the exercise of bad judgment. At other times the explanation is less flattering. Even in Canada we have police officers who have become "Fuhrmanized." Like Marcia Clark's "star" witness, who did more than anyone or anything else to secure O.J. Simpson's acquittal, there are police officers who, like many members of the public, have lost faith in the system. These officers believe that criminals have too many rights, and that they are being asked to fight crime with one hand tied behind their backs. They are the public servants who hold the heads of the dying victims, who stand in the pools of blood while they collect evidence from the bodies of victims, who transport rape victims to the hospital, and who tell mothers and children that their loved ones have been murdered. They are the first to be shot at or struck. They therefore develop an understandable but uncommonly deep disgust for crime and see themselves as members of a team that is to serve and protect the innocent against the common enemy, the guilty. Some come to believe that the apprehension of a criminal is more important than the rules of law that can impede their investigations, and they forge ahead, too often undermining the very prosecution they are attempting to assist. And when this happens, it is "the system" that takes the credibility hit, not the officers who have violated constitutional rights. It is the fault of courts for being too lenient.

Much of the crisis in confidence rests with the politicians. Politicians who are anxious to cash in on the political dividends of being hard on crime are prepared to capitalize on the public panic. In doing so, they validate or legitimize the public fear and the public perception that justice is not being done. A cycle of fear, affirmation, and more fear is created. To be sure, it must be an incredible temptation to exploit the opportunities that the law and order agenda presents. Crime is an easy political issue. If you have to choose sides, who would not choose law and order over crime, or victims' rights over the rights of criminals? So when there is a judicial decision that sparks public outrage, even if that outrage is caused by a failure to understand completely what has happened, the case is sure to attract a political response. Points are won by feeding the perception that there is a law and order crisis and then offering to solve it, a tactic opposition politicians are particularly adept at. They drive the government into what can be precipitate action, by making it look inert and uncaring. And in those cases where the blame can be deflected from itself to the courts, even the government is happy to participate. It claims the high ground, moderating what are perceived to be the excesses of liberal courts, so the Canadian public can be safe. In this way it undermines the reputation of the judiciary. Worse, it sometimes imperils justice itself, as the repressive legislation that is inspired by political pandering cuts deep into basic principles of criminal law.

It was a sobering spectacle on the eve of the last federal election to watch the main political parties vying for the law and order vote by trying to prove which one would be harder on crime. Even Priscilla de Villiers, president of CAVEAT, one of the leading victims' rights organizations in the country, said, "I am enormously concerned by the continuing use of victims as a football in the political arena." God bless her for having the integrity to say so. For political gain, victims had become the political "flavour of the month."[4] In the process, both victims and the credibility crisis in the criminal justice system were being exploited.

It is perhaps asking too much to count on politicians to help polish the tarnished image of the administration of justice. Many are too busy cultivating their own images as champion crime-fighters to appreciate the damage they are doing. For others, political expedience counsels silence. This means that the job of reclaiming public confidence falls to those of us who are responsible for administering the system on a day-to-day basis and who see it in operation. It falls to lawyers, and, to the extent that their offices allow them to do so, to judges as well. I suppose this is as it should be. Those of us who toil inside of the judicial branch of the system are best situated to do it. As well, as much as I hate to admit it, we are also more responsible for the criminal justice system's credibility crisis than anyone else.

I make this admission with great reticence, not because I do not want to accept my part of the blame, but because I would not want to damage the sterling reputation of my profession. According to the most recent poll on the matter, lawyers were still ahead of the Zambian bot fly in species popularity, and I would not want to be responsible for altering that order. Still, the truth is that the greatest blame rests with those of us who are trained in the law, primarily because, as a profession, we have become smug and complacent about public opinion. It is easy to see how this has happened. One of the characteristic features of the Western legal tradition is that law becomes a specialized body of knowledge that is practised by a learned profession. This is a natural, indeed inevitable, outcome in a society as complex as our own. Given that we are the specialists, it follows that we know more, and given that we know more, it is easy for us to feel that it is our right and responsibility to make the decisions.

The public should expect that, to some degree, we might resent criticism of what we are doing. Why is it, for example, that, apart from when vasectomies are being performed, the public rarely says to a surgeon, "Hey, doc, you should be making that cut a little shorter," whereas it feels quite comfortable saying to lawyers, "You should not have excluded that evidence"? It is natural, I suppose, for we lawyers to say to the public, "Stand back. We are the professionals here." The thing we have to appreciate, though, is that our status as a learned profession does not mean that the law belongs to us. We lawyers have simply been entrusted with it so it can be used for the benefit of society. We therefore have a duty to account to the Canadian public by demonstrating that we are using it well, on society's behalf. We have an obligation to explain in understandable terms why the system is the way it is and why we do what we do. Yet we have not convinced the Canadian public that we know what we are doing, and we have allowed the press to create the impression that we do not.

This is unfortunate. As anyone who knows the slightest thing about relationships of trust appreciates, it is not enough that those holding the power use it in the best interests of those to whom their duty is owed. They must demonstrate that they are discharging that duty by equipping their beneficiaries with the knowledge required to judge their performance. As a profession, we have failed to make this connection. The system we lawyers have built is being judged harshly largely because it is so misunderstood, and we must bear the blame for that.

Our failure to provide the public with the information necessary to judge our performance accurately has done more than contribute to the impression that the criminal justice system is failing, when it is not. It has also undermined in the public opinion much of the value that is being offered. Because public opinion has been cultivated in the absence of sound information, many of the views that are being expressed are both simplistic and ideologically based, with the prevailing ideology being that the system is "in general too easy on offenders."[5] Most members of the public want the system fixed so that accused persons have fewer rights, it is easier to gain convictions, and sentences are longer and more punitive. Their call for harsher and more punitive laws has caused many lawyers and judges to see the public not as the body that they must account to and accommodate, but as the enemy to be guarded against. We legal practitioners often find ourselves having to protect the basic principles of the system from public demands. We even find ourselves using the *Canadian Charter of Rights and Freedoms*, and clever lawyering, to guard the administration of justice against politicians when they are prepared to trade sound policy for popular vote. Like trustees who administer property on behalf of beneficiaries who have not yet come of age, we decide that we know best. We act like benevolent dictators, resolving legal controversies in what we perceive to be society's best interests, notwithstanding the wishes of the public.

To a degree, I will defend this kind of paternalism because it is not just a gratuitous manifestation of the reputation for intolerable arrogance that we in the legal profession seem to be so adept at cultivating. This kind of paternalism is the natural by-product of having a system that is operated by a learned profession. It is driven not by conceit, but by principle and precedent, and by the fact that even an informed public will, from time to time, lose sight of the systemic needs of the administration of justice. When Kenneth Parks was acquitted of killing his mother-in-law because he had been sleepwalking when he stabbed and bludgeoned her and her husband, the Supreme Court of Canada was fully aware of what the public reaction would be. Justice La Forest remarked candidly that this decision might, in the eyes of some, harm the credibility of the criminal justice system. That comment was as insightful as if someone had remarked, on seeing the Titanic, that it was a big boat. But he went on and, quite appropriately, said that these criticisms should be discounted because they would be made by people who reject the underlying values of the system.[6] When Justice Lamer, now the Chief Justice of Canada, was considering when courts should throw out evidence that the police have discovered by violating the constitutional rights of a suspect, he rejected the suggestion that the decision should be based on the views of the majority of Canadians, even though the law he was interpreting told him specifically to reject evidence only where the reputation of the administration of justice would suffer if it was received. "Members of the public generally become conscious of the importance of protecting the rights and freedoms of the accused only when they are in some way brought close to the system either personally or through the experience of friends or family," he said.[7] That being so, courts are the "only effective shelter for individuals and unpopular minorities from the shifting winds of public passion."[8] Speaking specifically of the *Canadian Charter of Rights and Freedoms*, Justice Lamer explained that the "Charter is designed to protect the accused from the majority, so the enforcement of the Charter must not be left to the majority."[9]

In at least one respect, Justice Lamer and Justice La Forest are right. Judges cannot allow public opinion to influence the decisions that are arrived at in individual cases. Even if it was feasible to do so, in a system governed by the "rule of law" it would be wrong for a judge to ask how the public would want a particular case resolved. On the most famous occasion when the crowd was asked to make the decision, it chose Barrabas. No. Asking the public how to respond to particular cases would be no better than opening the jail-house door to the mob who has gathered outside. It is the responsibility of every judge to be like Atticus Finch, who in Harper Lee's classic novel, *To Kill a Mockingbird*, propped a chair up against the jail-house door and stared the mob down, saying, "You are not coming in. This case will be resolved according to law." This restriction is not because the Canadian public is like the great unwashed, too ignorant and savage to be fair, but because of the significant cultural gap that has developed between lawyers and lay people. In a phrase, courts administer justice according to "long-term community values." Members of the public tend to judge the administration of justice according to whether it convicts and punishes adequately those whom they believe to be guilty.

As jurists, we are trained to allow overarching concern for the long-range performance of the administration of justice to interfere, from time to time, with the correct outcome of a particular case. We do this because we know that more injustice would be done by a single-minded campaign to punish the offender in every case than by recognizing that at times the conviction of the guilty comes at too high a social or moral cost. Things are not as simple as they were in the days when the entire community would convene to decide whether Thor should be banished from the fire or have his head crushed with a rock because he had violated some tribal taboo. A criminal trial is no longer just about the guilt or innocence of the offender. The entire administration of justice goes on trial every time a citizen is hauled before a judge and threatened with punishment. Indeed, it has been said that "the quality of a nation's civilization can largely be determined by the methods it uses in the enforcement of its criminal law."[10] The entire nation goes on trial with every suspect. The public interest in a fair trial process requires that, in some cases, competing considerations will outweigh the truth and that some who are guilty will have to go free.

I am confident that members of the public are thoroughly capable of understanding this responsibility. If they do not understand it now, it is because we lawyers and judges, the trustees of the system, have failed to keep the beneficiaries advised, and because we have allowed the system of criminal justice to become obscenely complex. It is a morass of technical laws and sophisticated concepts, born of experience and honed into a body of rules and practices over hundreds of years by lawyers speaking a language only they can understand. Unless explained with care, its mysteries are beyond the reach of most members of the public, and they even tax the skills of earnest law students. We would go a long way towards restoring the credibility of the administration of justice if only we would seek to explain the system to the general public.

Of course, the credibility crisis is not so simple. Although, in my view, misunderstanding is the main problem, it is hardly the whole story. A significant contributing cause is that those of us within the system have been making promises we cannot keep. We have done so by representing to Canadians that we can reduce crime by punishing offenders. The truth is that we can no more reduce most kinds of crime, particularly violent crime, by sentencing offenders than we can turn back the clock to spare a crime victim from the pain and indignity of falling prey to criminal conduct. Yet when we sentence offenders, we speak incessantly about specific and general deterrence. We claim that by punishing them we will teach the criminals before the court and other potential criminals that crime does not pay. And we talk a great deal about rehabilitation and restorative justice. We cling to the naive belief that we can take men and women who are alienated, impoverished, angry, addicted, desperate, unintelligent, disturbed, or conscienceless and turn them into model citizens by scaring them, or by ordering them to take therapies or do community service. No wonder the Canadian people judge the criminal justice system to be failing. We veritably invite Canadians to judge our work by our success in reducing crime, and then we invariably fail to deliver.

The truth is that, for most offences, a criminal trial is nothing more than an elaborate ceremony in which we reaffirm our values as a society, demonstrate our solidarity with the victim, invite closure for the community, and show that we will hold wrongdoers accountable whenever possible. Punishment is an indispensable but often useless component of this ceremony. There is an ugliness about it that inspires denial, but if we were honest we would admit that, in the main, our criminal justice system responds to a primal stirring in the human beast for retribution. It is the archetype of the Judeo-Christian philosophy that gave life to our system. God metes out punishment because it is a deserved reckoning, and we are His hapless imitators. It is only the revisionist rationalizations of more modern and squeamish thinkers that make us equate punishment with improving society. If we want to regain our credibility with the public, those of us within the criminal justice system have to admit this limitation to ourselves and then communicate it to the public. We only harm the credibility of the administration of justice by continuing to claim that it can perform miracles.

Granted, this is an unflattering, some would say shocking, portrayal of what we do. At first blush, standing naked in its retributive pallor, it seems to fit the creed of those who believe that we are being too soft on criminals. But those people will be disappointed if we ever do choose honesty over self-delusion. Exactly the opposite will happen. A public who judges us by our success in reducing crime can continue, in clear conscience, to call for harsher penalties and repressive measures, making the criminal justice system far crueller than it needs to be. In stroking the public conscience by telling the Canadian people that the prosecutorial arm of the administration of justice is a socially constructive institution that will make their homes and their streets safer, we shield them from the hard reality that we are punishing to return pain. If we would only admit that punishment does little more than satiate our felt need for making criminals accountable, we would be far more circumspect and merciful. We would also have a better sense of the true cost to society of acquitting a guilty person. Doing so sometimes does mean that our streets are made less safe, but most often it does not. What we usually lose when this happens is not our security, but rather our ability to bear witness to ceremonial justice. That is by no means a trivial loss, but it does temper the sense of catastrophe that so often follows when it appears that someone has gotten away with it.

Still, even public education and honesty about the limits of the law will not be enough to vault the administration of criminal justice into the top ten favourite public institutions. We will also have to go at least one step further if we want to improve its public profile. Those of us within the system have to be modest enough to appreciate that we may not have things entirely right. We have to accept that it is our responsibility to shape our system so that it reflects long-range public values. While we cannot change the law to respond to public clamour, particularly to resolve specific cases, we have a responsibility to look for patterns of public response and to listen to what the public is saying. At the same time that Justice Lamer cautioned lower courts against allowing the public mood to influence the outcome of decisions, he admonished courts not to "render . . . decision[s] that would be unacceptable to the community, when that community is not being wrought with passion or otherwise under the stress due to current events."[11] What he was seeking to reject, then, was not the values of the community, but uninformed opinion, fed by passion and outrage. We have to take every measure to ensure that the system reflects those long-term community values that are not at fundamental odds with the long-term community interest. While it is probable that the scientific weakness in polling and other social science methods for verifying community opinion will always leave room to debate about what the public really thinks, there is an unquestionable truth about Canadian public opinion and the administration of criminal justice that we can ignore only at our peril. The Canadian people want criminals to be held accountable, whenever possible.

As I will seek to demonstrate in this book, this wish means three things for those of us who administer the system of criminal justice. First, it means we will have to punish those criminals who are convicted. It is not enough to heal them or reconcile with them. We have to punish them in ways that are proportionate to the harm they have done, and we have to stop allowing them out on parole. Second, it means we have to continue what we have only recently started — namely, putting a higher premium on discovering the truth. Our courts have been working to reduce the mindless technicality of law, replacing it, where possible, with rules that better pursue their underlying purpose. We have to continue in this direction and, indeed, go further than we have. Third, we have to be cautious about the criminal conduct we choose to excuse. We have to resist the temptation to define more and more crime as pathological. To do this we have to exercise inordinate caution in letting behavioural scientists into our courts. They know less about human behaviour than some of them claim, and even less about justice. By the same token, we have to be particularly cautious in dealing with excuses that exploit our desire to be culturally sensitive or politically correct.

There is one other matter of great urgency that needs to be addressed: the role of the victim in the criminal justice process. This issue has become a major theme in criminal law reform. Much has been done, and there is room to do more, but this is an exceedingly dangerous issue. The demands of some groups threaten to turn the criminal justice system on its head. It is imperative that those of us who administer the system find ways to include the victim to the greatest extent possible without destroying the foundation of the system or jeopardizing innocence, and by explaining in credible terms why the "victim" cannot gain a full seat at the counsel table. If we do not explain this matter with clarity and persuasiveness, Canadian politicians, in the name of the public, will whittle the statue of Justice into a sharp stick, one chip at a time.

This book is my attempt to make a contribution in the fight against the criminal justice credibility crisis. There is a risk that I will only add to it by criticizing some of the current practices that I think are ill-advised and which undermine the public's faith in the criminal justice system. It is my view, however, that it would be worse to ignore these failings. We can do more for our credibility by being frank and honest. Those discussions will, I trust, not detract from the main mission I have undertaken. I am thoroughly convinced that the broad outlines of our system of criminal justice are sound and that, if they are explained well, the public will agree. I am confident that those members of the public who are interested in understanding why people get away with murder will be able to appreciate why we set the standard of proof so high that we systematically turn people free who are probably guilty. I think that if this reasoning is explained properly, they will come to understand that it would be indecent and dangerous for society to do anything else. I am also certain that interested members of the Canadian public will be able to accept the tragic need to allow some who are no doubt murderers to shelter under the inevitable "technicalities" in the system. If the issue is explained properly, they will come to understand that a system without technicalities, or one that chooses to give the benefit of technicalities only to those it likes, is not a system of justice at all; it is no more than a facade behind which those who might harm and oppress the weak and unpopular can hide. I am also certain that the Canadian public will be able to accept that while we have to take the opportunity to use the system to aid and express solidarity with victims, they cannot be allowed full rights of participation in the criminal process. The risk in trying to do so is that we will punish the innocent to give comfort to those who are mistaken, or who would abuse the system.

It is entirely possible that I have underestimated the degree of sophistication of the Canadian public. It may be that most people already understand these things, but that in their despair over the apparent failings of the system they have allowed them to slip their mind. If this book serves as nothing more than a refresher in the lessons of history or in the agenda of the criminal justice system, it will have been worth the work. If the cultural gap between courts and the public can be closed, either through explanation or reintroduction, and the public chooses to judge the criminal justice system according to the long-range values and interests it pursues, the credibility crisis can end and the system of criminal justice will be able to function as it should. And, in addition, it may also help to move lawyers up a few notches on the favourite species list, perhaps even past the common ground slug.

CRIME AND
PUNISHMENT

CHAPTER 2

In Defence of the Need to Punish

For those who prefer to avoid the stress of big city living, the small northern Ontario community of Webbwood, "Pop. 600, Home of Barbara Hanley, Canada's first female mayor," is a good place to live. Webbwood is far enough west of Sudbury to avoid the poison that spews from its nickel mines smelters. The town comes upon you quickly as you drive down Highway 17. If you are not watching the road signs carefully, you normally find yourself barrelling through at highway speed. The Ontario Provincial Police who are posted nearby usually have little else to do other than back onto a gravel sideroad to wait for speeding vehicles or clean up after car accidents.

Irene and Anthony Goodchild seemed much like any other family in the community, although a little better off than most. They both had jobs. Anthony, like many men in the region, made his living in the mines. Irene worked at the Revenue Canada office in Sudbury, a beneficiary of the commitment of the federal government to keep the community alive with regional government offices when the mining industry began to sag in the early 1980s. Within a year of their marriage in 1982, Irene and Anthony were blessed with a daughter, and then with three more over the next five years. The girls loved to horseback ride and to pick the blueberries that grow as large as grapes in the tangled brush along the highway. Anthony, for his part, took advantage of what the near north has to offer, spending his spare time fishing pickerel or hunting around the many lakes and rivers that dot the region. By northern standards, the Goodchilds seemed to be living the good life.

By 3 June 1994 Irene Goodchild was sitting at her desk behind a blue-cloth divider, wondering how it had happened. How does the death of a marriage come about? She held her hands in front of her mouth like a teepee, with her thumbs resting on her chin, thinking back to the day, a year before, when Anthony found out about her affair. She wondered whether deep inside she wanted him to know. Why else would she have

left the birth control pills in the cupboard? Not much of a clue for a husband with a vasectomy, she chided herself. Would he really kill himself?
she wondered. Would he really kill her if she took the girls? Lord knows
he was more than hinting at it. She thought about how close he was to
the girls, and about how they loved him. She thought about how she had
tried, going with him at his request to marriage counselling sessions even
though she knew it was pointless. She felt it was a bit pathetic that he
kept on going by himself after she quit. That was bad enough, but now
things were getting out of hand. His constant suicide threats were even
more pathetic. He was becoming paranoid. I can't take it, she thought.
The constant spying. Accusing me of passing out lewd photographs of
myself. It's not doing the girls any good. I'm getting out.

"You coming, Irene?" She looked up. It was her boyfriend.

"Yeah, let's go."

Everyone from the office was going to a barbecue. It would do her
good to get away for a while.

As the evening wore on, Irene was enjoying herself. Only the occasional phone call from Anthony was keeping her from forgetting it all. He
was becoming progressively more angry. Too late now, she thought. I may
as well have a good time while I'm here and face the music when I get
home. "If he calls back," she hollered to the hostess, "I'm not talking to him."

Long after midnight Anthony called back again. When Irene refused
to come to the phone, he asked the hostess whether Irene's boyfriend was
there.

"Yes, he is, Anthony."

"Fine. Tell her her bags will be packed when she gets here."

At around 5:00 a.m. Irene drove down the empty highway and
turned her car slowly up the drive, wondering just how ugly it was going
to be when she went inside. As the car lights caught the front lawn, she
could see her clothing strewn on the grass. The door was locked. When
she tried the key, Anthony was on the other side bracing the door shut.

"You're not getting in," he bellowed.

"Let me in or I'm calling the police."

"You're not getting in."

She went next door and rang the door-bell, waking her sister-in-law.
"I need to use the phone," she said. "Anthony won't let me into the house."

She assured the police officer that the children would be in no danger. "Ma'am," he cautioned, "you have a legal right to be in the house, but
it's best if you stay away until he cools off."

Over the protests of her sister-in-law, she went back out. She tried
the door again. "Get lost, Irene," Anthony responded.

Irene left the door and made her way to the side of the house. Sliding the basement window open, she climbed through. The lights were on. A shotgun was lying on the couch. The gun cabinet door hung open. Anthony heard her coming through the window and rushed down the basement stairs. "Put the gun away, Anthony," she said, as she grabbed it and placed it back in the cabinet. "I'm not going to let an asshole kill himself. Come to bed and we'll talk about it in the morning."

She regretted having agreed to let him have his guns back for hunting season. It had obviously been a good idea when his counsellor had persuaded him to remove them from the house.

Anthony slept fitfully, if at all. At 8 o'clock he gathered the girls up. They were upset because they had been awakened by the scene a few hours before and were afraid that their dad would shoot himself. Tears rained down his cheeks as Anthony kissed them and sent them to his sister's, assuring them it would be all right. He phoned his sister to tell her that the girls were coming so he and Irene could talk things over.

The last worldly sensation Irene felt was the blast of a twelve-gauge shotgun, fired from a distance of 2 to 3 feet into her lower neck. She had finally left Anthony, but not in the way she had imagined. Shortly after 11:00 a.m. there were no OPP cars backed onto the gravel roads that meet Highway 17 near Webbwood. They were all parked in the Goodchilds' lane.

◆   ◆   ◆

Anthony Richard Goodchild is now on probation. The custodial period of his sentence, eighteen months in a provincial reformatory, expired on 21 August 1997. He did not even serve the full eighteen months. He was already on parole by 12 October 1996, when the Ontario Court of Appeal upheld his sentence. The public was appalled. The Sudbury open-line talk shows were abuzz with callers, letters to the editor were sent off, and protests were staged. The sentence, for many, brought the administration of justice into disrepute.

It is easy to understand why this sentence was considered to be outrageous. Members of the public would conclude that it was simply too lenient to act as a deterrent to other potential offenders. They would wonder why the cost of killing a human being is less than a year in jail, followed by parole and then probation. What kind of message is that? The public would be disturbed that within a year there was a killer walking in its midst. How does this protect society? Of equal importance, the public would feel that the sentence simply fails to express its outrage at the crime. Symbolically, it devalued the life of Irene Goodchild.

In my view, the criminal justice system is to blame for much of the disquiet that this sentence, and others, have caused. It has brought it on itself, but not because its sentences tend to be too lenient, although some undoubtedly are. The criminal justice system has harmed its own reputation because, for too long, those of us within the system have fed the unrealistic public expectation that we can reduce violent crime by prosecuting and punishing offenders. We cannot. We have not been forthright about this result or about the considerable limits of the law. But we are not alone in our complicity. The press has aided and abetted our failure. Too often it fails to send accurate messages when we sentence in high-profile cases.

The False Promise that Punishment Will Reduce Crime

Eighty-eight percent of those persons surveyed by the Canadian Sentencing Commission in 1987 believed that the purpose of sentencing is to protect the public.[1] No doubt people believe the same thing today. We in the criminal justice system feed that expectation. We claim that ours is a "reductivist" system — in other words, a system designed to reduce the amount of crime. Without distinguishing between the various kinds of offences, we promise to reduce crime by the sentences we impose in a number of ways. Often we purport to rehabilitate offenders so they will lose the urge to engage in criminal conduct. We rely primarily, however, on "deterrence" — the idea that by attaching negative consequences to criminal behaviour, we can make the price of crime too high for the offender and for other like-minded people. We also promise to reduce crime by removing criminals from society by locking them up. The truth is that, for most offences, and for violent offences in particular, we cannot make a serious dent in crime by sentencing offenders, since none of these techniques is effective. The real reason we sentence in many cases comes down to retribution. Often we simply punish for punishment's sake. In the interests of the administration of justice, we had best start admitting it, both to ourselves and to the public.

REHABILITATION

The theory of rehabilitation is that the offender can be taught not to offend, or be offered treatment that will remove or reduce the tendency to do so. The first "penitentiaries" were founded on the theory that they would rehabilitate offenders. In the late eighteenth century, Quakers in Philadelphia decided that criminals should be put in cells with Bibles where they would repent and do penance, emerging as spiritually healed and contributing members of society.[2] Although there is a good deal of controversy about the concept of rehabilitation, we have learned one thing with absolute certainty: locking people up does not rehabilitate them, regardless of the kind of crime they have committed. Incarceration would not rehabilitate criminals even if the Gideons put Bibles in every cell. Government commissioned reports have consistently come to this conclusion.[3] It is widely recognized that "[p]rison can be an expensive way of making bad people worse."[4] As a 1977 report of the Solicitor General of Canada put it: "Growing evidence exists that, as educational centres, our prisons have been most effective in educating less experienced, less hardened offenders to be more difficult and professional criminals."[5]

The reasons are obvious. As the Le Dain Commission observed in 1973, criminalization "results from confining offenders together in a closed society in which a criminal subculture develops."[6] Criminal loyalties and values are nurtured, and extensive underworld contacts are made. If criminals carried business cards, prisons would be the ideal place to hand them out. Moreover, many prisoners brutalize and terrorize one another. The lessons learned in prison are not the ones taught in civics class, regardless of the good intentions of prison chaplains and correctional officials.

The concept of "rehabilitation" was the panacea that was held out by the helping professions during the 1960s. It is a positive, non-cynical idea and, for that reason alone, it is an attractive one. It expresses the archetypal spirit of redemption. It proclaims not only that people can change and be resocialized but that we can develop systems that will help or even make them do so, even after they have grown to become criminals. For a time, this intriguing idea became one of the principal objects of punishment, but, for the most part, it has been a failure. Although many offenders have no doubt benefited by the various programs and sentencing initiatives that have been taken, overwhelmingly the promise of rehabilitation has not been realized, regardless of the offence charged and whether the offender is sentenced to jail or not. By the late 1970s it had become apparent that efforts at rehabilitation, both within and outside the penitentiaries, were largely unsuccessful.[7] Even the defenders of rehabilitation have recognized this outcome. They now argue not that rehabilitation efforts have worked, but that the goal of rehabilitation, because it has never really been given a chance,[8] should not be abandoned.

There is some truth in this claim. Programs for offenders tend to be underfunded, understaffed, and inadequate. It is not uncommon for prosecutors and courts to discover that probation orders have not been carried out because there was no room for an offender in a program. But even if we did dedicate ourselves more completely to the goals of rehabilitation, there is strong reason to believe that many if not most offenders cannot be rehabilitated by court order, whether they are in custody or not. The causes of crime are deep and complex, presenting insurmountable difficulties in addressing them.

Criminologists are far from agreeing on the causes of crime. Most modern criminologists believe, however, that there is some truth in most of the leading theories of crime that have developed over the years. None of these theories, though, allows realistic hope for rehabilitating the criminally oriented through the sentencing process.

Some theories about criminal behaviour are environmental. They assert that crime is caused primarily by the social conditions in which people live. Theories of varying degrees of sophistication have pointed to poverty, economic inequality, education, unemployment, the breakdown of the family, cultural conflict and racism, as well as the general social breakdown that accompanies the modernization of society.[9] There are even environmental patterns with homicide. "Canadians convicted of murder are, for the most part, socially disadvantaged. They approach life with poorly developed social skills, lacking what we might call social intelligence . . . They are typically working class or poorer."[10] The Peter Demeters and Helmut Buxbaums are the exception. But even if the environmental sociologists are right and there is a causal connection between environment and crime, how do you rehabilitate without removing the environmental causes of crime? Do not look to the penal system to remove poverty or economic inequality, to bring families back together, to abolish racism, or even to educate or find work for offenders. Environmental causation undermines the promise of sentence-based rehabilitation. It is naive to believe that post-offence therapy and life-skills training can erase the "deep psychological scars from years of emotional stress or social and physical deprivation."[11] Social re-engineering, to the extent that it can reduce crime, is beyond the competence of the criminal justice system.

According to some theories, there are born criminals. Crime has a biological basis. The more primitive theories, now thoroughly discredited, are intriguing. Franz Gall believed that the size of various portions of the brain was linked to criminal behaviour. He developed an elaborate basis for measuring skull size and shape to identify those with criminal traits.[12] According to Cesare Lombroso's "atavism" theory, some people are atavistic and thereby innately criminal. Atavists can be identified by examining them for "stigmata," including such things as "ears of unusual size," "fleshy, swollen or protruding lips," "receding or protruding chin," anomalies of the hair, and even excessive tattooing.[13] How much faith can you have in a list of symptoms that, tattoos aside, describes some members of the royal family as accurately as it does the inmates in our criminal institutions?

The search for scientific, biological explanations for crime has not ended with such quackery. Heredity has been a prime candidate for theories of criminal behaviour.[14] It suggests itself because criminal conduct frequently runs in families. Adoption and identical twin studies have been conducted to verify the hypothesis by ruling out the influence of the shared family environment as the real cause. A review of the studies that have been done prompted one researcher to conclude cautiously that genetics may play a role.[15]

Chromosome abnormalities, especially the XYY syndrome, have also been studied extensively. Males with an extra Y chromosome are disproportionately represented in criminal institutions, primarily for less serious offences. But these males tend to have lower intellectual abilities, which may provide a more accurate explanation.[16] They tend to be from poorer families, where living conditions might contribute to chromosomal abnormality. In other words, it may not be the chromosomes that are the problem. The propensity to commit petty crime may be caused by the poverty that produces XYY males.[17] The same is true of hyperactivity and other learning disabilities. Research suggests a link between these conditions and crime, but the nature of that link is questionable. Learning disabilities, like lower intelligence, inhibit socioeconomic success, creating environmental conditions that may predispose people to crime.[18] Learning disabilities are often associated with low self-esteem because of failure, which may itself be the real cause of crime among those who are learning disabled.[19] Recently there has been increased interest in the impact of hormones and body chemistry, including testosterone levels, bodily changes brought on by menstruation, and problems with neurotransmitting chemicals like serotonin[20] or with central nervous system functioning.[21] There are also those who put their faith in intelligence tests to predict criminal behaviour.[22]

Assuming there is truth in these theories, or in any one of them, and that we are prepared to be politically incorrect enough to recognize the truth despite the stigmatization that would ensue, what promise does this hold for rehabilitation? Very little, one would expect. The criminal justice system cannot make people smarter, or change their genetic makeup or the shape of their heads.

Finally, there are the psychological and psychiatric theories of crime. The most desperate are the Freudian-based theories, according to which the personality can become warped at crucial stages of development. One of the critical periods is between six and eight months when the "ego" develops. The ego is the rational portion of our personality that orients us towards problem solving and enables us to delay gratification. The "superego," or conscience, develops between the ages of three and five years of age. Then the child goes through the oral, anal, phallic, and genital stages. (I am not certain whether it is a good thing or not, but those of us over twelve are in the genital stage.) Mess with a kid at the wrong developmental stage and a criminal might be born.[23]

There are other personality theories that have been less influential. But criminologists tend not to focus on mental illness or mental disorders as a cause of criminal behaviour because they are factors in only a small percentage of crimes. Most experts believe that psychotics, including schizophrenics, constitute such a small percentage of criminals, even relative to the general population, that there is no meaningful association between psychoses and crime.[24] Mental disorder cannot begin to explain why crime in general, or even violent crime in particular, occurs. It has been estimated that only 5 percent of homicides are committed by persons who are mentally ill.[25]

The one possible exception to the loose link that exists between crime and mental pathology is the psychotic or sociopathic personality. Sociopathy or psychopathy is a personality disorder that has been defined as follows by the World Health Organization:

> Personality disorder characterized by disregard for social obligations, lack of feeling for others, and impetuous violence or callous unconcern. There is a gross disparity between behaviour and the prevailing social norms. Behaviour is not readily modifiable by experience, including punishment. People with this personality are often affectively cold and may be abnormally aggressive or irresponsible. Their tolerance for frustration is low: they blame others or offer plausible rationalizations for their behaviour which brings them into conflict with society.[26]

You can see the problem this definition gives to criminologists. No. The problem is not that this looks like a job description for lawyers. The problem is that the concept of sociopathy or psychopathy is pointless as an explanation for criminal behaviour. The proof that a person is a psychopath or sociopath is found in chronic acts of deviance, especially crime. It therefore becomes no more than "a pejorative label hung upon lawbreakers because of their non-conformist behaviour, rather than a diagnosis of clear-cut psychological impairment."[27]

Even if mental illness or personality explains criminal behaviour, how do you rehabilitate? Do you drug or brainwash? C.S. Lewis described as "official straighteners" those who would try to assault the personality and integrity of their "patients" without gain.[28] If crime is linked to personality disorders, or to mental illness, rehabilitation has a tough row to hoe.

Whatever the underlying causes of criminal predisposition might be, the fact is that most crime is situational. This is particularly so with homicide. In 1988 Neil Boyd undertook a study which showed that 80 percent of homicides in Canada involved family or acquaintances[29] and were crimes of passion in which alcohol, sexual betrayal, separation, and divorce played the predominant role.[30] A high percentage of the killings were committed by men between the ages of sixteen and forty. (Boyd put the figure at 90 percent; according to Statistics Canada, between 1985 and 1995 males of all ages accounted for 87 percent of killings.)[31] Bearing this pattern in mind, Boyd noted that there was a dramatic increase in homicide rates between 1966 and 1975, after which rates stabilized. During that period the homicide rate increased from around 1.2 killings per 100,000 to about 3 per 100,000,[32] and then declined to approximately 2.5 per 100,000, or approximately 650 homicides per year.[33] (That pattern held until 1993, when it dropped dramatically to around 2 per 100,000.)[34] Boyd sought to explain the increase that had occurred between 1965 and 1975. He observed a number of social changes that might have had a bearing, including exploding divorce rates after the liberalization of the divorce laws, a 50 percent increase in alcohol consumption, and the expansion and distribution of illegal drugs. Perhaps most significant was the demographic change during that period. Baby-boomers, the population bulge that occurred between 1946 and 1955, were reaching the crime-prone years in 1966. We did not have more poverty in the 1960s and early 1970s; we did not have less education; nor do I suspect that we had more people with lower intelligence, misshapen heads, bigger ears, or a greater number of people with ego and superego damage. What we had was a greater proportion of younger men in situations where anger, hatred, quarrel, and revenge occur than we had in the past.

To the extent that crime is situational and demographic, what, if anything, does this tell us about the use of sentencing to reduce crime in general, and crimes of violence in particular? To answer those questions, it is important to distinguish between rehabilitation and "offender control." Whereas rehabilitation involves changing the predisposition of the offender to commit crimes, offender control has no such pretensions. It simply seeks to reduce the opportunity for a potential criminal to offend. For example, assume that a young man has been convicted of assaulting and threatening his partner while intoxicated, and that the two are no longer together. Even if he is incarcerated for a short time, he will be placed on probation as well. Some of the terms would be meant to rehabilitate him. He might be made, for example, to attend alcohol counselling and to participate in anger management sessions. If he is rudderless, he might even be ordered to seek and maintain employment. Other terms, however, would be aimed more at preventing him from doing further harm, given his demonstrated ability to do so. He would be prohibited from communicating or contacting the victim, he would be told not to possess any weapons, and he would be ordered to abstain from alcohol. To the extent that he was following these control orders, they would reduce the risk of his further offending. It would not be, however, because we have successfully changed the spirit of the man. It would be because we have, for a time, removed the irritants most likely to lead him into trouble, given who he is. For this reason, probation orders and other community-based sentences are not pointless, even if they do not succeed in rehabilitating offenders. If a court order had deprived Anthony Goodchild of his guns, Irene might still be alive today. But let us not be fooled. The extent to which the imposition of terms and conditions on offenders can reduce the incidence of crimes, particularly crimes of violence, is marginal. It works only in those cases where we can accurately identify potential offenders before they have done serious damage, and only where the offender is prepared to follow the order. If the offender is not, there is little that can be done. Restraining orders are impressive-looking documents, but they do not stop bullets. The sad truth is, we are not very good at remaking people by court order. Those who change do so because they are highly motivated to, not because we have ordered them to shape up. All we can really do is provide those who have the desire and ability to change with the facilities to do so. For this reason, we cannot expect significant gains in reducing crime, particularly violent crime, by rehabilitation through sentencing, no matter how many rehabilitative programs we have or how much money we throw at them.

DETERRENCE

The theory of deterrence has two components. The first, known as "specific" or "individual" deterrence, is that punishment will discourage the offender from committing further offences in the future. The second, known as "general deterrence," is that punishing offenders will discourage other like-minded people from committing offences.

Based on its 1987 study, *Sentencing Reform*, the Canadian Sentencing Commission gave up on specific deterrence. It acknowledged that the claim that punishment is effective in reducing the tendency to reoffend is undermined by rates of recidivism (or repeat offending), the apparent "undeterrability" of certain groups of offenders, and the "acknowledged fact" that most prison inmates have been convicted on prior occasions.[35] Anyone who has the time should sit in provincial court and watch offenders being sentenced. As a prosecutor, I became so accustomed to finding a copy of the criminal record in the file that if there wasn't one, I would look around the floor to see if I had dropped it.

In spite of our failure to intimidate offenders from reoffending by punishing them, we continue to rely on specific deterrence as a justification for punishment. If we are going to send a first offender to jail, our preference is to give a "short, sharp" sentence that will "send a message" to him or her. This practice shares a philosophical kinship with giving a child a sharp smack to the back of the head, and is probably about as effective. It is, however, a lot more expensive.

General deterrence, the theory that punishing offenders will intimidate others into being law-abiding, is even more central to our theories of punishment. For the most hated crimes, those involving sexual assault, violence causing bodily harm, robbery, and drugs, the primary sentencing principle is general deterrence. Trial judges are overruled by appeal courts when they fail to give general deterrence sufficient weight in sentencing offenders. Yet, paradoxically, most of the crimes for which we emphasize this sentencing principle are the kinds of offences that are most resistant to general deterrence.

The official position appears to be that we must accept the general deterrence theory as a matter of faith, but that we cannot put too much faith in it. The Canadian Sentencing Commission asked Professor Cousineau of Simon Fraser University to review the latest literature. He concluded that "there is little or no evidence to sustain an empirically justified belief in the deterrent effect of legal sanctions."[36] In spite of this report, the commission could not bring itself to reject the intuitively appealing notion that if people know there is a heavy cost associated with their conduct, they may, as rational people, opt not to engage in that behaviour.[37] But even the Sentencing Commission was guarded in its assessment. It cautioned that there is no reason to believe that legal sanctions can be used to deter specific crimes, or to believe that making an example out of a particular offender will have any effect on other potential offenders. It therefore concluded its discussion of general deterrence by saying that "deterrence is a general and limited consequence of sentencing."[38]

A moment's reflection will demonstrate why general deterrence is so ineffective. Deterrence is based on theories of rational decision making. It presupposes that actors weigh to a nicety the pros and cons of their acts before acting. The most dangerous criminals do not fit that model. They are not people renowned for their good judgment and considered action. At the same time, the most horrendous crimes do not lend themselves to this kind of judgment. Sexual offenders give in to vile urges. Assailants strike out in anger. Homicide, in particular, is primarily a crime of passion. It is only rarely a contract hit or a neatly planned exercise. It is more often the worst result of the free reign of jealousy, rage, vindictiveness, hatred, and anger, the most powerful of human emotions. Even when not spontaneous, it is still most commonly done in the throes of extreme emotion. In 1995, by no means an exceptional year, 9 percent of killers committed suicide, almost invariably immediately after they had killed.[39] If these people are not afraid to inflict mortal violence on themselves as the price for their crime, what makes us think we can deter them by threatening a cell with a television?

Some Canadians believe that the television in the cell is part of the reason that general deterrence does not work; we are not hard enough on criminals. If we ratcheted up the sentences, they believe, and began to treat criminals as criminals, we might just reduce crime. In fact, there is "a great deal of empirical research in the United States and elsewhere [that] has shown that crime rates are not greatly affected by changes to the severity of penalties imposed."[40] The Canadian Sentencing Commission came to the same conclusion.[41] This result has been effectively demonstrated in Canada with respect to the offence of murder. Murder rates did not rise with the abolition of capital punishment in 1976. They went down and stayed down. One of the great American ironies is that those states with the highest murder rates are the same ones that invoke the death penalty most frequently.

The Ontario Court of Appeal was recently asked to increase the typical sentencing range for men who attempt to murder their female partners. Sentences for that offence range around ten years. The Court was right to reject the submission that imposing higher sentences would discourage men from trying.[42] By definition, these men are attempting to succeed in killing their spouses. If they succeeded, they would get life imprisonment, subject to lengthy parole ineligibility. How can anyone think that a man who knows he might get life if he succeeds is going to sit down and say, "OK. If I fail they are going to give me twelve years instead of ten, so I had better not do it." This is simply silly. Even at twenty or thirty or even forty years, there would be no difference. The violent among us are destructive actors, not constructive thinkers.

Cesare Beccaria, sometimes called the father of criminology, was a proponent of general deterrence. He nonetheless sensed that employing brutal punishments would do nothing to reduce crime rates: "The countries and times most notorious for severity of penalties have always been those in which the bloodiest and most inhumane deeds were committed, for the same spirit of ferocity that guided the hand of the legislators also ruled that of the parricide and assassin."[43] Savage punishments reinforce savage attitudes in some people. For the just, savage punishments defeat themselves. They can cause a humane public to rebel against the values demonstrated by the administration of justice, thereby undermining the educational effect of criminal prosecutions. Experience has shown that they can even cause courts to rebel by finding technical ways to prevent imposing the punishment.[44] When felons were executed for minor felonies in England, judges became creative in finding ways not to convict.

Even if the theory of general deterrence is sound, its promise is easily defeated in practice. It is universally accepted that to be effective systematically, general deterrence depends more than anything else on the certainty of punishment. That is why high-profile RIDE programs and high police presence in crime areas can help produce a reduction in crime rates, but an abstract fear of being caught is tremendously less effective. Some commentators have added that the punishment must also be swift for general deterrence to work. For reasons we can do nothing about, punishment in our system is neither certain nor swift. In terms of the certainty of punishment, with the exception of homicide, where detection and conviction rates are high, only a very small percentage of offenders are even sentenced. This is partially because of the chronic underreporting of most offences, and partially because some crimes are simply not solved by the police. There are also incredibly high attrition rates for most offences. Complaints tend not to get to trial, either because there is insufficient evidence, the complainants recant, witnesses disappear, the accused disappears, the matter is judged not serious enough to proceed, or the case otherwise falls through the cracks. Some cases end up in acquittals. A leading English academic, Andrew Ashworth, estimates that, in Britian, only 3 percent of actual offences end up at the sentencing stage.[45] The John Howard Society of Alberta estimated that the clearance rate by conviction in Canada in 1987 was unlikely to exceed 20 percent.[46] Even if both these figures are gross underestimates, they demonstrate poignantly that we will never attain certainty of punishment, no matter how much money we throw at the system or how much we tinker with its rules.

All indications are that general deterrence, in the form of creating conditions through the punishment of offenders that will make others decide not to offend, is woefully ineffective for most crimes. It is particularly so for crimes of violence. If the marginal return of general deterrence was the only gain to be made by incarcerating violent offenders, it would not make economic sense to do so. Our continued reliance on it as a reason for the punitive sentencing of such people is therefore misleading and distorting. It creates a public expectation that cannot be satisfied.

INCAPACITATION

The theory of "incapacitation" is simple. Kill the criminals, send them to Australia or Devil's Island, or put them in the dungeons. Put them where they cannot hurt anyone.

Unfortunately, achieving effective incapacitation is more difficult than it sounds. First of all, let us be honest. Incarcerating violent offenders does not put them where they cannot prey on anyone anymore. It puts them where they cannot prey on those of us on the outside. They are still able to beat, rape, and abuse one another. Some may say, better them than us. But let us not think we are preventing dangerous people from being dangerous. We are only altering the cast of potential victims.

Now that we have cried that tear, we can return to the basic question. How effective and how feasible is incapacitation in protecting the rest of us? Speaking generally, the reduction in crime that can be achieved by incapacitation is probably not as great as we would hope. Look at the United States. It has a staggering rate of incarceration, yet it still has crime rates, particularly violent crime rates, that astound Canadians. The Americans have over a million people living in jail,[47] yet increases in incarceration rates have not led to a decrease in the amount of crime.[48] As Julian Roberts wrote in a report for the Canadian Sentencing Commission: "Recent research has demonstrated the futility rather than the utility of incapacitative sentences."[49]

Why is this so? Advocates of incapacitation argue that it is because Americans are still not jailing people for enough time. In fact, research based on patterns of reoffending tends to contradict this conclusion. It suggests that the gains to be made by increasing sentences would, in fact, be minimal. Although I am always reluctant to accept such statistics at face value, an American study estimated that establishing a three-year minimum term for offenders would decrease the overall crime rate by only 2.1 percent. Increasing it to a five-year minimum would decrease it by less than 5 percent.[50] Whether these "guesstimates" produce accurate information or not, they give reason to believe that the general gains in crime rate reduction through incapacitation will be less than dramatic.

At the same time, incapacitation by incarceration is prohibitively expensive. In 1995–96 the cost of keeping an inmate in federal custody in Canada for a single day was $126.71,[51] about the same as it costs the rest of us to stay in a fine hotel. In that year, Statistics Canada estimated that each inmate costs the taxpayer an average of $42,300 per year.[52]

Because of the modest gains to be made in crime reduction through general increases in sentencing tariffs, and the expense of doing it across the board, the practice of what is known as "selective incapacitation" is gaining support. Where it is practised, efforts are made to identify kinds of crime that tend to involve repeat offending by the same offenders, and to focus investigation and prosecution on known or suspected recidivists. It is a strategy that many police forces are now using with break and enter offences. Ottawa police credit a 15 percent reduction in property crime to their practice of targeting multiple-case offenders for investigation and prosecution, although increased and active police presence in high crime areas has no doubt contributed.[53]

Unfortunately, selective incapacitation simply does not work as well for other kinds of offences. For market-based offences like drug trafficking, pimping, book-making, and obscenity, for example, incarcerating offenders tends to open up the market for others. But what about homicide? Can we make society safer by increasing the period of incarceration for convicted killers? All indications are to the contrary. Although it does happen, murderers tend not to kill again.[54] Indeed, murderers who have been paroled are much less likely to have their parole revoked than other released offenders because they are significantly less likely to get into trouble.[55] Again, this result stems from the nature of the crime of homicide. It is most often a crime of passion, occurring under particular pressures and in a unique context that is unlikely to recur.[56] Of course, there are the Paul Bernardos and the Clifford Olsons. There is no doubt that incarcerating serial killers, serial rapists, and the like reduces the number of victims. But these kinds of offenders tend to be the exception rather than the rule, so, even by using incapacitative sentences on these people (as we do), we manage only an imperceptible dent in crime rates.

There are two ways in which we use incapacitative sentences in homicide cases. The first is the minimum sentence of life imprisonment for murder, coupled with long periods of parole ineligibility, which applies to all murderers. To the extent that this incarceration is done to protect the public, it is a blunt and inefficient way, since few convicted killers go on to kill again. The alternative technique is the more rational one. It involves attempting to identify specific individuals who are dangerous through dangerous offender applications.

A dangerous offender application involves a hearing, held before the judge who is sentencing the accused on a serious personal injury offence. If the judge finds that the offender is a threat to the life, safety, or physical or mental well-being of other persons, he can be declared a dangerous offender. Whether he is a dangerous offender will be determined based on a history of repetitive behaviour, or of non-repeated behaviour that is of such a brutal nature that it is clear that the offender is unlikely to be inhibited by normal standards of human conduct. Once declared a dangerous offender, he will be sentenced to indefinite incarceration. There will be periodic reviews, but he will not gain his release again unless he can demonstrate that he is no longer a danger to the community.

It is obvious that the law requires a mechanism like this, but it is an option that has a definite downside. While some cases are obvious, we are not very good at predicting who is likely to reoffend. As the Canadian Sentencing Commission put it, "the problem with predicting future delinquent behaviour and thus of identifying the most dangerous offenders *is yet unsolved*."[57] This failure is widely accepted to be true among social scientists, even by some supporters of the practice who are prepared to forge ahead with selective incapacitation anyway.[58] To the extent we are committed to this path, we best be careful. When we err by being too aggressive, we create both a minor and a major tragedy. The minor tragedy is that we use up badly needed resources incarcerating an offender who need not be incarcerated. The major tragedy is that we will have deprived a citizen of his or her liberty pointlessly, and without moral justification.

There is another significant cost to using selective incapacitation. The realities of fiscal policy require us to free up prison space so that dangerous, repeat offenders can spend longer in jail. In the United States, those jurisdictions that are trying selective incapacitation are reserving prison space for their most dangerous offenders so they can serve longer periods of custody, while having the less dangerous offenders serve their time in the community. In Canada, we are moving quickly in this same direction. We have developed the infamous conditional sentence that allows offenders who do not pose a danger to the community to serve their sentences in the community, and we are attempting to treat dangerous and non-dangerous offenders differently when it comes to parole eligibility and early release. Our attempt to reserve our limited prison space for the truly dangerous has been something of a public relations disaster, as many members of the public, as well as politicians, second-guess the decision of judges about who poses a danger to the community and who does not. Editorials and open-line shows decry the leniency of the conditional sentence, even where the offender does not pose a continuing threat. The irony is that in trying to make the streets as safe as possible in an era of fiscal restraint, the impression is being created that we are making the streets even more dangerous.

SUMMARY: WHY PUNISHING DOES NOT REDUCE VIOLENCE

Sentencing offenders, particularly to incarceration, will not reduce crime rates for most offences. Rehabilitation is largely a myth. Specific deterrence does not work. As a general strategy, incapacitation is neither feasible nor effective. And it is only blind faith that supports our contention that punishing offenders can intimidate others into not committing sexual offences, drug offences, and crimes of violence. Yet most of us claim that we sentence to protect society.

Reductivism is a particularly bankrupt idea when it comes to homicide offences. Rehabilitation has little to do with sentencing killers. It is not a factor for murder. When we sentence murderers to life in prison it is not so that we can remake them as better people. Even in manslaughter cases, rehabilitation, beyond alcohol or drug counselling, is rarely a significant objective. Even where it is, how successful will it be? The emotional cauldron that produces atypical albeit extreme violence in the family setting, the statistically most significant environment for homicide, is so situational that the offender often does not pose a continuing risk to the community. And in those cases where aggression and violence is the state of nature for the offender, we face the insurmountable hurdle of remaking the man. For the same reason, with the possible exception of the truly premeditated or profit killing, general deterrence cannot make a dent in homicide offences. And, with the exception of the likes of Clifford Olson, fortunately few in number, locking most killers up for generations can hardly be justified on the basis of incapacitation. We cannot justify punishing most violent offenders on the basis that doing so will reduce crime and make society safer.

Does this make me a weak-kneed, mealy-mouthed liberal who would simply let killers go? Not a chance. With rare exception, we should hit those who kill intentionally and hit them hard. In most cases, a harsh sentence will even be appropriate for those who have committed manslaughter or driving offences causing death. Jail the offenders, and make it for a long time. Why? Not because it will make society safer, but because it is the right thing to do.

The Real Justification for Sentencing Violent Offenders

The historical justifications for punishment are not based on the utilitarian fantasy of reducing crime. The most primitive justification is vengeance. We want to hurt those who hurt us. A slightly more sophisticated concept of vengeance is the theory of "requital": "The wrongdoer should suffer a harm equal to or similar to what he has inflicted . . . [I]n Exodus 21 (24) we read 'eye for eye — tooth for tooth — hand for hand.'"[59] Then there is the theory of "lustration," or "purification," in which the community has been defiled because a taboo has been broken. An idea found in Greek mythology, it requires community atonement to cleanse or heal.[60] And there is Hegel, who regarded crime "as the negation of" legal order. Punishment was needed to negate the negation and restore order to the community. It was as though there would be no balance or closure without punishment.[61]

Some justifications for punishment found in philosophy, theology, and literature focus on the needs of the offender. "Expiation" is closely related to "lustration." It requires the offender to atone for the sake of his soul. The punishment purifies. It is the Catholic purgatory, and the penance of Judeo-Christianity.[62] H.L.A. Hart explains that Dostoyevsky believed that, psychologically, the criminal needed punishment to heal his lacerated bonds with society. In the novel *Crime and Punishment*, "Raskolnikov the murderer thirsts for his punishment" and is all but destroyed by its absence.[63]

All these theories, like the more gentle utilitarian justifications we mouth today, share one thing in common: they seek to justify punishment. The fact is, though, that the deep, unflattering human thirst to punish pre-exists all these ideas. They only seek to explain it. The urge to punish, as ugly as it may be, is archetypal. It has been found in every society and in every age. Whether rooted in the good of society, or in the good of the offender, humans have felt the need to punish since the beginning of time. Yet modern humans are embarrassed by the impulse to do so. We lawyers have traditionally been ashamed of justifying punishment as retribution. We prefer to think of it as a constructive, utilitarian enterprise that will reduce crime. In only 3.7 percent of the 650 sentencing cases examined by the Canadian Sentencing Commission in 1988 did the sentencing judge even mention "retribution" as a reason for the sentence.[64] It is as though people can declare themselves civilized when they rise above their "primitive" urges and desires. It is not unlike Victorian society, which feigned disgust at nudity and sexuality, but lost its elegance when producing its share of children as the night fell. Because an idea is ancient does not make it "primitive": it may make it natural and indispensable.

This deep urge to see justice done through punishment cannot be denied, and it is folly to ignore it. We must not forget that when we established the modern criminal justice system, we took away the right of citizens to use self-help to punish those who had hurt them. We never said, "It is morally wrong for you to want to hurt those who have hurt you." We said to them, "Do not worry about doing justice. We will do it for you." We did this to make society more peaceful and law-abiding by removing the blood-feud and vigilantism, and to ensure that the job of punishing was done with the balance and impartiality that we believe few victims can muster. That is precisely why punishment is essential. It helps to maintain respect for, and reliance on, the law. Members of society, both victims and potential victims alike, expect something to be done.

Recently, George Fletcher, an eminent criminal law theorist, spoke of punishment as a way of "expressing solidarity with the victim":

> The minimal task of the criminal trial . . . is to stand by victims, to restore their dignity, to find a way for them to think of themselves, once again, as men and women equal to all others. Convicting and punishing the guilty is our way of expressing solidarity with those who have fallen prey to the pervasive violence . . . When we fail to act, when we let the guilty go untouched, we betray the trust that enables people to live together in peaceful interdependence.[65]

Fletcher's warning not to betray the trust that enables people to live together suggests more than the simple pragmatic pandering to a demanding public's base human instincts. Emile Durkheim believed that the wrongdoer is punished in order to demonstrate to all people the abhorrence of the criminal act. This retribution "preserves the moral ideal of the people."[66] Punishment inculcates moral values and binds the community together. "[I]t highlights and reinforces the moral boundaries of society" and "enhances social solidarity among conforming members."[67] This theory of punishment is known as "denunciation."

In a CBC radio broadcast in 1962, J.D. Morton gave an address that reflected similar thinking. He described the criminal trial as a morality play. He compared law to another of society's chief institutions — organized religion. Like a religious celebration, the trappings and ceremonies of the trial are an elaborate drama "staged in furtherance of the great general end . . . that citizens should so conduct themselves as to avoid the types of behaviour which society has legally condemned." Denunciation is not aimed, he said, at the criminal, "who, despite the process, goes on to commit a crime." It is aimed more at the ordinary citizen "who is susceptible to such conditioning."[68] In this sense, denunciation is distinct from general deterrence, which purports to reduce crime by discouraging potential offenders. Denunciation is meant to prevent the *creation* of potential offenders by reinforcing the values of the law-abiding. It does not promise to reduce crime. It promises to keep societal values relating to the decent treatment of others alive and vibrant so that crime does not increase.

In short, to the extent that punishment assists in controlling crime rates, it does not do so by intimidating potential offenders into being good. It does so by reinforcing basic values for those who are law-abiding in nature, thereby keeping them from wanting to do harm to others. In *Doctor Zhivago*, Nikolay Nikolayevich made this basic point when debating the merits of punishment with Vyvolochnov, a shallow man who missed the subtlety of great ideas and simplified things to fit his meagre understanding. Nikolayevich, probably wasting his words, said to Vyvolochnov:

> Wait, let me tell you what I think. I think that if the beast who sleeps in man could be held down by threats — any kind of threat, whether of jail or retribution after death — then the highest emblem of humanity would be the lion tamer in the circus with his whip, not the self-sacrificing preacher. But don't you see, this is just the point — what has for centuries raised man above the beast is not the cudgel but an inward music: the irresistible power of unarmed truth, the attraction of its example.[69]

We need criminal law and we need to punish, because not all men have risen above the beast. Not all have that "inward music," or, at least, not all hear it at all times. When we punish, we reaffirm those values that the bulk of society holds sacred, and it is the dissemination of those values which truly serves as the wall against crime.

The whole idea of punishing to inculcate values is abhorrent to some. It is particularly abhorrent to civil libertarians because it proclaims "that the state has a moral mission — that the state must know right from wrong and impose its view of the right."[70] This kind of thinking, it is feared, has enabled societies to punish "immorality," even when the only harm it does is to the sensibilities of others, such as the consumption of mild drugs, homosexuality, suicide, obscenity, gambling, blasphemous libel, and prostitution. This is certainly true, but along with the right to inculcate appropriate values in a system that respects both individual autonomy and group rights comes the responsibility to use the criminal law with restraint. Recognizing that we strike back at crime because it offends us does not require us to claim the right to use it to strike back at everything that offends us. The appropriate reach of criminal law should not be confused with the reason for punishing criminal offenders.

Others find it abhorrent for society to claim the right to punish, for punishment is the infliction of pain and the infliction of pain is evil. For this reason, the concept of restorative justice is gaining currency. Calling for a system of "offender responsibility, reconciliation and restoration," J.W. Mohr observed that "[t]here is . . . little difference between the crime committed by offenders and those we commit in the name of sentencing."[71] Perhaps Mohr is correct. We are simply not ready as a society, though, and I doubt we ever will be, for a system that hugs its criminals, particularly its violent offenders, and asks them to be nicer and to fix what is most often unfixable. While the moral high ground in the debate certainly belongs to those who would forgive and build bridges, any effort to build a criminal justice system around "reconciliation" for serious crime is a rose-coloured fantasy that expects more than mere humans can give. While the urge to be constructive and reconciliatory has an important place in sentencing, it will never form the blueprint for a criminal justice system when it comes to violent offences. Patting the likes of Clifford Olson on the head and saying, "Rejoin the community, Cliff," is like trying to pet a frothing dog.

While reconciliationists can claim the moral high ground, reductivists cannot. C.S. Lewis makes the point more effectively than I could. He called for a return to retributivist theories of justice precisely because it was more humane to punish than to "cure" criminals. He was afraid of the assault on human integrity that rehabilitationists practise and considered their claim to humanity to be duplicitous and dishonest:

> [These "humanitarians"] are not punishing, not inflicting, only healing. But do not let us be deceived by a name. To be taken without consent from my home and friends; to lose my liberty; to undergo all those assaults on my personality which modern psychotherapy knows how to deliver; to be re-made after some pattern of "normality" hatched in a Viennese laboratory to which I never professed allegiance; to know that this process will never end until either my captors have succeeded or I have grown wise enough to cheat them with apparent success — who cares whether this is called Punishment or not? That it includes most of the elements for which any punishment is feared — shame, exile, bondage, and years eaten by the locust — is obvious. . . .
>
> . . .
>
> Of all tyrannies a tyranny sincerely exercised for the good of its victims may be the most oppressive. . . . [T]hose who torment us for our own good will torment us without end for they do so with the approval of their own conscience.[72]

The notion that criminals are abnormal and in need of healing was offensive to Lewis. It was offensive not because he craved blood through punishment, but because it left little room for "justice" and mercy: "If crime is only a disease which needs cure, not sin which deserves punishment, it cannot be pardoned. How can you pardon a man for having a gumboil or a club foot?"

The quest for retribution, the need to express solidarity with victims, the desire to reinforce basic standards of decency through punishment, or the need to hold wrongdoers accountable so that the law-abiding do not become demoralized — the basic need to punish however you might wish to explain it — does not have to be a harsh and uncompromising one. Indeed, it has been found that the utilitarian goal of the "protection of the public" is the justification used by a majority of the judges for the longest prison sentences.[73] Retribution tempered by objectivity, proportion, and mercy may well support less extreme penalties than rehabilitation, specific deterrence, general deterrence, incapacitation, or any of the other utilitarian fantasies. It is not an immoral foundation for a criminal justice system. It is pragmatic because it responds to public needs that are real, even if they are based in emotion. More important, it has more room for justice, forgiveness, and proportion than utilitarian philosophies do. But most important of all, if we are honest with ourselves, it is what we in the legal system in fact already do. We punish. We do not cure, nor do we reduce crime. By denying this reality we fail to appreciate the possibility of restraint.

In 1996 the Supreme Court of Canada rendered a decision that distressed those who believe that we have risen above the need to "punish" for punishment's sake. For the first time, the Court went out of its way to endorse "retribution" as a legitimate and central component of the sentencing process.[74] Chief Justice Lamer was careful to explain that retribution is not vengeance. It is not vengeance because vengeance represents an uncalibrated act of harm upon another person. Vengeance is self-help, and it is motivated by anger and emotion. Retribution, by contrast, is an objective, measured response that reflects the moral blame of the offender, the degree to which the conduct deviates from societal norms, and the harm the offender has caused. Unlike vengeance, it is a restrained response. It is related to, but distinct from, denunciation. Denunciation is a symbolic, collective statement of society's condemnation.

By reaffirming that retribution is a measured response, Chief Justice Lamer was reinforcing that the most the law can demand of an offender is an eye for an eye. We never take more because we believe that our moral right to use an offender as the instrument for sending messages is limited by the degree of his moral blame. The sentence must be proportional to the moral fault of the actor and to the harm done. This does not mean that the law always takes an eye for an eye. Retribution and denunciation are not the only values that require consideration. We have other values that need to be reinforced, including, where appropriate, mercy and compassion, so long as they are not doled out in soft-headed measure. There has to be room to recognize that people find themselves, often through little fault of their own, in compromising circumstances. They may be immature or have less intelligence than others, they may be destitute when they steal, they may be battered and strike back with excessive force, they may have been poorly socialized through no fault of their own, or they may be subject to provocation that may well have confounded the judgment of ordinary people. There is room to account for these variants, particularly in a retributive system.

Of equal importance, there also has to be room to be pragmatic. There are times when being principled is self-defeating. If a short period of custody will cost an offender a job, thereby increasing the risks of alienation from the community, why would we choose to use this offender to send the message? If an offender is young and impressionable and the offence relatively minor, why would we choose to enrol that offender in crime school by sending him or her to jail? If we attempted to send the message by using jail for every crime and every offence, our system would crumble and collapse under the cost. If we can satisfy the needs of justice without jail, why would we not do so? In short, recognizing that we sentence to punish does not require that we punish harshly or unpragmatically. It is the primary reason we sentence, but it is not the sole ingredient in the recipe for determining the length or nature of the punishment.

None of this argument is radical. The Canadian Sentencing Commission came to much the same conclusions, although it preferred to do so more euphemistically. It rejected "retribution" as a theory of punishment, but accepted the transparent balm of "just deserts" in which society is entitled to punish offenders to the extent of their moral fault and the damage they cause. It also rejected the efficacy of sentencing in reducing crime. In the end, it found the social utility in punishing offenders to rest in the "imperative" that "the law abiding not be demoralized by the perception that there is no accountability for seriously blameworthy behaviour." Even with the fine language, this assertion strikes me as indistinguishable from scratching the public itch to punish seriously wrongful conduct. When it came time to state its theory of punishment, the commission said: "[T]he fundamental purpose of sentencing is to preserve the authority of and promote respect for the law through the imposition of just sanctions." If there is some reduction of crime in the process, that is a nice touch, but it is not the purpose of sentencing. Exactly right.

It is critically important, in the interests of the credibility of the system, that those of us within it spend more time spreading this message, and less time claiming to be reducing crime. As a leading criminologist, Julian Roberts, has said: "The problem with tying the sentencing process to the goal of reducing the crime rate is that the public is primed to expect reductions in the crime rates as a result of changes in sentencing policy."[75] As a result, citizens call for changes in sentencing policy, including more frequent and lengthier prison sentences. Worse, they feel that the promise of societal protection is betrayed by sentences like the one received by Anthony Goodchild, no matter how appropriate they might be, thereby putting pressure on courts to punish unjustly. The repute of the criminal justice system takes a hit, even though it is working as it should be.

The Goodchild Sentence

The vast majority of Canadians believe that, in general, sentences are too lenient. Surveys most commonly reveal that 80 percent of us hold this view. In a society as diverse as ours it would be difficult to get an 80 percent consensus on almost any issue, including global warming or life on Mars. The same pattern holds true in Australia, England, the Netherlands, and the United States. Research internationally, including in Canada, has demonstrated that the more information people are given, the less harsh their sentencing expectations are. Ignorance of court practices, and the reasons for them, fuel dissatisfaction. The public tends to be tolerant and trusting, even of a wide range of sentences, when provided with enough information.[76] Perhaps if the facts were known to the public, as they were to the court that sentenced Anthony Goodchild, the case would not have inspired the anger it did.

The first point to appreciate is that Anthony Goodchild was convicted of manslaughter, not murder. In other words, the finding of fact made by the trial judge was that he did not mean to kill his wife. He had taken the gun out to shoot himself. She walked into the room. He turned while holding the gun and it accidentally discharged, tragically striking her. The reason this case was not simply a blameless accident that falls outside of the realm of criminal law is that she died as a result of his unlawful act of carelessly using the firearm.

I have the same reaction on hearing this version of facts as you probably do. I, too, am sceptical. This is not the first time I have heard this one. According to Beverley Joan Ratten's husband, for example, she was "accidentally" shot to death while he was holding a gun, only minutes after she dialled 911 and screamed hysterically, "Get me the police, please."[77] Similarly, Timothy Randall Lemky claimed to have shot his girlfriend, Michelle Cummins, when the gun he was holding got knocked to the floor and went off when he was trying to pick it up.[78] My all-time favourite hair-trigger story, one that Tom Sawyer would probably call a "stretcher," was given by Ruth Piche to the court, after she had provided a totally different one to the police.[79] According to Piche's testimony, she had taken the rifle from the weapon rack in the bathroom so she could shoot herself, and on seeing her partner, Leslie Pascoe, inert on the couch in an alcoholic stupor, she decided to go and kiss him once more before she died. It was the kiss from hell. She should have put the gun down first, for she blew a hole in poor Leslie's head. If guns fired as easily as these cases suggest, there would be dead hunters lying all over northern Canada. But, I suppose, it can happen.

Still, the trial judge did not have any choice but to proceed on the basis that the killing of Irene Goodchild was an accident, albeit one that was careless enough to warrant punishment. The Crown had dropped the murder charge and accepted a plea of guilty to manslaughter. By definition, manslaughter is an unintentional killing. That is what Anthony Goodchild pleaded guilty to, and that is therefore what he was convicted of. Justice Bernstein, the trial judge, could not disregard this plea and sentence him on the basis that the killing was intentional. You can sentence someone only for what they are convicted of, not for what you think they might have done.

Still, the Crown prosecutor sought to have the judge sentence him as an intentional killer who had shot his wife in an act of rage. Given that the Crown prosecutor, by withdrawing the murder charge, had represented to the court that the crime was a manslaughter, the judge had no choice but to refuse that invitation. No doubt the community would have had more confidence in this verdict if it had been arrived at after trial, and perhaps the Crown should have refused the plea and allowed the evidence to fall where it may. But on the evidence available, the Crown prosecutor apparently concluded that the most she could establish with any confidence was that Irene Goodchild died accidentally at Anthony Goodchild's hand. The judge seemed to agree. Based on the evidence the Crown did have, which was read into court, Justice Bernstein said:

> We don't know if it was near-accidental pulling of the trigger or an act of rage resulting from some perceived wrong. On the basis of the agreed upon facts read in in this case, the lack of any previous violence within the marriage by the accused, the accused's obvious reaction earlier that morning when his wife first returned home to propose suicide, I conclude that the victim's death was caused while the accused had the gun out in the first instance to kill himself. No other conclusion on the basis of the evidence would be appropriate. To find otherwise would be to engage in mere speculation.

We can all have our suspicions, and it will always bother reasonable people that perhaps Goodchild got away with murder, but no one can be sure. I suspect, however, that most of us agree that the criminal justice system cannot afford to entertain such doubts. It must sentence offenders on what it knows, not on what it fears. As a result, the court could not treat this case as one of domestic violence. Anthony Goodchild was being sentenced for a culpable accident — a simple, tragic carelessness, or a "near-accidental pulling of the trigger" as the judge put it. That being so, the judge had no choice but to treat him the same way as any other person who, through the careless use of a firearm, causes the death of another. If his gun had discharged in a duck blind, killing a friend because he had handled the weapon carelessly, would the sentence have caused the furor it did? That is effectively the crime that Anthony Goodchild was convicted of — a careless but accidental discharge of a firearm. When we judge the criminal justice system we have to bear the precise facts in mind.

What other information did the judge have to help him in his sentencing? A long list of character witnesses came forward who spoke glowingly of Anthony Goodchild's love of family, his loyalty, his reliability, and his generosity to others. Based on the character references, the opinion of two psychiatrists that he was not dangerous, and the absence of any evidence of a criminal record or of abuse or attempted dominance of his wife, the judge concluded that Anthony Goodchild was not an ongoing threat to the community. On the evidence before him, he would have been wrong to have concluded otherwise.

When Anthony Goodchild was in jail pending his bail release, there was concern for the emotional well-being of his children. Their conduct improved when he was released, and all four daughters were given an opportunity to address the judge. In the judge's assessment, "[t]he evidence of the children and others makes it obvious that their relationship with the accused is the most important thing in their young lives." A social worker testified that they were clinging to their father for "security, predictability and nurturance." All the professional evidence before the court "stressed the importance to the children's well-being of having continuing and very regular contact with their father."

In a case where the sentencing was based on the premise that the killing was intentional, these kinds of considerations would be disregarded. To allow a man who has killed his wife to pray in mitigation that his children will be without a parent if he goes to jail is like the wornout joke in which the man who has killed his parents asks for leniency because he is an orphan. On the evidence before him, though, the judge was not sentencing a wife killer. He was sentencing a man who posed no danger to the community, who had accidentally but carelessly shot his wife, and whose daughters were in emotional crisis and who needed him with them, in the community.

All this evidence would have made it easy for the judge to have imposed a non-custodial sentence. There are enough precedents for it: accidental killing; upstanding citizen; strong reasons to keep him in the community. But, to his credit, the judge felt the weight of the need to have the sentence in some way express society's repugnance at the act of a man, even one in great emotional turmoil, who had taken the life of another by loading a gun in the distraught state he was in, while inside of a dwelling house, causing such a tragic consequence. He said: "The law recognizes above all the sanctity of human life and judges have a duty to reflect that in sentencing. Sympathy for the children and to some extent for the accused would be misguided if it resulted in a failure to reflect the disapproval of society for the taking of a human life."

What is the value of a human life? The sentence of Anthony Goodchild was never meant to suggest that it is eighteen months followed by three years probation. Irene Goodchild, mother, friend, and human being, was worth infinitely more than that. Yet the relevant question in any rational criminal justice system is not the value of the human life that has been lost. The only question the criminal law is equipped to answer is, What is the value of the sentence this man should receive? It is a composite question that requires answering: What is the degree of moral blameworthiness for this offender? How much harm did he cause? And what factors are there that may cause us to take less than an eye?

Given what Anthony Goodchild was convicted of, his was not a lenient sentence. A man who accidentally but carelessly killed his wife was sentenced to eighteen months in jail so that the criminal justice system could make a point to those of us who are law-abiding. I wonder if this case would have caused quite as much contempt for the criminal justice system if it had been reported this way in the newspapers. And I wonder whether it would have been condemned as a sentence that fails to protect society if we in the criminal justice system were to admit openly that even if we were to send Anthony Goodchild away for an eternity, our homes and our streets would become no safer.

Conclusion

If those of us in the criminal justice system were less squeamish about admitting that we cannot reduce crime by sentencing violent offenders, I suspect we would produce two very beneficial results. First, society might learn to rely more heavily on better crime prevention initiatives, including funding for battered women's shelters, women's resource centres, and addiction and alcohol treatment programs. Society might even decide to do more to identify and ameliorate the social conditions and predisposing factors that cause violent crime. The fact is that we could do more to reduce violence by reducing substance abuse, particularly of alcohol, than by sentencing offenders. By promising to reduce crime by sentencing violent offenders, those of us in the criminal justice system have become both enablers and whipping-boys. We have enabled members of society to do little about the causes of crime while blaming us for failing to protect them from it.

Second, by admitting that we cannot reduce most kinds of crime by sentencing offenders, particularly violent crime, we might increase the credibility of the criminal justice system, which is only tarnished by our habit of constantly making promises that cannot be kept. In the process, we might reduce the public tendency to insist on harsher and harsher sentences in the expectation that they will reduce crime. To accomplish these benefits, we have to stop using general deterrence as a leading sentencing principle in cases of violence. We should acknowledge that it is just a sideline benefit that might occur in some cases. We will have to be frank about the considerable limits on our ability to rehabilitate. More important, it will require open and public acknowledgment that our criminal courts are punitive rather than healing institutions. We punish people who commit serious offences because they deserve it and because we, as a society, need to know that there are consequences for criminal behaviour. And we need the public to know that this punishment will be done in an impartial, balanced way, with the needs of retribution and denunciation being tempered, where appropriate, by pragmatism and compassion. To accomplish all of these goals, we need change nothing about the way we sentence. We just need to be more honest and accurate in describing why we sentence.

Conditional Justice

A t the time of her court appearances, Lisa Ferguson did not wear her thirty-five years well. Both life and lifestyle had been hard on her. On 24 November 1993 life and lifestyle proved to be even harder on her common-law husband of three years, Vincent Foley. That was the evening that Lisa Ferguson shot him to death.

Vincent Foley and Lisa Ferguson had been living together for three years or so, along with Lisa's young son. They lived on a small hobby farm raising eighteen beef cattle in Woodlawn, Ontario, not far from Kanata, the home of the Ottawa Senators. Vincent worked on and off as an elevator repairman while Lisa tended to the farm. The setting may have been idyllic, but these people did not live in bliss. According to neighbours, when the countryside became quiet at night near Woodlawn, it did not always become tranquil. Vincent could sometimes be heard shouting and cursing. Neighbours said the relationship was abusive on both sides. According to Lisa, though, the real abuse, the kind that shatters bones and the human spirit, was one-sided. She claimed that Vincent, a man who at least one neighbour said he had seen sober only once, abused her physically, sexually, and psychologically. She had left him on at least three occasions because of his abuse, but always returned after he promised to stop hurting her.

When Lisa Ferguson was abused by Vincent Foley on 24 November 1993, she decided not to leave. Instead, she killed him. The tragedy of that evening, an event that would cause Lisa to attempt to end her own life three times, started when she had complained to Vincent about how unreasonable he was being, expecting her to do the chores and to get his supper. He responded by striking her a number of times and grabbing her by the side of the face and throwing her down a flight of stairs. After she had lain at the bottom of the stairs for a while regaining her breath, she retrieved a rifle, loaded it, and went looking for him. He was not in his room. She went downstairs into the kitchen. He was not there. She saw him in the living room lying on the couch, the final resting place, it seems, of a number of abusive, alcoholic men. There she shot him, first once, and then again. At the trial she testified that he was coming towards her at the time. When she had called for the ambulance, though, she provided a different story. She can be heard on the 911 tape that was played to the jury saying, "He's beat on me so many times. He's passed out cold and I shot him."

At her trial, her soft-spoken, highly experienced attorney, Leonard Shore, presented evidence to establish that Lisa Ferguson suffered from "battered woman syndrome." Given the quality of her counsel, it would have been an effective presentation. Dr. Fredrick Shane, the best-known expert in the field in Canada, was called on her behalf. According to the theory of battered woman syndrome, women suffering from it can predict, through experience, the onset of violence, but they lose the ability to escape from it. They become trapped in a cycle of abuse that robs them of their self-esteem and self-control. The fear builds, and in some cases they come to believe they have no way out. There is no point in going to the police. There is no point in running away. They come to believe, the theory goes, that they must kill to save themselves. This perspective is not one they acquire through their own fault. It is the product of an escalating pattern of abuse which ultimately robs them of their powers of self-determination. Violence no longer remains a matter of choice; it becomes a matter of survival. This was what Dr. Shane said happened to Lisa Ferguson.[1]

Had he been right, she would not have been guilty of anything. The Supreme Court of Canada modified the defence of self-defence in 1990 to make it available to women suffering from the syndrome who, while reasonably fearing death or great bodily harm, form the reasonable belief that they have no choice but to kill.[2] The defence is remarkable because it allows women to use fatal force, even though the threat they are defending against is not immediate. Battered woman syndrome theory purports to explain how it is reasonable for women to believe that they cannot protect themselves simply by leaving or summoning the assistance of the police or asking for the help of others. The abuse robs them of control, rendering them helpless to the point where self-defence becomes their only option.

A conceptual problem arises in applying the theory of battered woman syndrome. It has aptly been pointed out that "it is hardly a sign of helplessness to acquire a gun and to kill one's psychological captor."[3] Whether it was scepticism about the battered woman syndrome theory, the divergence between Ferguson's testimony and the 911 statement, or a simple refusal to accept the law's opinion that abused women are justified in killing their abusers based on fear of future attack, the jury did not buy it. They convicted Lisa Ferguson, but not of murder. In what may well have been a compromise verdict, they convicted her of manslaughter.

I do not like quibbling with a jury verdict, but there was no compelling legal basis for this result. In a self-defence case, the accused is either guilty of murder because she was not acting in self-defence or is innocent. There is no half-way house in which the law says, "This was almost self-defence, so let us split the difference and call it manslaughter." It is all or nothing.

There are, of course, legal bases for reducing an offence from murder to manslaughter. As in the Goodchild case, a killing can be manslaughter when the accused does not intend to kill or to cause bodily harm that the accused knows is likely to cause death. That was not this case here. Even though Ferguson testified that she did not intend to kill Foley, there does not seem to be much question about her purpose: she clearly meant to fire gun shots into his body. That is why she armed herself and went looking for him, and that is why she pulled the trigger twice. It wasn't a case where she could realistically say, "I only wanted to wing him."

There are other legal devices for reducing an apparent murder to a manslaughter. One is the so-called defence of drunkenness. For murder charges, this "defence" recognizes that some impaired people are too intoxicated to have the intent to cause death. Their inebriated state alters their perception of reality and blunts their ability to make the link between actions and results. Contrary to popular misconception, you are not entitled to this defence simply because you are intoxicated by alcohol or a drug when you kill. It is not even enough that the alcohol or drug has loosened your inhibitions and made you braver or more aggressive than you otherwise might have been. Nor is it a defence that the drink or drugs have caused you to act out of character. You have a defence only if you did not intend to do what you did — in this case, to cause death or bodily harm that you know is likely to cause death. The intoxication merely provides evidence that may account for the fact that you did not appreciate the natural consequences of your actions. When this defence works during a murder trial, you do not walk away free. You are convicted of manslaughter rather than murder.

This scenario hardly describes Ferguson. She was an experienced drinker. She had a prior impaired driving conviction. More important, based on the evidence and the submissions of her counsel, when it came time to sentence her after she was convicted of manslaughter, the trial judge sentenced her on the grounds that she needed help to overcome an alcohol problem. The ten beers she drank over the day of the shooting did not rob her of her faculties to the point where she did not know what she was doing. Her testimony made it clear that she knew exactly what she was up to.

This was not a staggering drunk who swings a bottle at an annoying drinking buddy in an alley. She had the wherewithal to evaluate her lot in life and to complain to Foley about it. She had the ability to rise from the floor, gather herself, seek out a weapon, and go hunting. While the alcohol may have contributed to her readiness to use fatal force, it did not undermine her ability to know that if she pointed the gun and shot, Foley was likely to die. This was not a case for the drunkenness defence.

All that was left, then, was the partial defence of provocation. Available only in homicide cases, it does not provide a complete defence. Instead, killers who take a life intentionally while provoked are not convicted of murder. They are convicted only of manslaughter.

The defence of provocation is a controversial concession to human weakness. It is the remaining vestige of an old rule that gave defence to men who killed their wives' lovers. The idea is that even ordinary people can snap under the stress of provocative and wrongful acts or insults. It is available only if the killer loses the power of self-control and acts "on the sudden," before the passions have had an opportunity to cool. As well, the defence is available only if an ordinary person in the position of the accused would also have lost the power of self-control. This qualification is required so that the defence cannot be used by unusually excitable or pugnacious people who lose control easily.

The trial judge chose to interpret the jury's verdict that Lisa Ferguson was guilty only of manslaughter as one based on the defence of provocation. Part of the foundation for a provocation defence was indeed present in the Foley killing. Vincent Foley had done the wrongful act of assaulting Lisa Ferguson by striking her and throwing her down the stairs. It was unlikely, however, that she had lost the powers of self-control and was in the throes of passion when she shot him. The defence sought to portray her as a woman who, because of the history of abuse, had made a reasonable decision that she had to kill her abuser to protect herself. A killing cannot at once be the result of a loss of self-control and a measured act of self-defence. The classic provocative act emerges because it "strike[s] upon a mind [so] unprepared for it, that it must make an unexpected impact that takes the understanding by surprise and sets the passions aflame."[4] According to the evidence, this abuse was not unexpected. It was part of a pattern that was so common that, as a battered woman, Ferguson had supposedly acquired the ability to predict the onset of Foley's violence.

It is also a matter of some difficulty to claim that this killing was on the sudden. Had Ferguson poked a knife into Foley immediately after he struck her, it would have been. But, according to the evidence, Foley had time before he was shot to leave the scene of his assault, lie down, and pass out on the couch, and Ferguson had time to catch her breath, retrieve and load a gun, and seek out her prey. This lapse in time does not necessarily undermine completely the suddenness requirement for the defence, since suddenness is such an imprecise concept and there was psychiatric evidence to suggest that the time that passed may not have been sufficient to negate the provocation factor. At the very least, though, the time that passed clearly weakens any claim that this was a provoked killing.

I do not challenge the weak technical basis for the manslaughter verdict in order to criticize members of the jury. I agree with the judge when he said they did the right thing. They did not come to this conclusion because of the law, however. They did it either because they misunderstood the law, applying one or more of the defences with inappropriate generosity, or because they understood it and decided to render a manslaughter verdict in spite of the law. Perhaps they were simply not ready to condemn her to life in prison, given the mitigating factors that were present. If that is so, the jury ought to be applauded.

A jury cannot be asked for reasons for its verdict, nor can jury members be questioned about it afterwards. It is an offence in Canada to discuss jury deliberations. There are a number of unconvincing reasons for this practice, but it is well established. Since juries never have to answer for their decisions by providing a legal basis for the results they arrive at, they effectively have the power to refuse to apply an unjust law or to apply a law unjustly. In Quebec the attorney general of the province was unable, for example, to get a jury to convict Dr. Henry Morgentaler of committing abortions, even though the evidence against him was clear. This same power also allows compromise verdicts to be arrived at. This jury did not believe that the Foley killing was a true case of self-defence, either because members did not like the state of the law or the evidence satisfied them that the claim of self-defence was not available. Nor did the jury believe that murder was an appropriate result. Their deliberations might therefore have sawed off at manslaughter.

It is not unusual for murder charges to end up with manslaughter convictions. Data collated in 1993 show that 30 percent of those charged with first-degree murder who are convicted are actually convicted of manslaughter, while a staggering 75 percent of those charged with second-degree murder who are convicted are convicted of this lesser offence.[5] More than half the murder charges where convictions are obtained and where the Crown initially alleges that the death is intentional, therefore, end up being sentenced on the basis that the death was unintentional or provoked.

It is difficult to believe that more than half the people who are killed by others away from the roads and highways of our communities have been the unfortunate victims of unintentional killings. Without question, many manslaughters are really murders in disguise.

There are many reasons why murders often result in manslaughter convictions. In some cases a jury has legitimate concerns about whether an accused who intentionally assaulted another really intended to cause death. Sometimes the partial defences of provocation and drunkenness convert murders into manslaughters. Even though technically the defences of provocation and drunkenness are narrow, a jury will normally have to be told about them because there will be some evidence of either on the trial record. In close to 50 percent of all homicides, the killer is under the influence of alcohol and/or drugs,[6] and, in most, the killing is an act of emotional impulse. There is plenty of opportunity for jurors to accept either of these defences where they have a sympathetic accused or a difficult case.

Often, though, the manslaughter conviction is the product of plea bargaining. Prosecutors size up their case. Sometimes they believe that, technically, it really is a manslaughter case and that justice requires that they agree to an appropriate verdict being rendered. Often, though, they agree to accept the plea because their case is weak. They are afraid that if they go to trial, they may lose it entirely. Prudence dictates that they accept a manslaughter conviction, even though they may think it a murder, so the accused does not get off scot-free.

One has to wonder whether this is not what happened in the Goodchild case. Recall that the Crown agreed that the case was a manslaughter and not a murder. When it came time for the sentencing phase, however, it was clear that the prosecutor did not accept the accidental discharge theory of the defence. She urged the judge to find that Anthony Goodchild had killed Irene intentionally during a rage. The only way in law to marry the theory of the Crown that this was both an intentional killing and a manslaughter is for this case to have been a provoked killing. Yet there was no evidence of provocation that could satisfy the legal defence. Leaving aside the difficult question of whether Irene's adultery or her decision to stay out until she was ready to come home amount to a "wrongful act or insult," this killing occurred hours after Irene's return. No one, with the possible exception of Anthony Goodchild, who claims not to remember any of the events, has any idea what, if anything, she said or did that was provocative when they were together that morning. The decision to take a manslaughter plea by the Crown was almost certainly a pragmatic one, inspired by a weak case in which a complete acquittal was conceivable. As distasteful as it is, there are times when prosecutors have to make such choices.

Sometimes Crown prosecutors agree to accept manslaughter or even lesser convictions where a murder verdict appears to be unduly harsh. This compromise happens often in cases involving battered women. Battered woman syndrome evidence has not resulted in a rash of acquittals of abused women who kill, although there have been some. It has resulted, however, in a large number of manslaughter pleas, as women, afraid to risk full conviction, accept the Crown's offer to treat an intentional killing as a manslaughter.[7]

This practice of accepting pleas to lesser charges is almost routine in "mercy killing" cases. Sometimes the Crown agrees to a manslaughter plea. In others the Crown has consented to a plea to the non-homicide offence of administering a noxious substance. In these cases, the unremitting minimum punishment of life imprisonment for murder is simply out of line, and reasonable people therefore choose to keep the letter of the law from applying with blunt and inappropriate force.

The practice of treating murders as manslaughters reflects a serious problem. It is not a problem with the integrity of juries or prosecutors, or of judges who accept manslaughter pleas in what are evidently murder cases. Rather, it is a problem with the law of sentencing in murder cases. Murder is one of the few offences that bears a minimum penalty. Every murderer must be sentenced to life imprisonment, with lengthy periods of parole ineligibility. The very least that someone convicted of second-degree murder can expect to serve is ten years in jail. Without a special order to the contrary, first-degree murderers can expect to serve at least twenty-five years. By contrast, manslaughter produces much lower penalties. Although it, too, can be punishable by life imprisonment, the life sentence is not mandatory. Indeed, no one who is convicted of manslaughter receives a life sentence. Ninety percent of manslaughter convictions produce custodial sentences of three years or less. In Ontario, only 53 percent of those convicted of this offence even go to jail. In Nova Scotia, the median manslaughter sentence (half the sentences were longer and half shorter) is six months. Quebec is the only "get tough" province when it comes to manslaughter. In Quebec, nearly all manslaughter convictions, 97 percent, result in jail terms, and the median sentence is nine years,[8] but that is still a long way from the sentences imposed for murder.

The variation in manslaughter sentences is partially regional, but huge variations occur even within a province, or within a city, or even between different cases decided by the same judge. Not all manslaughter cases are equal. They range from the near-accident to compromise verdicts in murder cases. They result from the acts of both the negligent gun owner and the irate provoked killer, and the offenders include both drunken brawlers and battered women.

Although there is less diversity among murderers, it is equally clear that not all murders are the same. Indeed, it is clear that not all murders warrant life sentences. One need look no further than the case of Robert Latimer. On 24 October 1993 twelve-year-old Tracy Latimer died of carbon monoxide poisoning. In a statement to the police, Robert Latimer, her father, described how he lifted Tracy from her bed and placed her in the cab of his truck in a shed. He hooked up a hose to the exhaust of the truck and fed it into the back window of the cab. He turned on the truck and left her to die. Once she was dead he returned her to her bed, where her mother found her when she returned from church. After he gave this statement, Latimer showed the police the equipment he had used to kill her.

Tracy Latimer was a human being. To the extent that any of us are, she was a child of God. But in her total innocence, she was a child who lived a hell on earth. Ravaged by severe cerebral palsy, she was a quadriplegic, so debilitated that she was bedridden most of the time. She could laugh and cry, but her brain damage was so substantial that she could not communicate at all. She did not even know her name. She could not sit up on her own, roll over, or focus her eyes. She suffered seizures every day of her life, at first every minute, but, with the assistance of drugs, five or six times a day. Her muscles tightened when they should not because her brain could not control them. She would twist up in pained, cramped contortions. Doctors, intent on relieving the agony, cut the muscles "at the tops of her legs (so her hips would not dislocate), her toes, her heel chords, her knee muscles and so on."[9] Stainless steel rods were put on either side of her spine to straighten her body to alleviate stomach cramps and to keep her lungs from being pinched shut. Regularly enough to require keeping a bucket nearby, she vomited when her parents engaged in the laborious task of forcing food into her mouth with a spoon. She was due to have more surgery to reduce the agony of a dislocated hip. It was going to take her a year to recover.

This child suffered more in twelve short years than most of us combined will feel in a lifetime. This was the child that Robert Latimer loved and could not stand to see suffering anymore. He killed her not because of anger, hatred, jealousy, or evil, but because he wanted what he thought was best for her. Because he killed her, he was charged with first-degree murder.

When he first came to trial, Latimer was tried by a jury of his peers and convicted, although only of second-degree murder. In finding him guilty of second-degree murder, this jury was being generous. The killing had all the indications of a first-degree murder. It was as planned and deliberate as killings get. Nonetheless, the break he received did not go far enough to achieve justice. The law still required a life sentence for this devoted family man, a father of four who was by all accounts a loving, caring, nurturing parent who actively participated in Tracy's daily care, and that is what he received. The law would settle for nothing less than life, even though he posed no risk to the community, was in no need of rehabilitation, and had acted without evil intent. Because of the state of the law, on the day he was sentenced he was told he could not even ask to be released to his family and his farm until he had served ten full years.

What Robert Latimer did was very wrong. He had no right to play God. He had no legal right to reach that breaking point where he could no longer watch Tracy suffer. He had no right to decide whether Tracy's life was worth living. His legal obligation was to care for her and provide her with the medical care she needed. According to the facts as found by the jury, he had to be punished. But not like this. A life sentence for this killing is cruel and self-defeating. It was particularly obscene to punish Latimer in this way, given that others have walked the same road without receiving this kind of punishment.

Daniele Blais, of Montreal, drowned her six-year-old autistic child in the bathtub in November 1996. Her frustration and the stress of caring for the child brought on a depression that, while profound, was apparently not enough for a mental disorder or "insanity" defence. Instead, it was agreed that she should plead to manslaughter.[10] On 2 July 1997 Blais, who had held her struggling six-year-old's head under the water till he stopped fighting, received a twenty-three-month suspended sentence. She did not go to jail. She was released into the community on terms and conditions to assist her in coping with what had happened.[11] Her child was not even killed to alleviate his suffering; he was killed to alleviate hers.

A husband and wife in Nova Scotia smothered the wife's father with a pillow when he was terminally ill with lung cancer. The Crown agreed not to proceed with murder, and the pair received probation and community service.[12] A nurse poisoned a terminally ill patient with potassium chloride. He was allowed to plead guilty to the lesser offence of administering a noxious substance and he received a suspended sentence.[13] A northern Ontario doctor named de la Rocha used the same drug to hasten the death of a women who was begging to have the tubes taken from her trachea. He received a suspended sentence as well. The prosecutor, David Thomas, felt that he had to prosecute and to seek a period of custody, but he could not justify a murder conviction in his own mind. Even though he believed that Dr. de la Rocha intended to kill his patient, he accepted a manslaughter plea: "[W]hen it got down to the crunch, I have to confess that I had a great deal of difficulty with the case. As one who has prosecuted what I will call real killers — child killers, sex slayers, thrill killers — I had a very hard time casting Dr. de la Rocha in the same sinister light as these other types of men."[14]

This reaction is not surprising. Dr. de la Rocha is not like these men. Not all killers are alike, and not all killings are alike. Making them all share the same minimum penalty is preposterous: it is too rigid to be just. To be sure, most killers deserve long prison sentences, but not all of them do. We nonetheless carry on with a system in which justice is left to the discretion of prosecutors or to the resourcefulness of juries. Where prosecutors and juries are not prepared to disregard the law, the law tells us that we are to put people like Robert Latimer at risk of jail "for life," leaving the judge with no choice in the matter.

Fortunately, the saga of Robert Latimer did not end with his life sentence. He earned a new trial because the Crown had tampered with the selection of the jury. The prosecutor had arranged for the police to investigate some of those whose names appeared on the jury list before jury selection to find out their views on mercy killing. This incomprehensible error by the Crown involved prior contact on behalf of one of the parties with persons who would be expected to judge the case neutrally and impartially. It raised the perception that the jury that was ultimately selected may not have been impartial. As a result, the jury's verdict of second-degree murder had to be set aside, and a new trial was required.[15]

When that retrial was held, Latimer was tried only for second-degree murder; the first jury had already acquitted him of first-degree murder, so he could not be tried on that charge again. The second jury again convicted him of second-degree murder, only this time the judge, Justice Noble, refused to follow the law. In a controversial ruling, he held that to impose a life sentence on Robert Latimer would violate his constitutional rights. It would be "cruel and unusual" treatment or punishment. He therefore claimed the legal authority to exempt Latimer from the minimum sentence dictated by law. Instead, he imposed a sentence of one year's imprisonment, to be followed by one year of house arrest.[16]

Justice Noble took this course in large measure because of the huge public outcry that followed the first sentence and because members of the jury were visibly shaken, after they convicted Latimer, when they learned that the law required a life sentence. They had undertaken the exceptional step of recommending to the judge that he become eligible for parole after serving only a year in jail. The Crown has since appealed the sentence, arguing that the judge had no power to do as he did, so

Latimer's travails are far from over. It will take another decision by the Supreme Court of Canada to settle this case.

Maybe the Crown will prove to be right and the judge did overstep his authority. The judge's decision certainly required creativity, a kind of creativity that does little for legal certainty. But even if the Crown is correct on the narrow legal question of whether judges have this power, the more basic question remains of whether it was just to prosecute Robert Latimer under a law that gives no regard to circumstances when it comes to his sentencing. Under our system as it currently stands, we do not seem to worry about this point. The prosecutor decides, and justice becomes a matter of discretion to be pushed along by personal philosophies rather than by a rule of law.

The temptation to do the right thing in the face of an unjust law can produce curious legal decisions, none more interesting than the recent prosecution of Dr. Nancy Morrison, a well-respected and, by all accounts, compassionate Halifax physician. Dr. Morrison was alleged to have hastened the death of a terminally ill patient, Paul Mills, in Halifax in November 1996. After a police investigation, she was charged with first-degree murder, the same offence that was used to prosecute Paul Bernardo and Clifford Olson, subjecting her potentially to the same minimum penalty — life in prison.

The man that Dr. Morrison allegedly killed was going to die, most probably within hours if not minutes, but his body was hanging on. He was a shell of his former self, ravaged with cancer. After ten surgical procedures, Mills was no longer even healing from the operations. His infection had filled his lungs with putrid fluid that stole the space needed for oxygen, and the infection was irreversible. A meeting was held with the family, and the medical team was advised of Mills' wish not to be kept on life support. The process of dying would be allowed to go on without medical intervention, without the heroic and futile efforts to stave off the inevitable. It was time for Paul Mills to die.

The tube that helped force oxygen into his damaged lungs was removed. But he kept drawing air, his whole chest heaving and quivering instinctively and pointlessly to sustain his life. Although not fully conscious, he was in obvious agony. He was given pain-killing drugs through the IV that had been attached to his leg. When no improvement in his apparent comfort level was being achieved, the dosages administered reached astronomical, almost unprecedented proportions. The medical team was in disbelief that he was still hanging on, still suffering pointlessly. So Dr. Morrison is alleged to have injected potassium chloride, a drug that, in large enough doses, can stop the human heart, into his IV line. Within seconds his heart stopped. Months later Nancy Morrison's heart would almost stop, as sixty police officers descended on the QE II Health Sciences Centre and arrested her for murder.

After great public pressure and some reflection, the Crown prosecutor rethought his position. He announced that he would be changing the charge to manslaughter, stating publicly that the penalty for murder would be unconscionable if applied to Dr. Morrison. The Crown asked the police to lay a new charge, alleging that Nancy Morrison had committed manslaughter. The Crown would then withdraw the murder charges and proceed on manslaughter alone. But the police refused. Dr. Morrison was properly charged, they felt, and it was their job to lay the charges, not the Crown's. So the case went forward, alleging murder.[17]

When she ultimately had her preliminary inquiry to see whether there was enough evidence to justify a murder trial, a provincial court judge ruled there was not. It was possible that Paul Mills died from natural causes or from many of the other drugs that had been administered to ease his suffering. It was also possible that the IV tip had become dislodged from his vein. Had that happened, the drugs that had been administered, including the potassium chloride, would have pooled in his body cavity and been absorbed into his muscles. They would not have killed him. There was some basis for believing this had happened because the pain-killing drugs had not had their expected effect and an autopsy had failed to show Dilaudid in the liver, which would have been expected to accumulate there in trace amounts given the quantity of that drug that had been administered through the IV. Whether the Crown could prove that Dr. Morrison contributed meaningfully to Mills' death was a real issue.[18]

The judge was no doubt correct to wonder whether the Crown could ultimately prove that Dr. Morrison killed Paul Mills. But that was not his function at the preliminary inquiry. Technically, his job was to decide whether, on the evidence, a reasonable trier of fact (a superior court judge or jury) could conclude that the actions of Dr. Morrison contributed to Paul Mills' death. The evidence showed that she selected a drug, potassium chloride, that had no purpose relevant to the man's condition at the time, a drug known to cause death by stopping the heart. She had already administered another drug to lower his blood pressure — again, not a medically prescribed treatment — but it failed to kill him. She administered the potassium chloride immediately after a nurse had remarked to her that the only thing that would end his suffering was KCL, the name for potassium chloride. She injected it directly into the man's IV line, telling the nurse she was injecting KCL. Immediately after the drug was injected, his heart stopped, precisely the effect one would have expected. In context, given her apparent purpose, the drug, and the result, a reasonable jury could certainly have concluded that her actions contributed to his death. Technically, the case should have gone forward to trial, and, for that reason, the Crown has brought an application to a superior court judge to overturn the preliminary inquiry judge's decision.[19]

If the Crown succeeds in its application and remains committed to the prosecution of Nancy Morrison, we can only hope that it will stay true to its word and prosecute her only for manslaughter. To try her as a murderer and subject her to the minimum penalty of life imprisonment would not just be bad justice. It would be an abomination. To even think of Dr. Morrison in the same breath as Paul Bernardo or Clifford Olson is preposterous. To strive to give her the same treatment as they received would be an obscenity.

The saga of all these cases is that good justice can be attained in some homicide cases only by twisting the law to avoid the minimum penalty for murder. This price is thoroughly unnecessary and it brings the administration of justice into disrepute. When a law inspires this much creativity, when prosecutors and juries are prepared to disregard it to avoid brutality, and when judges resort to clever characterization to avoid its implication, it ought to be changed. The minimum sentence for murder ought to be scrapped.

Striving to find ways to keep killers from being punished too savagely also takes its toll on those rules of law that reduce murder to manslaughter. Self-induced intoxication, which should exonerate only rarely, becomes too common a justification for murder verdicts, sending inappropriate messages to the community. We purport to have a restrictive concept of provocation, crafting significant limits on the operation of the defence, but then we rely on it to excuse acts that go far beyond its boundaries. We abuse the law to assist battered women where we fear that an acquittal will be too generous, but a life sentence too extreme. In the process, we are making these defences dangerously wide, increasing our tolerance for what are sometimes feeble excuses. We call murders "manslaughters" even when they are not.

None of this tinkering can improve the public perception of the law. And we are doing it all unnecessarily. We do not need minimum sentences to achieve significant jail time for those who kill intentionally without mitigation. They would receive substantial sentences without the minimum penalties. While trying to send the message that we are hard on killers, we have done nothing more than put ourselves in the position where reasonable people often have to be hard on law, justice, and on the credibility of the system.

The Ferguson Case: Conditional Sentencing

When the jury chose to render a manslaughter verdict, stretching the law out of shape in the process, the entire vista of sentencing options opened for the trial judge: the minimum penalties for murder were avoided. The options available to the judge included the new sentencing tool — the conditional sentence. A conditional sentence enables a judge to permit an offender who is not a danger to the community to serve the sentence in the community. The judge sentences the offender to a period of incarceration, but crafts a series of conditions that the offender must obey. The offender is then released into the community. If the offender breaches any of those conditions, the privilege of serving the sentence in the community can be lost and the judge can order the offender to serve the sentence, or any part of it, in jail.

While many of its advocates cited the futility of incarcerating non-dangerous offenders as the reason for adopting this kind of sentencing device, the immediate genesis for the conditional sentence was the incredible cost of incarcerating offenders, coupled with the habits that had developed in this country. Even though many Canadians feel that we are too easy on criminals, Canada has one of the highest rates of incarceration of any country in the Western world. Only the United States, some of the former Soviet bloc countries, and possibly Switzerland jail more people per capita.[20] Many of those incarcerated in Canada have committed property-related offences. One in four provincial reformatory prisoners who were jailed in 1995–96 were imprisoned for non-payment of fines.[21] Although libertarians have argued for years that we unjustly sentence too many people to jail, it took a fiscal crisis to achieve a sensible sentencing policy. This device allows us to make room for those who deserve to be in jail by keeping those who should not be there out of jail.

The conditional sentence is a useful and constructive device. Justice Marc Rosenberg of the Ontario Court of Appeal called it "a rational response to the problem of allocating scarce resources for the administration of justice."[22] It is also as rational a device as there is for pursuing the elusive goal of rehabilitation. To the extent that there is any realistic hope of assisting offenders to rehabilitate themselves, we know with certitude that it cannot occur while they are in jail. It can occur, if at all, in the community.

Although the conditional sentence is a useful and rational device, it is also a tremendously dangerous one from a public relations perspective. It threatens, if used too readily, to undermine public confidence in the criminal justice system. The conditional sentence is not a free ride, but it is not jail either. Even though it can involve restraints on the liberty of the convict, including, in extreme cases, house arrest and the wearing of monitoring devices, it is not significantly retributive. It simply does not have the punitive aura that is typically required to denounce serious offences and to achieve retribution. Still, these limitations do not mean that it is without any value as a form of punishment. It would be easy to underestimate the humility and pain that can be inflicted by requiring people to "report," to obey curfews, and to follow other court-based orders that non-convicted people are not subject to. Conditional sentencing has a role to play in punishment and denunciation, but at what point does its inconvenience and opprobrium fail to express a fair measure of censure or a fair assessment of moral fault?

Parliament chose to deal with this problem by making the conditional sentence available only if the accused is sentenced to less than two years, and only if the offence does not carry a minimum period of incarceration. What Parliament did not do, and what many believe it should have done, was to disqualify those convicted of crimes of violence or serious bodily harm, including sexual offences.

The belief that conditional sentences should not be available for such offences is understandable. It is one thing to spare property offenders from jail, where it is otherwise called for. It is quite another to spare violent offenders. The fact is, though, that it would have been foolish to have prohibited absolutely the use of conditional sentences for violent offences. As I have been at pains to demonstrate, not all offenders and not all offences are equal. In isolated cases, there can be compelling reasons for a conditional sentence, even for offences of violence. The conditional sentence also has some advantage from a law and order perspective. It has more teeth than other options, such as the suspended sentence,[23] for having the offender remain in the community. If conditional sentences were not available for violent offences, judges who were convinced that it would be best to have the offender serve a sentence in the community could simply suspend the passing of sentence and place the offender on probation, as they have always done. Many manslaughter sentences end up with probationary orders. I would rather have such offenders on conditional sentences, which make it far easier to have miscreants thrown into jail if they fail to live up to their conditions. It would be ironic if the stricter community sentence option, the conditional sentence, was used for non-violent offenders while the less effective suspended sentence was being used for violent offenders.

Having said this, the availability of the conditional sentence does present the significant risk that courts will fail to craft sentences which sufficiently denounce violent conduct, or which fail to accomplish retribution. Only in cases where there is palpable and compelling mitigation should a conditional sentence be used for a crime of significant violence or devastating carnage. There is a serious risk that judges, trained in the tradition of viewing sentencing as a device for reducing crime, will underestimate the importance of denunciation and retribution and will use the conditional sentence in inappropriate cases. Already there have been examples of unsuitable sentences. On 10 October 1996 a sixty-five-year-old woman in Richmond, Ontario, received a conditional sentence for attempting to arrange the murder of her daughter after her husband had been sent to jail for sexually assaulting the girl.[24] While she was under the pressure of a domineering husband, she was not subject to duress in the legal sense. The crime was despicable and heinous, crying out for jail. Similarly, on 5 May 1997, Don Dumoulin received a conditional sentence after being convicted of two counts of dangerous driving causing death and one count of dangerous driving causing bodily harm. The truck he was driving flipped off a highway ramp, killing two women standing below and leaving a baby with permanent brain damage. Dumoulin had a criminal record, including an impaired driving charge, and he was convicted again for impaired driving even after the fatal crash.[25]

Unquestionably one of the worst examples of a judge misusing a conditional sentence is the case of Kim Tran. After her husband, Vi Hoc Phung, admitted that he was in love with a younger woman, she waited for him to drift off, then took a meat cleaver and lopped off his penis, which she promptly flushed down the toilet. She told the police she did it "because [she] loved him so much." Now she is separated from him, and he from his penis, while she serves a two-year conditional sentence during which time she is studying life skills and learning English as a second language.[26] Without question, the conditional sentence in cases like this understates the criminality of the conduct. In my opinion, the same criticism applies to the Lisa Ferguson sentencing.

Ferguson received a conditional sentence. A well-respected and experienced trial judge sentenced her to two years less a day for shooting Vincent Foley, and then ordered her to serve it in the community. This was a compassionate and pragmatic decision, but it is not one that should have been arrived at. Ferguson should have been required to serve her sentence in custody. Justice Mercier, the sentencing judge, examined the sentencing issue almost exclusively from the point of view of the needs of the offender. By doing so, in my view, he failed to pay sufficient attention to the principles of denunciation and retribution. As a result, the sentence does not begin to express the full extent of her criminal conduct.

In those aspects of the decision that deal with Lisa Ferguson, Justice Mercier was characteristically perceptive and unquestionably correct. He was right to conclude that Ferguson does not pose a danger to the community and that she is not at risk to reoffend. He was right to note that the evidence showed her to be remorseful. He was correct that sentencing her to jail would not be likely to provide any measure of general deterrence. He was even correct to find that she would be better off outside prison — but, then again, who would not be? From a purely utilitarian, crime reduction perspective, Justice Mercier was absolutely right. Lisa Ferguson should not be in jail.

What I cannot agree with is his conclusion that the "strict conditions" that he imposed on her conditional sentence "satisfy the objective of denunciation" as is required by the facts of the case. Community service? Counselling? Alcohol abstention? Lisa Ferguson intentionally shot a man to death. When she did so she was not acting in self-defence. I doubt she was even provoked in the legal sense. She was drunk, angry, sick and tired of being abused, and no doubt afraid, but she took the law into her own hands, seeking Vincent Foley out and then shooting him, not once but twice. Even if she was provoked in the legal sense, provocation does not justify murder. It mitigates it, but does not cancel it out. It is a concession to human weakness and emotion, not a justification. We cannot forget that killing is almost always the product of excessive, unconstrained emotion. Provoked killings and drunken killings, save in the rarest of cases, must be denounced, and there must be some retribution for the wrong done. Ferguson's is not one of those rarest of cases. Once self-defence was rejected, this was little more than a run-of-the-mill domestic killing in which the anger needed to kill was fed by blows rather than by jealousy, infidelity, or frustration. While the circumstances call for some compassion and mitigation, they do not bear the full burden of converting a homicide sentence into a community sentence.

Certainly, on the evidence before the judge, Vincent Foley had brought this tragedy on himself to a large degree. But even though the evidence in the case painted Foley as a brute and a drunk, he was not, to use a Deep South expression, "one of those people who just needed killin'." Even if he was, "He deserved it, my Lord," is not yet a defence plea that is heard in our criminal courts, although we sometimes come close in cases involving battered women. If we, as a society, had taken the opportunity to punish Foley for his abusive conduct, we would not have exacted his life as the wages of his sin. Nor did Ferguson have any right to do so. Her conduct needed to be censured and denounced in a more meaningful way than the conditional sentence allowed.

Society, and no less the family of Vincent Foley, expects more punishment for a killing than a community-based sentence, unless there is far more mitigation than was present here. Not disproportionate and unfair punishment, but a punishment that reflects what the accused was convicted of. If this was a manslaughter, it was on the periphery of a murder. Even with the threat of jail hanging over her head, Ferguson's 240 hours of community service and rehabilitative terms relating to alcohol treatment and anger management simply fail to do it. This sentence does not inspire respect for the administration of justice because it defeats the reasonable expectations of the community that there will be punishment.

Although the tragic case of Lisa Ferguson called for compassion and understanding, given that she had been dragged to the breaking point by abject cruelty, her act did not call for the punitive aspect of her sentence to be effectively disregarded. While numbers like "life," or twenty-five, ten, or possibly even five years would have been excessive, we should not have reduced her sentence to the mere shadow of incarceration. We cannot lose sight of the fact that she had left Vincent Foley on several occasions. There was no evidence that he had pursued her, or stalked her, or intimidated her into coming back. There was no basis for believing that her will was so broken by years of abuse that she lay herself down and took it, helpless to find a way out. If she wanted to, she could have left. She did not.

In coming to his sentencing decision, Justice Mercier relied on experts. He was influenced by the probation officer's plea that Lisa Ferguson be allowed to remain in the community, and he was influenced by the opinion of a psychiatrist that incarceration would interfere with her rehabilitation. The views of the probation officer should simply have been ignored, and those of the psychiatrist should have been put into the perspective of the overall sentencing function. Experts are not in the business of doing justice: the court is. Their opinions on how to sentence are therefore worth little or nothing. As the eminent English jurist Patrick Devlin said: "The sentence must be no longer than is justified by the gravity of the crime and must not fall below the least that retribution demands. This is the lawyer's objective. The penologist's objective is to send the prisoner back to the world changed for the better."[27]

When judges begin making "changing the prisoner" the primary objective of sentencing in violence cases, it is time to trade the black robes for white ones. Lisa Ferguson, who could no doubt use assistance in improving the quality of her life, did not need rehabilitation to protect society. Yet she received a masterful rehabilitative sentence. In the bargain, in my opinion, neither society nor the family of Vincent Foley received justice.

When Robert Latimer's counsel stood before Justice Noble he asked for a conditional sentence, for the same treatment that Lisa Ferguson received. The judge said no: "I'm not quite frankly inclined to consider a conditional sentence in this case . . . It's just in my view, the nature of the crime, albeit one that was committed for altruistic reasons, is just too serious."[28] Dead right. And Vincent Foley didn't even die for altruistic reasons.

The conditional sentence, with its premises that the offender is not a danger to the community and its focus on probation-like terms rather than punishment, is bound, unless great care is exercised, to cause courts to lose sight of the sentencing mission. This is especially so if we underestimate the importance of the denunciatory and retributive aspects of sentencing in the case of violent offenders. Fortunately, appellate courts are now recognizing this, and it is likely that this message will work its way to trial judges. If it does not, instead of operating as a rational sentencing device, the conditional sentence will contribute to the public malaise over the failings of the criminal justice system. It will ultimately defeat itself because politicians will make it more rigid, or possibly even abolish it. In the end, a valuable sentencing tool will become lost.

The Injustice of Parole

P ress Release, 22 January 1993:

> Anyone knowing the whereabouts of Nicole Marguerite Mattison is asked to contact the Metropolitan Toronto Police. Mrs. Mattison has been missing since 2 December 1992 when she was last seen walking east on the south side of King Street West at Spadina Avenue. She is fifty-three years of age, five foot 10 inches tall, and weighs 150 pounds. She has blond hair and was wearing a multi-coloured jacket, maroon slacks and black shoes at the time of her disappearance. She was also wearing two gold chains, one with a pendant with the inscription "Live, Love, Laugh."

"Live, Love, Laugh," thought Constable McGreal when he received the missing person's report from Nicole's husband, David, a month before the press conference. "There hasn't been much loving and laughing in that marriage." He had worked with David Mattison at the downtown 52 Division, where Mattison was a police sergeant. He recalled how David would come to his place with his girlfriend while Nicole sat at home. McGreal could never understand it. David, an astute investor, probably had more than a million dollars, maybe a couple of million. "Why don't you just split things down the middle and let her go her way and you go yours?" he would say. But they stayed together. It wasn't because David loved her. In January 1991 he told a marriage counsellor that he would rather do five years for killing her than fifteen years living with her. "Perhaps they stay together because Nicole won't let go," he thought. "Why else was she always phoning around looking for him?"

Maybe they felt they had to stay together for the sake of their two grandchildren. Nicole and David had lost their eldest son, Lionel, in a car accident in northern Ontario three years before and they had custody of his two children. While that tragedy may have kept them together, it did not make them any closer. It simply increased the stress and tension. Things got so bad that David ultimately took his girlfriend to Florida and boasted to Nicole about it. Indeed, he had probably done so again only a few weeks before Nicole went missing; he had gone to Florida without her at the same time that his girlfriend had taken her vacation. This was not a happy marriage.

Constable McGreal couldn't help feeling nervous about the missing person's report. It made no sense. Why had David waited nineteen days before reporting Nicole missing? When he did file the report it just felt wrong. He had told McGreal that on 2 December he and Nicole had an argument while in the car. She got out at the busy intersection, slammed the door, and punched the passenger window, shattering it, before walking away.

It was not the account of Nicole punching the window that caused McGreal to doubt the story. Nicole worked as a jail guard and was a stocky 5 feet 10 inches. She was feisty, too. On at least one earlier occasion she had used a knife to threaten David, who is as large as any Tim Horton's cop. But this report didn't seem right. As McGreal was later to explain:

> The whole thing didn't make sense. If I hated my wife and was reporting her missing, I'd be sitting down with a beer. I'd say good riddance. But he was very uptight. Ask a simple question like "What colour's her eyes?" and there'd be a long story about it before he'd finally explain what colour her eyes were.[1]

Why would she just walk away from the money? If she wanted out she would sue him, not disappear.

From the start, foul play was suspected, and fifty-eight-year-old David Mattison, who had brought Nicole back from France in 1961 after being posted there with the armed forces, was the only suspect. Even if the police in Brentwood, California, O.J. Simpson's territory, don't suspect the husband when a wife dies or goes missing, police everywhere else on the planet do.[2]

The ironic thing was that Nicole was not really missing — at least not entirely. The police in Hamilton, Ontario, had her leg; they just didn't know it was hers. The leg, which had clearly been severed intentionally, had been found washed up on the beach a few weeks before. Tissue samples from the leg were being sent off to the United States for DNA analysis, along with samples taken from Nicole's relatives. Even though the police responded at the press conference that the disappearance of Nicole was unconnected to the grisly discovery, they had their suspicions. On 26 March 1992, when the laboratory results were returned, David Mattison was arrested and charged with the first-degree murder of his wife.

This is the kind of case prosecutors dread. Instinct makes you confident that you know what happened, but the evidence is incredibly weak. You have grounds to arrest and charge the suspect, and no real choice but to proceed, but you know that your chances of succeeding are poor. Plenty of motive, a flippant remark to a marriage counsellor a few years before that could be construed as a threat, body parts, and suspicious behaviour — but no witnesses, no crime scene, no autopsy, and, to make matters worse, prior aggression by the victim. The case was assigned to prosecutor Mary Hogan. She would later spend her time assisting in the prosecution of Paul Bernardo and had earned the nickname "Maximum Mary" for her unrelenting sentencing positions.

Like most accused killers, Mattison applied to be released on bail so he would not have to wait in jail for his trial to start. Murder bail hearings are different from the simple hearings that are held for routine offences. Most bail hearings take place before a justice of the peace within hours of the charge, with prosecutors and even defence lawyers largely winging it because they do not have time to do otherwise. By contrast, lawyers prepare meticulously for murder bail hearings, which tend to be protracted affairs, sometimes lasting more than a day. These hearings are done before superior court judges. Most often, fear of releasing a killer into the community keeps judges from granting the request, and suspects are kept in jail pending their trials, often for a year or more. When Mattison was ordered released, it became agonizingly clear to Hogan just how weak her case was. It was time to consider doing a deal. Within a few months she reached an agreement with Mattison's lawyer, Austin Cooper, a leading Toronto counsel who had earlier defended Susan Nelles successfully in the Hospital for Sick Children debacle. Rather than risk life in prison for murder, Mattison was prepared to plead guilty to manslaughter. In return, he would give a videotaped statement to the police that would provide them with the facts that would be given to the judge, and the Crown would agree to a sentence of between ten and twelve years in prison.

To a prosecutor, ten to twelve years in prison does not sound bad. Ten years is a long time. It is enough time to turn pudgy six-year-old children into young adults, capable of producing their own pudgy children. It is enough time to give a handsome, fit, smooth-faced thirty-five-year-old man thinning hair, deep lines around the eyes, and a bulge over the belt that won't go away, no matter how many situps are done. In the scheme of things, it is a monumental slice out of any life. As a plea-bargained sentence, compared with the risk of nothing, which is a real prospect in a case like this, it is almost a no-brainer. You buck up and take it.

Detective Sergeant Warr, the investigating officer, no doubt felt some apprehension as he turned on the video camera. Would they get the real story? Nicole Mattison was not going to be there to tell her side of it. Only David Mattison was, and he had reason to come up with a version that would enable the judge to agree to the deal.

Mattison spoke of how stormy the marriage had been. In early December, while the thoughts of most turn to the coming holiday season and even those who are normally cranky seem to be in good spirits, David and Nicole Mattison had a horrendous fight. He had gone to visit her at their home in Fonthill, near Niagara Falls. The fight started over the way he had disciplined their nine-year-old grandson for a bed-wetting episode. Nicole, he said, called him names and swore at him. As she got more irate, she grabbed a kitchen knife and threatened to cut herself with it, then came at him, chasing him and jabbing the knife towards him. He took his revolver and shot her.

This version of facts was suspicious, but no one could prove otherwise. In reporting David Mattison's account when it was read into court, Thomas Claridge, a courts reporter with the *Globe and Mail* observed: "There was no explanation of why the handgun was 'at hand.' Elsewhere in the statement Sgt. Mattison was described as having been on sick leave from the police since Oct. 13, 1991, suffering from a job-related injury."[3] This man, who had already lied to the police, had provided a troubling account. From there, things got even more distressing. He panicked, he said, and felt he had to get rid of the body. So he took her corpse and threw it into the trunk of his car. He drove to the couple's Pickering home, east of Toronto. There he got out his tools. He used a utility knife and a hacksaw. He dismembered and beheaded his wife's body. He put the head in a tin can. Then he cut off Nicole's fingertips so that, if her arms were found, they could not be identified. Like the butcher he was, he wrapped the body parts, using garbage bags. He placed her remains in the trunk of his car. He drove, no doubt cautiously to avoid a chance encounter with the police, to the Burlington Canal. There he dropped the remains of Nicole Marguerite Mattison into the frigid water and watched them sink. When he returned home, he set his car on fire to destroy the evidence and blamed his orphaned grandson's carelessness for the blaze.

Even if his story was entirely true, David Mattison had taken the road from self-defence to the unspeakable inhumanity of self-preservation. With all its warts, this was the version of facts that was provided to the sentencing judge. As Detective Sergeant Warr was later to say: "There's nothing good about the case. . . . But what I think and what I can prove are two entirely different things."[4]

The guilty plea was done before Justice David Humphrey, who before going to the bench had been a lawyer of legendary skill and humour. Folklore has it that he once ran from the stands and tripped a player who was going to score in a CFL game against his home team. But there would be no room for humour or spectacular antics on this day. As Justice Humphrey said, this case was "a tragedy of monumental proportions." He commented how David Mattison, who had served the people of his community for years and whose life spiralled downwards after the death of his son, had degenerated to the point where he could engage in such "callous and disgusting behaviour." Based on the evidence presented at the sentencing hearing, Justice Humphrey nonetheless agreed to the joint proposal. On the evidence available, the killing had been provoked, therefore manslaughter was an appropriate verdict. The sentence had to reflect this fact. On 11 June 1993 David Mattison stood and the community watched as Justice Humphrey told him he was going to jail for ten years. When Justice Humphrey spoke those words, he knew Mattison would not spend all that time in jail. Mary Hogan knew it too, but there was nothing she could do about it.

While ten years is a significant slice out of any life, three and a half years is a much smaller slice. It may seem a long time for someone who is working towards a BA degree, but as a prison term on these facts it would seem to the public like "Bugger All." On 27 November 1996 Mattison was moved from the minimum security camp at Beaver Brook, where he had served most of his time in custody, to Keele Centre, a community corrections centre, or half-way house, in downtown Toronto. Just under three and a half years into his ten-year sentence, he was on day parole, free to enjoy the city during the day. You may have sat next to him at a Blue Jays game or had a coffee next to him at the Eaton Centre. He applied for and was denied full parole in December 1997. He is up for parole again in September 1998. If he succeeds, he will have served just half his sentence in some form of detention. Even if he fails, the worst he will do is to remain in custody until the Christmas season of 1999, when he will be given statutory release. Unless he breaches the conditions of his release, he will watch the millennium change from the comfort of his own place, some six and a half years into his ten-year sentence.

Many Canadians hate the parole system. They believe that release on parole is granted too early, too often, and to the wrong people.[5] As it does with many detested aspects of the criminal justice system, this dislike exists, at least in part, because Canadians do not fully understand the system and are basing their distaste on false assumptions. They overestimate how often parolees commit offences while in the community, they exaggerate how often parole is granted, and they tend not to understand the difference between, or the operation of, parole and other forms of release.[6] This confusion is not surprising. The process of being released from prison is so complex that even many criminal lawyers do not understand it. Many wave to their clients as they march off to jail, not knowing exactly what their sentences mean, while the judge often sits there wondering the same thing.

Discontent with the parole system cannot be attributed solely to misunderstanding. Even if Canadians understood the system better, they would not like it. In my view, the system of early release that we have is simply not a part of the criminal justice system that can be defended in rational, convincing terms. This is so for a number of reasons, not the least of which is that it makes the solemn ceremony of sentencing look like a pious fraud. It is as though every sentence comes with a ready-made asterisk above it. That asterisk leads to a footnote that says, "When we say 'ten,' we may really mean three and one-third, or we may mean six and two-thirds or some other number, but we only rarely mean ten."

The word "parole" originally described the word of honour given by a prisoner of war of the officer class who was allowed to live at large or even to visit his home, so long as he promised not to escape or to fight anymore.[7] It was a matter of honour between officers, a reciprocal arrangement made between those with the power to protect themselves from the full brutality of war. Now it is one of several mechanisms for protecting convicts from the full brutality of prison. It is no longer a matter of honour at all. Instead, it is the sleepy vestige of an earlier era when we believed that prisons could rehabilitate and that offenders, like young puppies, could be scared into behaving appropriately by being punished.

The mechanisms for early release from prison are not difficult to explain, but they are nonetheless complex. One of the reasons they are complex is that both the provinces and the federal government play a role in the penal corrections system. Prisoners serve the custodial period of their sentence either in provincial reformatories or in federal penitentiaries. This is an idiosyncrasy of Canadian federalism. Generally, those who are sentenced to two years less a day go into the provincial system. Those who are sentenced to two years or more become federal prisoners and go to the "pen." The rules for early release differ in some respects for federal and provincial prisoners.

I recall as a prosecutor seeking a penitentiary sentence for a young man who had escaped from a provincial reformatory. I was asking for a sentence that would, coupled with the time he had left on his existing sentence, amount to twenty-six months. Defence counsel fought hard against a penitentiary sentence. He wanted a combined sentence of eighteen months that would keep the accused in the provincial system. The judge sawed off, as often happens, and sentenced the offender to what would amount to twenty-two months. His lawyer looked relatively jubilant, having defeated my efforts to upgrade the young man from a "reformatory" prisoner to the inmate of a "pen." But then his client piped up:

> "Your Highness," he said to the judge, trying to imitate the grovelling he had just seen from the two lawyers. "Please don't give me 22 months. Either give me the 18 my lawyer wanted, or I'll take the 24, but don't give me 22 months."

The whole court erupted in laughter as the judge, like a Burger King cashier said, "Have it your way," before sentencing the man to twenty-four months. As we were walking out of court an experienced defence lawyer explained to me that the accused wanted to go to the "pen" because he would be released sooner than if he went to the provincial institution. The prisoner knew more about the correctional system than I, the judge, and his lawyer, yet he was the only one of us who was not paid for his legal work.

The primary reason for the complexity of the law of early release is that, apart from making a papier mâché head to leave in bed before crawling through the prison sewer system or having your moll rent a helicopter, there are a number of ways that a convict can end up outside prison before his sentence has expired. These ways include "temporary absences," "day parole," "parole," and "statutory release."

Although there are a number of possibilities, in a simple case a federal prisoner has a "parole eligibility date" that will fall one-third of the way through the sentence. At that time, the prisoner can apply for parole. If parole is granted, the offender has been judged not to pose an undue risk of reoffending and is released into the community to assist in his or her rehabilitation.

"Day parole" is a more limited form of release, in which the offender is normally able to enter the community by day to engage in some structured pursuit of work or study, only to return to custody at night. Eligibility for "day parole" normally arises after one-sixth of the sentence has been served.

Those who are not given full parole are normally given "statutory release." This privilege enables all but the most dangerous offenders to be released into the community after two-thirds of their sentence has expired, whether they have been paroled or not. Offenders who have committed violent offences, sex offences, or serious drug offences can be made to serve their entire sentence if there are reasonable grounds to believe that they will commit an offence causing death or serious harm, a sexual offence against a child, or a serious drug offence.

"Temporary absence," as the name suggests, is a mechanism for allowing convicts who have not yet been paroled and who have not yet obtained statutory release to go into the community for specific purposes, such as to attend court, to go into hospital, or to participate in rehabilitation programs. These absences can be escorted or non-escorted.

Each of these forms of release is known as "conditional release." The releases are conditional because legislation, and corrections officials, impose terms and conditions on the released offender. If the offender breaches any of those terms, or there is reason to believe that there will be a breach of those terms, the privilege of being released can be lost and the offender reincarcerated.

As a result of the various modes of "conditional release," few offenders actually serve their entire sentence. In 1995–96, for example, only 5 percent of those who were released from federal penitentiaries had completed their sentences; all but 417 of 7998 of the convicts who were released that year had served less time than the judge told them they would.

Contrary to popular belief, the main reason for this early release is not parole. In 1995–96 the parole grant rate for federal inmates was only 34 percent,[8] enabling a total of 3024 offenders to be released on parole. Because parole is denied so often, the main reason for the early release of inmates is "statutory release." In 1995–96 it accounted for the release into the community of 4457 of the 7998 inmates.[9] It can easily be seen, then, that between parole and statutory release, early release is the overwhelming norm. Quite simply, taken together, parole and statutory release have taken the fun out of the prison break.

Conditional Release

The *Corrections and Conditional Release Act* states that the purpose of conditional release is: "to contribute to the maintenance of a just, peaceful and safe society by means of decisions on the timing and conditions of release that will best facilitate the rehabilitation of offenders and their reintegration into the community as law abiding citizens."

Officially, then, the main purpose of statutory release is rehabilitation. An examination of the Act and its history reveals that conditional release is also counted on to accomplish other purposes as well. For example, some prisoners are released on compassionate grounds. Historically, the primary function of early release was to encourage offenders to be of good behaviour while they were in jail; although this is no longer one of its major purposes, it is still a factor in parole decisions. Without question, however, one of the major considerations is simple economics. Although it is nowhere stated in the legislation and is flatly denied as official policy,[10] prison overcrowding and its associated costs argue powerfully in favour of early release. Parole and statutory release have significant budgetary implications that cannot be ignored. Most offenders serve, on average, approximately half their designated sentence. Simple arithmetic suggests that if all prisoners were to serve their complete sentence, prison populations would be close to double. We cannot afford, either socially or economically, to have that. Anyone who criticizes the parole system has to understand this reality and make allowances for it.

PAROLE

Those who are granted parole are released so they can finish serving their sentences in the community. They have been judged by the parole board not to present an undue risk to society, and to be persons whose rehabilitation will be assisted by allowing them to integrate slowly into the community.

As indicated, most convicts, including those convicted of violence and sex offences, are eligible to apply to be released into the community by way of parole after serving one-third of their sentence, or seven years, whichever is less. This is the parole eligibility period for those convicted of manslaughter. It is the regime that applied to David Mattison, who became eligible to apply for full parole three and a third years after he was convicted.

The period that must be served before parole eligibility is longer for murderers. When sentenced, those who have received life sentences for second-degree murder are told that they will not be eligible for between ten and twenty-five years, depending on the discretion of the trial judge. Generally, first-degree murder convicts are told they cannot apply for parole until twenty-five years have expired. The "faint hope" clause, section 745.6 of the *Criminal Code*, allows those convicts who have served fifteen years without eligibility for parole to apply for a reduction in their ineligibility period. To date, most section 745.6 applications have been successful, reducing the parole ineligibility period in 70 percent of the cases.[11]

Occasionally, violent offenders can become eligible for parole sooner than the normal one-third period. In exceptional cases, accelerated parole can be given to an offender who is terminally ill, whose physical or

mental health is likely to suffer serious damage from continued incarceration, or whose incarceration would impose excessive hardship because
circumstances have changed since the time of sentence. These people can
be released only if they are considered unlikely to reoffend. If Corporal
Klinger of *MASH* fame had worn pin-stripes instead of a U.S. Army uni-
form, this is the early release plan he would have opted for.

Inmates who have not committed offences of sex or violence and
who are in the penitentiary for the first time will normally be entitled to
"accelerated parole." Correctional officials are required by law to refer
their cases to a parole board at least three months before they have served
one-third of their sentence, although this referral can be done sooner. The
parole board must then decide at least seven weeks before the convicts'
normal parole eligibility date whether to grant parole.[12] In theses cases the
board has less discretion. The parole board *must* approve the accelerated
parole unless it has reasonable grounds to believe that the convict will
commit an offence involving violence before the expiration of his or her
sentence.[13] Assuming that all officials wait until the last minute to do their
jobs, this means that a convict who has no history of violence and who
has received a three-year sentence for impaired driving causing death will
be granted full parole after serving ten months, regardless of behaviour
while inside.

STATUTORY RELEASE

Statutory release has replaced "remission" as a mechanism for gaining
early release from prison. "Remission," which had been around since
Confederation, allowed offenders to shorten their sentences by good
behaviour. We have been through numerous elaborate formulae. Each was
premised on the theory that, if inmates know they will be released earlier
by behaving well in the institution, prison officials will have an easier time
maintaining discipline. Most recently, prisoners could earn up to one-
third of their sentence for good behaviour.

Originally, the time off for good behaviour was "remitted" or forgiven, and the offender simply left the prison as a free man or woman
after the sentence remission was cashed in. A three-year sentence would
become a two-year sentence. Then we abolished sentence remissions and
moved to a system of "mandatory release." Prisoners could still earn time
off for good behaviour, but they would be under community supervision
while on the outside until their original sentence expired. Now we have
gone one step further, moving away from the requirement that inmates
earn their sentence reductions. We have a system that *automatically* entitles most inmates to be released once they have served two-thirds of their

sentences, whether they have been of good behaviour or not. They can be the most obstinate, unrepentant troublemakers and they are still entitled to be freed after two-thirds of their sentence has been served.

The idea of time off for good behaviour died because it was not working. Appearing before the Daubney Committee in 1988, the Commissioner of Corrections testified that he had his doubts about whether remission did very much to improve institutional behaviour. He testified that it had lost its purpose because it had become almost automatic.[14] The practice was not only ineffective but offensive. Why reward prisoners for doing what they were supposed to be doing anyway? The Daubney Committee recommended that time off for good behaviour be abolished, and their proposal was ultimately accepted. Earned remission no longer exists. Instead, we automatically let most prisoners go after two-thirds of their sentence has been served, good behaviour or not. Why? The idea is that even those who have not been paroled still require a period of community supervision and adjustment before being released entirely. The belief is that society is better served in the long run by these people being released early so they can be reintegrated slowly, with the support of corrections officials. How long do they need to be integrated? One-third of their sentence seemed a familiar figure. Why not keep that as the measure?

Exceptionally, the most dangerous prisoners do not receive this early form of release. During the early 1980s there was considerable pressure to abolish mandatory supervision because of public fear that particularly dangerous convicts were being freed without finishing their sentences. Since prison officials were responsible for remission-based release, the National Parole Board could not prevent convicts from being turned loose, no matter how dangerous it considered them to be. What the National Parole Board could do, though, was to order the detention of any inmate who was likely to reoffend. It decided to use this power to rearrest prisoners released on statutory remission whom the board considered dangerous. As a result, we endured for a time the silly ceremony of "gating": corrections officials would escort the inmate to the gate for release on statutory remission so he could be ceremoniously arrested on a parole board warrant once he crossed the threshold and be taken back inside to serve the remainder of his sentence. This cruel and silly practice was stopped because the courts ruled it to be unconstitutional, but Parliament responded immediately with legislation that achieves the same result, albeit more sensibly. This legislation allows the parole board to prevent the release of the most dangerous offenders. Under its terms, the parole board can order the continued detention of offenders who are in prison because of violence, sexual offences, or drug offences, provided that evidence at a detention hearing shows there are reasonable grounds to believe that, if released, they are likely to commit an offence causing death or serious bodily harm, a sexual offence involving children, or a serious drug offence. In 1995–96, 483 federal inmates were denied statutory release and detained under this authority.[15]

The Release of Dangerous Offenders

It can be seen that the government has moved steadily towards a policy of reducing access to early release for dangerous offenders, while attempting to release non-violent offenders from jail as early as possible. Coupled with the conditional sentence, these initiatives are intended to reserve precious prison space for those whom society should lock up. Parliament has recently taken additional steps in this direction. Those who are declared by a sentencing court at the time of their convictions to be "long-term" offenders can be subject to up to ten years of community supervision after their sentences have expired. "Long-term" offenders are sexual offenders who pose a substantial risk of reoffending, where there is a reasonable possibility of controlling the risk of reoffending in the community.

By attempting to clear out prisons for violent and dangerous offenders while reducing our dependence on prisons for property-related and less serious offences, it is clear that recent legislation is heading in the right direction, at least from a resource management perspective. The continued use of the parole and statutory release model to get there, however, is fraught with problems.

The False Promise of Parole and Statutory Release

The theory behind both parole and statutory release is that they allow society to maintain control over offenders for a period of time after they are released so they can gradually wean themselves from the nurturing milk of supervision. Inmates who have completed their sentences before being released are free to do as they want. They are not subject to the power of corrections officials, for they have done their time. If an offender is released before completing a sentence, conditions can be imposed and the progress of the offender can be monitored until the sentence has expired. It is believed by those who support a parole and statutory release model that this community supervision period improves the chance that the convict will become a contributing member of society in the long run.

How compelling is this belief? Take parole first. The fact is, there are serious problems with the whole idea. A prerequisite for granting parole for most convicts is that they not present an undue risk of reoffending. The implicit assumption must be either that paroled offenders never presented an undue risk of reoffending, even when initially sentenced, or that the time they spent in jail has reduced their propensity to commit offences. But prison does not reduce the risk that an offender will offend again. Government commission after commission has concluded that prison has a debilitating rather than a rehabilitative effect.[16] There is simply no basis for believing that criminals will be less dangerous after they have served a portion of their sentence than if they had served no time in custody at all, yet this is a major premise of parole theory.

The next assumption is that the relevant parole board will be in a position to predict who is likely to reoffend. Save in rare cases, it is not. As criminologist Neil Boyd has observed:

> Members of our national and provincial Parole Boards are not really any more accurate than the rest of us in their predictions of an individual's readiness for release. The best guesses are based on past criminal record and age, not on any specialized psychiatric or psychological expertise. Beyond such objective measures, the prediction of future criminal behaviour is little more than speculation. It is, as a number of researchers have demonstrated, no better than flipping coins in the courtroom.[17]

There is no doubt that members of the national and provincial parole boards work hard and have the best of intentions, but even if they have full information, their job is as precarious as betting on the horses. While there are some sure bets, parole boards are required to make this assessment for every potential parolee. More often than not they will be doing little more than guessing. In many cases, it seems, they are guessing without the benefit of full information. The Auditor General of Canada found in his 1995–96 review that the National Parole Board has a tendency to rely too much on the offender's version of the initial crime and that important information is often missing from the files. Sixty parole cases were audited at random and, in more than half, pre-incarceration information about the offender was missing or incomplete; in 17 percent, no information had been received from the prosecutor, and in 18 percent police information was incomplete.[18]

Parole theory also depends on another, more fundamental assumption: that an offender who is supervised in the community for a period will be less likely to continue to offend than an offender who is simply shown the prison door at the end of the sentence and told to leave. This belief rests on faith in the ability of corrections officials to rehabilitate offenders, a faith that must be called into question based on the woeful record of rehabilitative sentencing measures. Rehabilitation is an elusive objective, primarily because it requires that lifelong attitudes and value systems be changed. It ignores the fact that much of the crime that occurs is personality based and that it is no easy feat to change a human being. In some cases crime may even be linked to innate physiological or psychological conditions. Often offenders do not want to be rehabilitated, some to the point where they would rather sit out two-thirds of their sentences than participate in rehabilitation programs.[19] Others participate in available programs simply to fool parole officials into granting early release.

Casting aside these observations, there are insufficient resources to allow for the meaningful rehabilitation of those who are on mandatory supervision, even if it were possible. In 1995–96, 120,300 offenders were serving sentences in the community. Of those, 16 percent were on parole or statutory release, while the rest were on probation. This number represents a 50 percent increase over the last decade.[20] In the 1987 Canadian Sentencing Commission report, surveyed corrections officials reported, in significant numbers, that their caseloads were too high to allow for effective supervision.[21] Since then, government spending on adult corrections has decreased in real terms.[22] We have far fewer resources than we did ten years ago when things were already bad.

The Auditor General of Canada noted that even when inmates are still in the institutions, they are seen by their case management officers only once every one or two months for forty-five minutes.[23] How do you drum twenty-five years of anger out of a young man by chatting with him for 1/2000th of his time, while he spends the rest with guys who have homemade tattoos across their knuckles? Corrections officials and rehabilitative programs are overburdened, both inside and outside the institutions.

Not surprisingly, the Canadian Sentencing Commission was not impressed with claims that gradual release will reduce the tendency of those released from prison to offend:

> Research shows that whether an offender is released with or without conditions has almost no effect on recidivism rates. Waller (1974) found that release on supervision merely postpones rather than prevents subsequent recidivism. When clients are no longer under conditions they offend at rates similar to those who have not been subject to conditions.[24]

The fact is that while it may be possible through effective community supervision to reduce the conditions that predispose an offender to offend, such as through restraining orders, random drug testing, alcohol prohibitions, residential placements, employment programs, and constant monitoring, community supervision does not increase rehabilitation rates. Once community supervision ends, the offender is no more likely to have been effectively rehabilitated than one who is simply released at the end of his sentence. Even during community supervision, there continue to be problems. In 1995–96, 3164 of 7481 convicts released from federal institutions, or 44 percent, were returned into custody. Two-thirds of those who were returned were sent back for breaching conditions such as alcohol abstention or for associating with known criminals, but one-third of those who were returned, or approximately 14 percent of all released offenders, had committed a new offence while on community supervision.[25] While less than 2 percent of federal prisoners who were on community supervision committed violent offences in that year, a rate of one violent offence for every fifty people is far greater than the ratio among the general population.[26] If these people will not remain law-abiding when under community supervision, they are not going to be rehabilitated after community supervision ends.

Even if it did work, parole is unacceptable because it replaces the judgment of the judge, whose sentence is arrived at in the interests of justice, with the judgment of committees and bureaucrats who make their decisions not according to the demands of justice, but according to the interests of manageable community risk and the self-deluding pursuit of rehabilitation. At the time of sentencing, rehabilitation and incapacitation are only two of the factors a judge will consider. At the time of parole, they become the only considerations. There is no place in parole decision making for the board to consider denunciation, to express solidarity with the victim, or to accomplish retribution, yet these factors, along with temporary incapacitation, tend to be the real reasons for incarceratory sentences in the first place. It makes no sense to have a parole system that pursues different objectives in administering a sentence than those pursued by the courts that have proclaimed those sentences.

The importance of the gulf between the punitive aspect of sentencing and the rehabilitative goal of parole cannot be overstated. When a judge sentences an offender, rehabilitation will be a consideration. If the judge believes that rehabilitation is the correct goal to emphasize, he or she will generally choose a non-incarceratory sentence or a short period of jail, followed by probation. What is only a secondary and often an irrelevant feature of the incarceratory sentence for the judge becomes the essence of the sentence for the correction official. Sentencing and parole operate at cross-purposes, often pursuing inconsistent goals.

Those who defend the parole system deny that there is a gulf between sentencing practices and the parole regime. They seek to minimize the difference between sentencing and parole decisions by arguing that parole does not lengthen or shorten sentences. It merely affects "the way of serving the sentence."[27] They claim, as well, that when they are releasing offenders, they are merely administering the sentence of the court.[28]

All these justifications are as transparent as wet cheese-cloth. Allowing someone to be in the community on conditions is closer to probation than it is to prison. Converting prison into probation is not a simple matter of sentence administration or tinkering with the mode of sentence; it is a matter of evisceration. Although serving time in the community is a sentence, it is very different from the one the judge has proclaimed. It has only a shadow of the denunciatory or retributive properties of incarceration.

Official corrections policy goes so far as to deny that early release undermines the denunciatory or punitive aspects of the sentence. The National Parole Board believes that the punitive portion of the sentence is finished when parole eligibility arises. As the former chairman of the board put it, "Parole cannot be granted until the denunciatory portion of the offender's sentence — as determined in [parole] regulations as the parole eligibility date — has been served."[29] In other words, Justice Humphrey was intending to punish David Mattison only for the first third of his sentence. If that is so, what were the last six and a half years supposed to be for? Providing him with a place to live? While there is a great deal about the purposes of sentencing that is unclear, one point that is certain is that judges who send people to jail do not do so thinking that the denunciatory or retributive portion of the sentence ends one-third of the way along. Euphemism and rationalization cannot change the fact that the parole system is at loggerheads with the sentencing process.

Parole officials are not to blame for this discord; rather, it is the legislation that supports the parole system. Corrections officials are simply carrying out their legislative mandate and, contrary to public perception, they most often do it with commitment, trying their best to come to the right decision. Those of us who work in the courts cannot get off of the hook so easily. We bear a good measure of the responsibility. We have allowed the gulf between sentencing and parole to remain obscure because, like corrections officials, we never tire of taking the high road and claiming that we sentence to reduce crime rather than to punish. If we were more frank and open in admitting the punitive aspect of sentencing, it would be much more difficult for those who support parole to operate under the pretense that parole and judicial sentencing are two hands that share a pair of matching gloves.

What, then, of statutory release? In some respects it suffers from fewer problems than parole. It is better in the sense that it is marginally more honest. Most inmates are released without the pretense of predicting whether they are likely to reoffend, and they are released without any pretensions about their having been rehabilitated enough by the prison experience to be set free. Yet statutory release still suffers from many of the problems that parole does. It, too, depends for its existence on the myth that compulsory community supervision following incarceration is a form of rehabilitation. Like parole, in the false pursuit of rehabilitation, it too is permitted to dull the punitive aspects of incarceration.

In at least one respect, statutory release is even more offensive than parole. For all but the worst offenders it is an automatic statutory discount, given regardless of good behaviour, attitude, or promise. It is a gift, bestowed on these wonderful citizens, "just because." It is as though we had fallen into such a habit of crediting up to one-third of the time off that, when the original reason for doing so disappeared (encouraging good behaviour), we simply manufactured a new reason (gradual reintegration) to keep up the practice. We should always be suspicious of legal rules that take on new explanations to outlive their original reason for existing.

There is yet another, more fundamental reason why the parole and statutory release systems are unacceptable: they compromise the main purpose for the criminal prosecution. We prosecute and punish offenders because society demands that criminals be held accountable. The criminal trial is the way in which society comes together collectively and publicly to determine whether an accused person has violated basic community norms. Where the offender is guilty, the sentence is the way that society measures and expresses the degree of the offender's accountability and its commitment to the values that have been breached. It is the discharge of the obligation that society owes to the victims, who, in the interests of civilization and civility, it has deprived of the right of self-help. Canadian society, like every country, race, and creed in every millennium and continent, expects and depends on ceremonial punishment. As a civilized society we have learned to temper retribution and denunciation by proportionality, restraint, openness, objectivity, and, in some cases, forgiveness, but we have not been willing or able to discard the compelling need to punish wrongdoers. Those of us who felt sick when the O.J. Simpson verdict was announced were not upset that the Americans had lost the opportunity to rehabilitate the man; rather, it sickened us that someone generally believed to be guilty was not going to be held accountable. That is what the criminal trial is primarily about. Its whole purpose is to determine whether we must hold the accused accountable through punishment. Speaking of the criminal trial, Sir James Fitzjames Stephens said that "the sentence is the gist of the proceedings. It is to the trial what the bullet is to the powder."[30]

What role do parole and statutory release play in this process? Together they serve to mask the real sentence an offender will receive, taking it from an open and public courtroom where it is clear and resonant, and muffling it under the babble of incomprehensible, bureaucratic mumbo-jumbo and little-known statutory provisions. The real meaning of "ten years" can only be understood in terms of "parole eligibility dates," "statutory release dates," "revocations," "suspensions," "terminations," "accelerated parole eligibility," and the musing and speculations of labcoats and bureaucrats about when a man is new. The judicial sentence, as announced with solemn ceremony to the community as an expression of denunciation of the crime and of solidarity with the victim, is butchered into some fraction of a sentence at a later date. We have built a system in which the public, and even the lawyers and judges, have no idea what a sentence really means. It is a matter of great mystery how we, in the system, can justify telling the public that David Mattison is going to jail for ten years when we know that this is not going to happen.

Parole and, to a lesser extent, statutory release are unacceptable to those who are interested in justice on another ground. They exacerbate the unequal treatment of offenders and have an inflationary effect on sentences. Although technically it is wrong to do so, many judges allow the prospect of early release to influence the sentences they pronounce, inflating sentences beyond those that are appropriate for offences.[31] All for what? So that after the offender and the sentence have been locked behind what are effectively closed doors,[32] we can pursue the futile policy of rehabilitation in preference to the objects of sentencing that are pursued by a judge in open court.

It is time to be frank. To the extent that parole and statutory release are premised on the promise of rehabilitation, they are an elaborate failure. The fact that most convicts do not reoffend while on community supervision cannot be the measure of the success of early release. The reason for parole and statutory release is not to reduce offences during the continuation of the sentence. The most effective way to do that is to make convicts serve their entire sentence. The reason for early release is to assist in the reintegration of the offender into the community as a rehabilitated person. The relevant question, therefore, is not about rates of offence during community supervision but whether early release enhances long-term rehabilitation. There is no reason to believe that it does, and every reason to believe that it does not. As one critic has said:

Whatever else can be said of parole, it is surely the weakest link in the chain that is supposed to protect the public. By putting the focus on the reliability of risk assessment and on the need to protect society, the advocates of parole only compound the most damaging error of the criminal justice system: making promises it cannot possibly fulfill.[33]

The truth is, we continue to engage in the early release exercise for two insufficient reasons. The first is sentimental. The more gentle among us have an abiding but naive belief that we can rehabilitate our worst offenders, even against their will. In supporting the parole system the Daubney Committee, in the face of evidence to the contrary, simply asserted that it "believes that people can and do change; it rejects the notion that nothing works." Sure people change, but when this happens it has less to do with the legal system than we like to believe. As if sensing the enormity of the challenge, the committee commented that "there appear to be no constructive ways to foster positive changes in offenders beyond making the attempt."[34] Fine, but do we perpetuate an elaborate parole and statutory release structure to deal with our most intransigent offenders solely so we can say we tried?

The second reason why we continue to engage in community supervision is that it makes economic sense to do so. It is infinitely cheaper than continuing to incarcerate offenders. In 1995–96 each inmate cost the taxpayer on average $42,300 per year. Community supervision, while still a staggering figure, came in at $9145.[35] In an era of "accelerated parole" and statutory release that operates regardless of good behaviour, it is simply unconvincing to suggest that early release is not dollar driven. If economics is the real reason for community supervision, we should admit it openly so we can look for better ways to accomplish economy than by defeating judicial sentences. We should continue to do what we have recently begun by being more selective about whom we jail and by jailing fewer people. The unalterable price of open, honest sentencing, in which considerations of justice and accountability are used to determine the length of sentences, is that we have to use jail as a last resort. Whenever incarceration is not absolutely necessary to punish or denounce criminal behaviour or to incapacitate the obviously dangerous, it should not be used. As a society we have to accept liberal resort to conditional sentences and other community-based options for our less serious offences. We also have to expect judges to impose shorter sentences. If judges have been ratcheting sentencing numbers up to account for "real time," then justice demands, if early release is abolished, that sentences reflect this change. It would make for a more consistent and credible system.

I, for one, would rather have a system in which a judge makes a solemn, public, denunciatory pronouncement that someone like David Mattison will receive and serve a six-and-a-half-year sentence than to have the one we have now, where the convict is told that he will receive ten years in the penitentiary, but serves only a fraction of that time. I would rather have a sentence of community service with restitution and fines for property offenders than fill our jails so full of crooks that we have to let killers and rapists out early. I take that position not because of fear that paroled killers and rapists will, like a band of Vandals or Visigoths, run out of the gates of prisons to ravage and smite innocent villagers. These people will be no more or no less dangerous if released early than they would be if released at the last minute. I take that position because, as a matter of justice, it is simply wrong to blunt the denunciatory and retributive aspects of prison sentences with early release, especially when it is done under the pretense of improved rehabilitation. In the interests of keeping the criminal justice system open, credible, effective, and acceptable to the public, both rehabilitative parole and statutory release should be abolished.

Temporary Absence Passes

"Temporary absence" passes allow prisoners in both federal and provincial institutions who are not on parole, and who have not received statutory release, to be away from the prison. These temporary absences can be escorted, meaning a responsible person is meant to be with the prisoner, or they may be unescorted.

There are times when it is necessary to allow convicts to leave prison. For example, the offender may be ill and require a medical visit or even hospitalization, or a close family member may die. Even an ounce of humanity suggests that there has to be a mechanism for allowing prisoners to attend to such business. The temporary absence pass, or TAP as it is called, is also available for other reasons that might evoke less sympathy. They can be provided for offenders who do not present an "undue risk to society" where "it is desirable for the offender to be absent from [prison] for medical, administrative, community service, family contact, personal development for rehabilitative purposes, or compassionate reasons, including parental responsibilities."[36]

Time limits are imposed on most temporary absence leaves. Although medical leaves can be for any period, including entire sentences, there are limits on the frequency and duration of other passes. Unescorted temporary absences are also limited in the sense that there are waiting periods for inmates in penitentiaries, which vary according to the length of the sentence. For most federal sentences the waiting period is six months, or one-sixth of the sentence, whichever is greater. Lifers have to wait until within three years of their parole eligibility dates. For provincial inmates there are no such limits. They can be given unescorted temporary absence passes immediately. Indeed, sentencing judges sometimes make recommendations for immediate temporary absence passes to allow offenders to work or to look after children. It is up to administrative officials, however, to make the ultimate decision.

As with any system, there can be abuse. In the days before conditional sentences I prosecuted a man for a white-collar offence and fought very hard to have him put in jail. I succeeded in getting a reformatory sentence of one year. This period could not repay the retirees whom, together, he had effectively bilked for close to a million dollars, but it would be a hard time for a soft man and seemed punishment enough. I learned the following week that he had spent one night in jail and then was released on TAP to work in the United States. Medical evidence had been produced by his lawyers that both physically and mentally his health was endangered by incarceration. To prove the point, he apparently spent most of his one night in the detention centre hanging onto the leg of the superintendent's desk in his orange jump-suit. He was pried loose and shown the door the next day. He spent the year not in jail, but working as a professor. I can tell you that, aside from marking examinations, being a professor is not a form of punishment. I often wonder how, if he was so fragile, he managed to keep himself from gripping the leg of the counsel table when he was trying to look dignified and innocent during court hearings.

I was outraged by this outcome — and not because the man did not go to jail. I would have accepted the decision of the judge to allow him to serve his sentence in the community had that been his order. But it was not. The judge, who weighed the complex amalgam of sentencing considerations and who was unmoved by the same medical evidence, had ordered the man to jail for something more than a humiliating pit-stop, and that order was defeated. The whole prosecution seemed as if it had been an expensive joke.

This was a case where the punitive aspect of the sentence was defeated through manipulation by the inmate and by the failure of the administration at the institution to pay sufficient regard to the judgment of the sentencing judge. Sometimes, however, the punitive aspect is defeated wholly by the administration. The Daubney Committee, while largely supportive of temporary absence passes, expressed concern about their inappropriate use: "It has been made available to some who would appear to be high-risk inmates for the 'rehabilitative' purpose of celebrating birthdays, attending sporting events and going on shopping excursions. In the Committee's view, these represent inappropriate uses of an otherwise highly successful program."[37]

Recently a Newfoundland judge refused to sentence a woman to jail for a $27,000 fraud. The reason he gave was that he "didn't want to fool people." He said that if he did sentence her to jail, corrections officials would simply use their temporary absence powers to release her back into the community immediately after she had been sentenced. The Crown appealed the sentence. The Newfoundland Court of Appeal held that the trial judge had erred because it was wrong for him to base his sentence on what corrections officials might do. His job was to sentence and theirs was to administer the sentence. The Court of Appeal nonetheless lambasted provincial corrections officials. They had provided evidence to the court that they had a policy of granting temporary absence passes as soon as practicable for all offenders sentenced to less than six months who are considered to be at low or moderate risk of reoffending, so they can serve their sentences in the community. The policy also provided that where such offenders receive greater than six months, they will normally be granted temporary absence passes after one-sixth of the sentence has been served.

Without mincing words, the Court said that the practice of using temporary absence passes to grant permanent release was illegal and could undermine confidence in the criminal justice system. It observed that some might even see this practice as demonstrating contempt for the court. Of course it would. The executive branch of the government is responsible for enforcing court ordered sentences, not frustrating them.

Recent amendments to the legislation require that non-medical releases cannot exceed sixty days without reapplication. This restriction would prevent blanket policies like the one that had been adopted in Newfoundland, but it will not prevent parole boards who are so minded from granting a series of temporary absence passes, which could effectively keep an offender out of jail.

It is not only in Newfoundland that these passes have been used to deal with prison overcrowding. In some parts of the country, some prisoners sentenced to serve intermittent (usually weekends) sentences of less than ninety days are told when they arrive at the jail for the weekend that they should go home because there is no room at the inn. Some lawyers have reported that, in urban centres, overcrowding has prevented penal administrators from administering short sentences. Offenders are simply given temporary absence passes within hours of their arrival at jail, in some cases for the duration of their sentences.[38]

Most often, though, TAP is employed to assist with rehabilitation efforts. The passes can be used to permit offenders to reside in half-way houses, and most provinces have established temporary absence programs to enable prisoners to work, study, and to reintegrate themselves in the community. They are used, in effect, to "test drive" some convicts to see how they perform, before day parole or parole are granted. David Mattison found this out. By March 13 of 1996, while his wife lay mouldering in various parts of Ontario, and less than three years after newspapers reported that he had been jailed for ten years, he was given six seventy-two-hour unescorted passes for family contact with unspecified family and a common-law wife.[39]

I do not intend, by citing inflammatory examples, to slag the entire temporary absence program or to suggest that corrections officials are using it improperly as a matter of routine. Temporary absence passes could not possibly be abolished entirely in a humane system, and there is no reason to doubt that, for the most part, corrections officials use their authority consistently with the legislation. What I do want to suggest, however, is that there is a serious problem with the legislation. Again, temporary absence passes are used primarily to assist with the rehabilitation and personal development of inmates when that is not why offenders are sent to jail. If we would simply admit that a long weekend pass is not going to change people, the public would not have to endure such pointless and infuriating leniencies. While temporary absence passes are clearly necessary for some purposes, we should not be using them as an adjunct to the failed parole system or to defeat judicial sentencing by allowing incarceration to become community sentencing.

Early Release, Murder, and "Faint Hope"

When the death penalty was abolished in 1976, it was replaced with minimum life sentences for murder, coupled with parole ineligibility provisions. First-degree murderers cannot even apply for parole until they have completed twenty-five years of their life sentences. Second-degree murderers cannot apply for at least ten years. Many must wait longer because judges are empowered to impose parole ineligibility of up to twenty-five years for second-degree murderers, and they are using this power with increasing frequency. In 1987 as many as one-quarter of second-degree murderers were told they had to wait longer than ten years. Now the number may be closer to half.[40]

These are harsh sentences. To put them into perspective, before these provisions were passed, those who had committed capital murder but whose death sentences were commuted served an average of 13.2 years before release.[41] The price paid by capital murder convicts for the abolition of the death penalty was that the period of actual incarceration for first-degree murders has more than doubled.

At the time these changes were made, Parliament held out a "faint hope" to those who received sentences that included parole ineligibility of fifteen years or more. It provided, in what is now section 745.6, that they can apply, after they have served fifteen full years, for a reduction in their parole ineligibility. The primary purpose of the application is to enable the decision on parole ineligibility to be considered in light of new information or factors that could not have been known at the time of sentencing, and that might justify a lesser sentence. The application is heard by a jury in the province where the murder had occurred. Although the jury cannot order the release of a prisoner, it can reduce parole ineligibility, enabling the inmate to request release from the parole board. The jury can declare the convict to be eligible to apply for parole immediately, or it can reset the parole ineligibility period so that the convict will have to go back to jail for a further but shorter period before applying.

The "faint hope" held out by section 745.6 turned out not to be so faint after all. Of the sixty-nine reviews that had been done as of January 1997, fifty-four have resulted in some reduction in parole eligibility. As of that date, close to half of the successful applicants were on full parole or day parole and twenty-five remained incarcerated. A number of those who are still in jail are there because, while their period of ineligibility has been reduced, their parole eligibility date has not yet arrived. Once they are allowed to apply it is almost certain that the success rate for gaining early release through section 745.6 will prove to be even greater than its current 50 percent. Parole eligibility reviews promise to be big business. There are currently 214 eligible applicants. With more than 2000 inmates serving time for first- or second-degree murder, the application rate for reviews threatens to explode over the ensuing years.[42]

The faint hope clause has drawn a significant degree of public criticism, particularly when it was known that the notorious serial child killer Clifford Olson would be bringing an application. The provision has been criticized primarily because it requires the families of murder victims to relive the crime as the matter is dragged through yet another court hearing. It has also been criticized because it demonstrates leniency to killers, because there is public fear that it threatens to allow the release of dangerous people into the community, and because it undermines the initial judicial sentence.

As a result of public pressure, the government has recently changed the law to make it more restrictive. One of the changes was to remove the right to apply for those prisoners who have committed multiple homicides. Another requires that a judge must examine the application before the review is ordered. If it has no reasonable prospect of succeeding, no review will occur. Unfortunately these amendments did not get passed in time to stop Olson's application, which went ahead because a law that alters the punishment for a crime cannot be applied retroactively. At the time Olson was sentenced, multiple murderers could apply. Even the new judicial vetting procedure could not stop Olson's review because his application had already been filed under the previous process, which entitles him to an automatic review. As a result, everyone had to endure the pointless spectacle of his application. Not surprisingly, his application was denied, and all that was accomplished was that Canada's most offensive human being received more headlines.

To be sure, section 745.6 applications are distasteful, even for those of us who are not offended at the prospect of releasing convicted killers who have served more than fifteen years in prison. They are expensive and distressing for the families of victims. They would not be needed, however, if the minimum sentence for murder was removed and parole was abolished. Judges could sentence murderers to real time, which could be identified to reflect adequate punishment and denunciation for the crime in all the circumstances. This flexibility would enable sentences to reflect that not all murders, or even all first-degree murders, are equal, and it would bring some certainty and proportionality to those sentences that are imposed. For patently dangerous offenders like Clifford Olson and Paul Bernardo, dangerous offender applications instead of life sentences could be used to secure indefinite incarceration.

The irritating spectacle of section 745.6 applications is a remnant of a system that pursues inconsistent policies. We perpetuate the simple-mindedness of minimum sentences for murder so we can denounce and express our abhorrence with intentional killing, but then we worry that those we convict may not be dangerous enough to justify locking away for so long. The faint hope clause can be dispensed with when we choose to recognize that murder sentences are denunciatory by nature, and when we stop treating all murders as though they are the same.

Conclusion

David Mattison is an excellent candidate for parole. He has a long history of good character, he has been a contributing member of society, he has the financial means to support himself, he has a common-law spouse who is supportive, and, according to his psychological profiles, he does not present a high risk to reoffend. Efforts by the parole board to require counselling before he was granted day parole proved largely fruitless because the corrections counsellors did not believe he required it.[43] But what do these circumstances have to do with the sentence he received, and why should they affect the sentence he is required to serve? He was sentenced because of the need to denounce his conduct and to punish him for it. He was sentenced because his actions did not make the grade of self-defence and because he had contributed to the provocative atmosphere that led to the killing. He was sentenced because his callous and brutal act of concealment and his efforts at escaping detection lowered him far enough into the depths of depravity as to mute any natural human tendency towards compassion, understanding, and leniency. The judge knew when he sentenced Mattison to ten years that he has a long history of good character, that he has been a contributing member of society, that he has the financial means to support himself, and that he poses little or no threat to reoffend. The members of society who followed the case also knew these facts. So, too, did Mattison when he instructed his lawyer to accept the plea bargain. What has changed? Only his sentence. A stout effort to denounce and punish intolerable behaviour has in his case been weakened by day parole, and it will prove to be undermined entirely either when he is granted parole or when he has served six and a half years and becomes eligible for statutory release. These changes will all be done in the name of reintegrating into society a man who has no need for rehabilitation. What he needs is to be punished. What society needed was to express adequately its disdain for his repulsive conduct. Things went off of the rails, though, when David Mattison left the system of justice for the system of "corrections."

GETTING
OFF ON
TECHNICALITIES:
THE RULE
OF LAW

CHAPTER 5

Defining Crime

When our children were born it was in a hospital. I watched anxiously on each occasion as the nurturing hands of the obstetricians gently coaxed each one from their mother's body while I stroked her hair and rubbed her shoulders. The enduring image of birth that I have is witnessing the wet, chalky-grey complexions of our children turn flush and pink with the glow of new life as their first taste of lung-drawn oxygen coursed through their tiny bodies. There has been, and will be, no happier time for me.

When Brenda Drummond lay on her bathroom floor, her brown hair matted and dank with sweat and her face flushed and contorted with pain as she delivered her son, Jonathan, I cannot begin to imagine what it was like or what she was feeling. Only two days before, during the late afternoon of 28 May 1996, she had gone into that same bathroom in the small Ottawa Valley hamlet of Carleton Place while her two daughters played in the house. There, she inserted a pellet rifle into her vagina and fired it, propelling a pellet through the soft skull of her unborn son. It came to rest in his brain. Brenda was far luckier than Patricia Denner, another Ottawa area woman who only six months later bled to death from a collapsed uterus after she delivered, and then stabbed to death, her newborn child in the kitchen of her home. Unlike Patricia and her baby, Brenda and Jonathan were taken to the hospital and both survived.

At first, Jonathan Drummond did not appear to be in trouble, but within a few hours of birth he developed a severe infection. The medical staff at the hospital was puzzled. Desperate to find the cause, they x-rayed the young boy. The x-ray revealed a small metal object embedded in his brain. Further examination revealed a minuscule injury to his scalp. When asked about it, Drummond denied knowing how the injury had occurred. Finally, two days later, after the boy had developed meningitis and his life was in peril, she revealed what she had done. The pellet was surgically removed, saving Jonathan's life.

A country prosecutor, earnest in his conviction that what Brenda had done was nothing short of criminal, charged her with attempted murder. She had, after all, taken a firearm and blasted a projectile into the brain of a helpless child, a child who shared her breath and her nourishment and who could not possibly have been more dependent on her for his well-being. The rank cruelty of doing such a thing was staggering and, as a simple matter of human decency, it seemed to cry out for justice.

But was it an act of cruelty or was Brenda herself a casualty in this bizarre event? Why did she do it? The psychiatrists who came to be involved in the case have concluded she did not know that she was pregnant when she fired the rifle. It is not unknown for women to carry children full term without knowing they are pregnant. These women seem to suffer from clinical depression and, to protect themselves from the stress and problems a new child can create, they delude themselves wilfully, or psychosomatically, into thinking they are not pregnant. The prevailing wisdom, for example, is that Patricia Denner, a heavy woman, was not conscious of her own pregnancy. It is clear that her husband did not know of it. Patricia had left her bed the night the child was born to watch television, complaining of indigestion. The next day her young son discovered her dead body and that of the baby, who had been stabbed and placed in the sink. There were signs that she had tried to clean up the mess. Psychiatrists have offered the opinion that when she was confronted with the shock of her child's birth, she attempted to eliminate it to protect her belief that she was not pregnant.

The psychiatrists who examined Brenda Drummond and consulted on her case came to a similar conclusion. Like Patricia Denner, Brenda was by all accounts a loving and capable mother. She was a good, hard-working person with no prior criminal involvement and no history of violence. As a result of marital difficulties, she was left largely on her own with her two daughters. Then a co-worker who had been providing her with emotional support through her troubles committed suicide. This resulting shock may have pushed Brenda into mental illness. In summarizing the psychiatric opinion relating to Brenda Drummond, Judge Inger Hansen, the trial judge who presided over her prosecution, wrote:

> The psychiatrist concluded that Mrs. Drummond suffered from a mental illness and major depression which was severe and caused various symptoms, suicidal ideation, and excessive preoccupations. Her lack of awareness of her pregnancy even in its late stage, was most likely the result of her own depression, with inattentiveness to her own body functioning, being "over-absorbed" in her inner preoccupations of a psychotic intensity.

Psychiatric mumbo-jumbo? Perhaps. While it is easy to believe that her actions, seemingly so out of character, resulted from mental illness, it is more difficult to accept she would have fired a pellet into her vagina if she did not know she was pregnant. If true, this was the most bizarre suicide attempt in the history of humanity and it was incredibly bad luck that there happened to be a baby in the way. The judge was able to avoid having to decide whether the psychiatrists had it right. The case would turn on a more technical point. Even assuming that she had intended to kill her child when she fired the gun, would she be guilty of attempted murder?

Almost seven months after the shooting, only two days before Christmas, Brenda Drummond sat in court in the small town of Smith Falls, Ontario, her husband beside her, waiting to hear the answer. Judge Hansen was about to decide after two days of legal argument whether she could even be tried on the charge. Her lawyer, Lawrence Greenspon, both bright and flamboyant, had argued that, legally, it was not possible for her to have committed the offence of attempted murder because the child she shot was not a human being. In the circumstances, he said, her actions did not amount to an offence. The implications of his argument struck many observers as staggering. If he was right, then according to law she could have fired the pellet gun six times into the child's brain had she wanted to. She would have been free to spear her unborn child with a fireplace poker or to crush its skull by bashing her womb had she so desired. Legally, she could have injected poison into him and it would not have mattered that his central nervous system was fully developed or that he might linger in excruciating agony for hours before dying. He was not a human being. If her lawyer was right, in law, the yet unborn Jonathan Drummond had less protection from her actions than a dog, a laboratory rat, or even her neighbour's car would have. Had she intentionally scratched her neighbour's car, she could have been prosecuted criminally for mischief to property, but the criminal law would leave her free to kill or torture her unborn child only two days short of its birth.

Defence counsel had precedent on his side. Two British Columbia midwives, through actions that amounted to extreme negligence, caused the death of an unborn child while it was in the birth canal. They were charged with criminal negligence causing death. They were acquitted because the child had not yet been born alive at the time of their negligence.[1] There have been similar cases elsewhere. In 1970 in California a man named Keeler, on discovering that his ex-wife was pregnant by her boyfriend, crushed her abdomen with his knee, explaining as he did so, "I'm going to stomp it out of you." He was true to his word. His blows crushed the foetus' skull. The California Supreme Court decided that this despicable man was not a murderer because the baby was never born alive. As a stillborn child it had no protection in law, even for actions occurring while it was alive in the womb. Keeler was guilty only of aggravated assault against his ex-wife.[2]

After argument, Judge Hansen agreed that Brenda Drummond could not be prosecuted for attempted murder. Her lawyer had been right. The attempted murder charge as well as the related charge of using a firearm in the commission of an offence were therefore thrown out. In the end, Drummond pleaded guilty to the far less serious offence of failing to provide the necessities of life. Her offence was not in shooting the child, but in not telling the doctors after he had been born alive that she had shot him when he was in her womb. Once born, Jonathan earned the protection of the criminal law, and that law required his mother to provide him with all the necessities of life, including proper medical attention. By not disclosing the nature and origin of his medical problem, Drummond failed in her duty. She was placed on probation for thirty months.

The technical explanation of why it would not have been attempted murder even if Brenda Drummond had been trying to kill her unborn child is straightforward, despite the fact that the homicide provisions of the *Criminal Code of Canada* are preposterously complicated. Under the *Criminal Code*, homicide may be culpable or non-culpable. Culpable homicide is then classified as murder, manslaughter, or infanticide, but in each case culpable homicide requires that the death be caused to a "human being." Obviously you cannot be guilty of "murder" for killing a gnat or even something as cute and lovable as a baby harp seal. The section protects human beings. So the legal issue is whether a foetus is a human being. According to the *Criminal Code*, it is not. Section 223 (1) provides:

> A child becomes a human being within the meaning of this Act when it has completely proceeded, in a living state, from the body of its mother whether or not
>
> (a) it has breathed,
> (b) it has an independent circulation, or
> (c) the naval string is severed.

Jonathan was simply not, according to the *Criminal Code*, a human being when his mother fired the pellet into his skull. He was still in his mother's body at the time. If he had died immediately from the wound, she could not have been charged with murdering him, or with manslaughter, or even with infanticide, since killing something other than a human being is not a homicide offence. As defence counsel put it, to convict her of attempted murder would be to hold her criminally responsible for failing to accomplish something that would have been legal had she succeeded, and that, of course, cannot be.

The Crown prosecutor presented creative and clever arguments to convince the judge to rule otherwise. Section 223(2) provides that you commit homicide if you injure a child before its birth, provided the child dies after its birth from that injury. A Manitoba man named Prince was convicted of manslaughter in the death of a child who died twenty minutes after being born alive from stab wounds sustained when Prince stabbed the child's mother in the abdomen while she was carrying the child.[3] Under section 223(2), had Jonathon died in hospital from his infection, Brenda Drummond could have been convicted of murder. This possibility made the defence argument untenable, argued the prosecutor. Surely the law would not find someone guilty of murder if a child assaulted while *in vitro* dies after being born, but guilty of nothing if that child lives, even in a vegetative state. In each case, the same actions done with the same intention could produce diametrically opposed legal results, depending solely on sheer chance. If the child succumbs to its injuries, those actions and that intent amount to the offence of murder, but if the child manages to languish indefinitely from the assault, the same actions and intent are perfectly legal. Should guilt depend solely on the physical fortitude of the victim? That simply makes no sense. Fix it, he told the judge, by interpreting the relevant sections of the *Criminal Code* so that even children who stay alive after being born are protected.

It is impossible to disagree with the prosecutor, at least to this extent: the current law does not make sense. Unfortunately for the prosecutor, though, while it is a good idea for the law to make sense, it does not always do so. The irrational state of affairs in which unborn children who die immediately in the womb from assaults are not protected by law, but those who survive only long enough to be born are, did not emerge by design. It is the result of the decision of the Supreme Court of Canada in *R. v. Morgentaler*,[4] which struck down as unconstitutional the law against abortion. Had Brenda Drummond attempted unsuccessfully to kill her child while it was in her womb prior to the decision in *Morgentaler*, she could have been convicted of attempted abortion. She would have been trying to terminate her pregnancy, albeit by incredibly unorthodox means and at a preposterously late stage, without the prior approval of an abortion committee. When the abortion law, which was intended to provide a measure of protection to foetuses, was struck down as unconstitutional, a gap was left in the law.

Many people feared that the judge would seek to close the gap by somehow finding that the foetus was a human being. In both the domestic and the international press, the Drummond case came to be about the right to abortion, a fact Drummond's defence counsel sought to exploit in his legal arguments on her behalf. Holding his fingers two inches apart, he cautioned the court that it could not go even "that far" in recognizing the rights of the unborn without diminishing substantially the liberty of the mother to control her own body. To her credit, Judge Hansen avoided being drawn into the abortion debate: "The tragic events . . . and the charges that are challenged, do not require this court to deal with questions of morality. At this point the Court's focus is on the vexed question of whether Brenda Drummond has been charged with an offence known in Canadian law."

While a fine judge, Judge Hansen is neither a moralist nor a legislator. She is a judge, with knowledge of the law superior to that of members of the public but with no higher claim to knowledge about correct public policy. No doubt cognizant of the arguments in favour of providing at least a finger spread of protection to the foetus while at the same time being circumspect enough not to show her own views, she said, "[N]o matter how desirable it may be, I cannot construe section 223 in a manner that removes the words at the end of 223(2): '[A]s a result of which the child dies after becoming a human being.'" If the law is to be changed to protect those who die before becoming "human," or to penalize attempts to kill *in vitro*, it is for Parliament to do so. The Drummond case was not to be decided on Judge Hansen's views on this controversial issue. It was to be decided the way a lawyer should decide — as a simple matter of legal interpretation, or of law, regardless of the consequences.

Although I have great sympathy for both Jonathan and Brenda Drummond, I, for one, do not like the law the way it is. Leaving aside the abortion question, the current law draws indefensible lines. One second after birth, the full panoply of criminal protections is yours. One second before, and you have less legal status than a Volvo. Get hurt *in vitro* and die after you are born, and your assailant may be a murderer. Die before you arrive, and he is just a guy. Suffocate in the birth canal, and the midwives present a bill. Get dropped after you've made it out, and they are criminals. What a law! Despite this disparity, it would have been very wrong for Judge Hansen to have tried to remake the law to make it sensible. It was simply not her function to do so. The definition of crime is a matter for Parliament.

Prime Minister Kim Campbell's government had tried to respond to the *Morgentaler* decision with legislation that would have protected late-term babies like Jonathan while preserving medically required late-term abortions, but the legislation died on a tied vote in the Canadian Senate.[5] Had one senator forgotten to take his prunes that day, his cramps might have kept him from his vote and we might today have legislation that would have criminalized what Brenda Drummond did. Such is the fickle fate of criminal justice. But even the inability or unwillingness of politicians to tackle this politically charged issue would have provided no authority to the judge to solve the problem by treading outside of her proper sphere. Judge Hansen, in refusing to find that the law protected Jonathan, was not being an irresponsible and callous person, oblivious to the rights of the young child. She was a judge doing her job by respecting the "rule of law." That is what the Drummond case was really about: not abortion, and not psychiatric jargon that is so counter-intuitive that, rightly or wrongly, it invokes laughter in some quarters. It is about the proper role of our criminal courts of justice and the commitment to the rule of law.

The rule of law, like many legal or jurisprudential ideas, can be expressed with a simplicity that makes it at once comprehensible and potentially misleading. Its most familiar description is found in A.V. Dicey's *Introduction to the Study of the Law of the Constitution*. In its simplest terms, the rule of law means that persons are to be ruled by law, not by the arbitrary or discretionary power of others, and that the law applies equally to all persons. What does it have to do with Brenda Drummond? If a judge, in deciding the guilt or innocence of an accused, resorts to her personal view, or even to her perception of society's view about what is right or wrong or what should or should not be criminal, then the rule of law is being flouted. The question for a judge even in a criminal case is not whether the actions are right or wrong, laudable or despicable, responsible or dangerous, but whether the act is prohibited by a rule of law. For a judge, guilt is never a moral question. It is always a technical one. When it ceases to be a technical question and becomes a matter of personal judgment and choice for the judge, we are allowing ourselves to be ruled by judges, or people, rather than by law. For this reason, technicality in some measure is not something to be feared. In a democracy it is something to be welcomed. Should the fate of Brenda Drummond, and potentially of the abortion debate, depend on whether the judge she appears before is pro-choice or pro-life, or should it depend on the rules that have been identified in advance by the society in which she lives? To ask that question is to answer it. The rule of law is intended to preserve the liberties of all of us, even if it means for some of us that there will be no justice. The fault, if there is fault to be ascribed in this case, is not with the criminal justice system nor with Judge Hansen. It is with Parliament for failing to fill the gap created by the *Morgentaler* decision.

The model for resolving legal controversies in our society has been described as follows:

> Our Anglo-American legal systems have preserved their historical stability through a model in which the legal system is dominated by legal values and structures which have survived over an extended period of application. They have avoided emphasizing the particular personality of the judge, his unique prejudices and the complex psychodynamics that occur among the various participants in the legal process. . . . In such a model, the judge functions as an umpire and the sense of justice is kept tidy because all of the participants are accountable to the rules, including the judges. . . . In liberal democracies a commitment to the structured rule of law is deeply held.[6]

Why is the rule of law held so deeply in liberal democracies? Because of past experiences. Obviously, the central preoccupation of these concepts is the abuse of power. Like so many of our most hallowed principles, the idea of the rule of law has its origins in the history of England, a history marked by the ongoing struggle between "the people" and the Crown for sovereign power. This tradition gives the rule of law an impressive pedigree. It is one of the founding or constitutional concepts of our modern notion of democracy, and, as such, it should not easily be compromised. While its function historically was to give legitimacy to the act of controlling and ultimately wresting power from the king, its legacy is to protect modern democracies like ours from the kinds of abuses that occurred before the English Civil War. To make the point and to explain the concepts of the rule of law, it is best to examine those origins in greater detail.

The History of the Rule of Law

We have a romanticized view of life in Anglo-Saxon times, thanks to Hollywood. We think of Robert Goulet, with his perfect hair, singing "Camelot," or perhaps more recently of Richard Gere, angular, healthy, and clean, standing with legs slightly spread and a hand on the hilt of his sword while the wind gently tussles his locks. It was not like that. People were short, certainly dirty, likely pock-marked, and probably carbuncular. They wore no underwear and their clothing was like sack-cloth; they no doubt spent more time scratching themselves than most baseball players do. In Anglo-Saxon times, life was, to put it in Hobbesian terms, "nasty, brutish and short." Disease, famine, blood feuds, and the omnipresent risk of plunder from marauding villains and miscreants made life itself uncertain. To protect themselves, people were almost tribal, certainly clannish. It was, we have been told, "a wild time."[7] But even in those dark ages, it was not an entirely lawless time. What is now Britain was composed mainly of self-contained communities, each having its own crude legal system and political administration, each with its own rudimentary legal customs. There was, in a fashion, rule by law. Indeed, there has been no time in the recorded history of Western Europe when there was not legal order, in the sense of legally constituted authorities that applied law to settle disputes.[8]

The law administered in those pre-Norman communities came from local customs that were recalled by community elders, modified to some degree by broad rules that were found in the Dooms of Anglo-Saxon or Danish kings. These crude laws were accepted because of their antiquity, their status as custom, and the belief that they reflected God's choice rather than that of mankind. Even in such primitive times, efforts were being made both in practice and in theory to keep the law objective, so that the power of law-giving would not be abused.

After the Norman conquest of England in 1066, things changed. The Norman kings and their successors, the Plantagenet kings, set out to consolidate power. This objective required that the kings control the law. Control that, and you control society. So the kings sent judges out on circuit to settle disputes. The judges were astute enough to realize that their decisions would be effective only if they reflected the values of the people, so they resolved cases by finding out what the local customs were and by applying those customs, whenever possible. Over time, the king's judges began to meet to discuss their decisions. Judges began using each other's precedents and, in this way, our "common law" system was born.

Naturally, the growth in the power of the king's courts infuriated the local barons. The more powerful the king's courts were, the more powerful was the king and the less powerful were they. The barons tried to stop the king from taking control of the law. Indeed, the victory of the barons at Runnymede led to the *Magna Carta* (1215), and, while it addressed a broad array of grievances, a number of its provisions were designed to stem the increase in royal justice. In spite of this restriction, by the reign of Edward I in 1272, the king's courts had established their supremacy[9] and the law became increasingly centralized. The emergence of a strong centralized authority, coupled with the establishment of professional jurists, enabled the huge mass of inherited customs and precedents to be gathered and systematized.[10] Sophisticated legal concepts began to develop as these jurists sought ordering principles and procedures to guide their adjudication.

One of the casualties in developing an ordered body of principles and procedures is that the law becomes technical and therefore inaccessible to non-lawyers. Its practitioners acquire a monopoly of power. They are given the keys to the law, while those who are not trained become dependent on lawyers to enjoy their legal rights. The power of lawyers, coupled with the deep mysteries and technicalities of law, lead, in turn, to distrust. This suspicion is not a new phenomenon. During the reign of King James I, Dr. Bonham was fined for practising physic, or medicine, without a licence. A number of years before, King Henry VIII had granted a Royal Charter to the college of Physicians and Surgeons by letters patent, empowering the College to issue licences and to levy such fines. Bonham refused to pay and was arrested and imprisoned, and his leeches and bone-saws were no doubt impounded. The Lord Chief Justice, Sir Edward Coke, a lawyer of great renown, ordered his release. King James I asked Sir Edward to explain himself. "Unless one had studied the common law diligently, Coke told James . . . the requisite 'artificial reason' could not be acquired."[11] Imagine: the king, who claimed the right to rule and proclaim law by divine right, was told by a mere lawyer, "Sorry, King. This one is beyond you. Leave it to the experts, O.K.?"

This kind of arrogance is unlikely to endear lawyers to the public. Indeed, apparently it did not endear Coke to his own wife, who is reputed to have remarked with his passing, "We shall never see his like again, praises be to God."[12] (She would have had no way of knowing that someday lawyers would be as plentiful in North America as dung beetles are in the Savannah.) Nor is Coke's reference to "artificial reason" likely to inspire confidence. But Coke realized that the development of a technical legal system with fixed rules was a sign that civilization was dawning.[13] He also appreciated that it was the way to control the tyranny of those in power.

The biggest threat of tyranny through abuse of power was the king himself. King James I fancied himself above the law and answerable to no man. He was, by divine right, the Lord. In a speech to Parliament on 21 March 1601 he said:

> Kings are justly called gods for that they exercise in a manner or resemblance of divine power on earth, for if you will consider the attributes to God you shall see how they agree in the person of a king. God hath power to create or destroy, make or unmake, at his pleasure; to give life or send death, to judge all and to be judged accountable to none; to raise low things and to make high things low at his pleasure; and to God are both soul and body due. And the like power have kings: they make and unmake their subjects; they have

power of raising, and casting down; of life, and of death, judges over all their subjects and in all causes, and yet accountable to none but God only.[14]

No doubt by modern standards, King James seemed a bit full of himself. Paradoxically, it was the development of the technical and sophisticated legal system that the kings developed to consolidate their power which proved to be their undoing.

When the Norman kings first created the courts, their judges were drawn from the Curia Regis, or the King's Council, a large body composed of the leading nobility. It was through this council that the King administered the realm. Although the particular circuit judges had been delegated the power to decide cases and to declare law, the King's Council itself retained the authority to conduct judicial business as well. Its powers were both large and vague, and its procedures were "simple, speedy and informal compared to the common law courts."[15] The council also had superior powers to enforce attendance; it was unencumbered by precedent; and it was far more able to enforce its orders by simply dispatching the army. Unconstrained by clear rules, it often used its power, not to enforce the law impartially but to favour the powerful.[16] Frequently it did the king's bidding, ignoring the law in the process. "The layman feared and suspected it; and the lawyer hated it because it encroached upon his province."[17]

Things became even worse after the Wars of the Roses.[18] The king's courts proved to be anaemic in the chaos that ensued, because the power of the judges was limited by law and procedure. The King's Council was not so ineffective. So the Tudor kings looked to the council to assist in establishing order. Never mind that the council was unable to dispense justice in a neutral fashion because many of its members had been implicated in the riots and the oppression that had occurred.[19] The first matter of business was to regain control, and the council, with its extensive powers and the wide discretion it had to free itself from the strictures of established law, proved extremely adept. Indeed, there was so much work for the council that it created a separate judicial branch, the infamous Court of Star Chamber, which was also provided with tremendous powers unimpeded by the refinements of technicality.[20] Order was restored by savaging the enemies of the king.

When order was re-established by the end of the seventeenth century, the need for a specialized court with extensive powers to act without the impediment of the law had largely passed. The Court of Star Chamber and the King's Council, once instruments of order and efficiency in a time of great chaos, came to be feared as able instruments of oppression. "Under the Stuart Kings, the Star Chamber and the Council became the principal engines for enforcing the King's will. From instruments of peace and good order they became the means of defying the common law in the King's name."[21]

But not everyone was silenced. Opposition to the absolutist pretensions of the Stuart kings came from Puritans and common lawyers. The Puritans objected to interference by the king with the church, and interference with ideas and the freedom to express them. The common lawyers objected to the threat that the Stuarts presented to the law. Each believed that the king ruled subject to the law. As the historian Eusdon explains:

> The two groups roundly opposed the Stuart conception of the divine right of kings with theories that God and law ruled the world. . . . The Puritans and lawyers worked with the old idea of the limitation of power and applied it in a new political setting. In doing so, they fashioned one of the indispensable elements of contemporary democracy.[22]

When Parliament, largely composed of common lawyers and Puritans, gained ascendancy in 1641 after its long struggle with the Stuart kings, the Court of Star Chamber was abolished and the Stuart conception of the divine right of kings was defeated. The familiar adage that no one is above the law became a central tenet of political theory, and so, too, did the firm conviction that, in a democratic system, people must be ruled by law and not by the arbitrary power of others.

I know it is difficult for most people to think of lawyers as champions of democracy, and I doubt that Puritans appreciate the association. I have heard it asked, "What is brown and black and looks good on a lawyer's neck?" and I have heard it answered, "A doberman." I have never heard the same thing said about a Puritan. Together, though, lawyers and Puritans gave birth to the Canadian concept of democracy and to the rule of law. When you detest technicalities and despise the specialized knowledge that is the province of lawyers, remember that both lawyers and the law they administer are instruments of liberty and democracy. So laugh heartily the next time some film director shows you a dinosaur picking a lawyer off a toilet and chowing down, or some Hollywood mogul produces a movie called *Liar, Liar* about a lawyer (and here, you might think, is the redundant part) who is incapable of telling the truth. Just remember: it is to us that you owe your freedom — oh yes, and to the Puritans too. And one more thing. Celebrated lawyer Edward Greenspan cleared up another common misconception during a recent speech:

> Let me tell you a little-known historical fact. Shakespeare's famous tribute in *Henry IV*, Act IV, Scene II: "The first thing we do, let's kill all the lawyers." When Shakespeare wrote this famous phrase, his s's had a large loop and looked like l's. What he really wrote was: "Let's kiss all the lawyers." He truly loved lawyers.[23]

So you should feel the urge to kiss a lawyer. If you cannot control this craving, be quick about it: lawyers bill out their time in six-minute blocks.

The Rule of Law Today

The lessons that this period in history gave us continue to influence the development and application of our criminal justice system. As a society, we continue to insist that the fate of our citizens, like Brenda Drummond, be determined according to law and by law alone. The result, of course, is that if there is no law against doing an act that society comes to consider to be reprehensible and worthy of punishment, then the actor cannot be punished by the state. This restriction has long been recognized as having its greatest importance in criminal cases, where the liberty of citizens is most at risk. In 1949 a young man named Frey became bored and, not having a television, decided he would take his ladder and prop it up against a Mrs. Fedoruk's bedroom window in an effort to catch her undressing. Mrs. Fedoruk was preparing for bed and glanced out the window, only to stare into Frey's face. He did not stop to exchange pleasantries but galloped away at full flight with the ladder under one arm. Mrs. Fedoruk's son, on hearing his mother scream and gathering what had happened, grabbed a butcher knife and gave chase.

I remember doing the same thing as a teenager — giving chase, that is. I was at a friend's house when his mother screamed. We, too, chased a young man who was running with a ladder. I did not have a butcher knife, nor was I quite certain what I would do if we apprehended the pervert. Like young Fedoruk, we caught him. Unlike Frey, this young man calmly explained that he was looking for odd jobs around the neighbourhood and wanted to check to see if the window ledges needed painting so that he could find prospective customers. We decided to let him go with a sharp "Don't do it again." I am glad we made that choice, given what happened to Fedoruk. He decided to detain Frey. Then a policeman came. The officer did some investigation and arrested Frey. For their troubles, both Fedoruk and the policeman were sued by Frey for false imprisonment — successfully. They breached his rights by holding him against his will!

How could this suit come about? It happened because of the rule of law. According to law, the powers of police officers and citizens to detain or arrest other individuals are strictly limited. In order for the police and Fedoruk to have arrested Frey legally without a warrant, Frey had to have been committing a criminal offence. While being a "peeping Tom" was decidedly rude, it was not a criminal offence under the *Criminal Code of Canada*. The arrest was therefore wrongful, and actionable as a false arrest.

The British Columbia Court of Appeal would have dismissed the suit despite this fact. It ruled that even though nothing in the *Criminal Code* applied to Frey, he was nonetheless committing an offence at common law for which he could be arrested without warrant. At common law, the court reasoned, it is an offence to breach the king's peace, and Frey had done that. This ruling requires some explaining, given that the peace that was disturbed was Mrs. Fedoruk's. The king was not even there. The point is that Frey's actions, by their nature, were apt to provoke a violent, retributive response. Such violence would disturb the public peace. Since the king is the figurehead of the public, Frey's conduct would disturb the king's peace, making it a criminal offence.

This clever basis for finding that Frey was justifiably detained and arrested disturbed the Supreme Court of Canada. If everything that could provoke a violent, retributive response was criminal, would that make adultery an offence or insulting words a crime? Could a fan be arrested for wearing a Toronto Maple Leafs sweater to a game at the Molson Centre in Montreal? While cheering for the Maple Leafs might be an intensely embarrassing thing, it should not be criminal. Justice Cartwright overturned the decision of the British Columbia Court of Appeal and upheld Frey's lawsuit, holding:

> I think that if adopted, [the Court of Appeal's technique of using the common law offence of breach of the King's peace to identify offences] would introduce great uncertainty into the administration of the criminal law, leaving it to the judicial officer trying any particular charge to decide that the acts proved constituted a crime or otherwise, not by reference to any defined standard to be found in the *Code* or in reported decisions, but according to his individual view as to whether such acts were a disturbance of the tranquillity of people tending to provoke physical reprisal.

So ended the ability of judges to define conduct as criminal because, in their personal view, it disturbed the king's peace. Indeed, the Court went even further:

I think it is safer to hold that no one shall be convicted of a crime unless the offence with which he is charged is recognized as such in the provisions of the *Criminal Code*, or can be established by the authority of some reported case as an offence known to the law. I think that if any course of conduct is now to be declared criminal, which has not up to the present time been so regarded, such declaration should be made by Parliament and not by the Courts.

Since *Frey*, it has been the law in Canada that only Parliament can create criminal offences. Judges cannot, regardless of how distasteful or offensive the actions of an accused person might have been. Indeed, the *Criminal Code* was amended four years after the *Frey* decision to make this clear.[24]

We did not have to go so far in protecting the rule of law. In England, after all, even after King Charles' execution, the courts continued to use the common law to define and even create new offences. Common law decisions are based on precedent and principle, and when the common law develops properly, the application of the common law still constitutes rule by law. In the late nineteenth century an eminent English lawyer, Sir James Fitzjames Stephen, drafted a Criminal Code for India. In it he attempted to include the principle ultimately adopted in *Frey* v. *Fedoruk*: "*nulla crimen, nulla poena sine lege*" — no one shall be punished for anything that is not expressly forbidden by law. As Professor John Willis reported immediately after *Frey* was decided, this principle caused some English judges to criticize Stephen's code when efforts were made to introduce it into England. He reports the famous English jurist, Baron Parke, as saying:

My objection to the proposed measure is founded on the danger of confining provisions against crimes to enactments and repealing in this respect the rules of common law, which are clear and well understood and have the incalculable advantage of being capable of application to new combinations of circumstances, perpetually recurring, which are decided, when they arise, by inference and analogy to them and upon the principles on which they rest.[25]

Willis reports that when Stephen's draft *Criminal Code* was modified and adopted for Canada in 1893, Sir John Thompson said when introducing it into the House of Commons: "The common law will still exist and be referred to, and in that respect the code . . . will have that elasticity which has been so much desired by those who are opposed to codification on general principles." As Willis points out, it is precisely this elasticity that Justice Cartwright sought to avoid in *Frey*.

If the elasticity is taken from the law, it cannot be moulded easily to fit new situations as the need is perceived to arise or as society evolves. Critics of *Frey* point out, with great purpose, that in these complex times Parliament is not able to respond and resolve every issue that arises by passing legislation. When the court sees reprehensible conduct, it should be able to take the initiative and address it. Is it not preposterous that Frey, a peeping Tom, gets to sue those who tried to hold him accountable for his outrageous conduct, simply because Parliament had not thought to create a criminal offence for the despicable act of peeping Tommery? And is it not unconscionable that Brenda Drummond can shoot her foetus with impunity? Had she walked into the hospital saying "Hey. Take care of this kid. I shot him in the head just before he was born," she would have got off scot-free. Surely, it is argued, courts should be able to fix these kinds of gaps in the criminal law. If we take a step back, though, and consider the long-term interests of justice, we might have more sympathy for the implications of the rule of law. The Drummond case, and the legacy of *Morgentaler*, arguably provide a strong illustration of why the rule of law is an important safeguard that cannot be disregarded as a simple matter of expedience. Remember, Parliament had been unable to resolve what rights to give to a foetus. If there is such deep division on whether conduct should be criminal that no clear majority emerges through the democratic process, then that conduct should not be criminalized. Regardless of one's views on abortion, the criminal law, society's bluntest instrument for controlling and shaping human behaviour, should be used solely as a last resort, and only when there is an appreciable consensus that the conduct deserves to be criminalized. If we leave it up to a single judge or a panel of judges to decide, even using the common law method to identify criminal conduct, the criminal law cannot help but proliferate, moving into areas where it is simply not necessary or desirable.

Justice Cartwright recognized that the common law method, while it is capable of resolving legal questions, is prone to manipulation and the influence of personal perspectives. In theory we rely on precedent and principle to resolve decisions, so that even common law decisions are the product of law rather than the choice of the adjudicator. Still, there is a gulf between theory and practice. Speaking of precedent, a leading American legal commentator, Jerome Frank, said in the same year that Frey took out his ladder:

> Lawyers and Judges purport to make large use of precedents; that is, they purport to rely on the conduct of judges in past cases as a means of producing analogies for action in new cases. But since what was

actually decided in the earlier cases is seldom revealed, it is impossible, in a real sense, to rely on these precedents. What the Courts in fact do is manipulate the language of former decisions. They could approximate a system of real precedents only if the judges, in rendering those former decisions, had reported with fidelity the precise steps by which they arrived at their decisions. The paradox of the situation is that, granting there is value in a system of precedents, our present use of illusory precedents makes the employment of real precedents impossible.

The decision of a Judge after trying a case is the product of a unique experience. . . . [The] "decision is reached after an emotive experience in which principles and logic play a secondary part."[26]

I know that Frank is being too harsh. To make his point, he exaggerates greatly the extent to which judicial decisions are the product of emotion and politics rather than the reasoned use of precedent, although he unquestionably has a point to make. Even the best-intended judges applying the common law method are going to be influenced in how they view the law by the implication of their decisions. Given the natural tendency to allow personal preferences about outcome to affect legal decisions, if we remove the power to create new offences from judges, we reduce the risks to the rule of law. To put a human face on it, imagine that judges have the power to create criminal offences to deal with what they perceive to be a social evil. Imagine further that in courtroom 1 the Honourable "Judge" Joe Borowski is presiding.[27] In courtroom 2, the Honourable "Judge" Henry Morgentaler is the judge. Do you think that Brenda Drummond would be treated the same way in each court? Not likely. What kind of "system of law" would there be if the legality of conduct could vary according to what courtroom the case happened to be assigned to? The theory of the rule of law requires that everyone be equal before the law. Although not entirely indispensable to the rule of law, one of the most effective ways of ensuring that liberty is not curtailed by the mere will of others is to ensure that criminal conduct is defined solely by Parliament.

Of course, it would be naive to believe that we could remove the risks to the rule of law entirely by preventing judges from creating offences. As a practical matter, even when a law has been passed by Parliament, courts have the ability to extend the scope of the criminal law by the way they interpret it. In spite of the best of intentions, written words are often an empty vessel capable of being filled with the meaning that is attractive to the reader. Judges who apply written rules therefore have the capacity to influence the reach of the criminal law in profound ways. This outcome is unavoidable. To reduce the threat that this reality poses to the rule of law, it has long been recognized that judges have a duty to interpret the criminal law strictly in favour of the liberty of the accused. Since the rule of law is intended to preserve liberty by constraining the powers of government, where the reach of a penal provision is not entirely clear on its face, it is considered to be better to resolve the ambiguity in favour of the accused. If an accurate interpretation cannot be assured, it is preferable to err by construing the law more narrowly than Parliament intended rather than more broadly. This preference, of course, helps those who are charged with offences, but it does so to preserve the liberty of us all.

To be honest, it is a bit misleading to suggest that this principle of "strict construction" grew from a conscious effort to preserve the rule of law. In fact it emerged with similar sentiment to protect not only the liberty but also the lives of members of society. In seventeenth- and eighteenth-century England, those convicted of most felonies were sentenced to die, even when their crime may have been comparatively minor. The judges who administered the law had problems with this system. After all, they were to be the agents who would deliver an unjust death. They therefore invented a number of techniques so they could avoid imposing what they considered to be an oppressive and unconscionable penalty. One of those techniques was "strict" or narrow construction. One commentator has illustrated the effect that strict construction had at the time by listing examples of cases where rules were narrowly interpreted to avoid convicting and then dispatching accused felons:

> It was variously held that a "colt" was not a "horse," and that a statute proscribing the stealing of *horses* did not extend to the theft of one horse only; that the misappropriation of "goods, wares and merchandise" did not extend to the wrongful conversion of mere "money"; that a "heifer" could not be considered a "cow" where both terms appeared in the statute in apparent contradistinction; that a theft that occurred at about nine-thirty in the evening did not occur "at night"; and that a "warehouse" was not necessarily a "warehouse."[28]

This highly technical if not contrived reasoning is the kind of legal mumbo-jumbo that irritates the public, as opponents of strict construction are quick to say. Professor Livingston Hall uses the example of the Lindbergh kidnapping to do so. One of the issues in the case was whether Bruno Hauptman was guilty of first- or second-degree murder. If the murder was not premeditated, it would be second-degree murder unless Hauptman killed the baby while committing a major offence; as a policy matter, persons who kill while committing major criminal offences like robbery, sexual assault, or break and enter are treated more harshly than those who are not committing other offences when they kill. The law is designed to discourage the use of violence to assist in the commission of these serious offences. For this reason, Hauptman's guilt of first-degree murder could conceivably turn on whether he had broken into Lindbergh's home before killing the Lindbergh baby. If Hauptman did, the killing would clearly be first-degree murder. If he did not break in, the killing might not be first-degree murder. The fact that there can be any question about this matter is probably startling to many. Everybody knows that Hauptman (or the intruder, for those who hold to the view that Hauptman was wrongfully convicted) "entered" the upstairs bedroom window with the aid of a home-made ladder. But did he *"break and enter?"* If the word "break" is interpreted strictly and if the Lindbergh's upstairs window had been open, Hauptman would not have "broken" in. He would have simply entered, without having to "break" anything. The distinction could make the killing second-degree murder. This argument drove Professor Hall to the following comment:

> The public is already impatient with the refined, and for practical purposes unnecessary, distinctions embodied in the penal codes. To make Hauptman's conviction for murder in the first degree turn on whether the window in the nursery was open or shut . . . does not commend itself to the average man. Strict construction of such statutes has completed the degradation of the substantive criminal law in his mind.[29]

Fortunately, the doctrine of "strict construction" is no longer applied as some hypertechnical avoidance strategy enabling judges to cop out and keep from doing their duty in applying the law. In Canada we resolved the open window issue by ruling that it is a break and enter to climb on in through an open window, but not before we had a short flirtation with the attractions of strict construction. In *R. v. Jewell*[30] the Ontario Court of Appeal acquitted a man of break and enter because the doors to the house he entered had been left open wide enough to allow him to slip in. This decision was later ruled to be incorrect by the Supreme Court of Canada because it made no sense: it would distinguish between fat burglars and thin ones, said the Court.[31] I agree. There is already too much discrimination against the rotund to warrant convicting them of actions that the svelte among us can commit with impunity. More important, though, is that interpreting a statute in favour of the accused should be done only when the statute is ambiguous or unclear. If the purpose of the provision is clear, a meaning should be applied that gives effect to that purpose, even if the intention could have been better expressed. Given the purpose behind the law of break and enter, it would be preposterous to hold that the law was not meant to include those who gain entry through open doors or windows, notwithstanding that this interpretation was the old common law rule. The risk of violence and of loss of property is as great when the burglar finds an open window as it is when he has to jimmy the thing first.

The decision in *R. v. Paré*[32] illustrates the limits of the doctrine of strict construction. Marc-André Paré, then seventeen years of age, lured Steeve Duranleau, a seven-year-old boy, under a bridge and sexually assaulted him. The boy swore he was going to tell on Paré. Paré tried threatening him. Concluding that the boy was going to tell despite the threat, Paré decided to kill him. He held the boy's face down for some two minutes. Only then did he begin to strangle him with his hands. He then bashed his head several times with an oil filter. Finally, he took a shoelace and strangled Steeve some more, ultimately killing him. As in the Lindbergh case, the issue was whether the murder was first or second degree. The *Criminal Code* would make it first-degree murder if Paré caused the death of the young boy "while committing" an indecent assault. There was no question he killed the young boy, and there was no question he had indecently assaulted him. Paré's position was that he did not kill the boy "while committing" the indecent assault. He had finished his assault. He argued that strict construction required that this provision be interpreted in favour of his liberty, so he should be convicted only of second-degree murder. If Parliament had wanted first-degree murder to include killings that occur after committing a sexual offence, it would have said so. His argument got him nowhere. Justice Wilson agreed that the seriousness of imposing criminal sanctions demands that reasonable doubts be resolved in favour of the accused, but found that it was not reasonable to suggest that Parliament meant to draw a distinction between those who kill during the commission of an indecent assault and those who kill two minutes later to avoid detection. An interpretation that captures those who kill as part of one continuous sequence of events forming part of the same transaction better expresses the policy considerations behind the provision. Paré was still involved in the same transaction in which he had sexually assaulted Steeve when he killed him. Only two minutes had elapsed, he was still at the scene, and he had not yet escaped. Strict construction is only to be used where the policy behind the provision does not give clear meaning to the phrases that are employed.

This is a sensible, inevitable approach. Moreover, in theory it poses no threat to the rule of law. The construction that advances Parliament's purpose is selected, ensuring that the offence applied is the one that Parliament created. Unfortunately, reliance on Parliament's purpose to resolve ambiguous questions of construction does not remove entirely the danger that is posed for the rule of law. The particular "intent" of Parliament is at best an elusive thing. Strictly speaking, it makes no sense to speak about parliamentary intention. It is fanciful to assume that all who are involved in the passage of a piece of legislation believe it to mean precisely the same thing. Policy analysts may identify the problem to be cured, drafters will pose and develop solutions, ministers responsible for the legislation will "sell" the product, and parliamentarians, many of whom are non-lawyers, will vote on it based on executive summaries rather than the language of the legislation. Indeed, more often than not they vote on it according to party loyalty or because of party discipline, without any clear sense of what particular provisions might mean. Left to discuss what they have created, these players would be unlikely to agree. As important, it is demonstrably false to suggest that Parliament had any intention as to how the specific case before the court is to be resolved. Legislators act on generalities, while courts are asked to resolve specific problems. Parliamentary intention, therefore, is largely an abstraction, especially when the question is asked, "How would Parliament want this case resolved?" For these reasons, while the exercise of statutory inter-pretation is conceptualized as the process by which courts give effect to the intention of democratically elected officials, the reality is that courts play an integral role in the legislative process. Through interpretation, they become partners in the development of legislated rules. The way they choose to perform that role has a critical influence on the rule of law.

The reality that there is no identifiable legislative intention has enabled some to argue that the rule of law is largely a fiction that should not interfere with the ability of judges to provide meaningful solutions to real problems. They urge that judges should not attempt to bind them-selves by the text of the legislation, but rather should adopt "postmodern" interpretation techniques. They should provide legal solutions after con-sulting the legislation as well as cultural, professional, and personal mate-rials. "These include linguistic conventions, legal principles, factual and cultural assumptions, as well as knowledge and experience that is more personal and idiosyncratic. Working with these materials, a court may construct a meaning . . ."[33]

It is one thing to sacrifice the rule of law by adopting postmodern construction techniques when construing statutes that do not result in the criminalization of its citizens. It is quite another to convert the pragmatic realization that the search for parliamentary intention is an illusive exercise into an invitation to judges to make the criminal law in their own image. The "postmodern account of interpretation" in which judges are asked to help solve social problems has its place, but that place is not in the criminal law. This is not to say that judges interpreting penal statutes should strive for preposterous or contrived constructions to assist those charged with offences. To do so would be a breach of their duty to apply the law. What the rule of law demands, however, is that judges have the humility to select *reasonable interpretations* that favour the liberty of the accused over those interpretations that happen to accord with their own views of what the law should look like. The reality that legislative interpretation will invariably require the participation of the judge in the legislative process should not be used to justify converting those judges into legislators. They are partners in the process of legislative governance, but they must play a decidedly different role from that of legislators, where the liberty of the accused is at stake. If anything, the reality that precise legislative intention is often illusive or even non-existent underscores the danger that exists in accepting that judges should see themselves as providing meaningful solutions to social problems. If they take too seriously the notion that there is no real legislative intention, they become free agents to do as they please, treating the language of the statute as nothing more than an inconvenience to be overcome in getting where they want to go. While it is true that precise legislative intention may be unfathomable, the general purpose of legislation is not, and it can well be consulted in identifying the reasonable range of possible interpretations. Without a clear and convincing indication that the purpose of the legislation is intended to make the kind of conduct the accused is charged with criminal, the accused should be given the benefit of the doubt. Otherwise, the rule of law becomes an empty promise, while our judges become unelected politicians with all but absolute power.

Conclusion

Rule of law values depend on the law being scientific. Scientific law is technical and, in a sophisticated society, necessarily complex. This complexity has made much of the law inaccessible to the lay person. Those values have also damaged, to a degree, the public perception of the law and its institutions. The public judges the performance of the law not according to "rule utility" but according to "case utility." In other words, they do not ask how the decision in question will assist in producing justice in the long run. They want justice in the particular case. And they do not always judge justice according to "law." If the law is correctly applied but produces a result that is offensive, many members of the public will describe the decision as unjust.

Certainly the victims of an unpunished crime will have this view. But justice is a complex concept. It is to be measured not only by the consonance between a legal outcome in a particular case and the morality or values of the society. Justice also has to be measured, as well, according to the integrity that legal institutions have demonstrated in applying the law of the people. Judges cannot be asked at the same time to rule by law and to decide cases according to what might have appeared to Solomon to be best. Our judges are talented, industrious, and dedicated professionals, but few have the wisdom of Solomon. Instead of relying on their wisdom, the lawyers who don judicial robes rely on the law. If the law is producing unacceptable results, or doing more damage then good, then it will have to be changed. When we are talking about the reach of the criminal law, the time to define what is criminal is not when a citizen is standing before the court. And the person who creates new offences so that reprehensible conduct can be punished should not be an unelected judge who can speak only for him- or herself in deciding what conduct should be punished and what conduct should not. The time to define activity as criminal is before the accused acts. The institution that does so has to be Parliament.

In this way, the rule of law both preserves liberty in society and gives integrity to the law and to the decisions that get made. In the bargain, it presents challenges to pragmatic adjudication or practical decision making. It prevents judges from resolving legal disputes by asking the functional question, "What is best here?" Instead, judges are required to ask, "Regardless of what is best here, what does the law say?"

If we confine ourselves to law, then we can produce bad policy, as some will conclude Judge Hansen did in Brenda Drummond's case. The Romans were aware of this problem:

> When Cicero argued for a more complex systematization of law, with clear definitions and abstract legal rules, the jurists "answered these strictures by polite silence." They had no reason to try to transform the Roman genius for consistent adjudication into a philosophical system. They had every reason to be suspicious of the applicability of the higher ranges of Greek philosophy to the practical needs of adjudication.[34]

Roman society, though, was much simpler than our own. It was largely monocultural and it was classist. The senators listening to Cicero had no need to be afraid of the influence that personal values can have on the equal and just application of law because they got to decide what the law was. Things are different with the criminal law in contemporary Canadian society. Criminal rules allow society to cage people or to place accused adults on probation, requiring them to "report" to a probation officer or to obtain treatment. When society claims the right to do these things, the "rule of law" takes on tremendous importance. While we think of the power to convict and sentence as one of the greatest protections that citizens in this country have from the truly injurious conduct of others, it also poses the greatest threat to the liberty of its citizens. History demonstrates this fact. History of long ago shows it with political crimes like sedition and crimes against religion, such as blasphemy. More recent years show it to be so with homosexual offences. Most recent years show it to be true with politically attractive causes like the prosecution of war crimes, pornography, and heterosexual offences. Law is politics, but its administration cannot be allowed to become politics.

One might well ask, "What is the big deal about the rule of law? It doesn't work anyway." That is only partially true. What has to be appreciated is that the rule of law, like all principles of law, is an ideal. It never has, nor will it ever have, absolute fidelity. It is beyond question that the law or the facts can be manipulated to produce desired results, as has so often happened in the past. That practice does not make the rule of law a useless principle. Indeed, if anything, the extent to which the law can be manipulated should be seen to make the rule of law all the more important. All any law or legal principle can ever do is slow down abuses, whether they be by the state, its agents, or by the miscreants who live among us. The question is, do we prefer a system in which the road to tyranny is paved, with tires stacked along the sides like an Indy track, or would we rather have a road to tyranny that has sizeable speed-bumps placed strategically along the way? Do not think of the rule of law as an obstacle. Think of it as a speed-bump.

As always, the road we choose is up to the judges and parliamentarians, but mainly the judges. The rule of law tells us this much. Parliamentarians, for their part, should avoid using broad or vague language in defining criminal offences wherever possible, although that cannot always be accomplished. No one expects Parliament, for example, to describe in intimate detail the forbidden poses and contortions that make erotica obscene. But where the law can be stated with clarity and precision, it should be. Judges, for their part, have to be humble in their task, appreciating that while they can have an impressive and appropriate influence on the law, they are neither law reformers nor politicians. They need to appreciate that the definition and range of the criminal law is a matter for Parliament, not them. They have to discharge their function with a commitment to the ideals behind the rule of law, even when they do not like the results that the rules produce, and especially when they know the public will not. To choose clever contrivance to catch a "criminal" who has the law on his or her side is in itself an offence. It is nothing less than a breach of trust and, in the long run, it does not do the public any good. It weakens the ability of the law to protect the public from government abuse, or from the politics of those members of the intelligentsia who have been given the privilege of serving as judges.

As for the public, it is hoped they will understand that law is, of necessity, technical and laden with abstract principles that can be used by criminals, no matter how heinous the crime. While some of the antiquated technicalities can be criticized, the existence of technicalities cannot be. After all, it was the process of making the law technical that liberated people from the tyranny of kings. Why would we bind ourselves by a necessarily complex law which can defeat results that, to the public, may seem more practical, sensible, or just? History provides the answer, and it lies in the abuse of power, the reduction of bias, and in the long-range interests of justice and democratic principle. That is why the rule of law has become part of the fabric of the Constitution of Canada. The preamble to the *Canadian Charter of Rights and Freedoms* introduces the *Charter* by asserting that "Canada is founded upon principles that recognize the supremacy of God and the rule of law." Killers and brutes get off on technicalities because it is in the long-range interests of justice and democratic principle to judge them according to law, no matter how undeserving they might be.

Getting Off on Technicalities

F rank Boyle was a nice man — everyone said so. He went to church every Sunday and took mail to people who could not get out. At eighty-six years of age he still lived by himself in a small home in an isolated community of 300 people in the interior of British Columbia, a place with the unlikely name of "Likely." He passed the time after his wife died feeding the birds and squirrels near his home on Cedar Creek Road. He smoked Sportsman cigarettes and drove a red Datsun pickup truck. He drove it so slowly and cautiously that when the pickup was found crashed in a ditch at the end of a long set of skid-marks, the local people knew that Boyle could not have been driving at the time. They were right. He was not driving because by the time the truck left his garage, Boyle's skull had been smashed five times with an iron bar. It had been smashed so violently that any one of the blows would have killed him. There was blood on the walls of the living room where the body of Frank Boyle lay face up on the carpet.

There is no longer any mystery about who killed him. In fact, the mystery lasted only a few hours. It was Michael Feeney, a twenty-two-year-old outsider, who descended on that quiet community like a plague of vermin, holing up in a windowless trailer in the back of some property his sister and her partner were renting. The judge and jury who tried Feeney knew he had done it, and they convicted him. Members of the British Columbia Court of Appeal who upheld his conviction also knew it. And so, too, did the nine Supreme Court of Canada justices, including the five who voted to throw out virtually all the evidence against him.

Whatever else it means to get off on a technicality, Michael Feeney surely did. When the legal system allows a person whom it knows to be guilty to escape punishment, it can only be for technical reasons.

For the RCMP officers stationed at Williams Lake, an hour's drive from Likely, 8 June 1991 was not a routine day. Frank Boyle's body had been found in his house by a neighbour at 8:20 a.m. The neighbour had checked on Boyle when he noticed his garage door had been left open, something that struck the neighbour as unusual. When the neighbour discovered the body, the police were summoned. Constable Hamilton arrived a little over an hour later, at 9:25, to secure the scene.

Staff Sergeant Madrigga, the non-commissioned officer who was in charge of the Williams Lake RCMP detachment, arrived on scene at 10:05 a.m. He took charge of the investigation. He entered the home with the trepidation that even experienced officers feel when arriving at a homicide scene. Few become hardened to the sight and smell of violent death, and the sight was worse than he had imagined. Boyle had not just been bludgeoned to death. His head had been bashed in repeatedly, and the small house had been ransacked.

Shortly after his arrival, Madrigga learned from bystanders that Boyle's vehicle had been found abandoned in a ditch about half a kilometre west of the Boyle residence. It had been driven off the road. The arrival of the officers at the scene brought the local residents out. Cindy Potter told the police that she had seen Boyle's truck in the ditch at 6:45 that morning. A few minutes earlier she had observed a man whom she knew as "Michael" walking in an easterly direction along Cedar Creek Road, although she had not seen him driving the vehicle. Michael was holding something in his hand — possibly a beer, or a coffee cup, or perhaps a stick.

Kelly Robert Spurn spoke to the police as well. He told them Michael lived nearby on property he was renting to Michael's sister, Angela, and her partner, Dale Russell. He also told the police that Feeney had crashed and abandoned a blue flat-bed truck at the same location earlier in the morning. That truck, belonging to Russell, had been stolen from Spurn's property. Spurn surmised that Feeney had probably been driving Boyle's red Datsun as well, given that both vehicles had been ditched in the same place, and in the same manner, within a short time.

This was enough for Staff Sergeant Madrigga. He suspected that Feeney had stolen the Boyle vehicle, and that being so, he also suspected that Feeney was the murderer. He concluded from having seen the crime scene that if the perpetrator had not cleaned himself up, he would undoubtedly be covered in blood. Accompanied by two officers, Constable Hamilton and Corporal Haggard, Madrigga went to the Spurn property where Dale Russell, Angela Feeney, and Michael Feeney were living. It was around 10:30 a.m. There he spoke to Dale Russell, who was trying to fix the blue flat-bed truck. Russell confirmed that Feeney had stolen the truck and that he had found it just down from the Boyle residence, exactly where Boyle's truck had later been discovered. He also told the police that Feeney had come home at 7:00 a.m. after a night of drinking and was now asleep in the small storage trailer behind the residence which he was renting from them. This trailer may have been humble, but for Feeney it was his home.

Madrigga made his way to the trailer and banged on the door. There was no answer. He yelled "Police." There was still no answer. He drew his gun, leaving it hanging at his side, cautiously opened the door, and leaned into the trailer. Coming out of the sunlight into the dark, Madrigga could make out a man lying on a bunk at the back of the trailer, apparently asleep. He entered the trailer, followed by Corporal Haggard, and moved the few steps to where the man was sleeping. He leaned over and shook the man's leg. "Wake up, police. I want to talk to you." Michael Feeney squinted as he leaned on his elbow. Madrigga could not see him well because of the poor light. "Could you get out of bed and step to the door, please." Feeney complied. Madrigga led Feeney through the trailer, his hand on the young man's back, as they moved the short distance from the bed to the door. Madrigga could smell alcohol and smoke on Feeney's breath. As the daylight caught Feeney, Madrigga could see that the shirt he was wearing was splattered with blood.

Feeney was arrested and handcuffed. Madrigga then instructed another officer to read Feeney his rights:

> It is my duty to inform you that you have the right to retain and instruct counsel without delay. You may call any lawyer you want. A Legal Aid duty lawyer is available to provide legal advice to you without charge and can explain the Legal Aid plan to you. If you wish to contact a Legal Aid duty lawyer, I can provide you with a telephone number. Do you understand?

Feeney did not respond.

"You are not obliged to say anything, but anything you say may be given in evidence."

Feeney was then asked again whether he understood. Always the type to be polite, Feeney replied: "Of course, what do you think I am, illiterate?"

"How did you get the blood on you."

"I got hit in the face with a baseball yesterday." Madrigga looked at his face. There was no sign of any injury.

Constable Haggard piped in, pointing to a pair of shoes that were strewn on the floor: "Are those the shoes you were wearing when you went out last evening?"

Feeney responded, "Those are the only shoes I own."

Constable Haggard noticed a package of Sportsman cigarettes and asked Feeney if he wanted them. He said no, but asked for his can of tobacco. Madrigga recalled seeing Sportsman cigarettes at the Boyle residence. He told Haggard to leave this package of Sportsman cigarettes in the trailer. It could be seized later when the police had a warrant, along with the shoes.

Michael Feeney was then led to the police car by the officers. They removed the handcuffs long enough to seize the shirt he was wearing. Then they put the cuffs back on him and left for the Williams Lake RCMP detachment, some seventy-five minutes away, with Feeney sitting in the back seat, behind a screen, shirtless, shoeless, and with his hands manacled behind his back.

Shortly after his arrival at Williams Lake, Feeney tried to contact a lawyer. At 12:17 he left a message at a lawyer's office, asking the lawyer to call him. At 12:23 he was told that a breath sample would be taken from him. The officers were intent on trying to obtain a statement from him and wanted to make sure before doing so that he was not drunk. They may have learned from the Lana Clarkson[1] case decided several years before that a confession obtained from an intoxicated suspect is worthless in court. Clarkson, who had confessed to shooting her common-law spouse with a shotgun while he slept on a couch, was acquitted because the police had not waited before interviewing her until she sobered up enough to make an intelligent decision about whether to speak to a lawyer before talking to them. Feeney was not advised that he was not compelled legally to provide a breath sample, so he did as he was told. He blew .08.

Feeney was then placed in a brightly lit observation cell at the detachment, where he was left for over eight hours. At 9:10 p.m., Detectives Pilszek and Grinstead began to question him. Soon after they started, Feeney said, "I should have a lawyer." The interview continued, the comment ignored. During questioning, Feeney admitted to striking Boyle and stealing his cigarettes and beer. He also told the police he had stolen cash from Boyle's house and had put it under his mattress in the trailer.

With a search warrant in hand that was obtained from a justice of the peace who had gone to the police station to order Feeney to be held in custody, the police drove back to Likely and re-entered the trailer. They took Feeney's shoes, the Sportsman cigarettes, and a wad of bills totalling $350 from under the mattress. The evening before, he had told a young woman that he did not have any money. At 3:05 a.m. the police reinterviewed Feeney for one and a half hours, trying to persuade him to do a videotaped re-enactment of the crime. Feeney, who had still not seen a lawyer, refused.

There must have been relief and a sense of pride in the detachment. The police had broken the case. They had their man, and they had caught him swiftly and without incident. No one in Likely need sleep in fear that night. What a case: blood, opportunity, motive established through Feeney's possession of the stolen property, his circumstantial association with the stolen vehicle, and a confession.

The next morning Feeney was fingerprinted twice. Those prints tied things up nicely. They matched fingerprints found on the fridge door at Boyle's house, as well as a fingerprint found on an empty beer can in the Boyle truck. Then the forensic evidence came back. A shoe print left on Boyle's wallet matched the print from Feeney's shoes, the blood on Feeney's shirt was consistent with that of the deceased, and the blood-spatter pattern on the shirt matched the "medium velocity splatter patterns" found on the walls at the scene of the murder. In 1981 this case would have been a dream investigation. But it was 1991, the era of the *Canadian Charter of Rights and Freedoms.*

The optimism about the "quick collar" must have faded for the police once the trial got under way and a *voir dire* commenced. A *voir dire* is a hearing that takes place during a trial to decide a legal issue that has arisen. It is often referred to as a "trial within a trial." Where a jury trial is being conducted, as it was in the Feeney prosecution, most *voir dires* are held in the absence of the jury. Because they involve questions of law, they are decided by the judge, not the jury. The jury decides questions of fact, using the evidence that the trial judge permits it to hear and to consider. In law, evidence, or information about the incident the court is inquiring into, is either admissible or inadmissible. It is admissible when the court is entitled to consider it when deciding what happened. It is inadmissible when the law prevents the court from using it. Many *voir dires* concern the admissibility of evidence. If jurors were able to listen to the *voir dire*, they would learn about evidence that the judge might rule to be inadmissible, information that they should not know about. For this reason, the press is not allowed to report what happens during a *voir dire* until the trial is over. The issue at this *voir dire* was whether the police had violated Michael Feeney's constitutional rights as guaranteed under the *Canadian Charter of Rights and Freedoms,* and, if so, whether any of the evidence they had obtained should be excluded from admissible evidence.

Staff Sergeant Madrigga sat in the witness box clutching the duty book that contained his notes. His duty book was wound shut with elastics so it could be opened only to the pages dealing with the Feeney investigation. The defence lawyer would be allowed to look at the duty book during Madrigga's testimony, and the lawyer had no business with the notes from any other investigations. Madrigga waited for the next question from the defence lawyer:

> Q: Okay. Now at that point, the three of you [the police officers] were going to see Mr. Feeney?
>
> A: That's correct.
>
> Q: Because you wanted to question him about that, right?
>
> A: That's correct.
>
> Q: And at that point as you are going to the trailer, you would agree with me you had no intention of arresting Mr. Feeney?
>
> A: No, I just wanted to check what he had been doing.
>
> Q: And, of course, you didn't have a warrant for his arrest?
>
> A: No, I did not.
>
> Q: Because basically there wouldn't have been enough information to obtain a warrant?
>
> A: That's correct.
>
> . . .
>
> Q: And from the time you went into the trailer, there was no suggestion that you were going to let Mr. Feeney walk out of the trailer and go away?
>
> A. If I had no further evidence. If I had — when I went in and talked to him, if I had nothing to indicate he was involved in this, I would — it was shaky if I would have had grounds for his arrest at the time, but I had to check it out because I had people ask or tell me that this person was in the area.
>
> Q: All right, so let's see if we agree on something. At the time you went into the trailer, you didn't feel that you had grounds for his arrest, but when you saw the blood spatter on him after looking at him, that's why you said —
>
> A: I have grounds to suspect he could have been involved, sir, and I would have been negligent in my duty if I did not check that out.
>
> Q: Oh, I'm not arguing that point, Sergeant. But you didn't have grounds for an arrest?
>
> A: Not for an arrest at that time.

There it was. Staff Sergeant Madrigga, a man trying his best to uphold the law, had just conceded that he had broken it. As incredible as it seems, he violated the *Charter* by arresting Michael Feeney, the murderer. How so? Consider it for a moment. Madrigga opened the door to Feeney's residence — his home, his dwelling-house — even though he did not believe he had reasonable grounds to arrest him, and walked in, uninvited. This is not like cousin Eddie poking his head in the door to see if anyone is home. This is a public official, armed by the state and given wide powers to curtail the liberty of citizens, opening the door to Feeney's home, gun drawn, and walking in. The law at the time was clear, and despite the heroic efforts by the dissenting justices in the Supreme Court of Canada to find to the contrary, Staff Sergeant Madrigga, sworn to uphold the law, had violated the law.[2] No doubt he did not believe he was doing so, but for citizens we say that ignorance of the law is no excuse. Can we say anything different for police officers who presumably are trained in the law?

According to *R. v. Landry*,[3] a 1986 decision of the Supreme Court of Canada, while a police officer can enter a dwelling-house to arrest someone for an indictable [serious] offence without a warrant, that officer must believe on reasonable and probable grounds that the person he is about to arrest has committed the offence and that the person sought is on the premises. He must also make a proper announcement before entering. The only one of these preconditions that was clearly satisfied in this case was that the officer believed Feeney was in the trailer, and, given what he had been told by Dale Russell, it was reasonable for him to have that belief. Beyond that, he was found by the majority of the Supreme Court of Canada to have breached the other requirements. By his own admission, he did not believe he had grounds to arrest Feeney when he entered the trailer. And, while it is an agonizingly close call, the majority of the Supreme Court found that even if he did believe he could arrest Feeney on what he had before he saw the blood, it would have been unreasonable for him to have held that belief. All the police had at the time was a circumstantial connection between Feeney and the Boyle truck, which had presumably been stolen after the murder. This was enough to make Feeney a suspect, but according to the majority of the Supreme Court, it was not enough to conclude reasonably that he was probably the killer. In any event, the knock, followed by "Police," did not constitute a proper announcement. Before an officer enters a private house to arrest someone who is inside, he should identify himself clearly as a police officer, explain why he is there, and ask for permission to enter. Staff Sergeant Madrigga had broken the law. In doing so he had violated the *Canadian Charter of Rights and Freedoms*, which, along with other parts of the Canadian Constitution, contains the most fundamental and important set of rules in our entire legal system.

Feeney's *Charter* rights were breached in a number of other respects as well. The police had violated his constitutionally protected right to counsel. He should have been told of his right to counsel immediately on being detained, and he was detained the moment the officer, gun in hand, touched his leg and told him to get up. Yet Staff Sergeant Madrigga waited until he had Feeney in the light and had observed his shirt before telling him about his right to a lawyer. Even that did not end matters. There were still more problems. When the rights were read, they had been incomplete. The police did not provide adequate information about how Feeney could get immediate, free legal advice. As well, the law requires the police to refrain from using a person who is detained as a source of information or evidence until that person has had a reasonable opportunity to call a lawyer. The police should not have been asking Feeney about the blood on his shirt, or his running shoes, while in the trailer. They should have waited until Feeney had been given a chance to speak to a lawyer. Even then the police were not done violating his right to counsel. They breached his right again by questioning him at the station after he indicated that he should speak to a lawyer, and after he had left a message to have a lawyer contact him. They should have suspended their questioning immediately, providing him with a reasonable opportunity to speak to counsel.

As for the search warrant that the police obtained from the justice of the peace, it too was defective. To be valid, a warrant must be based on sworn evidence (called an "information") that discloses reasonable and probable grounds to believe that an offence has been committed and that there will be evidence at the place to be searched. This search warrant was based on information obtained during Feeney's unlawful arrest, including the blood on his shirt and the observation of the Sportsman cigarettes in his trailer. It was also based on confessions that had been obtained in violation of Feeney's right to counsel. The law does not allow unlawfully obtained evidence to be used to get a search warrant.

Feeney's fingerprints were also improperly taken from him, thereby further violating his constitutional rights. Fingerprints can only be taken from persons who have been arrested properly for indictable offences. Feeney had not been lawfully arrested.

In fact, the majority of the Supreme Court of Canada did not stop with the conduct of these police officers when identifying the *Charter* breaches. The Court went so far as to hold that even if Staff Sergeant Madrigga had met the four conditions that the Supreme Court had spelled out eleven years earlier in the *Landry* decision, he still would have been breaching the *Charter* by entering the trailer. *Landry*, the Court ruled, was a pre-*Charter* case and was no longer good law.[4] Under the *Charter*, an officer cannot enter a dwelling-house to arrest a suspect without a warrant, save perhaps in exceptional situations. At the time Feeney was arrested, the police did not have a warrant, nor were there exceptional circumstances.

The *Landry* case was controversial from the time it was decided. It was controversial because, in it, the Supreme Court of Canada had created new police powers, and there is a longstanding principle of law that new police powers should be created by Parliament rather than by the courts. The courts should not be seen to restrict the liberty of Canadian citizens. Prior to the *Landry* decision, it seemed to be the law that the only time an officer could enter a dwelling to arrest a suspect was after "hot pursuit." Hot pursuit, as the name suggests, involves the uninterrupted process of identifying a suspect and then pursuing him with the intent to arrest him. If he enters a dwelling-house in an effort to avoid arrest, the police can follow him in. In *Landry*, the Supreme Court extended the power to enter to make an arrest to cases where there is no hot pursuit, provided the officer has reasonable and probable grounds to believe that the suspect is in the residence.

In *Landry*, the Court decided to extend police powers as a matter of simple pragmatism. There was a gap in the *Criminal Code* at the time. The *Code* did not give any power to police officers to enter private dwellings to arrest suspects. Chief Justice Dickson reasoned in *Landry* that unless the police are given that right, then suspects can obtain sanctuary from the law by staying in their homes. Quasimodo leaning off the bell tower of Notre Dame Cathedral, triumphantly screaming "sanctuary," may be good theatre, but it is not good public policy. If Parliament is not going to sort out this quandary, the courts should. So, on behalf of the Supreme Court of Canada, Chief Justice Dickson expanded the power to enter dwelling-houses.

When Michael Feeney's case came before the Supreme Court of Canada, however, the Court had a change of heart. At the very least, reasoned the Court, without an emergency, the police should at least obtain a warrant before barging into someone's home to make an arrest. Even though the *Criminal Code* did not provide for arrest warrants that authorize entry into dwelling-houses, the *Feeney* Court held that justices have the power to issue such warrants and that police have the duty to obtain them before entering to arrest suspects. The sole exceptions are cases of hot pursuit and emergency situations, as when danger is presented to other occupants or there is reason to believe that the suspect is about to destroy evidence.[5]

Given this reasoning, even if Staff Sergeant Madrigga had followed the law in *Landry*, he would still have violated Michael Feeney's rights. What did the Court expect him to do? Had he hopped in the car and driven to Williams Lake to find a justice of the peace to request a warrant to enter to arrest Feeney, the JP would have thought him crazy. She would have said two things: "You don't need a warrant — read *Landry*," and then, "I don't have the power to give such a warrant — read the *Criminal Code*." It was no doubt an incredibly frustrating experience for Staff Sergeant Madrigga to learn the Supreme Court decision: it told him he had been constitutionally bound to do something that would, at the time, have been impossible.

Yet this last breach was moot, or unimportant, in the larger scheme of things. Apart from failing to obtain an unobtainable warrant, the police had committed numerous breaches of the law. And, because of the many breaches of Feeney's constitutional rights, the majority of the Supreme Court of Canada decided that they had no choice but to throw out the unconstitutionally obtained evidence — the bloody shirt, the blood analysis, the shoes, the Sportsman cigarettes, Feeney's fingerprints that matched those on the fridge and the beer can, the confessions, and the cash under the mattress. What did the Crown have left after this evidence was done? That Feeney was seen walking away from the area where Boyle's stolen car had been abandoned, that he was near the residence when the murder could have occurred, and that he had abandoned another stolen vehicle in the same area earlier that morning. Does this evidence prove beyond a reasonable doubt that Michael Feeney killed Frank Boyle? You could not even get convicted in Iraq on this kind of evidence. The Crown in British Columbia is nonetheless retrying the case, perhaps with the assistance of evidence that was not used during the first trial.

Justice L'Heureux-Dubé disagreed with the majority of the Supreme Court of Canada, along with two other justices. She denied that constitutional rights had been violated and held that, even if they had been, the evidence should nonetheless be admitted. She warned that excluding this evidence was probably going to lead to Michael Feeney's acquittal during his retrial. Justice Sopinka, speaking for the majority, was unrepentant:

> If the exclusion of this evidence is likely to result in an acquittal of the accused as suggested by L'Heureux-Dubé J in her reasons, then the Crown is deprived of a conviction based on illegally obtained evidence. Any price to society occasioned by the loss of such a conviction is fully justified in a free and democratic society which is governed by the rule of law.

There is that pesky rule of law again. It may make it necessary to let the murderer go because of technicalities.

For the record, I, for one, am not convinced that the Supreme Court of Canada had to throw out all the evidence in this case. In my view, the need for the legal system to address the allegations against Feeney — with full information — was far more pressing than the need to address the constitutional violations of the police. Still, while I may disagree with the application of the law by the Court in *Feeney*, I endorse completely the sentiment expressed by Justice Sopinka. Even though *Feeney* may not have been an appropriate case to do so, there are times when the rule of law requires the acquittal of the guilty. We have no choice but to accept this consequence, however painful it may be.

Justice in the Long Run

I alluded earlier to different utilitarian goals of the justice system. A rule utilitarian is someone who believes in the value of rules and what those rules can accomplish in the long run. A case utilitarian measures the utility or usefulness of the criminal justice system not according to its long-range promises, but according to the results it attains in the particular case. To a rule utilitarian, the legal evisceration of the Crown case in *Feeney*, or in any case for that matter, is to be measured against the extent to which the rules of law that are applied represent good policy and correct principle. To a case utilitarian, the legal destruction of the Crown case against a known killer is nothing short of obscene. Letting someone like Michael Feeney go free is simply unacceptable. A true case utilitarian might want to ask Justice Sopinka, the spokesperson for the majority in *Feeney*, whether the price to society occasioned by the loss of Feeney's conviction will be worth it if he bashes somebody else's head in for the promise of beer, pocket money, and cigarettes that you don't have to roll yourself. That is a powerful question, one that presents real problems for the rule utilitarian.

Rule utilitarians like myself hate to be frank and to say, "That will be tragic if it happens, but the risk that it will is something we all have to live with, just as we all have to live with the risk of automobile accidents and the release of carcinogens by factories that employ whole communities." I hate that answer even in the abstract, for it simply sounds too glib. Remove that answer from the abstract and it becomes even more offensive. It can be removed from the abstract by imagining what it would be like if Michael Feeney, or some other killer who has been released on a technicality, comes to prey on your family or your friends. Nothing that any rule utilitarian could ever say is likely to convince a victim or the family or friends of a victim that releasing the killer was the right thing to do. As cruel as it may sound, however, that is precisely why we do not have victims draft our laws. That is why being a victim is not a prerequisite to holding judicial office. If tragedy brings us too close emotionally to an issue, we may be among the last to have appropriate perspective. The harsh reality is that, as a society, we cannot afford to be pure case utilitarians.

The problem that a pure case utilitarian has is that the best way to ensure that criminals are found guilty is to remove all investigative, prosecutorial, or judicial impediments to the truth. Give the police absolute power. Tell them they can go anywhere they want whenever they want, and take anything they want. Give them the authority to enter private residences, to peruse hospital records to find drug users and drunk drivers, do DNA typing on everyone, take everyone's fingerprints, have everyone's photo in police mug books, arrest anyone for questioning, or hold people for investigative purposes. Then give the prosecutor absolute authority. Let the prosecutor change the charge against the accused partway through the trial, or lay charges that are unlikely to succeed in the hope that they will. Remove constraints on the judge. Let the judge admit whatever evidence he or she wishes, or allow any questions to be asked in whatever order he or she chooses. Allow the judge to force accused persons to take the stand during their trials so they can explain themselves. That is the way to achieve case utility.

You do not, of course, have to be a hard-core civil libertarian to reject this vision. As G. Arthur Martin, the pre-eminent Canadian criminal law judge of the last half-century and an eminently practical man, observed: "It has been truly said that the great distinction between the methods of totalitarianism and those of democracies is that in the totalitarian State the end justifies the means, whereas in democracies we often give up ideal ends because we renounce the means necessary to achieve them."[6] If we want to be effective case utilitarians, we need only one rule: the ends justify the means. Sometimes, though, the price of the truth is simply too high.

Even if we wanted all technicalities to be removed, it would simply not be possible to do so. Professor Mellinkoff, in a book called *The Conscience of a Lawyer* (a title some will say gives whole new meaning to the term oxymoron), defends the use of technicalities in these terms:

> Any system of justice has its procedures, its technicalities, the details by which it takes laws out of the books and puts them to work. It is often only a choice of procedures that separates savagery or tyranny from civilized life. Head-hunting is a procedure; so is the rack. Whether you are presumed guilty when charged with a crime or presumed innocent until proven guilty is a technicality.
>
> Our particular choice of technicalities distinguishes us from men who are not free. '[T]he most celebrated writ in the English law,' 'the great and efficacious writ,' of habeas corpus is a technicality. For want of it men in our English past and men in other lands today have been

kept caged without conviction of any crime, often without even being told why they are deprived of their liberty.

There are other procedures of law which may delay the day of reckoning for a guilty man as surely as they preserve the liberty of an innocent one. The privilege against self-incrimination, for example. . . . The privilege reinforces the presumption of innocence, requiring the accuser to gather evidence to prove a man guilty rather than to resort to the simpler, faster expedient of squeezing his genitals until he confessed. A technicality.

The suspicion of gossip formalized in the rules against hearsay testimony. The right to confront one's accusers, and to cross-examine them. . . . Technicalities. Technicalities learned the hard way of history.[7]

The first point being made by Mellinkoff is that every system of law has its procedures and technicalities. Without procedures and technicalities, there is no "system of law." To enforce the law that applies to citizens like Michael Feeney, there has to be a process for doing so. We need to engage in some process of investigation, some process of charging, and we need to have some process for trying, judging, and then punishing offenders. There is a name for a process by which the law is enforced without the benefit of rules: it is called a "mob." The sad fact is that we need rules and technicalities to define the process. Without them there is nothing to guide and constrain the police, the prosecutors, or the courts other than their own values, priorities, and beliefs. Without rules, those who administer the law would be left free to make up the rules and procedures as they went along.

As a society, we have rejected this option for a number of reasons. The first has to do with the basic principle of equality. Simply put, if we did not have rules and procedures, the law would not be applied equally or consistently. To ensure the equal application of law, there must be rules to give direction and instruction. There must be rules about how a court conducts its process, how judges perform their role, how prosecutors behave, and how the police conduct their investigations. Without rules, there is absolute power for the police, for judges, and, heaven forbid, for lawyers.

The second reason why we have procedures and technicalities is that technicalities are indispensable, even to the accomplishment of case utility. In other words, we need technicalities to get the verdict right. A number of our most infamous technicalities are rules of evidence, designed to advance the truth. For example, when Peter Demeter was being tried for murdering his wife, he attempted to introduce a statement made by a prison inmate, which claimed that the inmate, and not Peter

Demeter, had killed Christine Demeter. Demeter could not call the inmate as a witness at his trial because the man had since died. The confession by this man that he, and not Peter Demeter, had killed Christine Demeter was rejected by the court as inadmissible because of a technicality known as the hearsay rule. This rule is offended any time a statement that has been made out of court is being presented to a trial court as an accurate account of what happened. There is usually no way to test the reliability of the statement because the person who made it is not there to be cross-examined. There was an appreciable risk that the statement was a false contrivance designed to get Demeter off. The man who made the confession had nothing to lose by taking the rap. He had terminal cancer at the time and was already under a life sentence. The hearsay rule, a major technicality, is intended to advance the truth, and in this case, because the evidence was excluded, it may have assisted the Crown in obtaining a conviction.[8]

Another rule prevents courts from receiving the confessions of accused persons which have been obtained by the police through the use of force, threats, bribes, or other things that might make the confession involuntary. There are several reasons for the rule. The most saleable is that if an accused person has confessed involuntarily, his confession may not be true. It is worthless. Put a thumbscrew on my fingernail and I'd likely confess to shooting Kennedy before you even started to tighten it. This technicality results in many confessions being thrown out.

The problem with any such rule is that the baby can get thrown out with the bathwater. Because rules are, by definition, general, perfectly true confessions are excluded along with false ones. One need go no further in making the point than to introduce the case of *R. v. Horvath*.[9]

Otto Joseph Horvath, seventeen years of age at the time, was on a tear in the early evening hours of 16 June 1975. He had stolen his step-father's car keys from his mother's dresser and gone to his workplace to steal the car. He spent the evening racing around Vancouver with three young ladies in the vehicle, leaving the scene of two automobile accidents he had caused. When he made it home at midnight, he was greeted by the police. They were not interested in the car theft or his accidents. They arrested him for the murder of his mother, whose body had been found lying on her bed in the late afternoon "with her head bludgeoned to a pulp."

Within twenty minutes, an interrogation commenced at the police station. It proceeded from 12:10 a.m. until 3:10 a.m., without a break. Young Horvath was sitting in a chair that was wedged between two police officers, one of whom, Corporal Delwisch, was 6 foot 3 and 225 pounds. The officers peppered Horvath with questions, each in turn, for the full three hours. They emphatically accused him of lying and told him, with reference to his demeanour and his way of answering questions, to "pack up that nonsense." The trial judge considered the entire atmosphere to be oppressive. Even the Crown psychiatrist acknowledged that the atmosphere would give Horvath a sense of being threatened.

The next day Horvath was taken to the RCMP headquarters, ostensibly for a polygraph, or lie-detector, test. He was left waiting for an hour. He was then brought into Sergeant Proke's office, where he remained for the next four and a half hours. No effort was made to administer a polygraph test. Instead, he was subjected to what the trial judge referred to as "the most skilful example of police interrogation that ha[d] ever come to [his] attention in [his] thirty-six years as a lawyer and a judge."[10]

During the entire interview, the events were being surreptitiously recorded. Initially Horvath said he could remember nothing about his mother's death and denied his involvement, although he admitted to being troubled by something locked away in his mind. After more than an hour of questioning, Proke left the room. Horvath began to talk to himself, not realizing that the recorder was on or that the police could hear what he was saying. He denied any involvement and swore vengeance against whoever had killed his mother. Proke then returned and continued to question Horvath. He asked Horvath whether he could see his mother's image in the bed with blood around her. After a period of further unsuccessful questioning, Proke left again. Horvath continued to talk to himself, only this time he recounted how his mother had begged him to kill her and how he had finally acquiesced. As if speaking to his mother, he promised her he would never tell.

Proke returned again and questioned him further. He confronted Horvath with his soliloquies, and Horvath repeated the story. Proke left, and Horvath again tried speaking to his mother, apologizing for revealing her request that he kill her. Finally, twenty minutes later, Corporal Delwisch, the larger of the two officers who had first interviewed Horvath, took a conventional written statement from him. After the statement was done, Horvath accompanied the police to Burnaby Mountain and helped them find a baseball bat, gloves, and bloody socks. Even though this evidence could not be connected to the crime without Horvath's statement, the police unquestionably had their man.

The Crown psychiatrist, Dr. Stephenson, described Horvath as having a sociopathic personality, making him impulsive, hedonistic, reckless as to consequences, and boastful. This discription troubled the trial judge and he asked Dr. Stephenson to listen to the tapes. Dr. Stephenson did, and then he reported back. Based on what he knew of Horvath and what he had heard, it was his opinion that Horvath had initially repressed the memory of whatever had happened. In describing the interrogation technique to the trial judge, Dr. Stephenson said that Sergeant Proke had skilfully played upon Horvath's "feelings and latent pleasures to bring the material into his consciousness." More important, he concluded that Proke, whether deliberately or not, had adopted a hypnotic tone and cadence to his questions. Judging from the nature of the youth's response, Dr. Stephenson expressed the opinion that Horvath had slipped into a mild hypnotic state, which lasted through the first two soliloquies. Under questioning from defence counsel, he agreed that persons who are hypnotized are more susceptible to powers of suggestion.

Based on Dr. Stephenson's evidence and all the other proof presented during the *voir dire* into the admissibility of the confession, the trial judge concluded that during the four hours and four minutes of the interviews, the complete emotional disintegration of Horvath had occurred. His confession was not voluntary and should therefore not be admitted. The first statements made during the oppressive interrogation where also excluded as involuntary.

By the narrowest of margins, the Supreme Court of Canada ultimately agreed. Two justices concluded that a confession obtained through involuntary hypnosis should not be admitted. Two others adopted a broader rule, suggesting that confessions that are not the product of an operating mind are unreliable and should therefore be excluded. The confessions were therefore thrown out. Without them, the discovery of the bat and the socks and the gloves was not enough to convict Horvath. He was ultimately acquitted of murder at his retrial and was freed.

The *Horvath* case is a fascinating illustration because it demonstrates how rules, designed primarily to accomplish case utility by pursuing the truth, can distort the truth in particular cases. Our courts simply consider it to be functionally impossible to distinguish between true involuntary confessions and false involuntary confessions, so, according to law, they all have to go. They are dismissed in the long-term interests of the truth. Through experience, the legal system has learned that if we allow involuntary confessions into evidence for fear of throwing out a truthful confession, we will produce less accurate verdicts in the long run. Professor Alan Dershowitz in his book *Reasonable Doubts* explains:

> There are different kinds of truth at work in our adversary system. At the most basic level, there is the ultimate truth involved in the particular case: "Did he do it?" Then there is the truth produced by cases over time, which may be in sharp conflict. For example, the lawyer-

client privilege which shields certain confidential communications from being disclosed may generate more truth over the long run by encouraging clients to be candid with their lawyers. But in any given case, this same privilege may thwart the ultimate truth — as in the rare case where a defendant confides in his lawyer that he did it.[11]

Unfortunately, the Horvath story is not only a fascinating example of how rules sacrifice short-term truth in the interests of long-term truth but it is also a tragic story. It is tragic for those who believe that justice must be done, and who believe that the evidence showed beyond any doubt that Horvath killed his mother — hypnosis and emotional disintegration notwithstanding. It was even more tragic, however, for a young classmate of Horvath who came into his life shortly after he returned to school, having been acquitted on a technicality. Horvath killed her, too. Had his confessions to killing his mother been allowed into evidence, this young woman would probably be alive today. It would probably take a far better lawyer than I to convince her parents that the law has to countenance technicalities of any kind. Understandably, they might even detest those technicalities that are designed to arrive at the truth. Sometimes, so do I. The message, though, is that even if we were pure case utilitarians, we could not avoid technicalities, including those that can acquit the guilty.

The third reason why we cannot be pure case utilitarians is that, as much as we would like it to be, a criminal trial is not simply about the truth of the claim that the accused is guilty. Although the immediate objective of the trial is to make that determination, the truth of the allegation is not the only interest at stake. As Dershowitz has put it, "Our system of justice [including our trial process] reflects a balance among often inconsistent goals, which include truth, privacy, fairness, finality and equality."[12] This multiplicity makes the law complex and technical as well as unsatisfying. Unfortunately, ignoring these other interests would make it even less satisfying.

Since the *Feeney* case is largely about protecting privacy, perhaps that is the interest that should be used to illustrate the point. Privacy interests can arise during the course of any trial. They tend to arise, most commonly, in sexual offence prosecutions. Asking questions about the past sexual experiences of the complainant may have relevance in some cases. So, too, may the psychiatric or therapeutic records of complainants. Yet our rules do not allow accused persons to ask questions of sexual offence complainants about their sexual history in every case where it has some relevance, nor do we allow accused persons to see the psychiatric or therapeutic records of complainants in every case where they have some relevance. There are competing interests. The privacy and dignity of the complainant has to be considered. So, too, must the longer-term interests of encouraging complainants to come forward.

A British Columbia Court of Appeal case, *R. v. D.D.W.*,[13] illustrates dramatically how privacy interests can compromise case utility. The accused was charged with the rape of his sister. Shortly after the alleged rape, she discovered that she was pregnant. She gave birth and put the baby up for adoption. She denied having had intercourse with anyone else, claiming that her brother was the father. The accused, for his part, denied that he had had intercourse with her. His counsel wanted access to the adoption records so that the child could be identified and blood samples taken. Those samples could have gone a long way to proving the accused's innocence if they excluded him as the father. Yet the court refused to allow access to the records or to order the blood tests. The court had real and understandable concern about the trauma to the child, should he suddenly be dragged into the case, of discovering that his father was his uncle and that he was the progeny of a rape. According to the court, his privacy interests outweighed the interest of the accused in case utility.

What about privacy during the investigative stage? Ask yourself this question and answer it in all honesty. How would you feel if the police came into your house without reasonable and probable grounds to believe that anyone inside had committed an offence? I suspect that most Canadians — indeed, an overwhelming majority of them — would be outraged. I suspect that most police officers would agree that this entry should not be permitted. I doubt they have a problem that there is a law against it.

Bearing that response in mind, imagine that the events of 8 June 1991 had happened differently in Likely, British Columbia. Imagine that no one had seen Michael Feeney walking away from the accident scene and that the police did not have a suspect. It would nonetheless have been reasonable for the police to assume that the killer was still in that tiny community, given that the car he had stolen had been abandoned. With Likely being as small as it is, it probably would have been feasible for the police to search every home in town. Would it have been acceptable for them to have done so? Would it have been tolerable for them to enter every one of those homes to rummage through them looking for clues or suspects, even in cases where the homeowners refused entry? It would be an appalling spectacle. We want to protect our streets, but I doubt we want to do it to this extent.

This scenario raises the question: If the police should not be able to enter the homes of the townsfolk, why should they be able to do it to Michael Feeney, given that they did not have reasonable and probable grounds to believe that he had committed the offence? The rule that protects the privacy of the townspeople should have kept them out of his trailer. The police should simply have stayed out. And if they had stayed out, they may not have seen his bloody shirt or the Sportsman cigarettes. They never would have been able to arrest him to take his fingerprints, and unless he had a prior criminal record for which he was fingerprinted, they could never have linked him to the killing. In other words, according to law, unless they found other leads or evidence, they should never have caught him. That conclusion is a hard pill to swallow, but it is a necessary corollary of having rules that restrict police powers.

Protecting the Guilty to Save Ourselves

The truth is, we as Canadians tend not to object to the existence of technicalities. We like the technicalities that protect crime victims from abuse by defence lawyers. We like the technicalities that protect our privacy from the police. What we really object to is the use of technicalities by those we believe to be criminals. There is more than a little hypocrisy in this distinction. When defence counsel attempt to obtain the psychiatric records of complainants in sexual offence cases, there is broad-based public opposition. The complainant and the therapist or the sexual assault crisis clinics object. Often the Crown joins in, making dramatic arguments about individual integrity, invasions of privacy, and the sanctity of hospital or therapeutic records. In the end, our parliamentarians, smelling political mileage, jump into the fray on the side of the angels, putting an end to the spectacle, oblivious to the fact that in some cases these records will protect the innocent. Yet when the accused's therapeutic or hospital records promise to be helpful to the Crown, the Crown skips off with a warrant and grabs them. The prosecution uses such records to prove the blood alcohol level of the accused if it is a driving case, or the admissions made by the pedophile to his doctor or therapist where it is a sexual offence case. We Canadians applaud the investigative initiative. We support the hearsay rule when it keeps out a potentially concocted defence, but vilify it when it keeps out potentially inculpatory evidence. If we were honest, we would admit that it is not the technicalities we object to; we object to the use of technicalities by those who are accused of offences. When a person whom we not only suspect of being guilty but know is guilty uses those technicalities, we pass beyond dislike to contempt.

If we detest the fact that we *must* allow those who are guilty to use the law to shield themselves from detection and conviction, that is entirely understandable. It is like detesting taxes, or sickness, or death itself. If, however, we as a society detest the fact that we do allow those who are guilty to use the law to shield themselves from detection and conviction, we have a problem.

As nice as it would be, we cannot have one set of laws for the innocent and one for the guilty. Who would decide which set of rules to apply during the investigation — the police? Judges and juries, who are selected because they are believed to be neutral and impartial adjudicators, cannot always distinguish the truly guilty from the truly innocent even after trial. What makes us think that the police could do so with any degree of accuracy? The warrant requirement for searches and arrests, in which the police must convince a neutral, impartial justice that they have reasonable and probable grounds to believe that the accused has committed the offence, or that there is evidence of a crime in a building or home, developed precisely because, during the heat of the investigation, the police may not exercise sound judgment about when someone is probably guilty. The alternative to a warrant requirement is to have after-the-fact assessments of whether the police had correctly identified those who are probably guilty. But, by that time, a citizen has already been needlessly carted off and held in custody, or the privacy of the home has already been needlessly invaded.

It is not even possible to have one set of rules for the innocent and one for the guilty during the trial process itself. Innocence and guilt are supposed to be decided at the end of the trial, on all the evidence. That is why our judges direct jurors not to discuss the evidence they hear until all the evidence in the case has been presented. Even if we wanted it done, it would be impossible in most cases to tell whether the accused was guilty or not at the time when the rules of evidence were being applied.

But, most important, how much integrity would a verdict have if it was arrived at through the selective application of the law. The integrity of law and of the entire legal system requires that we all be judged by the same rules and by the same standards. The defining nature of a rule of law is that it is something that must be applied by those who administer the rules. If there is freedom not to apply it, it is no longer a rule. It is, at best, a suggestion that can be rejected by the police or the judge because of their own tastes, experiences, beliefs, and prejudices. It is difficult enough to be a black, or native suspect. Imagine being a black or native suspect in a system that makes no pretence to the equal application of the law?

There are also selfish reasons for agreeing to see the law applied equally to all. To enable the law to be applied as a matter of choice would debase society's legal institutions — institutions we have an interest in preserving. It would defeat both the appearance of justice and justice itself to permit those who administer our institutions to decide who gets the benefit of law. Moreover, it would undermine the integrity of all rules of law. It would deprive those rules of the ability to give benefit to any of us.

There is a compelling point in Robert Bolt's play *A Man for All Seasons* in which Sir Thomas More, the Lord Chancellor, is asked to arrest a man who is perceived by others, including Roper, to be a danger to the Lord Chancellor, and to be a man who has violated God's laws. More refuses because the man has broken no laws. When he is chastised for letting the man go, he replies:

> More: And go he should, if he was the Devil himself, until he broke the law!
>
> Roper: So now you'd give the Devil benefit of law!
>
> More: Yes. What would you do? Cut a great road through the law to get after the Devil?
>
> Roper: I'd cut down every law in England to do that!
>
> More: Oh? And when the last law was down, and the Devil turned round on you — where would you hide, Roper, the laws all being flat? This country's planted thick with laws from coast to coast — man's laws, not God's — and if you cut them down — and you're just the man to do it — d'you really think you could stand upright in the winds that would blow then? Yes. I'd give the Devil benefit of law, for my own safety's sake.[14]

The point that the laws are there to protect us all tends to leave ardent case utilitarians unmoved. Those among us who are most offended by the access of criminals to protective laws tend to be decent people who are not criminally inclined and who therefore believe that we do not need the protection of the technicalities that the criminal justice system has designed. We find it much easier to imagine ourselves being brutalized by criminals than by the police or the courts. For this reason, in *R. v. Collins*, in response to the argument that the decision to exclude unconstitutionally obtained evidence should be based on whether the general public would approve, Chief Justice Lamer observed that "members of the public generally become conscious of the importance of protecting the rights and freedoms of accused only when they are in some way brought closer to the system either personally or through the experience of friends and family."[15]

It is a measure of the success of the rule of law that many have trouble believing in it. We have the luxury of assuming that even without it, our cherished values would be protected. Why? We have learned to trust our officials because, for the most part, they have respected the rule of law. If they had been disregarding it all along, they never would have earned our trust. If they acted in a result-oriented manner, in which rules meant little and power meant everything, we would not trust them. We would not trust them if they were in the habit of entering our homes at will, carting us away without charge, and punishing us without trial. The point has been aptly made that it is difficult for dictators to get accustomed to the idea that the main purpose of law is, in fact, to make their task more difficult.[16] The price we pay for the luxury of our freedom, and it is acceptable coinage, is that it becomes more difficult for the police to be effective in catching criminals.

PROVING GUILT AND MAINTAINING INNOCENCE

CHAPTER 7

The Specific Allegation

L ake Taupo is a small but magnificent body of water that seems on a relief map to bore a hole into the middle of New Zealand's North Island. A three-hour drive south of that country's major city, Auckland, it is framed by three graceful mountains — Tongariro, Ngauruhoe, and Ruapehu. Much of the area around Lake Taupo is sacred to the Maori. Anyone who has been there would not be surprised. The lake sits in mystical environs, surrounded by hot springs, boiling mud pools, and vents that open from the deep recesses of the earth, spewing clouds of steam that climb through the trees and hang in the sky, creating an ethereal atmosphere. The many watercourses that give life to the central island have unique, varied colour, depending on their origin, depth, or the geological composition of their basin: a washed-out peacock blue, a deep emerald green, or the milky grey of the shallow glacier-fed streams that run in from the mountains. Tourists flock to the centre of the North Island to tour sheep stations or a buried Maori village, to watch Maori warriors perform their Huka, or war dance, to wet tied flies in the Tongariro River, the "fly fishing capital of the world," or to take to the water on jet boats — sleek, propellerless craft that can skim over shallow rocky streams and spin "360s" at heavy speed.

On a calm, beautiful January day, Barry Marshall was operating a jet boat full of tourists on the Waikato River on the edge of Lake Taupo when he spied what appeared to be the bloated stomach of a sheep floating in the water. He worked the boat closer. It was not the bloated stomach of one of the less fortunate among New Zealand's sixty million sheep but the swollen body of Peter Plumley Walker, his feet and hands still bound, with a rope hanging loosely about his neck. Marshall dropped the tourists on the dock and, acting on the instructions of the police, returned, tied a tow-rope to the body, and dragged the corpse slowly to shore.[1]

Plumley Walker, as he came to be known both in the media and in the parlours of New Zealand where everyone was talking about the case, had gone missing under mysterious circumstances several days before. His gold Ford Cortina had been found on fire in southeast Auckland. This was cause enough for worry, but Peter's state of mind the last time he had been seen added to the fear. After several years of separation that Peter had never wanted to accept, his wife had finally obtained a divorce decree. Disconsolate, Peter had wandered into his bank, withdrawn $200, and disappeared.

Ian Walker, Peter's brother, did not know of Peter's habits. Despite a veneer of conventional respectability as a well-known cricket umpire, Peter, a tall stately man with a magnificent white handlebar moustache, had led a secret life. He craved the unfathomable pleasure of bondage, and he would periodically set out to K road in Auckland, where any perversion can be gratified for enough money. When Ian began looking for his brother, he went into Peter's apartment to see if there were any clues to his disappearance. He found a small sheet of paper by the phone with notes written in Peter's hand. He could read the names and phone numbers of several women. An address on Rotomahana Terrace showed next to "4:30 Friday." From the magazines and letters scattered around the apartment, Ian knew that the names on the paper would belong to dominatrixes, women who would beat, bind, or even torture men, and occasionally even other women, for a price.

Following the leads contained in some of these materials, the police made their way to the impressive home of a middle-class woman. She answered the door. Yes, she provided domination services. Yes, she had sent a letter to Peter Plumley Walker's address describing what she would do to him after he responded to an ad she had placed in *Raunchy* magazine. No, she had never actually met him. Yes, the police could look around. In her diary the police found the inscription, "Peter — $200.00." It showed on Friday, 27 January, the same day that Plumley Walker was last seen. In the yard the police found cinder blocks that looked similar to one that a police diver had recovered from the bottom of the Huka Falls on the Waikato River. They found rope that appeared similar to rope that had been tied around the brick. On the curtains in the bedroom, they found blood. Forensic tests were ordered. The police were sure they had the case solved.

As anyone knows who has followed a different Walker case — the case of Albert Walker — circumstantial evidence can be enough to prove guilt. Walker was recently convicted of murdering Ronald Platt on the strength of powerful circumstantial evidence. He was convicted because he had motive to kill Platt to steal his identity; Platt's body, identifiable by the Rolex watch he was wearing, had been dredged up in a fishing net along with an anchor identical to one Walker had purchased, in an area where Walker's boat had been at the relevant time; Platt's belt was crimped as though it had been attached to something heavy like an anchor; and Walker had lied to Platt's girlfriend about his whereabouts. Although there were no eye witnesses and no admissions of guilt, Walker found himself caught by a different kind of net than the one that dredged up Platt. Albert Walker became enmeshed in a net of inexplicable coincidences.

Even though their proof was also entirely circumstantial, the police who were trying to solve the killing of Peter Plumley Walker and who had discovered the ad, the cinder blocks, the blood, and the diary notation, had the makings of a pretty good case. Fortunately, the woman was spared the indignity of arrest by the miracle of modern science. The cinder block was different from the one that had been dredged up, and neither the rope nor the blood matched the evidence that the police had obtained. Embarrassed, no doubt, by the police questions, her "Peter," still very much alive, confirmed her explanation for the diary notation.

Consider what would have happened had the cinder block been a match, even a common one. Assume that her "Peter," out of understandable shame, denied he knew her. Imagine if the blood on the curtains had yielded the same general blood type as Plumley Walker's. Coincidence can lead to miscarriages of justice. There is little that the law can do to prevent it from happening when the stars happen to align in the wrong way. In this case, however, there was a better suspect.

The police ultimately arrived at the tiny white house on Rotomahana Terrace in the trendy Remuera suburb of Auckland that bore the address found next to Plumley Walker's phone. A woman, Renee Chignell, then only nineteen years of age and previously unknown to the police, stood in the doorway. She wore her hair blond, had a tattoo running up between her ample breasts, and bore the defiant look of rebellious youth. She had recently left her employment as a masseuse so that she and her boyfriend, Neville Walker (who was not related to Peter), could open their bondage service. Neville, always handy with tools, built her the crude implements of her trade. Was she in the bondage business? Yes. Did she know Peter Plumley Walker? No. Had she been near Lake Taupo recently? Not in years.

In an impressive bit of police work, constables were sent to all the petrol stations between Auckland and Lake Taupo in the hope that some of the premises had security cameras. Maybe they had film from 27 or 28 January. And just maybe one of these films might show Chignell or Neville Walker near Taupo. Indeed, at one station they were both captured on film, sitting in their car eating meat pies while it was being gassed up in the early morning hours of 28 January.

The arrests of Chignell and Walker followed immediately after, but the investigation was far from over and the case was in no shape to bring to trial. More proof was needed, not to establish that the pair were involved somehow in Plumley Walker's disappearance (they unquestionably were), but in what way. In New Zealand's system of justice, as in our own, the government cannot prosecute someone for having had "something" to do with a suspicious event. A specific allegation is required. When someone is charged, the government must specify the precise offence it says the accused has committed, and it must prove that specific allegation beyond a reasonable doubt. There were still many possibilities. Although unlikely, it may have been that Peter Plumley Walker died of natural causes during the bondage session "like a man in a dentist chair," as one of the police officers suggested, and perhaps Chignell and Walker decided to get rid of his body rather than explain that they were in the business of selling bondage services. Perhaps they had been negligent, unintentionally causing his death. If so, as in Canada, they could potentially be guilty of the offence of manslaughter, but not murder. Or perhaps they intended to kill him for some reason, dispatched him in Auckland, and then dumped his body over the Huka Falls, thereby committing murder. Conceivably, they could have taken him to Lake Taupo alive and then thrown him the 10 metres over the falls, weighted down with a concrete block so he would drown.

The pathologist was unable to help out. There was water and sand in Peter Walker's lungs, normally indicative of death by drowning, but it could prove nothing, given that he had been thrown into the frothing base of a waterfall. Even a corpse would have water and sand forced into its lungs as it was lashed about by the swirling currents. There were modest bruises on parts of the body and injuries to the head, but none that would appear to have caused death. Most of the injuries were probably caused post-mortem as the body crashed along the rock walls as it was washed away from the falls. The cause of death, as shown on the pathology report, was "asphyxia/drowning?" — a conclusion too tentative to provide the needed answer. The police had the right suspects, but no solid theory.

As they had hoped, as soon as she was confronted with the videotape, Chignell began to talk. Detective Senior Sergeant Dewar, in an effort to get her to open up, had suggested that perhaps Plumley Walker died during a discipline session, in which case she would not be guilty of murder. He recorded what he claimed to be her response: "But it didn't happen like that." She explained that she had tied him up with a dog collar around his neck and hoisted him off the ground so that his feet were barely touching. She could see him turning blue, but decided to leave him there and left the room to have a coffee with Neville Walker. "I knew what was happening to him — his face looked so funny." She got her boyfriend to come and look at him. After they took him down, they wrapped him up in a blanket and drove to Taupo and dumped the body off a bridge. According to this statement, Chignell would have been guilty of murder at Auckland. That is where he would have died, and she would have caused that death by leaving him strung up.

Wanting to tighten the case, the police sought a written, signed confession from her. In New Zealand, oral statements are admissible, just as they are in Canada, as long as they are voluntarily given and the necessary rights to counsel are respected. Accused persons should know there is no such thing as an "off-the-record" statement. A written statement, however, makes it more difficult for the accused to challenge what was said. The police were therefore pleased when Chignell agreed to give a statement in writing. Unfortunately for the prosecutors, her written account differed in several respects from her previous oral statement.

In the written statement, Chignell claimed that she bound and hung Plumley Walker in the fashion that he wished and then left the room, as was her practice. She stayed away for some twenty minutes, longer than was her custom. When she returned, his hands were blue and she quickly let him down, whereupon he fell to the floor. Neville Walker came in and saw what had happened. They checked for a pulse and there was none. While they were deciding what to do, her mother arrived unannounced with fish and chips. Unable to do otherwise, they joined her for dinner and made small talk while the body of a naked man lay stiffening on their bedroom floor. After she left, they tied Plumley Walker's feet and hands so they could carry him more easily, drove to Huka Falls, and threw his body off the bridge. On this version, she would be guilty, at worst, of manslaughter, but not murder. The killing would have been unintentional, but would probably have been committed under circumstances that were sufficiently negligent to make it criminal. As in Canada, a criminally negligent act causing death is manslaughter. The police had a problem, though. Which version was true, and which crime had been committed, murder or manslaughter?

In the meantime, Renee Chignell was placed in a cell next to a young woman who later came to be known as "Witness A" to protect her identity. This young woman had been busted importing heroin and was facing a substantial prison term. Her partner had just received a thirteen-year sentence. Her lawyer contacted the police, advising them that Chignell had confessed to her and that, as a matter of conscience, she was prepared to help the authorities. Although the police denied that any deals had been struck in exchange for her evidence, she was immediately released on bail. Unfortunately for the prosecutors, Chignell's confession to this young woman differed from each of the two statements she had already provided to the police. According to Witness A, Plumley Walker had told Chignell some things that disgusted her. The Crown would later surmise that Plumley Walker had told Chignell the same story he had told another dominatrix — that he had been employed at a girls' school in Germany and been responsible for caning the girls, after which he would often force sex on them. After hearing the story, she bound him and gagged him as he had requested, and then left the room in disgust to tell her boyfriend what her client had said. The boyfriend then went inside and beat the hanging man, first with his fists and then with a metal bar. Having gone this far and fearing arrest, the couple later walked him to the car, drove him to Taupo, weighted him down, and, together, threw him into the water — vigilantes seeking a crude form of justice against a child sex offender. On this version, despite what some might consider their lofty motives, both Chignell and Walker would be guilty of murder at Taupo, rather than murder at Auckland.

Even if this last statement was the true one, it could provide evidence solely against Chignell. In New Zealand, as in Canada, a confession is admissible in evidence against the accused who confesses, but it cannot be used as evidence against a co-accused. It would be considered unfair for the Crown to use Chignell's statement as evidence against Neville Walker because Chignell, being an accused at the trial, could not be forced by Walker to take the stand and testify. Walker would therefore have no way to challenge her claims before the jury by cross-examining her. It would be fair, however, to use her confession against Chignell herself. If she wanted to challenge its accuracy or explain it away, she could always choose to testify in her own defence. The jury could therefore convict only Chignell on the basis of Witness A's statement.

In an effort to crack the case against Neville Walker, the police planted a jailhouse informant in his cell. He came to be known by the moniker Witness B, to protect his identity. This professional "snitch" left the cell beaming with self-appreciation: he had obtained a confession. According to Witness B's version, Chignell and Walker had strung their client up in chains, including one around his neck, and together they beat him, stopping when he cried out that he had had enough. They left the room for a coffee, and when they returned some twenty minutes later, Plumley Walker was slumped in the chains. Neville Walker tried to revive him, but could not get a response, other than the twitching of his arms. He and Chignell wrapped him in a carpet, binding it to make it easier to carry, and took him to Taupo, where he could be sunk forever. The body was still twitching when they threw it into the falls, but Neville Walker considered this to be nothing more than "nerves." They used their victim's car for the trip. The next evening they loaded their bikes inside, drove the car some distance from their residence, and lit it on fire, so that they could ride off as the flames destroyed all the evidence.

Essentially on this evidence, Chignell and Walker were tried and convicted of murder. Twelve jurors strong and true believed beyond a reasonable doubt that Renee Chignell and Neville Walker had intentionally killed Plumley Walker. The problem is that it was not clear that the jury had been unanimous in its conclusions about how the murder had happened. The Crown had begun the trial alleging that Plumley Walker was murdered at Taupo when he was thrown over the falls alive. As the trial progressed, the prosecutors decided to hedge their bets and went to the jury on the basis that Chignell and Walker killed him intentionally either at Auckland or at Taupo. The trial judge told the jury it did not matter which was true. It would be enough for the jury to be satisfied beyond a reasonable doubt that the pair had murdered Plumley Walker, regardless of how or where. Given that jury direction, it was not clear what the jurors had decided. Perhaps some of the jurors believed beyond a reasonable doubt that Chignell and Walker killed him intentionally in Auckland, and perhaps others believed they killed him at Taupo, or perhaps some or all were not sure what happened but concluded that, however it happened, it must have been murder. The New Zealand Court of Appeal overturned the murder conviction because of this uncertainty.

After the appeal, Chignell and Walker stood convicted solely of intentionally damaging Plumley Walker's car. If the Crown wanted its murder conviction, it would have to retry the pair. A retrial would not be "double jeopardy" because that principle only prevents a person who has been finally acquitted or convicted from being charged again for the same offence. Once the conviction was overturned on appeal, it was as though there had been no trial. The Crown could try again.

The Crown was now in a difficult position: it had to elect which of the two theories to go with. Did the pair kill Peter Plumley Walker intentionally in Auckland or in Taupo? The Crown elected to go with the Taupo theory. At the retrial, the jury "hung"; it could not agree on whether the accused persons were guilty. Jurors must be unanimous to reach a verdict of either guilty or not guilty. If they cannot do so, there is a mistrial.

The Crown did not give in. It decided to try Chignell and Walker a third time. Again, this was not double jeopardy because the second jury had neither convicted nor acquitted the pair. At their third and final trial, they were acquitted. Although there was grave suspicion against them, the Crown could not prove its case beyond a reasonable doubt. Even though on her least incriminating statement, Chignell had committed manslaughter at least, she was not convicted of any homicide offence. The irony is that had she provided only one story, she probably would have been convicted, either of manslaughter or murder, depending on the version. In a strange sense, then, the Crown had too much evidence. The jury simply could not sort out what had happened.

Occasionally this happens. I prosecuted a young man once for dangerous driving — for speeding through a picket line and striking a picketer. By the fourth union witness I knew that, regardless of what had actually happened, I could not get a conviction. Each witness told a different story. On their combined evidence, the car came from the left and from the right without turning and did a U-turn to go back to the picket line, sped up and slowed down as it approached the picket line, was going both 15 kilometres per hour and 60, and stopped a few feet past the picketer who had been struck, while not stopping at all. Incidentally, the picketer was on the left-hand side, right-hand side, and centre of the roadway when he was struck head on, while being clipped by the side of the vehicle. I made the mistake of having each witness mark a diagram of the accident scene with an X to mark the point of impact, and arrows to show the line of the car's entry. Before I was finished, the diagrams looked like a series of unrelated pages in a doodle pad. I have no doubt that all the witnesses were doing their best, but they left me in doubt as to what happened, and I was on their side. What would the judge think? Acquittal.

The most interesting issue for Canadian lawyers in the Plumley Walker saga is not that too much conflicting, incriminating evidence can cloud the record to the point where an acquittal is preordained, but that a jury, according to the ruling of the New Zealand Court of Appeal, must be unanimous not only about guilt, but also in its theory of what happened in order to convict. In Canada, jurors must be unanimous about guilt to convict, but they need not be unanimous in their theory about what happened. Although the case can be read more narrowly, this is the result of a Supreme Court of Canada decision arising out of the prosecution against Colin Thatcher.

It's Still Murder

Thatcher had been a cabinet minister in the provincial government of Premier Grant Devine until only days before the events of 21 January 1983. On that day, Thatcher's ex-wife, JoAnn Kay Wilson, was mercilessly beaten in the garage of her home with an unidentified sharp, curved bladed implement. She was then shot in the head with an aluminum jacketed bullet fired from either a .38 or .357 calibre handgun. Thatcher, whose hatred for JoAnn was well known after their rancorous litigation over the custody of their children and the $820,000 divorce judgment she had secured against him, was the obvious suspect. After an investigation produced a large amount of evidence, Thatcher was charged with her murder. He was tried on an indictment that alleged "[t]hat he, the said Colin Thatcher on or about the 21st day of January A.D. 1983 at Regina in the Province of Saskatchewan did unlawfully cause the death of JoAnn Kay Wilson and did thereby commit first degree murder, contrary to Section 218 of the *Criminal Code*."

An "indictment" is the legal document that sets out the charge against the accused for which he is to be tried. This document gives the judge and jury the power to try the charge against the accused — without it there can be no trial. The indictment also plays another crucial role. It specifies the charge that the accused is to meet. It advises the accused of the specific allegation, so he can come prepared to answer it, and it confines the power of the trial court. The judge or jury can convict the accused solely of the offences charged and those included within the charge, and of no others.

The challenge for the Crown in the Thatcher case was that it was not in a position to specify exactly what Thatcher's role in the murder was. Some of the evidence suggested that Thatcher committed the murder himself, whereas other evidence suggested that an unknown hit-man whom he hired had done so. The Crown position was that, either way, he "caused the death of JoAnn Kay Wilson," his former wife, and that he was a murderer. In Canadian law, a person need not commit the offence personally to be guilty of it. Someone who "aids or abets" the commission of a criminal offence is equally guilty, and hiring or counselling another to kill is as culpable in law as the actual killing. However it happened, Colin Thatcher caused the death of JoAnn Wilson and was, in either case, guilty of her murder.

Like the trial judge in the Walker case, the trial judge in the Thatcher case directed the jury that it could convict Colin Thatcher if it was satisfied that either theory had been proved. The jury convicted. Since juries provide what are known as "general verdicts," merely pronouncing "guilty" or "not guilty" without providing any reasons for their decisions, it was impossible to tell which theory they had accepted. Indeed, some may have believed that Colin Thatcher killed JoAnn Wilson with his own hands, while others may have concluded that a hit-man had done it. Unlike the case in New Zealand, the highest court in Canada said that this potential disagreement did not matter. The conviction was nonetheless a good one.

As the Supreme Court of Canada put it, the one proposition that the jurors were unanimous about was that Colin Thatcher was not innocent of the crime.[2] His conviction should therefore be upheld.

This decision must strike most people as simple common sense. Yet the notion that an accused person can be tried and convicted on alternative theories about what happened is a controversial proposition in the legal community. There are harsh critics of the *Thatcher* decision who believe that common sense cannot be allowed to get in the way of the law. They claim that Colin Thatcher should not be convicted without unanimity among jurors as to exactly what happened. As the Supreme Court of Canada said, however, why should this matter? The crucial legal question asked by the charge was whether he was guilty of murdering JoAnn Kay Wilson, and all the jurors agreed on that. Would the law have produced an acceptable result if Thatcher had been acquitted despite the fact that all twelve jurors were convinced he was a murderer? Hardly.

The Thatcher case does not reject the critically important and basic rule that the Crown must prove its specific allegation against the accused. It simply holds that the Crown's allegation that he was guilty of the murder of his ex-wife was specific enough, without having to specify whether he killed her himself or hired someone else to do so. The Crown must still make a specific allegation, and it is that allegation that must be proved beyond a reasonable doubt, just as it was in the *Thatcher* case.

History Lessons

The rule requiring a specific allegation does impose limits on what a court can do. It means that if the Crown were to charge someone with kidnapping, and during the kidnapping trial it became apparent that the accused had also sexually assaulted the kidnapping victim, the accused could not be convicted of sexual assault. He could be convicted solely of the kidnapping because that was the only charge he was being tried upon. The sexual assault is a different offence from the kidnapping. Why, in a rational system, would we not convict him of a sexual assault that has been proved beyond all reasonable doubt on the evidence? That question can only be answered by examining the historical development of the principle that accused persons are to be tried solely on the specific allegation made. Like most of the founding principles in our criminal justice system, this one emerged from objection to the abuses of the Courts of Star Chamber and the High Commission in sixteenth- and seventeenth-century England. The abusive conduct of these courts arose out of the Catholic inquisition, and gained momentum in England after the great religious schism as it became the Anglican inquisition.

The inquisition had its roots in the Fourth Lateran Council, convened in 1215 by Pope Innocent III. In an effort to end challenges to Catholic doctrine, the council developed a code of procedure that was to be used by ecclesiastical courts to assist them in uncovering heresy. This procedure was based on the Imperial Roman practice known as the "inquisition." By 1401, ecclesiastical courts were established in England and given the power to conduct inquiries to find heretics by using the inquisitory code. Those found guilty would be burned at the stake. Long before 1401, Pope Innocent IV had made the inquisition more efficient by approving the use of the rack and screw to assist in the inquiry.

In their religious zeal, the clerics who ran these ecclesiastic courts would seek out suspects by inviting informers to come forward under the promise of anonymity. The courts would even act on gossip that came to their attention. And they would allow those who had been found guilty of heresy to save themselves from death and torture by revealing the names of other heretics, who would then be arrested. As legal scholar Leonard William Levy put it, these poor souls

> revealed from their frantic imaginations whatever they thought the Inquisitor wished to hear. . . . A prisoner who confessed, abjured heresy, and proclaimed his penitence could prove his sincerity — and escape the stake if not prison — by betraying his friends, neighbours and family. If he refused, the inquisitor considered him impenitent and put him to torture again to reveal their guilt — and then dispatched him for execution. [3]

Those who were brought before the courts were aware that the inquiry was to determine whether they were heretics, but they would not know precisely what heretical acts or thoughts they were suspected of. "Heresy" is an incredibly vague notion and "the interrogators were members of the clergy, highly educated in religious dogma [while] the person on trial was usually illiterate."[4] The inquiry would begin with the suspect being forced to swear an oath. Then a secret examination would be conducted in which the interrogator would confront the suspect with "the mass of surmises, rumours and hearsay against him and demand his confession."[5] He could be asked to answer, under oath, any question the examiner sought to put. As Justice Salhany has explained in his book, *The Origin of Rights*: "This placed him in an intolerable position. If he told the truth, he might find that his answers could amount to a confession of a crime that he was not aware he had committed. If he lied, then he ran the risk of being charged with perjury."[6] The suspect, facing torture and gruelling questioning while being held incommunicado, could unwittingly be entrapped into some form of admission that would, in the eyes of the interrogator, be heretical. Between 1554 and 1558 alone, 273 subjects were burned at the stake.[7]

In 1558, shortly after Elizabeth I became queen, the power to investigate and punish heresy was transferred from the ecclesiastical courts to the queen. She could, by letters patent, appoint a body to perform the role of uncovering heresy. It was a great time for entrepreneurs with connections. You could get a royal patent to make linen, sell mustard or mead, or twist bodies on the rack, depending on where your talents lay. Shortly after, in an effort to assist in the establishment of a national Anglican Church, Queen Elizabeth established the High Commission by patent, which eventually became known as the Court of High Commission.

For a while the royal or common law courts tried to interfere because these practices violated basic common law principles. These courts had the authority to do so because, as the king's courts, they had the power to compel specialized courts and bodies like the Court of High Commission to comply with the rules of law. A largely ignored statute had been passed some two and a half centuries before which had purported to limit the use of the inquisitorial procedures to matrimonial and testamentary cases. Relying on that statute, the common law courts would issue writs of *habeas corpus* compelling the High Commission to release any prisoners in cases where the inquiry threatened to go beyond such matters, on the basis that the commission lacked the jurisdiction in such cases to apply their procedure. Because of royal pressure, however, the common law courts ultimately backed down and stopped ordering the release of those imprisoned by the Court of High Commission.

In 1633, four years after King Charles dissolved Parliament, William Laud was appointed as Archbishop of Canterbury. He brought a zeal to the job that had been lacking in his predecessors, and the Puritans were his main targets. To make their persecution more effective, sedition was added to the list of offences that would be subject to inquisition. Moreover, the assistance of the Court of Star Chamber, composed of the Privy Council and chief justices of the common law courts, was sought. That court had the power to impose particularly gruesome punishments, and it also had the power to suspend its normal procedures and adopt the inquisitorial process that had been favoured by the ecclesiastical courts. It was only too willing to do so.

In 1637 the trial of John Lilburne, a Puritan, brought the revulsion against the inquisitorial process to a head, ultimately causing its demise. At the time, no books could be published without licence from the Archbishop of Canterbury. Dr. John Bastwick, a physician, Henry Burton, a preacher, and William Prynne, a lawyer, all Puritans, had been arrested for publishing an unlicensed text about the Anglican bishops. John Lilburne, a twenty-three-year-old Puritan, met Dr. Bastwick in prison when he had accompanied his master to visit Bastwick. Lilburne discovered that Bastwick had written another pamphlet about the Anglican bishops while in prison, and he agreed to smuggle it to Holland, where it could be printed and then smuggled back into England and circulated. Lilburne enlisted the assistance of two others to help him.

After their trials, Bastwick, Burton, and Prynne were found guilty of sedition, fined 5,000 pounds, and sentenced to life imprisonment. The Court of Star Chamber overturned the sentences as being too light, and ordered the men to be mutilated by having their ears cut off and to be pilloried. In the meantime, the smuggled pamphlets had been discovered by the authorities, and Lilburne's two accomplices confessed, implicating John. In December 1637 Lilburne was summoned to appear before the attorney general's chief clerk to answer questions.[8] He refused and was placed in prison for two weeks. He was then brought before the dreaded Court of Star Chamber to be examined. Defiantly, he refused to take the oath. When the clerk requested that he take the Bible and swear, he said:

Lilburne: "To what?"
The Clerk: That shall true answer to all things asked of you.
Lilburne: Must I do sir? But before I swear, I will know to what I
            must swear.
The Clerk: As soon as you have sworn, you shall but not before.

He continued to refuse. He was imprisoned for a further six weeks. He was returned to the Court of Star Chamber, but again refused to swear. In his own report of the trial, he recounts his speech made in court:

I am not willing to answer you to any more of these questions because I see you go about by this Examination to ensnare me: for seeing the things for which I am imprisoned cannot be proved against me you will get other matter out of my examination.

[They] went about to make me betray my own innocency, that so they might ground the bill [the charge] upon my own words . . . .

. . . [I]f I had been proceeded against by a Bill [a charge] I would have answered.

Because of his contempt, the Lords of the Star Chamber fined him and ordered him to be imprisoned indefinitely until he would take the oath. He was also ordered to be whipped "from the Fleet to the pillory, a distance of two miles." When he was brought before the pillory, the court offered to spare him if he would take the oath, but he again refused. Despite being told not to, he spoke to the crowd that had gathered to watch his torment until he was gagged and left in the sun. His arms and legs were then shackled and he was thrown "into the worst part of the prison" and left without food for ten days. He survived only because other prisoners had smuggled him food. He spent the next four months in solitary confinement, and was then left to languish in prison. In the meantime, he continued to write pamphlets and to smuggle them out. Others, inspired by his courage, refused to submit to the oath, fuelling further public opposition to the court.

In 1640 King Charles, in desperate need of funds, decided to reconvene Parliament to assist him in raising money. Since its dissolution eleven years earlier, Parliament had come to be dominated by Puritans. Oliver Cromwell took up Lilburne's cause and, shortly after, his sentence was declared to be illegal. He, along with Bastwick, Prynne, and Burton, were released, and on 4 July 1641 Parliament abolished the Court of High Commission and the Court of Star Chamber. Lilburne, who became known as "Freeborn John" because of his courage and principles, became a hero — a symbol of fair principle and all that is right and decent. It bears notice, I think, that he was also guilty of breaking the law, a point that should offer some comfort to those who insist on proper procedures even for the guilty.

While there is much that is objectionable and offensive to modern sensibilities in this sad tale, perhaps the most troublesome feature of the process of inquiry is the trial without charge. As Morgan, a leading American legal academic, has said: "The offensive characteristic of the procedure of which the oath was a part was its requirement that a person who had not been charged by a formal presentment or accusation answer under oath all questions put to him by the proper ecclesiastical official."[9] Probably because I wear glasses, the thing that troubles me the most about this saga is the part about cutting off the ears. Contemporary legal scholars consistently feel, however, that the main objection to the inquisitorial procedure of the Court of Star Chamber and the Court of High Commission is the absence of a proper accusation relating to the violation of a known and pre-existing rule of law.

Why is this, of the many objectionable practices of the Court of High Commission and Court of Star Chamber, the one that has received the most attention by modern legal scholars? Why this emphasis on the need for a proper accusation before trial? In part it is because we in Canada, the United States, and Britain need not worry any longer about mutilation, the rack, and the screw. Fortunately, we can afford to focus on the more technical aspects of the process. And there are several powerful reasons why a specific allegation is needed. First, requiring a specific allegation enables the rule of law to be applied. "A specific accusation presupposes a specific offence in law."[10] If the allegation does not disclose an offence, the accusation can be attacked and quashed, thereby terminating the proceeding. This is what happened, of course, in the attempted murder trial of Brenda Drummond, the woman who shot her foetus in the head with a pellet. The allegation did not disclose an offence known to law. Second, the specific allegation identifies the conduct that is said to constitute the offence. This information enables the accused person to prepare a defence. If the accused does not know what the event being inquired into is, it cannot be investigated properly and the defence cannot be prepared. Third, the need for a specific allegation assists in preserving the neutrality of the judge or jury. It does so by defining the jurisdiction of the court to try the accused — the only charges that the court has power to try are those that are laid against the accused. If the court acts as both investigator and trier of fact by expanding the charges as the evidence unfolds, the ability of the court to remain neutral will be compromised. Fourth, the specific allegation keeps the inquiry focused so that the trial remains about what the accused is alleged to have done. The allegation defines the issue in which the court is interested, enabling the court to identify what evidence is important and what evidence is immaterial. This restriction is not only important as a practical matter to keep the conduct of trials efficient and economically viable, but it also protects the accused from being tried for who he is rather than for what he is alleged to have done on a particular occasion. Fifth, and perhaps most important, the requirement of a specific allegation is there to protect the liberty of us all. Imagine living in a system in which you could be brought before the authorities randomly, so that they could inquire generally into whether you have been abiding by the law. Before a civilized state can properly set its criminal process in gear against one of its citizens, there must be a reasonable basis for suspecting the accused of a particular offence.

A totally understandable and acceptable exception to the basic principle that the accused is to be tried on a specific allegation enables judges and juries to convict accused persons of "included offences" that have not been expressly charged. An "included offence" is nothing more than an offence that is less serious than the offence charged, which will necessarily have been committed if the accused has committed the offence charged. For example, an accused person may be charged with the offence of assault causing bodily harm, contrary to section 267 of the *Criminal Code*. To secure a conviction, the Crown will have to prove that the accused not only assaulted the complainant but also caused bodily harm — a non-trivial or non-transitory injury. If the evidence proves the assault but does not establish the bodily harm, the accused cannot be convicted of the offence charged, but he can be convicted of the separate, less serious offence of simple assault, contrary to section 266 of the *Criminal Code*, which does not require bodily harm. Even though the accused was charged with a section 267 offence and not expressly with section 266, he can hardly complain about being convicted of section 266 because, to have committed a section 267 offence, he would have to have committed an assault. The allegation of simple assault is necessarily implicit in the charge of assault causing bodily harm. None of the dangers that the rule requiring a specific allegation are intended to prevent are present when the accused is convicted of an "included" offence. This is why those persons accused of murder are often convicted of manslaughter. Manslaughter is an included offence in a murder prosecution.

Retroactive Injustice

As the rationales for the principle requiring a specific allegation disclose, there is a closely related rule, sometimes referred to as the rule against retroactivity. It requires that the specific allegation relate to the violation of a pre-existing rule of law. No matter how desirable socially, Parliament cannot use a new rule to prosecute the accused for an act that occurred before the law was changed. The rule is illustrated by the following example.

In 1907 and through much of 1908, William Ball and his sister, Edie Ball, were lovers. Indeed, they lived together. William was in the habit of introducing Edie as his wife, and she had a child by him. Edie even registered her brother as the father of the child. There would have been no reason not to do so because incest was legal at the time. At the end of 1908, however, the *Punishment of Incest Act* 1908[11] was passed in England, in part because of the notoriety that the Balls' relationship had received. As a result, the police decided to go after the Balls. They undertook a clever, if not time-consuming investigation. On a number of nights between June and September, constables took up surveillance outside the Balls' home. On each occasion when the kitchen light was extinguished, only one upstairs light would go on. After having observed this pattern on a number of occasions, the police made their move. They knocked on the door, which was answered by Edie Ball, wearing her nightclothes. The police entered and William Ball came down the stairs, hitching up his pants. The police searched the home and found there was only one bed in the residence fit to sleep in. Although they had not caught the Balls in the act, there was a strong enough circumstantial case to prove their guilt.

The Balls could not claim to have slept together out of necessity (it being so damn cold and damp in England) because the police had been clever enough to wait for summer to lay their trap. The trial judge was satisfied that the only explanation as to why the Balls would share a bed was that they had been up to their old tricks. Together with proof of their earlier amorous relationship and certain love letters found on the premises, he considered that the compromising circumstance provided enough evidence to convict, a finding upheld by the House of Lords, the highest appeal court in England.[12]

To a non-lawyer, this police investigation must seem like a great deal of bother. It was clear that prior to January 1910, the two had committed incest and had even admitted it. Why not simply prosecute them under the law once it was passed? The reason, again, is that pesky rule of law. The principle that no one shall be punished for anything that is not expressly forbidden by law means that laws cannot be passed retroactively to define, as criminal, conduct that was perfectly legal at the time it was undertaken. It would simply be unfair if this was possible.

This potential unfairness is sometimes explained on the basis that people should be able to identify in advance whether their conduct will be illegal. In the criminal area, this explanation is so out of touch with reality in the overwhelming majority of cases that it cannot possibly provide a reasonable basis for preventing the non-retroactive application of the law. Do you think Brenda Drummond called her lawyer just before shooting Jonathan to ask whether it would be OK? Did Frey leave his ladder against the side of the law library wall while he went inside to check whether he could be detained if he was caught peeping in the window? Do you think Edie whispered to William, "Not yet, Willy Ball. I have to check the *Gazette* first to see whether the incest laws have been proclaimed in force?" This is too silly to warrant further consideration. The fact is, it is unfair for a society to pass retroactive laws and to apply them against citizens regardless of whether those persons bothered to inform themselves of the law or not. We rely on the rule that everyone is presumed to know the law, in order to prevent accused persons from saying, "Gee. I thought it was OK." That same presumption has to apply to enable citizens to say, "This was not illegal when I acted." To allow the law to be applied retroactively would enable the state to act oppressively and unfairly against unpopular individuals or groups.

It has to be remembered that the law in general, and the criminal law in particular, can be used to oppress. The principle against retroactivity is a way to ensure that our courts and our legislators are acting with appropriate motives and are not seeking simply to persecute. It is a way to protect the legitimacy of our legal institutions. A system that cannot show that the act being punished was illegal at the time is one that can have no credibility. It would be unspeakable, for example, for today's society to coax gays out of the closet with assurances that sexual persuasion is a legitimate matter of personal preference, only to decide in the future to recriminalize homosexual sex and to punish those who engaged in such acts today. It would be intolerable for the Government of Canada to decide in the future, if the threat of Quebec separation abates, to pass a law against advocating the dissolution of Canada, and then punish today's separatists.

In these turbulent times, these are not idle concerns. Our standards as a society have changed both with respect to corporal punishment in the home and in schools, and with respect to sexual behaviour. Regularly now, prosecutions are being undertaken relating to incidents that happened decades ago, when many standards of behaviour were entirely different. Many of these prosecutions arise out of institutional settings where the custodians, often religious orders having strong disciplinary codes, used corporal punishment that, by today's standards, would be unacceptable. Many children were sent to these institutions by their parents so they could "benefit" by that discipline, and society as a whole accepted it. Even in ordinary schools, teachers strapped children, or used yardsticks and paddles to slap a child's behind. In these softer, more humane times I am grateful that I do not have to worry about my children receiving this kind of mistreatment, but I recognize that it would be contrary to the most basic principles of decency to punish people now who used these forms of discipline for carrying out what, at the time, was their expected role.

The same thing holds true with sexual conduct. A few years ago it was not uncommon for university professors to date their students. Many ultimately married former pupils. At the time, the universities did not punish these people. Instead, they sent representatives or congratulatory messages to the weddings. Now the amorous game-playing that leads up to such celebrations would, at best, constitute professional misconduct. It could, depending on the circumstances, even amount to criminal conduct. The *Criminal Code* provides that there is no consent to sexual relations where "the accused induces the complainant to engage in the activity by abusing a position of trust, power or authority." We are still working out precisely what "induces" and "abusing a position of trust, power or authority" mean, but the point is clear. Yesterday's standards are not today's, and in extreme cases the criminal law has been given a role to play in changing things. The abuse of the power imbalance by a person in authority can deprive even communicated consent and the conscious choice between evils by a complainant of its quality as real consent. If we tried to turn the criminal clock back now to prosecute men whose actions ten or twenty years ago were in breach of these contemporary codes of conduct, we would probably be well on the way to achieving job equity in executive positions. Many men would be in jail, opening up a good number of positions for women.

When the movie was released in the early 1970s, *The Summer of Forty-Two* was understood to be the story of how a twenty-something-year-old woman brought an adolescent boy to age with the gift of sexual experience while he, in return, helped her through the trauma of her husband's death. At the time it was considered to be a touching story that left most men, at least, thinking that the boy had been in the right place at the right time. If all this had happened in the summer of ninety-two, and the young boy was not yet fourteen at the time, he would be in therapy and we would have handcuffed the woman and taken her away for having committed sexual interference.

Now that we have used the criminal law to tell such people to stop, they had better, but should we use today's conception of crime to judge yesterday's behaviour? If it is acceptable for us to do this, heaven help the gay community should we someday return to the morality that was expressed in the *Criminal Code* only a few years ago. We have to judge the conduct of the time by the standards of the time. Simple decency requires it, and so, too, do the fundamental principles of the accusatory system.

At times, the principle against retroactivity, like all other liberating principles, can be a meddlesome rule. As discussed earlier, it enabled Clifford Olson to apply for a section 745.6 review of his parole ineligibility, even though the law was changed on 9 January 1997 to prevent multiple murderers from having their sentences reviewed. Those who kill one of their victims after 9 January 1997 can be prevented from applying for sentence review because of this change. Those who have completed their multiple killings before that date can continue to apply.

As always, fundamental principles are only as useful as the resolve of the courts to apply them. The skill and cunning that enabled lawyers to have been the defenders of democracy at an earlier time can easily be turned against the very liberating principles that lawyers have created. Even basic principles of justice can be no match for creativity. The history of the law has been marked by the tension between the need for the law to be certain, and its need to be flexible and responsive as issues arise. When the flexible interpretation of principles is seen to be needed, it can be accomplished, fundamental principles be damned. Consider the following illustration.

Back in the 1930s and 1940s, no one in this country imagined that it would become a refuge for Nazi collaborators. When the Deschênes Commission[13] discovered that it had, the thought of these people living the good life in a country as precious as our own was more than the Canadian people could bear. Something had to be done. The commission recommended that the criminal law be used to punish these men for their sins, and the Canadian government agreed. The shrivelling of their aging bodies and the thinning of their bones could be no defence to the atrocities they had perpetrated. The legal problem was that their acts of murder, rape, and pillage were not illegal in Canada at the time they were committed. Certainly, they would have been illegal had those acts taken place in Canada, but the reach of Canadian criminal law was well defined. The provisions of the *Criminal Code* applied "throughout Canada" and, save for some exceptions to deal with offences committed in planes and ships, and on off-shore platforms, acts committed away from this country would not constitute criminal offences in Canada. If someone had asked in 1944, "is it a criminal offence in Canada to commit robbery, unlawful confinement, kidnapping and manslaughter in Hungary," a lawyer would have said no. Because of clever lawyering, the answer to that same question now would be yes in some cases, notwithstanding the principle against retroactivity.

When they decided to tackle this problem, the government of Canada recognized that if it was to create new offences that could be used to prosecute war criminals, it would run into retroactivity problems. So it got clever. It decided to prosecute Nazis for offences that were already criminal in Canada at the time. Instead of creating new offences, Parliament would simply expand the jurisdiction or power of the Canadian courts to adjudicate acts that occur outside Canada. There is no bar on expanding jurisdiction retroactively so long as the offences were in existence at the time the acts occurred. So, in 1985, section 7(3.71) was added to the *Criminal Code*. That section gave judges the power to try acts committed outside Canada where those acts would have been against the law if they had been committed in Canada. To keep this power from being used to prosecute ordinary offences committed by foreign nationals in their own countries, the law provided that it could be used only where a criminal offence constituted a "war crime" or a "crime against humanity."

In the case of *R. v. Finta*,[14] the Supreme Court of Canada was asked to strike down this new legislation as unconstitutional on a number of grounds. The Court refused and upheld the law. In doing so, however, the Court did not rely on the government's technique for avoiding the rule against retroactivity. For reasons that are unimportant to the present discussion, it interpreted the new legislation as though it did, in fact, create two new offences, "war crimes" and "crimes against humanity." It therefore had to find another way to avoid the principle against retroactivity, or it would have to rule that Nazis could not be prosecuted using these provisions. It was able to do so. The Court saved the war crimes offences by recognizing that, as an exception to the principle against retroactivity, Parliament is entitled to create a retroactive law that provides for the punishment of individuals for engaging in acts that were illegal, though not criminal, at the time they were committed, where those acts are also morally objectionable. The exception is justifiable, the Court reasoned, because, if the act is illegal, the accused has no business engaging in it, and, if it is immoral, blame can be attached to him for having done so.

Before the Second World War, war crimes and crimes against humanity were recognized by Canada as being contrary to international law. Even though international law rules bind only countries and are not enforceable against individuals, it could still be said that, at the time of the Holocaust, war crimes and crimes against humanity contravened the law applicable in Canada. Moreover, war crimes and crimes against humanity are, without question, immoral. The Court therefore reasoned that war crimes were caught by the exception, and could be made criminal retroactively without violating the rule of law.

This is complex reasoning. It is a testament to Sir Edmund Coke's prediction that the law gains complexity as society does. While clever and complex, this exception to the principle against retroactivity was not invented by the Supreme Court of Canada. It was one of the *ex post facto* rationalizations lawyers have created since the Nuremberg trials to argue that those hearings conformed to the rule of law. Despite the prior existence of the theory, the Court's decision to adopt it as the law in Canada deserves condemnation, even by those who, like me, believe that Nazi collaborators should be punished notwithstanding that fifty years have passed. This exception is dangerous. It is a result-oriented contrivance that poses a clear threat to the rule of law. The same reasoning used in *Finta* could be applied to criminalize, retroactively, immoral conduct that violates a non-criminal domestic law. To take an obvious example, for a number of years now discrimination against homosexuals or racial minorities has contravened non-criminal rules of law found in human rights statutes. It would not be difficult to find judges who consider such discrimination immoral. Does this mean that, ten years from now, Parliament can pass a retroactive law allowing all those people who refused jobs to gays or Native Canadians during the 1980s and 1990s to be prosecuted criminally? Or what about sexual harassment? I am not talking about unwanted touching, which is already criminal. I am referring to sexually inappropriate comments, or invitations to sex made by employers and co-workers in the workplace. These actions are illegal, according to new interpretations of existing Human Rights Codes, and are tortious, meaning that the person harassed can sue for damages. If we discover that our use of human rights legislation and civil suits is incapable of stamping out sexual harassment, can we decide to try to deter such conduct by prosecuting as criminals those who have breached these rules in the past? While we, as a society, have to attempt to eradicate these odious forms of behaviour, are their practitioners really criminal? More to the point, can we justifiably change their status retroactively from idiots to criminals? There is nothing in R. v. *Finta* to prevent this change from happening. With the Court having denuded the rule of law of its authority, we are left to trust the government to be fair.

One thing that is troublesome to some about the principle against retroactivity is that laws that assist accused persons can be made retroactive. It is only the laws that injure or harm people that cannot be. For example, the government recently amended the *Criminal Code* to impose a minimum four-year sentence for persons found guilty of discharging a firearm with intent to endanger the life of another. Previously, there was no minimum sentence. Those persons who committed the offence before the amendment, even if convicted now, cannot be subjected to the minimum penalty. Only those who commit that offence after the amendment will be subject to it. However, if a sentencing provision is amended to reduce the penalty or change it in a manner that is beneficial to the accused, she can have the benefit of it. That is why Lisa Ferguson was able to receive a conditional sentence even though, at the time she intentionally discharged the firearm at Vincent Foley, all prison terms were served in jail until release on parole or by statutory remission. Had Ferguson waited a few years to kill Foley, the Crown could have charged her with discharging a firearm with intent to endanger his life, and the judge would have been unable to give her a conditional sentence. The judge would have had no choice but to impose the four-year sentence.

Those who find it distressing that criminals can benefit from retroactive application of criminal rules, while the public or the state cannot, have to appreciate that the principle against retroactivity is part of the rule of law. It is intended to constrain abusive powers by the government, not to disqualify the state from becoming more generous after the fact. This is why the recent Self-Defence Review conducted by the Minister of Justice into the sentences and convictions of women presently under sentence for killing their partners does not violate the rule of law, even though it is meant to enable these women to benefit from changes in the law of self-defence that occurred after they had killed their mates. It is a benefit to the citizen, not a detriment, and it can be applied retroactively.

Like all such procedural guarantees, both the requirement of a specific allegation and the rule that the offence charged must pre-exist the act of the accused, are technicalities. Like all technicalities, they can interfere with the ability of the system to punish criminal conduct. They necessarily produce the kind of unpalatable result I referred to earlier — at the kidnapping trial of the accused, even though the evidence shows that he had also sexually assaulted the victim, he can be convicted *at that trial* solely of the offence of kidnapping, despite that the judge or the jury have no doubt that he also sexually assaulted her. The police can later lay a sexual assault charge and have another trial, but it will rarely be feasible or advisable to do so. The act goes unpunished, other than as a factor that aggravates the seriousness of the kidnapping. Without clever lawyering, the principle against retroactive offences could well have derailed the war crimes prosecutions as well.

These kinds of results are difficult to accept. For Peter Plumley Walker's family, the exaggerated New Zealand commitment to these same principles was no doubt infuriating. Because of what history has taught us, however, the requirement of a specific allegation, and the principle against retroactivity, remain among the most fundamental principles in our criminal justice system. Technicalities? Yes. Unacceptable ones? By no means. Not having these technicalities would be unacceptable. Together they mark the first major premise of our system of trial. All criminal trials commence with a charge being laid. The charge must contain a specific allegation that the accused has violated a rule of law that was in existence at the time of the offence. The criminal trial is not an inquisition in which the court conducts a wide-ranging inquiry that uncovers and then punishes all the reprehensible conduct it finds. It is a narrow, focused inquiry where the matter in issue is whether the Crown can prove its specific allegation. If it were not, the criminal trial would become an unfair process, available as a tool of persecution rather than justice.

Presumed Innocent

They were so young: childhood friends, then "sweethearts," and then man and wife, he twenty-one and a half and she four years younger. Reginald Woolmington, a farm labourer at Cheeseman's farm at Castleton, near Sherbourne, England, went about his chores ahead of the sun on that cold December morning in 1934. His hands pulled almost by reflex as he milked the cows, his mind far from the task. He had hardly slept the night before. Violet had left him, taking their newborn son. Her mother, never one to mind her own business, had put her up to it.

After he finished milking, Reginald hopped on his bicycle and peddled down the wet road, somehow dodging rocks and tire ruts, the traction slipping occasionally in the mud. He entered his father's house and ate his breakfast in silence before grabbing his "Da's" hacksaw. He slipped into the barn and there, where it had always been kept for shooting rooks, he found the double-barrelled shotgun. He sawed off both barrels and carried them furtively under his long coat as he walked across a field, dropping them in a brook where they were unlikely to be found. His pant legs wet from the grass, he went back into the barn, taking the two shells that were there. He secreted the shells and the gun in a long pocket he kept in his field coat for carrying rabbits and went back into the house. There he found a piece of flex wire and wrapped it crudely over the stock and the stump of the barrel so it could be slung over his shoulder under his coat. He hurried out the door and bicycled to his mother-in-law's house, not noticing that the sun was well on its rise, brightening the lush green of the countryside.

Violet, although not happy to see him, opened the door when he knocked and he went in. "Are you coming back home?" Violet's aunt, Daisy Brine, who was hanging out the laundry in the back of her home next door, could hear the voice and recognized it as Reginald's. She could hear no answer. A door slammed. It was 9:15 a.m. She heard a voice in the kitchen, but could not make out what was said or who had spoken. She strained to listen, concerned that Violet and Reginald might be fighting again. "Bang." It was the sharp report of a shotgun, leaving nothing but the pungent smell of gunpowder as its rude echo quickly died out. Daisy began to move towards her sister's house in an uncertain run before halting, not sure whether to go on. Before she could settle on what to do, Reginald walked out of the kitchen and grabbed his bike, which had been left against the wall of the house. "Reginald?" "Reginald?" She asked him what had happened, but Reginald ignored her. As he boarded his bike, he turned and gave her a hard look, then rode away. Daisy found Violet dead on the floor. A single shotgun blast had torn through her chest, exploding her heart and ending her young life.

Almost by instinct, Reginald rode to his father's home. Meeting his mother in the drive, he said, "Ma, I have been up and shot Violet." Before she could muster an intelligible thought, he turned his bike, rode to Cheeseman's farm, and said to his employer, "I shall not be coming to work anymore, as I have shot my wife." He rode back to his father's again and wandered around the farm for some time. When his father caught up with him, he said, "I am going to kill myself now, Da." "Don't Reg," the older man replied. "It will be OK. We can help you." Reg ambled to the outhouse, the gun still slung over one shoulder, one barrel unfired. He put the barrels into his mouth, tasting the rusty metal. Then, just as suddenly, he slipped the wire off his shoulder and laid the gun on a bench. He staggered to the porch and sat in his tears until the constables came. When they did, he spoke to them: "I want to say nothing, except I done it, and they can do what they like. It was jealousy I suppose. Her mother enticed her away from me. I done all I could to get her back, that's all." When his short speech was over, they found a note in his pocket:

> Good bye all.
>
> It is agonies to carry on any longer. I have kept true hoping she would return this is the only way out. They ruined me and I'll have my revenge. May God forgive me for doing this but it is the Best thing. Ask Jess to call for the money paid on the motor bike (Wed.). Her mother is no good on this earth but have no more cartridges only 2 one for her and one for me. I am of sound mind now. Forgive me for all trouble caused.
>
> Good bye
> All
> *I love Violet with all my heart*
>
> Reg

Despite his candour on the day of his arrest and the apparently irrefutable admissions in the note, when Reginald next spoke to the police he denied he was a murderer. Like many after him, and probably a large number before, he claimed he did not intend to kill his wife. He brought the gun with him simply to scare her back to him by threatening to shoot himself. As he brought the weapon out from his coat and pulled it across his body to show her, it discharged by accident. As for the note, it was a suicide note written after her death, nothing more.

On 23 January 1935 Reginald Woolmington was tried for murder by jury at the Taunton Assizes. He scaled the steps to the witness box and swore it had been an accident. Despite the unlikelihood of his account, the jury could not decide and a mistrial was declared. He was tried again at the Bristol Assizes before the Honourable Justice Swift. A farm labourer, previously of good character, he was this time convicted of murder. He stood stoically as Justice Swift pronounced his sentence:

> It now only remains for me to pass upon you the sentence of the law, which is, that you, Reginald Woolmington, be taken from this gaol to a place of execution, and that you be hanged by the neck until you be dead, and that your body be afterwards buried within the precincts of the prison, and may God Almighty have compassion on your sinful soul.

Woolmington could not have understood, standing there hearing his fate being read to him in solemn voice by the bewigged judge, that his name would become famous among criminal lawyers in far-flung places like New Zealand, Australia, Canada, South Africa, and Bermuda, exotic lands he had never even dreamed of visiting. He could not have imagined that his name would become the mantra that defence lawyers recite when imploring courts to protect the liberty of all by choosing to err on the side of innocence rather than guilt. His fame would emerge not because of the tragic events of 10 December 1934, but because of what Justice Swift said as he tried to help the jury in understanding their task:

> Once it is shown to a jury that somebody has died through the act of another, that is presumed to be murder, unless the person who has been guilty of the act which causes the death can satisfy a jury that what happened was something less, something which might be alleviated, something which might be reduced to a charge of manslaughter, or was something which was accidental, or was something which could be justified.

In law, he said, the person who was holding the gun as it fired had to satisfy the jury that he did not intend to kill. If he could not, he must be found guilty of murder.

It is obvious to anyone with even a passing familiarity with the current criminal justice system that Justice Swift had it wrong. Viscount Sankey, speaking for the House of Lords, the highest court of appeal in England, told him so:

> Throughout the web of English Criminal Law one golden thread is always to be seen, that it is the duty of the prosecution to prove the prisoner's guilt.... If, at the end of and on the whole of the case, there is a reasonable doubt, created by the evidence given by either the prosecution or the prisoner, as to whether the prisoner killed the deceased with malicious intention, the prosecution has not made out the case and the prisoner is entitled to be acquitted. No matter what the charge or where the trial, the principle that the prosecution must prove the guilt of the prisoner is part of the common law of England and no attempt to whittle it down can be entertained.

Appellate courts like the House of Lords do not conduct trials. They simply decide whether there have been legal errors. There had been a serious legal error in Woolmington's case, so the verdict of guilt and the sentence of death were set aside and the matter was sent back to the Court of Criminal Appeal to decide what would be just. That court had the power to acquit Woolmington or to order a new trial. Sadly, the law books do not record whether Woolmington was ultimately hanged after a new trial, acquitted, or simply freed after the appeal. They are less interested in the people than the principles that emerge from the cases, and the principles espoused in *Woolmington* v. *D.P.P.*[1] are the most hallowed known to English and Canadian criminal law. Accused persons are presumed to be innocent until proven guilty, and the Crown has the burden of proving the guilt of the accused beyond all reasonable doubt.

It may appear curious that Justice Swift made a mistake with such basic and fundamental rules. In fact, there were precedents to support him. These precedents, which the *Woolmington* court said were wrong, had come into existence because common sense suggested that if someone does an act, the natural consequences of which would be to cause death, then it makes sense to assume that this person intended to cause death. To assume the person did not intend the natural consequences of the act is contrary to human experience and should not form the basis for a rule. We should assume that people intend the natural consequences of their acts, and then have them convince us to the contrary, if that be so. Such a rule would be better at arriving at the truth than one that flies in the face of human experience. Perhaps so, but we do not always choose our rules based on which ones will be better at arriving at the truth. There are other interests at stake. The presumption of innocence is quite obviously not about maximizing the truth; it is about minimizing injustice.

Ten Guilty Men: The Presumption of Innocence

As the term "presumption" in the phrase "presumption of innocence" suggests, we are meant to start a criminal hearing from the assumption that those who have been charged are not guilty. When you think about it, this is strange. Like our refusal to begin with the common sense assumption that persons intend the natural consequences of their acts, it is contrary to human experience and common sense to infer that those who are brought up on criminal charges are innocent. Although I have horrified other defence lawyers by admitting this point, we know that most of those who are charged are guilty. Even if we judge by guilty pleas alone, the percentage of guilty people in the system is in the vicinity of 80 percent. In 1992 in the Provincial Division of the Ontario Court of Justice, a court that probably handles the highest volume of criminal cases in the country, 286,160 pleas were entered. Of these, 230,414, or 81 percent, were guilty pleas.[2] Only 19 percent of those who were called upon to stand trial said they were not guilty. Of these people, many were ultimately convicted. It would be a conservative guess to say that at least half of all criminal trials end with convictions. The number is probably higher. Although some of the convicted are no doubt innocent, some of the acquitted are no doubt guilty. Is a 90 percent "guilt" rate for those who stand trial on criminal charges a fair estimate? We can only hope it is even higher. If 10 percent of those charged with criminal offences are entirely innocent, we had better do something fast. As a defence lawyer once said to me with envy when I was prosecuting, "Of course you usually win. You have an unfair advantage: the truth is on your side." He was right. The high percentage of guilty defendants probably means that if we were interested solely in being accurate as often as possible, we would start from a presumption of guilt, not innocence.

George Dzioba, an Ottawa assistant crown attorney, gives a mock jury address at professional conferences, and, with the aid of humour, makes the point effectively:

> Counsel for the defence has done his best to create the impression, Ladies and Gentlemen of the jury, that the presumption of innocence is some sort of magic incantation that will wash away all crimes, if repeated often enough, particularly in front of a jury. But that is not

so. . . . To my chagrin, I cannot deny that the presumption of innocence is one of the great and fundamental principles of our law, but
like all great and fundamental principles, it is in complete disaccord
with common sense and the facts of life. For consider this, Ladies and
Gentlemen: if a man is presumed to be innocent, then what is the
point in charging him? And if indeed, there is a point in charging him,
how can he then be presumed innocent? Nevertheless, despite this
flaw in logic, the presumption of innocence is there for the accused
to rely on, for the Crown to contend with, and for you, Ladies and
Gentlemen, to do with as you please.

In fact, most of the players in the criminal justice system do not presume innocence when an accused person is charged. The police certainly
do not. If they thought an accused person to be innocent, they would not
lay a charge. The miscarriages of justice that result from police impropri-
eties do not occur because the police prosecute people they suspect to be
innocent. They occur for exactly the opposite reason. They occur because
the police believe that the accused is as guilty as sin, so much so that they
fail to recognize, and in extreme cases even suppress, evidence that might
result in an acquittal. Prosecutors also believe that those they prosecute
are probably guilty. If they did not believe so, they would not be prosecuting them. They would withdraw the charges, not just because the
overwhelming majority of them are honourable people, but because they
have to live with themselves. Most prosecutors fear they will secure the
conviction of the innocent. They prosecute people they believe to be
guilty, the presumption of innocence notwithstanding.

It is not just the police and prosecutors who do not start from an
assumption of innocence. The reality is that from the time the system
cranks up, for many purposes it seems to proceed on the assumption that
the accused is probably guilty. Think about it. The first thing we do is to
order the accused to come to court and to stand, humiliated, before a
judge while the charges are read out in open court, or we arrest and throw
him or her in the clink. Would we do that to someone we presume to be
innocent? The presumptively innocent person who is arrested is handcuffed and stuffed in the back of a police car, driven to a station somewhere, and put in a cell that most often will have nothing but a steel bench
to sleep on and a stainless steel toilet without a seat. (We know from experience that presumptively innocent people often kick toilet seats off, smash
porcelain bowls, or tear up mattresses when they are first arrested.
Presumptively innocent people who are arrested are not usually in a good
humour.) We allow the police to hold these presumptively innocent peo-

ple for up to twenty-four hours before bringing them before a justice to determine whether they should be released pending trial. To add to the torture, the only person whom they have a right to speak to is a lawyer.

Arrested suspects often are ordered, after their bail hearings, to wait in jail for their trials, the presumption of innocence notwithstanding. While normally the Crown must "show cause" why the accused should be held in custody pending trial, those who are charged with murder must show cause why they should be released. If they cannot, these presumptively innocent accused persons are made to wait in jail for their big day, sometimes for well over a year. Then the day of the trial arrives. What do we do with these presumptively innocent accused people? If they have been in custody, we bring them from the jail in shackles and handcuffs and we escort them into the courtroom as they stutter-step along, clanking their chains like Jacob Marley. (Because they are presumed innocent we usually remove the chains before the judge or jury comes in, but not always.) When a jury is being selected, we go through an elaborate ceremony in which the presumptively innocent accused stands in a prisoner's box while each prospective juror is told to approach the accused. The two are then told, "Juror, look at the accused. Accused, look at the juror." While the ceremony is intended to satisfy the accused that the prospective jurors are members of the community who will well and truly try the case, it hardly appears so. Prospective jurors, confused by the arcane practice, glance uncomfortably at the accused as though the eyes of Medusa are about to stare back to turn them into gargoyles for the front of the courthouse. You can almost read their thoughts. "So this is what a pedophile looks like, eh." The accused, who has already been introduced as the one who is accused of some heinous atrocity, peers back from behind glass, feeling as though there is a sign bolted to the door identifying his species as "Hominoid Criminalus." This is a ceremony for the presumptively innocent? How would we treat the presumptively guilty?

When we have a superior court trial, even those accused persons who are not being held in custody will typically be locked in the prisoner's dock during the proceedings. Some judges allow the accused to sit at counsel table if the lawyers make the pretence that they need the assistance of the accused, but most often the accused watches the trial from behind bulletproof glass or through bars. One can picture the cartoon. The prisoner, laid out in the prisoner's box, bound, shackled, chained to a board, and gagged with the wired mask worn by Hannibal Lecter in *Silence of the Lambs*, looks unimpressed as his lawyer, while waiting for the jury to come into court for the first time, whispers to him in an assuring voice, "Don't worry. You are presumed to be innocent." Even when we take the chains off, this presumptively innocent accused is still left with the humiliation of being the only one in the courtroom locked in a box with a burly prison guard at the ready. When the presumptively innocent accused is believed to present a security risk, there are often several officers standing around the prisoner's box like sultan's eunuchs.

What does all of this say about the presumption of innocence? As long ago as the nineteenth century the point was made:

> [T]he so-called presumption of innocence in favour of the prisoner at bar is a pretense, a delusion, an empty sound. . . . The treatment of the prisoner negatives the presumption. If he is presumed innocent, why is he manacled? Why is he put in jail? Why is he let out only on bail? Why, when he is put on trial, is he put in the [prisoner's] dock?. . . How can a person be presumed innocent who is presumably guilty?[3]

Does this not all make a mockery of our hallowed "presumption of innocence"? For the most part, the answer is a qualified no. We would do well to get rid of the jury selection ceremony and to let more accused persons sit at counsel table, as they do in the United States and as was recommended after the inquiry into the wrongful conviction of Guy Paul Morin.[4] It may even be that we keep too many people in detention pending their trials, but, for the most part, our practices are as respectful of the presumption of innocence as they can be, without turning it into a credo of self-destruction. Those who believe otherwise exaggerate the function that the presumption of innocence plays. As will be seen, its primary role before the prosecution begins is to provide the accused with the "right to silence." Beyond this, common sense and necessity require that, prior to the hearing, it cannot be given full weight. What are we to do, after all? Arrest or charge no one because everyone is presumed innocent? Release suspects who we know have a history of not showing up for their trials? Should we release those suspects who we have strong reason to fear will go out and finish what they started or commit new offences? "Now, Mr. Bernardo. We are going to let you go, but you come back for your trial, you hear, and don't bother any more young women in the meantime." Should we stop shackling prisoners during transport even though they could not be handled by prison guards if they were left unshackled? Why not just hand them the keys to the paddy wagon? The role played by the presumption of innocence before the start of proceedings is to counsel restraint, not to abolish common sense. How does it do so? We have developed rules that limit the power of the police to arrest where they can secure the appearance of the accused at trial by less intrusive means, such as by summons or by getting them to sign a promise to appear, provided there is no reason to believe that the accused will commit further offences. We have developed standards of restraint that prosecutors are to use when deciding whether to proceed with a charge. We have created criteria that are meant to limit the power to hold offenders pending their trial. And we have a constitutional rule, the right to have a trial within a reasonable time, that is inspired by the presumption of innocence. It recognizes that it is impossible to administer justice without subjecting presumptively innocent people to great stress and stigma, and in some cases significant loss of liberty, but it guarantees that the trial will be held within a reasonable time. In a practical system, principle cannot always be given full flower. Before the commencement of formal criminal proceedings, we have no choice but to compromise the presumption of innocence in significant respects. Where the presumption of innocence does most of its real work, and where it can never be compromised, is during the trial. There it is counted on, more than any other rule, to prevent the innocent from being convicted.

The reason we have to have a presumption at all is that it is impossible to devise a system that can always distinguish the truly guilty from the truly innocent. "What happened" will rarely be so obvious that we will know "God's truth." The fact-finder, whether it be a judge in a trial held before a judge alone, or a jury in a jury trial, will do its best to decide what happened, using testimony and clues that are left behind, including fingerprints, spent shells, or the number and nature of the wounds. Those clues may not be definitive: they rarely are. Witnesses may have it wrong. They may be lying or simply mistaken, either because they did not observe things accurately or their memories have failed. Crucial evidence may go undiscovered. Expert witnesses may make mistakes in analysing information because of poor scientific technique or because they are purveying junk science and their theories and assumptions are not nearly as valuable as they suggest. The point is, if forced absolutely to determine what happened, our judges and juries would often be wrong. Since perfect justice cannot be attained in every case, the issue is: On what side do we err? The presumption of innocence tells us that we have chosen to err on the side of innocence. We have done so because we believe that it is the only choice that a decent society can make.

The role of the presumption of innocence in ensuring that doubtful cases are resolved to keep the innocent from being convicted means that we, as a society, pay a heavy price. This presumption is responsible for far more guilty people going free than all the hated legal technicalities combined. We acknowledged its cost more than 225 years ago when William Blackstone, the author of one of the most influential law books ever written, remarked: "It is better for ten guilty persons to escape than that one innocent suffer."[5] Even more extravagant numbers are sometimes provided. In the fifteenth century when all felons were capitally punished, a former Chief Justice of the King's Bench, Fortescue, wrote, "I should, indeed, prefer twenty guilty men to escape death through mercy, than one innocent man be condemned unjustly."[6] I have read passages claiming that it is better for one hundred guilty persons to go free than for one innocent person to be convicted.[7] The numbers do not matter because we have no way of adjusting our system so that we can accomplish precisely the appropriate ratio. Nor would we want to. Why? Because as a society we cannot knowingly accept the conviction of *any* innocent people. If we were to set up a system that was designed to accept the conviction of one innocent person so that ten guilty people or even one hundred people could be convicted, it would be an obscenity. A moment's reflection indicates why.

Consider what a criminal prosecution is and what we do to those we convict. The fact that "criminals," who for most of us are faceless people that we believe are different from us, are brought before judges and juries and punished for their conduct while the rest of us are at work, rest, or play, masks what a criminal trial is really all about. When a criminal trial is held, you and I and the rest of our society are getting together and alleging that the accused person has transgressed one of our basic and most sacred rules. The fact that our appointed agents, the police and the prosecutors, undertake the business of investigating and swearing out charges does not change the reality that it is we, the members of this society, who are prepared to censure and punish one of our own. That is why prosecutions are brought in the name of the queen, as the representative of all of us. It is we who are hiving off one of our members and preparing to punish him or her after solemn ceremony. It is not the judge or the correctional officers who punish those who are found guilty. Sure, the judge decides on the appropriate sentence, and the correctional officials see to the implementation of that sentence, but it is in our name and with our authority that they do it. It is as it was when citizens circled the adulteress and pelted her with rocks for her sins. While others now wield the rocks on our behalf, there is no avoiding it. We, as a society, are circling and injuring one of our own. We take convicts from their families and lock them away like zoo animals. We deny them the right to go where they want or to do what they want, when they want. We create computer records that stamp them, like a scarlet letter, with the epithet "criminal." We shun them, fear them, and hate them. As in a primitive society, we both figuratively and actually cast them out. They carry the stigma of their sins on earth, with no hope for real redemption. Sadly, there are times when we have to do it, but before we do it to a fellow human, we had better be sure. We had better not err, for if we do, we as a society are committing a foul transgression, and doing so with the blasphemy of calling it justice. We are taking one of our own who is innocent and bringing him or her to ruin. Could we really, in all good conscience, set up a system of justice that tolerated this injustice as the price of catching more criminals?

The theft that masquerades as our income tax assessments aside, when a crime is committed in Canada it will rarely have been committed by the state. It will have been committed by a private citizen or a group of private citizens without the assistance or encouragement of the state. The victim is created not by the state, but by the act of a criminal. The criminal is the wrongdoer. When the state punishes one of its citizens, however, it is the actor. It is the one inflicting the harm. When the state punishes someone who is innocent, it is a wrongdoer. That means that we, the members of the community, are wrongdoers. If we set up a system that tolerates this abuse, we are no better than the criminals we prosecute. The presumption of innocence reflects our belief that it is less evil for a society to fail to punish someone who has actually committed a crime than to punish someone who has not committed a crime. We believe it to be so much worse to harm the innocent than to fail in our efforts to hurt the guilty that we have adopted the glib and irksome mantra, "it is better to acquit ten guilty men than to convict one innocent man." If you do not believe that to be so, ask yourself whether you are prepared to be one of the innocents who spends years in jail so that society will be more successful in punishing more criminals. If you are not prepared to make that sacrifice, then, as a matter of conscience, you can have no quibble with the presumption of innocence.

The need to err on the side of innocence is not just a matter of sentimentality; it is a practical imperative. Despite the frequent protests over the acquittal of the apparently guilty, would we feel secure in a society that punished its citizens without clear proof of guilt? Would we respect its institutions? A lawyer said it well when responding to a suggestion made by an eminent judge that we should abolish the controversial right of accused persons to remain silent:

> The system is . . . designed to make absolutely certain that regardless
> of how many guilty persons are acquitted, every single person who is
> convicted is guilty. The conviction is to be so totally solid — beyond
> any reasonable doubt, in the unanimous opinion of the jury, proved
> even in the case of the accused's silence — that the whole community can really believe in the conviction.[8]

If the community cannot believe in the convictions that are handed down, respect for the institutions of the law cannot survive, and if those institutions are not respected, they become pointless. They would lose the power to support and instil appropriate values or to denounce inappropriate conduct. Instead of expressing solidarity with the victim, they would be seen to be expressing solidarity with mistaken, or even with perjuring, accusers. If the community cannot believe in the convictions its courts hand down, it will lose faith in the system, and the system will lose the ability to influence behaviour and to shape public morals and values. In short, it will destroy itself. The irony is that acquitting the guilty where it is necessary to do so to protect the innocent actually protects society. It protects society's moral authority, its stability, and its law-abiding ethos.

Reasonable Doubt

This hallowed presumption of innocence gives rise to two of the central rules in our system. The first is the requirement that the Crown prosecutor bear the burden of proof in a criminal case. The second is that the standard of proof the Crown must meet be "proof beyond a reasonable doubt." This first rule, the one assigning the burden of proof, is easy to describe. Imposing the burden of proof on the Crown means that the Crown has to present its evidence first and that the Crown will lose where the judge in a judge alone trial, or the jury in a jury trial, concludes that the Crown has not proved its case. As familiar as it is, the second rule, that the Crown must present "proof beyond a reasonable doubt" to convict, is much more difficult to describe. Indeed, efforts to do so have proven to be so unsuccessful that, in a jury trial, the most common question asked by jurors after the judge has explained the law is, "Can you please explain again about reasonable doubt?" To this day, it is difficult to find volumes of our criminal law reporting services that do not include appeals from errors made by trial judges when telling juries what reasonable doubt means. What reasonable doubt means, in fact, is so difficult to put into words that some even suggest that we not try. The Law Reform Commission of Canada, a body established to find areas of difficulty in the law and to recommend reform, prepared a study paper into the problem in 1973. This is what the Commission said:

> If the judge explains to the jury that the Crown does not satisfy its burden of proof unless the evidence convinces them beyond a reasonable doubt of the existence of all the facts the Crown must prove, there would appear to be little danger that the average juror would fail to understand. *Reasonable doubt is a doubt that is reasonable*; it is difficult to see how such a formula could be simplified or amplified to advantage.[9]

When a term is used to define itself, we know we have problems: "A reasonable doubt is a doubt that is reasonable." I would be disappointed to open a dictionary and find that definition or any other like it: "Rutabaga (n.): A Rutabaga."

In spite of the challenges it presents, the Supreme Court of Canada has decided that it is an error for a trial judge not to give some direction to a jury on what a reasonable doubt is. Because the appellate courts across Canada have been disagreeing among themselves for years over what a reasonable doubt is, the Supreme Court of Canada has also finally provided guidance in the form of a model jury direction.[10] One of the most important things the justices said is that jurors should be told that they cannot convict simply because they may think the accused is probably guilty. If they were to do so, they would be applying the standard that is used in civil cases, which is proof on the balance of probabilities, or proof on the preponderance of evidence, as it is referred to in the United States, and this would be very wrong.

The civil standard of proof is easy to understand. If the plaintiff's version is more probably true than not true, she or he wins. Although a number of things, including the racial compositions of the juries, the admissibility rulings of the judges, the skill of the lawyers, and the discovery of new evidence, all played an important part, the conflicting O.J. Simpson verdicts can be explained technically on the basis that the burdens of proof in each case were different. To convict him during the criminal trial, a jury had to find him guilty beyond a reasonable doubt — a prospect made difficult by the evidence of police corruption and the bungling of the forensic witnesses. To find him civilly liable, the evidence needed to show merely that he had probably killed Nicole Brown and Ronald Goldman. Time and again, in this country, criminal judges and juries acquit people who they think are probably guilty, but they acquit them because they have a reasonable doubt.

Why the difference? Why do we have to endure the acquittal of the probably guilty, even though probable guilt is enough for them to lose civil cases? We treat criminal cases and civil cases so differently because the issues are so different. In a criminal case, the question is, should we, as a society, punish this person with the most extreme form of official censure available? In a civil case it is who, as between the plaintiff and the defendant, should bear the risk of loss? The answer in a civil case is easy: the person who is probably responsible. A civil suit is also a private matter, whereas a criminal trial is an allegation by us, the state, against an individual citizen. While society must, as a matter of moral imperative, accept a higher risk of error than the citizen who is being prosecuted in a criminal prosecution, why should we make one citizen in a private suit bear a greater risk of error than another? It is therefore wrong for judges to direct criminal juries about reasonable doubt in terms of probabilities, lest they confuse the civil and criminal standards. The standards for succeeding are different because civil and criminal trials are different.

The United States Supreme Court recognized in 1970 that truth would likely be arrived at more consistently by allowing criminal verdicts to be rendered on proof on the balance of probabilities, but that the cost to society of pursuing the truth with single-minded vigour would be too high a price to pay:

> If, for example, the standard of proof for a criminal trial were a preponderance of evidence rather than proof beyond a reasonable doubt, there would be a smaller risk of factual errors that result in freeing guilty persons, but a far greater risk of factual errors that result in convicting the innocent.[11]

It would be much easier if we could think of standards of proof in terms of probabilities, especially if numeric probabilities could be assigned, but it is simply not possible. There may be some sense in saying that the balance of probabilities arrives when the odds are 51 to 49 in favour of the plaintiff, but in criminal cases, statistics are meaningless when it comes to defining proof beyond a reasonable doubt. Professor Dershowitz of Harvard University gives this illustration to his students to make the point:

> A fatal accident is caused by a blue bus in a town where 90 percent of the blue buses are owned by the A Company and 10 percent by the B Company. That is all the evidence presented at the criminal trial of the A Company. Is this 90 percent "likelihood" that an A bus caused the accident enough to prove that fact "beyond a reasonable doubt"?[12]

The students tend to respond negatively. Of course, they are right. Proof beyond a reasonable doubt is not being 90 percent sure, or even 99 percent sure. It is not a matter susceptible to statistical expression.

The dangers of relying on statistics can be seen from the American case of *People* v. *Collins*.[13] A robbery took place in Los Angeles. The robbers were a white blonde female, wearing a pony tail, and a black male with a beard. They escaped in a yellow automobile. Sometime later, on this description, two suspects were arrested. The prosecutor called a mathematics professor as a witness. He invited the jury to rely on their own assessment of the frequency of each of these characteristics in the general population and taught them how to identify probabilities by multiplying each variable to determine the probability of all the variables occurring simultaneously. He also invited them to accept his estimates:

yellow automobile, one in ten; man with moustache, one in four; girl with pony tail, one in ten; blonde-haired girl, one in three; black with beard, one in ten; interracial couple in an automobile, one in one thousand. The probability of all these characteristics occurring simultaneously, he said, was one in twelve million. How can you have a reasonable doubt in the face of that? The fact is, if all you have is some mathematical probability theory, you should have a doubt. How reliable are the estimates of frequency? Were the characteristics probabilistically independent? This technique also requires "equating the probability of finding a duplicate in one random selection with the probability of guilt." More important, it accepts the arbitrary assumption that this accused is not the exception to the probable. This is silly — trial by math prof. Far more important than these kinds of probabilities are the quality of the descriptions, the proximity of the pair to the robbery, whether anyone could identify them and under what circumstances, whether they were found in possession of the money or the guns, or whether they made any statements. We will never be able to translate the concept of proof beyond a reasonable doubt into statistics, however digestible they might be.

So what, then, is a reasonable doubt? We are often told it must be based on reason and common sense. It is a doubt that is not imaginary or frivolous. It must not be based on fantasy or on speculation. It must not be based on emotion or sympathy or prejudice. It must be based on the evidence or the lack of evidence. We are warned that it does not mean absolute certainty because absolute certainty — mathematical certainty — does not exist or rarely exists. Now go away and decide.

In my view, we have wasted an incredible amount of effort attempting to put "reasonable doubt" into other words. Instead of trying to explain to jurors what it means, a more relevant and important approach would be to explain why we have it. We should express to them the values it exists to protect. Although we do tell them that it is linked to the presumption of innocence, that is not enough. The essential point that must be reinforced to juries in particular, and to the public in general, is that it is incredibly serious business to convict someone of a criminal offence. As the Law Reform Commission of Canada said before lapsing into its circular definition: "A high standard of proof is now required in criminal cases and is justified by the purposes for which the criminal sanction is used, the seriousness of depriving someone of his liberty, the stigmatization of the accused that results from a criminal conviction, and the other economic and social consequences that a criminal conviction entails." Isn't the critical thing for a judge or jury to ask at the moment of decision, "Should we do all this to this person, on the basis of the evidence that the Crown has presented?" It is unquestionably far too late to dispense with the phrase "reasonable doubt." It is part of the fabric of our Constitution. I, for one, would feel much better if we simply told juries and trained judges to remind themselves what a criminal conviction means, and to caution them that they should not expose the accused to the calamity of conviction unless they are sure it is the right thing to do.

While this is its essence, there are other aspects of the concept that need to be fleshed out. In particular, given the natural tendency to believe it is so, it is important to acknowledge that guilt is not established simply because a judge or jury is satisfied beyond a reasonable doubt that defence evidence is false or untrue. The test for conviction is not whether an accused or defence witness is lying when testifying or presenting misleading evidence. It is whether the Crown has proved the guilt of the accused beyond a reasonable doubt. There is a natural tendency to want to deny information that may seem harmful, and even innocent people, faced with apparently damning information, may lie in an ill-advised effort to preserve themselves from wrongful conviction. For example, Donald Marshall, who served eleven years in prison for a murder he did not commit, falsely told a police officer that he was not in the park where the stabbing of Sandy Seale took place. He did so because he and Sandy had gone to the park to rob people and he was understandably worried about what that admission would mean for him. If he had told the same lie on the stand and been caught at it, that would not have made him guilty of the murder. A judge will warn a jury against making this mistake.

As a prosecutor I won a pyrrhic victory when prosecuting a young man who denied his participation in a drive-by shooting. I caught him in numerous lies and contradictions when I cross-examined him. Even though he could have mushed my face with one punch had we been on his terrain, we were in my alley, playing my game. Every time he said something, I took his foot and pushed it farther down his throat. There was no escape. Like a cat that had cornered a mouse, I toyed with him and then I ate him up. I was flush, basking in the glory of my own performance, and he was wet with sweat. When the judge returned a short time later to give his verdict, I gave the accused my best "Watch this" face by raising my eyebrow and tilting my head just so, and I sat poised in this fashion until the judge let the air out of my balloon by acquitting him on the more serious charges. His Honour congratulated me on proving beyond a reasonable doubt that the young man was a liar, but then pointed out the obvious: I had not proven beyond a reasonable doubt that he had participated in the shooting. The accused then sent a message to me with his facial expression, only I don't think he was trying to communicate "Watch this."

For the same reason, when a case becomes a contest of credibility, with the complainant and the accused telling different stories, it is a mistake for a judge or jury members to decide to convict because they find the complainant's story more believable. A trial is not a contest to see which side produces more credible witnesses. The accused is only guilty if the Crown witnesses are so credible as to remove all reasonable doubt of the guilt of the accused, in spite of any evidence the defence calls. This condition is a common and understandable source of frustration among complainants in sexual and domestic assaults who have to endure the spectacle of the accused leaving the courtroom with impunity. They think that the accused has been believed and that they have not been. In fact, this is rarely so. What more often happens is that the judge or jury's impulse to believe the complainant and disbelieve the accused may convince them that he is probably guilty, but it is simply not strong enough to justify convicting him.

It should be obvious that the two fundamental principles currently under discussion — the presumption of innocence and the requirement of proof beyond a reasonable doubt — not legal technicalities, are the true foe of those who feel that the legal system is letting too many criminals go free. Sure, it is true there are many technical matters that can cause "guilty" people to avoid conviction. But the overwhelming majority of acquittals occur not because of technicalities, but because of the presumption of innocence. At the end of the case, the judge or jury is simply not satisfied of the guilt of the accused and he or she is acquitted. Nowhere can this be seen more clearly than with the prosecution of sexual assaults.

Protecting Those We Hate

The prosecution of sexual assaults is unquestionably the most politically charged area of criminal law. It is a crime overwhelmingly committed by men, with the victims being women and children. The successful prosecution of sexual offence cases has, therefore, perversely in my view, come to be seen as an issue of gender equality. The prevalence of the crime, we are told, is of shocking dimensions. Historically, the system of justice has appeared unable or unwilling to deal with it. Although one must always be suspicious of statistics hauled out in aid of strongly held but controversial positions, we can be sure that the conviction rate in such cases has always been intolerably low. The legal system, egged on by effective political lobbying and by the conviction that it is simply right to do so, has been trying for the last decade to change this imbalance.

We have altered every rule of law that has been targeted as a technicality. Ancient, discredited rules of evidence requiring that there be independent evidence beyond the simple word of the victim have been abolished. So too has the old "hue and cry" rule, which assumed, preposterously, that any female rape victim would run to the nearest trusted person and "cry rape" if it had really happened. We have made it easier for children to testify. Where we feel it necessary, we put them behind screens so they need not look at their accuser or move them out of the court to testify through closed-circuit televisions. We let children pretape their allegations and play the video in court, an unheard-of breach of a number of established rules of evidence, and we are about to allow adult victims to do so as well. We let children sit on parents' laps while testifying. We allow hearsay evidence, in many cases. In rare cases we even clear courts to save complainants embarrassment, and we routinely suppress the complainant's name while the accused's appears in all the papers. We are more tolerant about proof of the prior acts of sexual abuse by the accused than we once were. We prevent complainants from being asked about their sexual experiences. We no longer listen to reputation evidence about the lack of chastity of the complainant. We allow the history of how the complaint came before the court to be narrated, something we used to prevent. We protect complainants from abusive character cross-examination. We make defence lawyers jump through hoops to get access to a complainant's therapeutic records. We bring "experts" into court with what, at times, is reckless abandon. Often their "science" is not much more dependable than reading tea leaves, yet we allow them to testify that, based on her psychological profile, the complainant has been sexually assaulted. And still? While there are no doubt more convictions than there once were, it remains difficult to get a conviction in front of most judges or juries in a sexual offence case where there are not multiple victims or where there is no independent confirming evidence. Why? Because sexual assaults happen in private places where the only witnesses are the perpetrator and the victim. The criminal allegations are often made years after the alleged assault. When the matter gets to court, it is her word against his. "He did this to me." "No, I did not." Remove all reasonable doubt with that exchange? It can be done in exceptional cases where the complainant is particularly credible, but not otherwise.

This is why it is nothing short of irresponsible for counsellors and therapists, or rape crisis workers, to advise women to bring criminal charges to attain closure. This is why it is tragic for complainants to come to court expecting to find someone who will validate their complaint by believing them. Sexual offence victims should come to court, by all means, but they should come to court seeking justice, not healing, and they should understand that no matter what the law does short of convicting everyone, their tormentors may, unavoidably, be the undeserving beneficiaries of the presumption of innocence.

Those who are unacquainted with the importance of the presumption of innocence often say, "But why would she complain if nothing happened?" A good question, but if we start our trials on the basis that a complaint is likely to be true if a complainant is prepared to put herself through the trauma of the criminal justice system, then we are not applying a presumption of innocence. We are applying a presumption of guilt. The fact is there are false complaints, though we hope they are few in number. Even if there are almost none, the challenge for the criminal justice system is in identifying them. Since we cannot do so with perfection, we have no choice as a decent society but to err on the side of innocence. We cannot effectively presume guilt where the accused cannot uncover a reason or motive for a false or mistaken allegation. While it is almost certain that we will be wrong more often by presuming innocence, the cost of being wrong less often is unacceptable. We will have to vilify, stigmatize, and punish innocent men, and in some cases women, so we can be more effective at discouraging the real offenders. Why have a trial at all if we are prepared to do so?

This is a distressing reality at a time when we are attempting to combat sexual offences. They are a blight on our society, and it is understandable that they are at the top of our political agenda. But this is exactly the time when the basic principles of justice — the presumption of innocence and the requirement of proof beyond a reasonable doubt — have their most important work to do. It is when society develops a strong fear of a particular kind of crime or conduct that its resolve to preserve the values enshrined in the presumption of innocence is most likely to wane. The kings and queens of England did not presume innocence when they feared rebellion in the seventeenth century. In Salem, those accused of witchcraft were not presumed innocent. The House Committee on Un-American Activity, led by Senator Joseph McCarthy, did not presume innocence. And in Great Britain, the birthplace of our system of justice, the Guildford Six and the Birmingham bombers were tried and wrongly convicted only a few years ago when fear of terrorism loosened the restraints of principle. As a society, we currently have a morbid fear of pedophiles. Open any newspaper or magazine and there will be articles about our "secret fear." Turn on the television and watch protestors holding vigils near correctional facilities to protest the pending release of a child molester. Turn the channel and watch neighbourhood groups chasing convicted pedophiles from their homes. How committed are we likely to be when the price of the presumption of innocence is that we will be setting child molesters free? But ask again: How can we as a society justify driving a person to these depths of vilification if we are not sure? The worse the crime, the more important the principles become.

A horrendous crime was committed in Ottawa recently. Reputed members of a street gang known as Ace Crew kidnapped four young people after breaking into a suburban home, and carted the teenagers back to an apartment that had been prepared in advance for carnage. Plastic sheeting had been taped to the walls and floor of a closet, obviously to keep the anticipated blood-flow from leaving incriminating signs of the violence that had been planned. One of the kidnap victims, Sylvain Leduc, then only seventeen years old, was savagely beaten to death. One of his female cousins, who had also been kidnapped, had a heated curling iron inserted into her vagina. The police arrived, likely saving the lives of two girls and the other young man who had been taken, but they were not in time to prevent the torture that permanently scarred their bodies and their spirits, nor were they in time to save Sylvain. Experienced police officers, accustomed to the ugliness that humans can create, felt their knees buckle when they saw what had happened.

A handful of suspects, mostly teenagers, were apprehended trying to flee the scene ahead of the sirens. Other arrests soon followed. Of the four young offenders who have so far been tried, only one has been convicted of homicide despite the Crown's having urged that all were guilty of murder. He was convicted only of manslaughter, as well as other related charges. The other youths were acquitted of all homicide offences but convicted of lesser charges, including assault. Why? Because there was a reasonable doubt about their guilt. They were at the bloodletting, but who did what? While the Crown's evidence did ultimately prove that the three adult accused were guilty of murder, it could not sort out beyond a reasonable doubt what role all the young persons involved had played, and they were acquitted of the most serious charges.

This outcome infuriated many in the community. Here is a gang that preyed on high school kids, whose members refuse to respect even the most basic values of the community. They live in a world of drugs, child prostitution, and violence. They are exploiters, users. Then they come to court asking us to give them the benefit of the doubt. Why should we? They have rejected those fundamental values they find inconvenient. Why give them the benefit of our values when it suits them? Why? Because the rule of law requires it. You either have a rule or you don't. If you have the power to choose not to apply rules that seem inconvenient or distasteful, they can no longer perform their function. These fundamental principles either apply to all of us in all situations or they are impotent — lifeless incantations incapable of protecting any of us. Who is going to choose whom to give the benefit of the law to? It is all or none, and none is too scary a prospect to even consider.

None of this is to say that we have to be so afraid of making a mistake that we lose our ability to convict. There are judges, fortunately very few in number, whose concept of reasonable doubt is so preposterously wide that they are unlikely to be convinced that their noses have two nostrils on the basis of the testimony of others. This happens, I suspect, because it is very difficult to look someone in the eye and declare, "You, sir, are henceforth branded as a criminal." Judges have to go home at night. They have to sit with their families, knowing they have sent others away from theirs. They have to know in their hearts and their minds that they have not been wrong in harming other persons in the most egregious fashion that the law countenances — by punishing them on behalf of society. When in real doubt, conscience, if nothing else, dictates acquittal.

The Stain of Lingering Doubt

Some believe that if we have to accept this margin, perhaps it would be better to adopt the Scottish practice of declaring that criminal allegations are "not proven" rather than declaring that accused persons are "not guilty." It has appeal because it stops short of "exonerating" those who have actually committed the crime, but cannot be found guilty because of the poor quality of the evidence or legal technicalities. This attraction is understandable, but as a matter of principle it is unacceptable. There are innocent people who are found not guilty. If "not proven" is meant to suggest that it is appropriate to stain those who have not been convicted with the continuing mark of unresolved suspicion, it is a horrendous compromise. To keep from declaring the guilty "not guilty," we will mark the innocent "charged but not proven."

Putting principle aside, though, the truth is that our habit of declaring the probably guilty "not guilty" amounts to much the same thing. It has, in fact, meant that an acquittal, even when communicated with the words "not guilty," is not an effective absolution, either in law or in fact. The legal point can be established quickly.

A man named Riley was charged with a sexual offence against a young girl named Christine. He claimed the allegation was false. To assist in his defence, he wanted to call one Morley Roswell to testify that Christine had made false allegations against him in which she claimed that when she was around twelve, Roswell had sex with her on a number of occasions against her will. Indeed, Roswell had been charged, based on her allegations, but was acquitted. Despite this, Riley was not allowed to use Roswell's testimony. In explaining why not, the Ontario Court of Appeal said that Roswell's acquittal did not necessarily mean that Christine's claim had been false. "Even if we had a proper record of Roswell's trial, a not-guilty verdict, standing by itself, could not establish that the prosecution was based on fabricated testimony by the complainant."[14] There are times when, even according to our legal rules, we refuse to treat a not-guilty verdict as meaning what it says.

Recently, I read in the paper about Debra Marquard's reaction to her acquittal on charges that she committed aggravated assault against her granddaughter by forcing her head into a hot oven to punish her. Marquard had originally been convicted by a southern Ontario jury, but that conviction was overturned on appeal because of legal errors relating to the admissibility of evidence. In her retrial before a judge alone she was acquitted. She expressed her relief on the stairs outside of the court, saying of the judge who had acquitted her that someone in the criminal justice system had finally believed her. It is doubtful the judge did. While his judgment fairly negates every strand of the Crown's case, when it came time to pronounce judgment, the judge said, "Under all the circumstances and having regard to the evidence in its totality, while I certainly stop short of finding Mrs. Marquard innocent, I am left with a strong sense of reasonable doubt."[15] In other words, I cannot disbelieve her beyond a reasonable doubt and so I will acquit her, but I cannot be sure that she did not do it. The right result, but hardly exoneration.

Even where judges do not express their doubts about innocence, few people who are acquitted have been able to rise entirely above the tainting suspicion that they may have gotten away with it. Using the medium of literature to enlighten us about human nature, E.M. Forster, in *A Passage to India*, describes how many reacted to the acquittal of Azziz on the false sexual assault charges brought by Adella Quested in the Marabar caves:

> They still believed he was guilty, they believed it to the end of their careers, and retired Anglo-Indians in Tunbridge Wells or Cheltenham still murmur to each other: "That Marabar case which broke down because the poor girl couldn't face giving her evidence — that was another bad case."[16]

Many of those who have been acquitted in Canada bear the same lingering doubt. They are not treated as though they have been exonerated. They are treated as though theirs was simply another "bad case." They never get over the stain of simply having been charged. This is a sad but unavoidable reality. One of the costs of the presumption of innocence, with its preference for erring by acquitting the guilty, is that unless a judge goes out of his or her way to proclaim the accused innocent, a verdict of acquittal concedes the possibility of error.

There it is, then. In all its splendour, even while conjuring up notions of human decency and the commitment to moral principle, the presumption of innocence has a negative side. At bottom, it is an admission that our ability to divine who is innocent and who is guilty is truly limited, that we expect to be wrong from time to time, and that we choose to allow guilty people to be the beneficiaries of our uncertainty. This admission is disheartening for a society that feels the need to prove to those who have wronged us, and to ourselves, that justice will be done. Still, as perverse as it sounds, we should be prepared to celebrate that our system is one that will allow for the acquittal of some who are factually guilty. We should be prepared to celebrate it because, if we were not prepared to accept the acquittal of the factually guilty, we would be convicting far more innocent people than we already are. If you cannot go so far as to celebrate it, lament it as a necessary evil in any society that is built on humanity and decency.

CHAPTER 9

Closing Our Eyes to Find the Truth

George Philmon had almost finished the drainage ditch. He pulled his hat off his head and wiped the sweat away from his brow with his shirt. Cupping his hand over his eyes, he looked up to see how high the spring sun was standing in the eastern Australian sky. "Lots of day left," he thought. He let the spade fall, deciding he needed a break. Then he thrust his hand into the side pocket of his dusty coveralls to grab one of the smokes he had rolled earlier that day. As he squatted down to shield his match from the stiff October breeze that blew in from the seaside, his eye caught something in the trench. It looked like cloth. He reached over and tugged at it with his thick fingers. It gave a bit, then ripped. A nest of small bones, barely hanging together in the unmistakable shape of a tiny human hand, fell out.

"My Christ," Philmon gasped, spitting out the skinny cigarette that had been hanging from his mouth. He scrambled to his feet and backed off for a minute, his heart pounding. Then, tentatively, his curiosity overwhelming him, he grabbed a nearby broom and swept away the dirt to free the body from its unnatural grave. Within minutes, he had unearthed two bodies that had been lying beside each other in the garden of the tiny house he and his family had been living in for the last two months.

By the time the police had completed the job of digging up the rest of the yard on Burren-street in Macdonaldtown, New South Wales, Philmon wanted to walk away from the accursed place. The bodies of five more infants had been found buried about the yard. He and his family had been living in the midst of a bloody graveyard.

Although it was not uncommon in 1892 for newborns to die of natural causes, from scarlet fever or other infectious diseases, seven infants found buried in unmarked graves in the same backyard made the prospect that they had all died from natural causes defy common sense. As hard as it was to fathom, it was obvious that someone had been killing babies.

The next day Constable Joyce, who had come up from Sydney to investigate, found his way to the home of John and Sara Makin. He wanted to speak to them because, prior to George Philmon, they had been tenants of the Burren-street property where the babies had been discovered. By now word had spread of the macabre discovery, and the Makins had been holding their breath, hoping that no one would approach them about it. Constable Joyce could see the fear in their faces from the time they opened the door and saw him standing there in his stiff navy tunic. After introducing himself, and without telling them why he was there, he said: "Are you people in the habit of taking in children to nurse?" Sara looked at John for a minute. John forced a smile and responded:

"No, we only took one child in Burren-street. My wife was receiving 10 shillings a week to nurse it. We had to wait for three weeks while the parents came and took it away. They said they were going to Melbourne."

"What were the parents named?"

"Don't recall. I think the woman's name was Wilson. Yeah, I think it was Wilson."

"You sure that's the only time you took in a child to nurse?"

"Sure. We have children enough of our own."

Constable Joyce thanked them and walked away, knowing who his suspects were.

On 28 October, less than two weeks later, John and Sara found themselves called as witnesses at an inquest that was being held in aid of the investigation. Constable Joyce nodded to them as they walked into the town hall, but he never smiled. His look sent a chill down Sara's back.

"John. They know something. I know they do," she whispered frantically. "They know something." She sat for a moment trying to calm herself, and then it dawned on her — a thought that destroyed any hope she had of regaining her composure. What if the police had been to the George-street property where they had lived before moving to Burren-street. "John," she pleaded, looking to him for reassurance. "You don't think they've been to George-street, do you?"

"Might be that they have, Sara. I guess time will tell."

But Sara could not wait for time to tell. When the proceedings adjourned for the day, she set out for a long walk in the fresh spring air to see what had been happening at George-street. She stood peering over the fence of her former residence, craning her neck to see if she could see into the back property. A young woman came to the door, with a child on her hip and a suspicious look on her face.

"Help you, Ma'am?" she hollered. She opened the door and walked up to Sara.

"Good evening. You don't know me, Ma'am . . ."

"Right. I don't."

"Sorry to trouble you, but I was just calling around. I was worried about my dear friends. They used to live here. I was wondering, well, I've been worried about them and I have been wondering if the police have been around."

"Yeah. They've been around."

"Really."

"Been diggin' up the garden too." She paused for effect. "Lookin' for babies."

"Oh my. They didn't find any, did they?"

"No. They dug, but they didn't find any."

"That must have been a lot of inconvenience for you."

"Not at all. Couldn't stop 'em very much, could I?"

She shifted the child to her other hip, looking suspiciously at Sara as her thin hair blew across her face. Sara paused for a second, then decided to ask: "Did they dig up your floor or just about the garden?"

"Just in the garden."

Sara's face registered pleasure at the news. "Good evening," she said awkwardly. As she turned and walked away, the woman could not stop herself from calling after her: "If they are such friends you should go and see them."

In the meantime, Amber Murray, a sixteen-year-old girl, was also deeply troubled by the inquest, but not for the same reason that Sara was. She walked fearfully into the police station and approached the constable who was standing behind the desk: "I'm here to find out if my baby is one of them that they found buried." Constable Jacobs overheard her. He walked over and introduced himself, and showed her to a bench. She sat down and nervously pushed at the wrinkles on her dress with her palms, trying to make them go away. He sat beside her. Looking down at the floor, she reluctantly told him her story.

She had been with a man, once, and she had become pregnant for it. Her father at first was going to turn her out, but then agreed to have her stay, provided she would find a home for the baby when it was born. The baby, whom she referred to as Horace, was received into this world, in solitude and confidence, in the back bedroom at the Murrays' home on 30 May 1892, where Amber had been cloistered for seven months. To avoid scandal, the baby was immediately secreted off to the home of a wet-nurse, a Mrs. Patrick. Amber's father had arranged to have Mrs. Patrick care for the baby until a permanent home could be found for it.

In those harsher times, when the state did not see it as its responsibility to take care of such matters, Amber Murray put an ad in the paper, leaving only Mrs. Patrick's mailing address, inquiring whether anyone would be interested in adopting the boy. She received a letter from a woman named "E. Hill." Mrs. Hill offered to meet to discuss the adoption at an address on George-street in Redfern.

On 25 June 1892 Amber Murray walked to George-street by herself so she could decide whether the Hills would be suitable parents. They invited her in and served her tea and biscuits with marmite. They told her how they had lost a child two years before and were anxious to adopt another. Then they introduced Amber to their two daughters, aged eleven and thirteen, who seemed happy and healthy enough. The Hills told her they would be pleased to adopt the child and to raise it and educate it. If she agreed to give them the child, they were even going to move to a healthier place in Hurtsville that would be better for the baby. All they requested in return was that she pay them a premium of three pounds sterling, far from a fortune but a difficult sum for a single mother to rustle up. Still, it seemed a fair price if it was going to be a good home. They promised Amber she would be free to visit when she liked.

A few days later, on 27 June, Mr. Hill and one of his daughters arrived at Mrs. Patrick's to pick up the child. Amber took the child from her arms, healthy and clean, kissed it softly, and handed it over to Mr. Hill's daughter.

A few days later, Mr. Hill came by again. He was supposed to have signed some papers that she had prepared, but he did not have them. He told her he had moved to Hurtsville and mentioned that it would be six weeks or so before they were settled enough to receive her for a visit at their place. Instead, he said he would bring the baby around to her for a visit, on a day that was not too wet or windy. He mentioned that the baby had a rash on its face and was not entirely well, but he assured the women that his wife was looking after things. Then, on 5 July, when Amber was out, Mr. Hill came by with a sick-looking baby, all covered with sores, which he showed to Mrs. Patrick. Amber, worried about her son, had gone out to Hurtsville to see him, but no one there had ever heard of the Hills. They had simply disappeared.

The day after she showed up at the police station, Constable Jacobs stood beside Amber Murray at the door to the town hall, waiting for the Makins to show at the inquest. When they arrived, they averted their eyes and pretended not to know her, but Amber knew them well enough. At that moment her worst fears were confirmed. Horace was dead. Shortly afterwards, the police arrested the Makins, not just John and Sara, but their young daughters as well.

John, who had been taken to a "watchhouse" to await trial, stood looking out through the iron bars, drawing on a cigarette. His cell mate, a ruddy-faced man, looked at his back: "What's your trouble, mate?" the man intoned.

"Baby farming," responded Makin. "I'm here for baby farming." He turned around and looked at his cell mate square in the eyes, surprising even himself with his candour, but he talked on. "They found seven. There's another to be found, and when they do I will never see the daylight no more."

He turned and again looked out the window at the eucalyptus trees. They stood in clumps nearby, but, in the distance, they seemed to meld together into a thick carpet of blue, green, and grey which ran up between the rock faces and slowly climbed its way into the Blue Mountains. Far off — where he wished he could be. "That is what you get for obliging people," he muttered. "And you know," he turned again to face the man, "I don't care for myself. Really, I don't. But they've locked up my children, too, Blanche and Florence. They're innocent. Was me that buried the babies."

When Makin's cell mate passed this intelligence on to the guards later that day in return for his freedom on a minor assault, the police had renewed reason to go back into the excavation business. Six days later, after pulling up floor boards on George-street and doing a more thorough dig, they found the corpses of four other babies. Then two more were disinterred from the yard at the Makins' current address. Thirteen buried babies, scattered between the three addresses associated with the Makins. The state of New South Wales was horrified, and the case of the baby farmers grabbed headlines across Australia.

After the George-street excavation was complete, Constable Jacobs asked Amber Murray to come to the station. Apologizing for having to do it, he asked her to look through the clothing that had been found on the bodies of the children. There was no sense having her look at the bodies because they were so badly decomposed. There, amidst the soiled and rotting cloth, she spied the remnants of a dress that had once been hers, the dress she had wrapped young Horace in before delivering him to the Makins. The Makins had never moved to Hurtsville. They had repaired from their George-street home during a dark and rainy evening only two days after receiving young Horace. When they left, they carted away their meagre belongings, but no one carried the baby. He had been left behind, buried in the back yard. The baby they showed to Mrs. Patrick was not even Horace. That child was no doubt one of the seven that had found a home under the red clay on Burren-street during the six short weeks that the Makins had lived there.

By the time the investigation was done, four other women had come forward. They, too, had given their illegitimate children to the Makins, who promised to adopt them. In each case the Makins were paid paltry sums of between two and five pounds. Although none of the other babies could be identified because of their state of decomposition, two of the women were able to identify clothing that Sara Makin had pawned at the shops near her home.

Because only the Murray baby could be identified, John and Sara Makin ultimately stood trial for his murder alone, although that was enough at the time to get them hanged. Out of an abundance of caution, the police laid two charges relating to the same killing. The first charged that they had murdered "the child described as Horace Amber Murray." Since the boy had never been baptized and his birth had not been registered, there was some issue as to whether, legally, there had ever been such a person, so, in the rude habit of the day, the second count simply alleged the murder of "the infant which was the illegitimate child of a woman named Amber Murray." It was on this latter count that John and Sara Makin were convicted of murder by a jury in a trial held before Mr. Justice Stephen at the Sydney Assizes.

The *Makin* case has since become famous among criminal lawyers throughout the British Empire, not so much because of its bizarre and outrageous facts, but because the case made its way across thousands of miles of ocean to the Privy Council in London, then the highest court of appeal in the British Empire. That august body of law lords, dressed in rich cloth and ermine, capped in horse-hair wigs, had to grapple with a troublesome legal question, one that continues to plague courts to this day. At the murder trial of Horace Amber Murray, was it appropriate to permit the Crown to prove, by inference, that the Makins had killed and buried the twelve other children in order to prove that they had murdered the Murray baby? Was it appropriate to call the four other women to say that the Makins had obtained children from them in the same bizarre fashion that they had obtained Horace Amber Murray? The Privy Council answered yes to each question, although the rule of law they defined, known generally as the "similar fact evidence" rule, has frustrated prosecutors for generations.

Protecting the Accused from His Past

Barring exceptional circumstances, the similar fact evidence rule denies prosecutors the right to attempt to establish the accused's guilt on one charge by proving that he has committed the same kind of crime before.

In the words of Lord Herschell, words still familiar to every criminal lawyer in those countries that once made up the British Empire:

> It is undoubtedly not competent for the prosecution to adduce evidence tending to show that the accused has been guilty of criminal acts other than those covered by the indictment for the purpose of leading to the conclusion that the accused is a person likely from his criminal conduct or character to have committed the offence for which he is being tried. On the other hand, the mere fact that the evidence adduced tends to show the commission of other crimes does not render it inadmissible if it be relevant to an issue before the jury, and it may be so relevant if it bears upon the question whether the acts alleged to constitute the crime charged in the indictment were designed or accidental, or to rebut a defence which would otherwise be open to the accused.[1]

In current parlance, this is taken to mean that we will never allow the judge in a trial by judge alone, or a jury in a jury trial, to rely on the "bad character" of the accused to help decide whether he is guilty of the offence. It is never appropriate to infer that since he is the kind of person who commits such offences, he is more likely to be guilty of the offence charged. On the other hand, there will be times when proof of other bad acts by the accused can be relevant for other purposes, and when this is so, if the proof is important enough, we will hear it. The net effect of this rule is to prevent the Crown in most cases from proving the past criminal activities of the accused. It is as though, subject to exceptions, everyone tried for a crime in this country is entitled to be tried on the assumption that he or she is otherwise a law-abiding person.

Not surprisingly, some see this practice as a deception and are infuriated by it. Recently, in Ottawa, the similar fact evidence rule spun its magic by keeping the jury in the dark about who they were really trying.

Brett Morgan was being tried for the murder of his partner, Louise Ellis, a woman whom he had met, strangely enough, while on a temporary pass from prison where he was serving time for having strangled a young woman a number of years before. The escorted pass had been issued so he could testify before the Supreme Court of Canada during a hearing that was held to determine whether David Milgaard had been wrongfully convicted.[2] Morgan was testifying that his cell mate, a man named Larry Fisher, had confided in him that he had committed a murder and that another man was serving the time for it. Fisher, a serial rapist, had long been an alternative suspect in the killing for which Milgaard had been convicted.[3] After Morgan's testimony, Louise Ellis, a freelance writer who had been sitting in during the proceedings, approached Morgan and complimented him on his courage. They began to correspond. When he gained his parole, with her assistance, he moved in with her. Within a year, both she and much of her money had gone missing. As soon as the police learned that she had been living with Morgan, a paroled killer, he became the suspect in her disappearance. Weeks later, her body was "discovered" by Morgan, covered in brush at the side of a rural road, a good distance from where her car had been found abandoned. Instead of being rewarded with the proceeds from Ellis' will now that she was confirmed dead, Morgan found himself under arrest for her murder.

Normally a jury would have been left totally in the dark about Morgan's manslaughter conviction. In an unusual move, defence counsel agreed that the jury should learn that Morgan was on parole for manslaughter at the time Ellis disappeared. It was the defence theory that the police zoned in on him as the suspect immediately on learning this fact, and that they manufactured a case against him instead of trying to discover what had really happened. He could not present that theory to the jury without admitting the earlier killing, so the jury learned about the conviction. What they were not told, however, is that Morgan's victim had been a young prostitute, who had lived with Morgan and his common-law spouse, and who had been strangled (the same method that the Crown argued had been used to kill Ellis). Nor were they told that Morgan had tried to strangle a former wife, and had choked yet another of his partners. They were not advised of the pattern of violence he had used and the abuse he had employed against the women in his previous relationships.[4] The jury had been asked to decide the case without this information. They learned it from the papers after the trial was over. Many Ottawans were outraged, even though Morgan was convicted. What if the jury had found him not guilty without knowing about his past? The culprit that deprived them of this evidence, if it be a culprit at all, was the similar fact evidence rule.

The similar fact evidence rule also caused problems for the Crown in the recent decision of R. v. Khan.[5] On 11 September 1990 the body of Mr. Khan's sister, Bibi, was found in a freezer in his Manitoba home. There were no signs of injury on her body. The coroner listed the cause of death as "consistent with asphyxia." Not surprisingly, the police found the death suspicious enough to investigate. How could she have ended up in the freezer? It was remotely possible, they figured, that Bibi had been reaching in for the fish sticks when she fell forward into the freezer and the lid dropped shut, thereby preventing her escape, but that was unlikely. They even considered the possibility of suicide, although terminal freezer burn is not a popular choice among those anxious to shed their mortal coil. No. The most sensible scenario was that her brother had tossed her in and sat on the lid until she stopped banging, a theory that appealed to the police, given that Mr. Khan held large insurance policies on Bibi's life.

The insurance companies joined the police in their scepticism about how Bibi died and refused to pay up. But the police, hampered by that niggling concept of proof beyond a reasonable doubt, finally decided not to lay charges because they believed they could not prove their case. The companies settled with Mr. Khan for a total of $137,500, which no doubt enabled him to keep up the insurance payments on his wife, Sureta.

On 4 January 1994 Sureta was also found dead in Khan's home. She died not in the freezer, but in the bathtub. There were no signs of injury and, again, the cause of death was listed as being "consistent with asphyxia." This time the police decided they had to charge Khan. Things were getting out of hand and the insurance companies were raising Cain. Coupled with all the other similarities, in each of the two cases the home had been locked at the time of the woman's death, Khan had discovered the body, and each woman had a therapeutic or sub-therapeutic level of drugs in her system.

The problem the Crown had was that it could not link Khan directly to either of the deaths, and there was no evidence of foul play. The Crown banked on the fact that a jury, hearing about the two similar suspicious deaths, each of which Khan stood to benefit from, would conclude that he had killed both women. One mysterious death of an insured relative might be possible to swallow, but two? It just smelled too bad, and a jury would be sure to see that. The Crown was right. After the trial, Khan was convicted on both counts. That conviction was overturned, however, because, according to the Manitoba Court of Appeal, the jury should not have been allowed to consider the circumstances surrounding Bibi's death when deciding whether he had killed Sureta, and it should not have been permitted to consider the circumstances surrounding Sureta's death when judging the charge involving Bibi. Each charge should have been decided on its own evidence. As it did in the Morgan case, the evidence failed to meet the similar fact evidence rule.[6]

Most of us would consider the excluded information to be relevant in both the Morgan case and the Khan case. No doubt Justice McKinnon appreciated the relevance of the evidence he excluded in the Morgan case. The Manitoba Court of Appeal also recognized that, as a matter of logic and human experience, the two incidents together increased the odds that Khan was a murderer, yet still they ruled that the evidence should not have been given to the jury:

There can be little doubt that the manner of Bibi's death, even without the evidence as to the death of Sureta, would arouse suspicion against the accused in the mind of a reasonable man. The facts proved as to the death of Sureta would certainly tend to deepen that suspicion, and might well tilt the balance against the accused in the estimation of a jury. It by no means follows that this evidence ought to be admitted.[7]

Because of the similar fact evidence rule, relevant evidence, information that could influence the decision of a reasonable person, was thrown out.

This sort of thing compromises the basic principle of the law of evidence. That principle holds that judges and juries should be allowed to consider any relevant and material information in coming to their decision. The reason is obvious. Truth is given high premium in a criminal trial. As Justice Cory said in a recent decision:

The ultimate aim of any trial, criminal or civil, must be to seek and to ascertain the truth. In a criminal trial the search is undertaken to determine whether the accused before the court is, beyond a reasonable doubt, guilty of the crime of which he is charged.

. . .

[T]he modern trend has been to admit all relevant and probative evidence and allow the trier of fact to determine the weight [or importance] which should be given to that evidence, in order to arrive at a just result . . . [T]his is most likely to be achieved when the decision makers have all the relevant probative information before them.[8]

Of course. Would a scientist attempt to explore a proposition of fact while blinding herself to relevant information? That would be a fundamental breach of the scientific method. Although a criminal trial is not and cannot be a scientific search for the truth because of our accusatorial system and our commitment to procedural fairness, we nonetheless accept that, as a starting point, we should try to get as much relevant information as possible before the decision maker. Judges and juries, when called on to make decisions about facts, should be given all the facts. They should not be blinded to them.

While common sense suggests that the best way to discover the truth is to give full access to information, the fact is that our rules of evidence tend to perform the opposite function. Almost all of them are exceptions to the basic principle of access to information. Instead of allowing judges and juries to consider information, they tend to define kinds of information that we will not allow them to have. The rules of evidence, the ultimate technicalities in our legal system, tend to be exclusionary for two reasons. They exclude evidence either because there are compelling reasons of policy that are believed to be more important than getting at the truth (a theme I will discuss in chapter 10) or they exclude evidence because experience has shown that the kind of proof being offered is not, in fact, helpful. Indeed, it is likely to prevent accurate decisions from being made.

Take, for example, an involuntary confession made by an accused person. How many of the confessions secured under rack and screw by the Courts of High Commission and Star Chamber were likely to have been truthful ones? It is not only torture that can elicit a false confession. In Toronto last year, a security guard named Jeremy Foster confessed to involvement in a series of sexual attacks so he could put an end to an all-night interrogation. After spending close to a week in jail, he was released after DNA tests cleared him.[9] Under pressure, he confessed to horrendous crimes that he did not commit. For this reason, involuntary confessions — those where the police use threats or promises to extract confessions, or use oppressive tactics to break the will of the accused — are not admissible in evidence. In such cases, the decision makers are prevented from hearing about those confessions, not to keep the truth from them but to prevent unjust convictions. Even though most of us, if called on to decide, would rather be told that the accused had confessed, experience has shown that we are more likely to convict falsely if we have been advised of involuntary confessions. They are therefore thrown out, like the garbage they are.

This is the same reason why triers of fact cannot be allowed, in the ordinary case, to learn about the past criminal conduct or character of the person they are trying. It is why we have the similar fact evidence rule. Like the confession rule, it exists not to hide the truth, but to prevent wrongful convictions.

The first reason why bad character evidence can mislead has to do with how simple-minded our reasoning about character can be. The relevance of raw character evidence rests, by nature, in prejudice and generalization. Consider what happened to a young clarinet player not long ago in Queensville, Ontario, a small town about thirty-five miles north of Toronto. A nine-year-old girl, his next door neighbour, went missing, ultimately to be found murdered. It was not long before the police investigation focused on this young man, initially for no reason other than that he was, according to notes taken by one of the officers, a "weird-type guy." He seemed to be just the kind of person who would abduct and murder a young child. When the FBI did a profile of the likely killer, in the minds of the officers it matched the young man, fortifying their "instincts."[10] At his first trial, the Crown even sought to use psychiatric evidence that he had a mental disorder, schizophrenia, to suggest that he was the type to commit this kind of attack. Well, the fact is that he was not the type, and, of course, he did not do it. Simple-minded prejudices about how the world turns contributed immensely to the mood in which this man, Guy Paul Morin, was so aggressively prosecuted that evidence was suppressed, testimony was manipulated into perjury to make it more effective, the importance of expert forensic evidence was exaggerated, and an innocent man was ultimately convicted wrongfully of being a killer and a depraved sexual predator. "He is the kind of person" is a shaky, dangerous foundation on which to solve crimes.

Apart from our penchant for simplifying life by painting things with broad strokes, there are a number of other bases for believing that proof of other criminal conduct or bad character can distort the outcome of criminal cases. The risk begins with the investigation. The fact is that police officers, as a matter of human experience, recognize that criminal offences are likely to be committed by practised criminals. When they have an eye-witness to any kind of crime, the police head directly to the mug-books to see if the witness can identify the offender. They do not take eye-witnesses to high school yearbooks or catalogues. They do not walk with them through crowded malls, or take them to entertainment venues where people tend to congregate in large numbers. They take them to the place that is most likely to yield fruit — to the pictures of experienced criminals. They start from the assumption, where identity is in issue, that the perpetrator is likely to be a criminal. By the same token, the first thing they do when there is a random sexual offence is to investigate known sexual offenders. They do the same with burglaries and robberies. They even do this in the movies. Who can forget the first response of the police captain in *Casablanca* when informed that there had been an assassination: "Round up the usual suspects." Looking at the usual suspects has an undeniable logic to it, but it is also extremely risky. Without question, the usual suspects are the people most likely to be falsely accused.

The logic in commencing police investigations with persons who, based on their records, are the type to commit the offence being investigated does not extend to the conduct of the criminal trial. It is not appropriate to commence a trial by identifying the accused as the criminal type. We are meant to start the trial from the presumption that the accused is innocent, not from the premise that "Well, he has done it before." Moreover, in our system the accused is entitled to be tried on the specific allegation before the court, according to the evidence relating to that charge. If we were to allow his past criminal activities to be proved, there is a risk that the judge or jury will become confused between the incidents, mixing up the facts of the previous criminal conduct with the evidence relating to the alleged offence. Far more important is the fact that we would be lowering the threshold of conviction.

I recall, several years ago, while driving home from court one evening, reflecting on an impaired driving case I had just won as a prosecutor. Something occurred to me that made me wonder whether I had obtained the conviction of the right man. I came into the house quite troubled and expressed my concerns to my wife, who is the epitome of a fair and reasonable person. In relating my story to her I made mention of the fact that the man had a number of prior impaired driving convictions. Her words of solace were as follows: "Don't worry, David. Even if he didn't do it this time, think of how many times he did and got away with it." I am sure she was right. I would bet my Bob Dylan collection that the police had not caught the man every time he ventured onto the roads in the company of "Jack Daniels." This was extremely seductive logic. Thinking that maybe he did owe us at least one conviction, I felt a tiny bit better, until I thought about it further. The problem with this "Ya win some, ya lose some" philosophy is that, while it may provide some rough brand of justice, it is not justice according to law, the only kind that the administration of justice can really afford to dole out. What kind of a legal system justifies throwing people in jail because they may have committed crimes for which they have not been caught? Ours is a system in which one of the fundamental principles is that the accused should be convicted solely on the specific allegation that is being made.

Then there is the risk of prejudice through emotion. Many decent people react to criminal behaviour with disgust. I do, and I feel entirely justified about it. But this, too, is dangerous. There is a risk that if too much is learned about what the accused person has done on other occasions, some of us will become so outraged that our emotion might overtake our reason. If we learned, for example, that Brett Morgan had strangled a young woman for no good reason, screaming "Die, you bitch, die," as he did, and that he had abused and choked the other women in his life, the outcome of charges involving Louise Ellis may have turned on our anger and hatred for what he is rather than on the proof of what he did. In the enlightening prose of one judge, proof of bad character, particularly proof of prior criminal acts, can "add more heat than light."[11] I feel much more confident about the Morgan conviction knowing that the jury was not given the inflammatory details of his propensity for violence against women. Justice McKinnon had been right to exclude the evidence. Without question, allowing the Crown to prove past criminal conduct lowers the requisite degree of caution required for a safe conviction, potentially confuses the trier of fact, and puts the accused in the difficult if not impossible position of having to defend more than one allegation at the same time.

For all these reasons, we do not permit proof to be presented where it reveals other discreditable conduct of accused persons. We do this not to hide the truth from judges and juries. Strange as it may seem, we exclude this relevant evidence to keep them from coming to the wrong conclusion, primarily because we are concerned that they will make too much of the evidence. It is best simply to keep it from them.

As the *Makin* case demonstrates, the bar on proving past acts of misconduct is not an absolute one. There are times when we allow evidence revealing the bad character or criminality of the accused to be presented. If the evidence goes beyond proving the general fact that the accused is the kind of person to commit this kind of crime, and it is so compelling that it is justifiable to run the risk that the evidence may be given exaggerated importance, we will let it in. As is often the case, this point can be demonstrated most clearly by relying on an extreme example. Bear with me, then, because the best one I can think of comes from the McCauley Culkin movie *Home Alone*. You remember McCauley Culkin, the short blond kid with generous ears who earned more money by the time he was eleven than you or I will ever see.

The two burglars whom Culkin terrorizes in the film had this "m.o.," or *modus operandi*, for those of us who are *au courant* with the trade lingo. Every time they broke into a house, one of them plugged the sink and turned the water on. It was their calling card. At the end of the film they are captured burglarizing a house, with the water gushing all over the floor. The tall goofy one with the nail hole through his foot and the iron burn on his forehead tells the police they have arrested the "wet bandits." Of course, this confession enabled the police instantaneously to solve all the other burglaries where houses had been flooded. This peculiar habit of the burglars linked them to each of those cases. Had this been a real case, you can be sure that proof of their last burglary would be admissible on each of their other charges. It would be admitted because this evidence is not informative merely because it shows that these are the kind of people who burgle. It performs the much more compelling, distinctive function of demonstrating their guilt for each burglary according to the reasoning that these burglaries are linked by an unusual *modus operandi*; they are, therefore, likely to have been committed by the same people, and, since these men use that peculiar *modus operandi*, they are likely to have committed each of these crimes.

This is a straightforward illustration of the kind of reasoning that was used in the *Makin* case to justify allowing the Crown to try to prove, on the murder charge involving Horace Amber Murray, that the Makins had killed twelve other babies. Unlike the "wet bandits," however, *Makin* was not a case where identification of those responsible was the key issue. The police could link the Makins to Horace without difficulty. The real work of the similar fact evidence in the Makin prosecution was to help prove that Horace had been murdered. It did so because the sheer number of dead babies and the circumstances in which they were obtained and disposed of showed that the Makins had been killing them intentionally. It gave rise to the irresistible inference that the Makins were engaged in a systematic course of conduct in which they obtained infants from their mothers for money, murdered them, and buried them. No other reasonable inference flowed from the evidence. Although it was remotely possible that Horace was the exception, expiring perhaps from SIDS or some other medical calamity, the prospect of that being so was undermined by the evidence that he was healthy when the Makins received him; that he had been in their care for, at most, two days before he died; that the Makins had sought to conceal their true identity when obtaining him; and that they attempted to conceal his death after it occurred. What the similar fact evidence did was to increase to the point of proof beyond a reasonable doubt the prospect that they had murdered Horace Amber Murray. It did not do so solely according to the general inference that they were the kind of persons to commit murder. Its relevance rested on the more specific inference that babies were being murdered in a systematic fashion, in circumstances strikingly similar to those young Horace had found himself in, increasing the prospect that he had met the same fate.

There are, of course, others who disagree with this assessment. They argue that, in truth, the only relevance of the evidence in the *Makin* case was to prove that they were killers. Jurors would simply reason that since they had killed before, they likely killed Horace. They argue that the kind of reasoning I have used, which seeks to distinguish between kinds of inferences, is too refined to be real, and that the "similar fact evidence" rule is a fraud if it purports to prevent character evidence from being used to conclude that the accused is the kind of person to commit the crime. In substance, they argue, this is what we almost invariably do when we let this kind of proof in. They can point to many cases where it is, indeed, difficult to disagree. There is strong reason to believe, for example, that this is how the rule is in fact being used in sexual offence cases where we want to prove that "Daddy" was sexually assaulting one child, by showing that he was also doing it to the other children. We often let this kind of proof in simply because the allegation seems to ring truer if it is being made by more than one person.

Those who make these arguments do not do so to suggest that we should never allow proof of prior acts of criminal conduct or bad character. They do it in support of their contention that we should have a simple rule that enables a judge to let such evidence in if it seems important enough; if its "probative value" outweighs the "risk of prejudice" it presents, it should be let in even if it does no more than show the propensity of the accused to commit the kind of crime in question.

Indeed, even the *Khan* case, although not analysed as such, seems to turn on the fact that the evidence, though relevant, is simply not compelling enough to allow in. The Manitoba Court of Appeal said that it was excluding the similar fact evidence for the more technical reason that there was no independent evidence that Khan caused the death of either woman, and no independent proof of the cause of death of either woman that could be linked to an act of murder. All that is true, but the same thing can be said about *Makin*; there was no independent evidence that the Makins, or either of them, had caused the death of young Horace, nor was there any proof of how he or any of the other babies had died. It is hard to resist concluding that what made the evidence admissible in *Makin* and inadmissible in *Khan* was the simple fact that by dearth of the sheer number of victims, the inference of murder was much stronger in *Makin* than it was in *Khan*. Had Mr. Khan left thirteen sisters and wives behind who had died from apparent asphyxiation, each leaving him the proceeds of their insurance, I suspect that the Manitoba Court of Appeal would have found a way to let the evidence in.

This is not meant as a criticism of the Manitoba Court of Appeal. Even when he proclaimed his famous technical formula for the similar fact evidence rule, Lord Herschell said in *Makin*:

> In their Lordships' opinion the principles which must govern the decision of the case are clear, though the application of them is by no means free from difficulty. . . . The statement of these general principles is easy, but it is obvious that it may often be very difficult to draw the line and to decide whether a particular piece of evidence is on the one side or the other.[12]

To a lawyer, this kind of comment is an admission that a rule is so complex technically that we will often get it wrong or at least disagree among ourselves about whether we have it right. When we see appellate judges make this point, we tend to duck. One thing we lawyers have learned about wise technicalities, though, even when they tax our abilities and challenge us, is that the process of trying is important. If we did not have the similar fact evidence rule and simply declared open season on such proof, we would be far worse off. By struggling to apply the rule, we run an appreciably smaller risk of distorting the truth by convicting the innocent.

Hearsay and Truth

There are many other rules of evidence that prevent decision makers from learning about facts so they will be better able to come to an accurate decision. The most significant one is the hearsay rule — the one that prevents a witness from telling us what he has heard someone else say. Generally speaking, we are interested in what the witness knows, not what he has heard. So, for example, in the *Makin* trial, we would allow Mrs. Patrick to tell us that, on 5 July 1892, John Makin brought a sick-looking baby around to her house and said it was Horace, but we would not allow Amber Murray to testify that "Mrs. Patrick told me that on 5 July 1892 John Makin brought a sick-looking baby around and said it was Horace Murray." The reason for the rule is essentially that if we do not hear about Makin's visit directly from Mrs. Patrick, we can have no confidence that it happened the way she said, or perhaps at all. We would want Mrs. Patrick to tell us this information under oath, subject to a perjury prosecution for lying, and we would want an opportunity to watch her as she said it so we could judge her demeanour. It is not enough for her to tell this story to Amber Murray out of court, and then to have Amber Murray repeat it while she is under oath. We are effectively being asked to rely on Mrs. Patrick, and we should have her oath that it is true. But most important, we would want to be able to cross-examine her about Makin's visit.

Cross-examination is the procedure used when a lawyer tries to test the truth or accuracy of what the opposing party's witnesses are saying. It is extremely unpleasant to have your word challenged at every turn, but it is during cross-examination that the decision maker gets the data needed to decide whether to rely on what a witness is claiming. There is no sense asking Amber Murray questions about how confident Mrs. Patrick was about the date when John Makin came around, or about what exactly he was supposed to have said to suggest that the baby he had with him was Horace, or about how much raspberry cordial she had guzzled before he arrived for the visit. As a general rule, we need the person whose information we are being asked to rely on to come forward, so we can obtain the information needed to evaluate what he or she has to say.

This rule, too, can result in the loss of information that may appear crucial to the case. But for a sage change in the law, it would have happened in the murder trial of Victor Nikolaevich Kharsekin, who was charged with a killing that occurred on the *Grigoriy Lysenko*, a Russian trawler that was anchored at the time in Bay St. George near Stephenville, Newfoundland. On 6 May 1991 Ivan Pedyura, a crew member on that ship, staggered into the ship's medical centre, bleeding profusely from a wound to his neck. He was holding a knife and he was pleading for help. Dr. Zuyko, the chief doctor, asked him who had wounded him. Pedyura responded, as best he could, "I was wounded by the second electrical mechanic," or words to that effect. Pedyura then lost consciousness. After fifteen or twenty minutes, Dr. Zuyko managed to revive him. He was told to communicate by nodding or using his eyes, but not to talk. Some thirty minutes later, the maintenance mechanic, Valeriy Kin, arrived. Pedyura was still conscious and had demonstrated that he could understand the questions he was being asked. Kin inquired who had stabbed Pedyura. The doctor responded, based on what Pedyura had said earlier, "The second mechanic." Pedyura was observed to be nodding in agreement. Kin replied "Kharsekin? Is that Kharsekin?" and Pedyura again nodded affirmatively. A short time later, Pedyura lost consciousness for the final time and died.

Kharsekin was ultimately arrested and confessed to the stabbing. After his first trial he must have written home, advising everyone in Russia that if you are going to kill someone, there is no better place to do it than in Canada. Both his confession and Pedyura's last words were thrown out, leaving the Crown with no case. Had this happened in his mother country he would have been convicted and dropped into the Gulag faster than he could have said "Solzhenitsyn."

Now, the confession was thrown out for reasons that have nothing to do with the search for the truth. It was dumped because Kharsekin's right to counsel had been violated. He was told that he had a right to a lawyer. This information was given to him in Russian and he apparently understood it, even though the language of human rights is not familiar in his homeland. The problem is that he was not told that Pedyura had died. This omission violated his right to counsel because it invalidated the choice he made not to bother speaking to a lawyer before making a statement. The assumption, as questionable as it may be, is that while he might have been prepared to give up his rights and confess simply to plunging his knife into another man's throat, he might not have done so if we had only had the decency to tell him that the man had died from the wound. This rule, which causes us to throw out dependable evidence because of policy reasons, is a bit hard to take, but it should not distract us now. I will discuss it in chapter 10. For now, our concern is with the hearsay, the statements made by Pedyura.

These Pedyura statements were "hearsay" because the Crown was seeking to have the jury believe Pedyura's word that Kharsekin was the stabber, even though, through no fault of his own, Pedyura was not going to be the one to tell us this. We would be getting Pedyura's information second hand through Dr. Zuyko and from the dentist who overheard them, Maketsgali Teneldikova, as well as from Valeriy Kin. None of these people were able to answer relevant questions that we would have asked Pedyura, such as whether he had some motive to accuse Kharsekin falsely, or whether he was even in the position to identify the stabber. So the trial judge held that Pedyura's statements were inadmissible.

To be sure, these statements were hearsay. But not all hearsay evidence is inadmissible. Over the years we have developed dozens of exceptions to the rule. For example, we have exceptions allowing business records to be proved, allowing voluntary confessions made by accused persons to be admitted, allowing for some admissions made by persons against their interest to be recounted, and allowing official government documents like death certificates and birth certificates to be filed. The Crown had argued that the statements by Pedyura fit into some of the established hearsay exceptions and therefore should have been received. It therefore appealed Kharsekin's acquittal.

There are two long-standing hearsay exceptions that have relevance to Pedyura's statements. The first, of ancient vintage, applies in homicide cases. Statements made by a person while in the hopeless, settled expectation of death, which are about the death, can be admitted even though they are hearsay. The theory is that what persons who are dying say, can be relied on because they are unlikely to want to meet their maker with lies on their lips. The idea is that even agnostics and atheists are likely to hedge their bets in their final moments, so that any natural instinct they may have for stretching the truth will be stilled. Since the statements are made in circumstances that virtually guarantee their reliability, there is no need to exclude them, even if they are hearsay. Given that they are reliable, we lose little or nothing by not being able to cross-examine the maker, who, of course, is otherwise disposed by the time of the trial.

My own view is that this rationale is rather silly. Even if we assume that atheists and agnostics do hedge their bets in their final hour, the rule does not account for the fact that lots of dying people have a hard time staying on the right page, so to speak. They are as apt to mutter nonsense as to be carefully considering whether it is prudent to tell one last lie, for old time's sake. But this is an old rule, so in a profession that gives legitimacy to ideas simply because of their antiquity, why quibble? The important point for present purposes is that this rule did not help the Crown in any event. It did not help because it is as narrow as it is old. The rule applies only to those dying declarants who know they are history before they speak. If they still hope to survive, the pressure to speak the truth will not be strong enough to sanitize their statements. The challenge for the Crown is in proving this point. The first hurdle is that compassionate folk witnessing a death do not usually say to the poor unfortunate, "Boy, Sam, you look like hell. You've had the biscuit. You're done for." They say things like "We will get you a doctor" or "You are going to be all right." Most statements made by the dying will not, therefore, meet this exception. But even in the absence of white lies about the prospect of survival, there must be a solid basis for concluding that the deceased has given up. In *R. v. Bedingfield*,[13] in 1879, a woman identified in the case only as a laundress, who had been rejecting Harry Bedingfield's boorish sexual advances and who had been threatened by him because of her refusal to accommodate him, found herself alone in a room with him. Moments later she staggered from the room with her throat cut so deep that her death was both imminent and assured. Anyone looking at her would have known as much. To read the decision is to be amazed at the number of pipes, veins, arteries, and other crucial tubes in the human neck, for they are all listed as having been cut by Harry. Still, she managed the words "See what Harry has done to me," and then expired. The jury never got to hear those words because, as Chief Justice Cockburn said, "at the time she made the statement she had no time to consider that she knew [she was dying]." In other words, she was not under the settled hopeless expectation of death that would give her words the necessary stamp of reliability to allow them to be proved.

As it happens, Harry cut his own throat as well, but not with the same vigour he had managed when attacking her, and he survived. On the other evidence against him, he was convicted, allowed to heal, and then hanged, but the "dying declaration" exception was from that point on made so narrow as to rarely, if ever, apply. It could not help the Crown in *Kharsekin* because there was no basis for concluding that Pedyura had given up all hope of this world.

There was another more recent but well-established exception that also seemed to the Crown to hold out promise in *Kharsekin* — the exception for "spontaneous utterances." The idea here is that some statements are made under such pressure of overwhelming events that the speaker will not have an opportunity to concoct a story. This modern exception would surely have permitted the words of the victim to have been admitted in the *Bedingfield* case because there is no way, given her predicament, that she would have thought, on her way out the door, "Good. My throat is cut. Now is my chance to frame Harry."

In another case, this exception was used to allow it to be proved at the murder trial of her husband that Mrs. Ratten called the operator from her home in the small country town of Echuca in Victoria, Australia, at 1:15 p.m. on 7 May 1970 and said in a hysterical voice, "Get me the police, please." That call had been cut off, and at 1:20 p.m. a police officer rang the house to find out what was going on. Mrs. Ratten was dead by that time, for Mr. Ratten told the officer so. Mr. Ratten would later testify at his trial that she had been accidentally shot while he was cleaning his shotgun. He knew full well that he would have an easier time trying to sell this bull puck if the jury did not learn about the 1:15 call; unless she was a psychic who had prognosticated the "accident" before it happened, the panicked request for the police by Mrs. Ratten made it obvious that her husband was in the process of threatening her immediately before the fatal shot. So Mr. Ratten wanted to keep that little detail from the jury on the basis that what his wife had said about wanting the police was hearsay. The Privy Council did not believe that it was, for reasons too complicated to discuss here, but it held that even if it was hearsay, given that she was under the pressure of a threat on her life when she placed her call, it was pretty unlikely that she took that opportunity to make a crank call to the emergency operator. Her claim to need the police was trustworthy enough to admit, even if it was hearsay, because it "was being forced from [her] by an overwhelming pressure of [the] contemporary event."[14] It was a spontaneous utterance, and therefore admissible pursuant to an exception to the hearsay rule.

Obviously, it would have been preposterous to have excluded Mrs. Ratten's statement. But as a general rule, the spontaneous exception rule is suspect. While it is true that persons caught up in the pressure of a significant event are not likely to lie, psychologists will tell you that people are less apt to observe events accurately in such circumstances. As a general rule designed to identify trustworthy statements, it is therefore troubling.

Be that as it may, the spontaneous exclamation exception did not help the Crown get Pedyura's statements in either. His statements were not forced from him by the pressure of the moment. He did not run down the hall in hysterics, screaming, "Help me. Kharsekin stabbed me. Please help me, help me." He was asked questions and he narrated past, albeit recent events. So the exception was not met and it could not form the basis for admitting the hearsay.

I know, as a matter of common sense, what Pedyura said seems to be entirely reliable, even if we cannot wedge it into either of these classic exceptions. He was conscious and lucid at all times. It is obvious that the incident had just happened so, even if we allow for the preposterous assumption that, with the passage of time, one is apt to forget who it was who stuck in the knife, there was absolutely no risk of Pedyura misremembering who did it. More important, he did not give some long, self-serving narrative in which he sought to explain why Kharsekin had stabbed him and why it was all Kharsekin's fault. He simply identified the stabber. As for the risk of a lie, it is impossible to imagine that Pedyura, while galloping off to the infirmary with his neck slashed open, was thinking, "Now is my chance to get that s.o.b. Kharsekin. Even though Rasputin Ivanovitch Ilya Gorbachev stabbed me, I think I will blame Kharsekin." What, then, about the risk that he was mistaken about who his assailant was? There were, I should now tell you, blood stains on Kharsekin's pants matching Pedyura's blood type. What kind of a legal system would throw out this kind of evidence when the witness, Pedyura, cannot be called to testify? Thankfully, not ours.

The door to the admission of the evidence in *Kharsekin* was opened in the sad case of Dr. Abdullah Khan. Not the Khan who is alleged to have killed his sister and wife, but the medical doctor who sexually assaulted a three-and-a-half-year-old girl while her mother, who had left the child in the doctor's office, was getting ready for her physical.[15] The sexual assault of this child came to light approximately fifteen minutes after the mother and daughter had left Dr. Khan's office. The child's mother was driving along, carrying on a conversation with the child:

"So you were talking to Dr. Khan, were you? What did he say?"

"He asked me if I wanted a candy. I said yes. And do you know what?"

"What?"

"He said 'open your mouth.' And do you know what? He put his birdie in my mouth, shook it and peed in my mouth."

"Are you sure?"

"Yes."

"You're not lying to me, are you?"

"No. He put his birdie in my mouth. And he never did give me the candy."

This is a hearsay conversation, but is there any doubt about its truth? This was a spontaneous statement, made by a young child immediately after leaving the office of a doctor whom she has no motive to lie about, which contained an age-appropriate description of a sexual act that would be too precocious for most three-year-olds even to contemplate. Best of all, it was expressed with a naivety that brings tears to one's eyes: "And he never did give me the candy." Any doubt at all it is true? None in my books, but if you are still hesitating about accepting it, which I suspect you are not, you should know that she was picking on a wet spot on her sleeve while talking to her mother. When analysed, it proved to be a mixture of semen and saliva.

At his trial, Dr. Khan argued that the conversation was inadmissible hearsay evidence. The trial judge agreed. It was clearly hearsay, and it could not fit the "spontaneous exclamation" exception because too much time had passed and the child was not under the force of pressure when she spoke. In her precious innocence, she was neither shocked nor startled. The evidence was therefore disregarded. To make matters worse, when the young child, by then five, was called to testify, the trial judge held that she was not a competent witness. She was too immature to provide reliable testimony. Dr. Khan was therefore acquitted. All the evidence against him had been booted.

Fortunately, the Crown appealed. Anxious not to lose reliable evidence, the Court of Appeal wedged the statement into the spontaneous exclamation exception, even though it clearly did not fit. The Supreme Court of Canada did much better. It changed the law of hearsay forever. It held that in any case where hearsay evidence is necessary because the witness cannot reproduce that information through testimony, the out-of-court statement will be admissible if it is sufficiently reliable to justify giving to the decision maker for consideration. It does not matter whether it falls into one of the established exceptions. If it is necessary and reliable, the evidence can be admitted.

In *Khan* it was a slam-dunk. If the child could not testify as a witness, the statement was necessary. Moreover, there was ample basis for the decision maker to accept that it was true. Sadly, Dr. Khan, seeing the writing on the wall, fled the country before he could be retried. The most we could do to him was remove his licence to practise medicine *in absentia*. What the case did for the law, though, was to break down barriers. It was the basis on which the Newfoundland Court of Appeal ordered a new trial for Kharsekin. The statements by Pedyura had to necessarily be admitted in their hearsay form because the poor man had died, and they were reliable enough to give to a jury. So the case was retried on a more complete factual record. Even with that record, though, there was still too much uncertainty about what happened on 6 May 1991, deep in the bowels of the *Grigoriy Lysenko*. Kharsekin was acquitted, and, when last seen, is reported to have been firmly of the view that Canada has the best criminal justice system in the world.

There are two things I hoped to illustrate in this chapter. The first is that there are many technicalities in the law of evidence that do indeed keep certain facts from the decision makers, but that often this is done not to hide the truth from them but to assist them in coming to it. It is entirely defensible to do this in some cases, such as where the information will do little more than paint the accused as some contemptible jerk who can call for no decency or restraint when it comes to determining guilt. The similar fact evidence rule, complex though it be, is necessary in these cases to ensure that if that contemptible jerk is convicted, it is because of what he is proved to have done, not because of who he is. The hearsay rule performs the same role. Remember, "hearsay" is the foundation for rumour and gossip, and most of it has no place in a court of law where the judge or jury members must carefully assess what they are told before choosing to believe it. Hearsay evidence is normally rejected because it will not often help us to find the truth. There is some information that we are just better off without.

The second point I hoped to make is that we are becoming much better at using the law of evidence to pursue the truth. Instead of using the time-honoured practice of relying on precedent to determine whether to admit hearsay evidence, the Supreme Court of Canada, to its credit, found a way to attempt to identify reliable hearsay on a case-by-case basis. Without this tool, much reliable evidence is simply buried. The Court's move to provide increased access to reliable evidence is not restricted to the law of hearsay. The Court in *Khan* also held that the young child should have been allowed to testify. It lowered the test of testimonial competence for child witnesses, and should, in my estimation, lower it even more, thereby allowing what children have to say to be judged on its own merits. It also crafted a rule that enables the statements of witnesses to be videotaped and taken on oath in advance of the trial, in case the witnesses become "forgetful" at trial, as frightened Crown witnesses often do. And in the case of *R. v. Nikolovski*, the Supreme Court of Canada further demonstrated its commitment to using the rules of proof to find the truth.

A video-camera at a Mac's Milk store caught a long and clear image of Nikolovski robbing the cashier, Mahmood Wahabzada. Wahabzada, the only witness, could not identify him in court, so the judge looked at the videotape and at the accused. Left in no doubt that Nikolovski was the robber, she convicted him. Of course, you might think, why would she let him off? A lawyer can think of lots of technical reasons why, but no good reasons, so the Supreme Court of Canada upheld the judge. The conviction stood. It was in this case that Justice Cory commented on the importance of giving decision makers access to relevant evidence, and it was here where he affirmed that the best way to find the truth, in most cases, will be to give the trier of fact all available information.

Dedicated pursuit of this principle will help to prevent people from getting away with murder, but it will do something that is even more important. Speaking specifically of the progress of scientific advances, Justice Cory made this point in *Nikolovski*:

> The admission of new types of evidence is often resisted at first and yet, later accepted as commonplace and essential to the task of truth finding. Fingerprint evidence may be the first example of scientific evidence leading to identification. Similarly, blood typing with its ever increasing refinements can be extremely helpful in identification. DNA testing is yet another example. It must never be forgotten that evidence of this type can serve to establish innocence just as surely and effectively as it may establish guilt. The case of Guy-Paul Morin serves as a constant reminder of this.[16]

The same is true of reliable, non-scientific evidence. It, too, can protect the truth and, in the process, protect the innocent. One of the complaints about the *Bedingfield* case when it was decided in 1879 was that, had the poor women uttered "See what Harry has driven me too," thereby indicating that she had committed suicide, the hearsay rule would have worked an injustice by excluding this evidence of Bedingfield's innocence. While there are times when we must hold back information to secure the truth, it cannot be forgotten that the path to justice is almost invariably through full knowledge. Rest easy. Our courts appear to be well aware of that.

Abandoning the Search for the Truth

N ew Year's Day 1985, 3:28 p.m, Cranbrook, British Columbia. He could hear the lawyer's voice over the black rotary phone that sat like a museum piece on the white linoleum table:

"Don't talk to them, Terry. I'm telling you. It can do you no good. You've said enough already. They are going to keep trying, but don't say anything more. Like I said, you have the right to remain silent. Use it. That's my advice to you. OK? You won't be helping yourself."

"Right."

When the call was done, Terry Burlingham sat there for a minute tugging at a loose thread on his jeans, spinning the black coil that hung from the handset of the phone. He got up from the table and moved over to the door, which he pushed open, motioning the police officers who were waiting outside the interview room. He was done. Detective Alan Green[1] and John Morrison stepped back in.

"He told me not to talk to you."

"Yeah?" Green smirked. "Big surprise."

But Burlingham had already told the police too much to suit a defence lawyer. When they had interviewed him earlier that morning, confronting him with the lies he had told them the day before about his whereabouts and what he had been wearing, he admitted that he had shot sixteen-year-old Brenda Hughes with a .410 gauge shotgun. He told them how he had broken into her house thinking no one was home, found her there, placed a pillow over the back of her head, pushed the gun up against the pillow, and just snuffed her out. He described the weapon he had used, saying he and a friend named Biddlecome had stolen two .410s during a break-in. He had sawed the barrel and stock off one of the guns, which he had used to kill Brenda.

Terry did not admit, however, that he had raped Brenda, although the evidence that he had was clear. Semen matching his blood type had been found in her vagina, her brother's bed had been disturbed, and her clothes were scattered on his bedroom floor. (Fibres from the sheets would ultimately be found on his clothes.) Her parents and her brother, who had left her alive and well when they went to church earlier that morning, had returned home to find Brenda naked and dead.

Instead of treating Terry like the animal they thought he was, the officers kept their tone conversational. It was all matter of fact. They knew there was nothing to gain by treating him like dirt. They still needed him to believe they were on his side.

"Terry. You told us you would give us the gun. Are you still going to do that?"

"I guess."

Not long after, Burlingham sat impassively in the back of the unmarked police cruiser as it pulled into the driveway of his parents' home. What would his parents say? They were already panicked enough when the police questioned him the day before, and things got worse when they returned that morning and arrested him for murder.

As he expected, their anxiety turned into absolute grief when he led the police downstairs and one of the officers came back up carrying the sawed-off .410 in a clear plastic evidence bag. They had raised a killer. Somewhere along the way, the boy they had once cradled, the boy that people once said was so cute and patted on the head, had grown up to be a cold-blooded killer.

Ignoring his lawyer's advice, Burlingham took the police to the Hughes residence, and showed them how, only two days before, he had ended the life of a girl who was just entering the prime of life. The police videotaped his re-enactment. In it he was ready to admit he had executed the girl in cold blood, but he could not bring himself to admit he had raped her. Murder was something his twisted sensibilities would allow him to acknowledge, but rape? He couldn't bring himself to admit that.

The police were pleased to have solved the Hughes killing so quickly, but they were not done with Terry Burlingham. On 9 October 1984, after Burlingham and his friend Biddlecome had stolen the guns, the body of twenty-year-old Denean Worms was found naked in a gravel pit in Cranbrook. She, too, had been shot in the back of the head at contact range with a shotgun — probably a small-gauge weapon like a .410. Like Brenda Hughes, she had semen in her vagina. Burlingham was the

Cranbrook killer — no doubt about it. They just had to prove it. In those days, before the forensic use of DNA evidence, they could not make an air-tight link through science. They had to build a case the hard way.

The following Friday, Officers Green and Morrison pulled into the police station in Kimberley. Burlingham was being kept there because the Cranbrook cells were closed for construction. He was brought to them in an interview room where, for the next several hours, they tried to convince him to admit he had killed Denean Worms. They had the tape recorder going. Burlingham, who had spoken to his lawyer again, was now convinced he should not speak to the police, but the officers were intent on changing that:

TB: He told me not to say anything.

AG: That's right. And lawyers always say that —. This is the same man, Terry, who is telling you that he won't defend you unless you give him $15,000. Now it's not our, y'know, it's, it's not for us to deny you, if you want to make a call to your lawyer, if you want to talk to him that's fine . . .

So, 100 percent up to you, if you want to talk to him about what's happening now, fine, if you want to talk to him just about the fee and see what kind of a friend he is, that's all right too.

Burlingham phoned his lawyer back and was again told not to talk to the police. The lawyer said he was leaving town and would not be back until Monday, but he would talk to him then. Burlingham hung up and told the officers he was not supposed to talk. Still, the questioning continued. It continued for hours.

Officers Green and Morrison tried to appeal to Burlingham by pretending to be his friends. Green told Burlingham it would do him good to talk to somebody.

TB: Well, that's what I told you and I told him I pretty well got to talk to somebody about it. He said to talk to me about it.

AG: Talk to him? This is your friend who wants $15,000 out of you, and you're going to talk to him?

TB: — talk to him — . . .

AG: It hurts if that's what you think of us. That's all you think of us, after all —

And so it went. The officers described how hurt they were that Burlingham seemed to prefer his lawyer to them and how, for his own sake, he should get the whole thing off his chest. Still, Burlingham persisted in his refusal to come clean, although, after a time, his fortitude seemed to wane enough to keep the officers' interest:

> TB: Okay, well that's what I'm saying, I'd like to. I'm not turning around and telling you guys that I won't talk to you about this Denean murder. Like, I'm not going to turn around and say anything until I talk to him first. So, uh, okay.

But the interrogation continued. The officers repeatedly denigrated his lawyer, saying there was nothing he could do for Burlingham that they could not; asking him why he felt he could trust his lawyer, who had gone away for the weekend, more than he could trust them, given that they were staying there with him; saying that the lawyer was in it solely for the money ("Hmh. All he's really been worried about is money, money, money, eh?"), how he was not interested in getting Terry help, and even that lawyers were "fast-talkers."

The whole time, the officers simply ignored the many statements Burlingham made to the effect that he did not want to talk to them until he spoke to his lawyer. The officers pressed on about how, if he followed his lawyer's advice, he would not get the help he needed. They explained that unless he cleared the air now, his parents would just be getting over the shock of the first murder when they would learn of the second. Why not give it all to them at once so they could get over it? The same with his girlfriend. The whole story should come out so she could deal with it. And the parents and the terminally ill grandfather of Denean Worms. They deserved to know the details so they could find out if she was tortured or abused before she died. Still Burlingham said he wanted to wait to talk to his lawyer.

Then the police played their ace. So far, not all the lab reports were back, they said, but when they were, Burlingham would be sunk. They told him that because the reports were not yet back, they had authority to offer him a second-degree murder charge on the Worms killing instead of another first-degree murder charge, but that the offer would expire before his lawyer returned.[2]

The interview ended, with Burlingham holding fast. He was returned to the cells, but he was not left alone. The senior officer in charge of investigations visited him, telling him that, in light of his refusal to talk, the police were going to tear his mother's house apart in a search. Still he did not bend. Then Officers Green and Morrison arranged for Burlingham to meet with his girlfriend. He returned from that meeting and spoke with the investigators.

"If I can use the phone to talk to some other lawyer, I will tell you where the gun is."

"The gun?" thought Green. "I thought we had the gun. He must have used the other stolen shotgun on Denean."

Deal. Burlingham was taken to the phone and he called another lawyer, who also told him to say nothing. But Burlingham kept his word. A deal is a deal. Immediately after the phonecall, he piled into a police car with the investigating officers and, in the cold black of the winter evening, with tiny tornadoes of snow scurrying along the roadways, he directed the driver to Fort Steel bridge, which hung over the Kootenay River. Holding his collar shut, he leaned over the bridge and pointed out to the officers where, months before, during the red and amber fall, he had thrown the .410 he had used to kill Denean Worms into the black water below. The officers peered over the bridge at the sheet of ice that covered the river. They thanked him and told him he was doing the right thing. He then directed them to the gravel pit where he had executed a young woman for no other reason than to satiate his twisted lust. Finally, he took them to the last destination on their macabre tour — to the location where he had secreted Denean's naked body. It was now midnight. The police had their confession, and the next day, after police divers bored through the ice, they would have a rusting shotgun that would be found right where Burlingham said it would be.

While the police divers snaked along the bottom of the frozen river with their flashlights that next day, trying to fetch their clinching evidence, Burlingham, feeling refreshed after a night's sleep, spoke to his girlfriend again. He could not bring himself to tell her everything yet, but he admitted that he knew something about the killing of Denean Worms and that he had showed the police where the gun was. An hour later, back in his cell, Burlingham was visited by other "friends" he had made, the ones in blue he had been spending so much time with the last day or two. They feigned disappointed looks. Sounding like a couple of car salesmen, they told him they had bad news about the deal they had made to charge him only with second-degree murder for the Worms killing:

JM: I don't know if you're going to be very happy with the Crown, but what they've been saying is that uh . . . they said that [we] had no right to make any deals with you and they're taking the — you know it's probably no surprise to you — but they're taking the . . . the uh . . . line that we decide on what charges are laid.

TB: Ya, that's not very fair to me, though, is it? . . . I mean . . . promises were made to me and they're not being kept . . . . So, what you're telling me is that it's another murder one charge?

> JM: I'm telling ya is that — what I'm telling you is that the Crown
> will not let us make deals and they're . . . they're the ones that
> uh . . . will decide on those sort of things, so that the problem
> is . . . that they're not bound to go by and uh . . . Like I say, it's
> a piss off for everybody concerned.

Yes, it was a piss off, but not necessarily for everybody concerned. I doubt it upset the police too much, and I know the Crown shed no tears. They got their evidence and could still charge the man with first-degree murder. Only Burlingham and his lawyer would feel aggrieved. But when the courts got through with this part of the investigation, it would be the officers and a sizeable portion of the Canadian public who would be pissed off. They would be furious because the Supreme Court of Canada would ultimately throw out the confession about Denean Worms, the gun that was used to kill her, and the statements made by Burlingham to his girlfriend. They were to be excluded from evidence because of the Court's belief that admitting this evidence would "bring the administration of justice into disrepute." At his trial for the killing of Worms, the jury would be asked to decide whether he was guilty, without the benefit of this overwhelming proof.

The *Charter* and the Gatekeepers of the Law

Without question, the police had violated one of the most sacrosanct of all constitutional rights: the right to counsel. This is a right that Canadian courts do not fool with because, forgive my lack of humility, lawyers are the gateway to the enjoyment of all rights and freedoms. The law is complex. Only specialists understand what rights and freedoms you have when you are detained by the police, and what is at stake. The public perception is filled with misconceptions. For example, most Canadians who watch crime shows on American television probably believe that you have a right to have a lawyer present whenever the police question you, so that he can hold up his arm with the Rolex watch on it and say, "Don't answer that," every time the police ask a good question. But that is not the law in Canada. Once you have talked to a lawyer, the Canadian police are generally free to ask you questions after your lawyer has gone, or after you have hung up the phone. You are entitled to the advice of a lawyer, not his or her company. You need that advice to know you are entitled to the right to remain silent, the right not to do re-enactments, the right not to go into police lineups, the right not to give bodily samples other than in alcohol driving cases unless the police have a warrant, the right to be released if not charged within twenty-four hours, and the right, if charged, to be brought before a justice of the peace for a bail hearing within twenty-four hours. Even if you have a vague idea about how far these and your other rights go, you will need advice on how best to enjoy them in the circumstances. If you do not know what your rights are, they are useless to you, so you need a lawyer to explain them, even if "all he's really . . . worried about is money, money, money, eh."

After the police advise you of your right to counsel, they must refrain from asking you questions or seeking to use you as a source of evidence until you have had the opportunity to speak to a lawyer. If you understand the right to a lawyer and you decide not to talk to one, that is fine — they can start to question you or get you to provide breath samples and such. But unless you let the police know that you do not wish to do so, they are to wait until you have been given a reasonable chance to consult with counsel.[3] If they had delayed giving you your right to counsel until after they have questioned you, put you in a police lineup, or made you do a re-enactment, it would be too late. By the time you spoke to your lawyer you may have acted without appreciating your rights and obligations. Unless you clearly and competently disclaim your right to a lawyer, the police are supposed to suspend any efforts to use you as a source of information. The police discovered this obligation after the case of Ronald Charles Manninen went to the Supreme Court of Canada in the early days of the Charter.[4]

Manninen was apprehended on a tip, two days after a Mac's Milk store was robbed. When he was arrested, Manninen, who apparently had experience with this sort of thing before the *Charter* went into effect, was quite impressed when the officer took out his card containing the new-fangled *Charter* rights and read them to him. After the officer was done, Manninen responded, "It sounds like an American TV program." When the officer read the card out loud again, Manninen, without knowing it, spoke some magic words: "Prove it. I ain't saying anything until I see my lawyer. I want to see my lawyer."

Today, lawyers recognize that request as a signal to police officers everywhere to stop asking questions immediately and get the man a lawyer. But not back in 1982. After introductions were made (Q: Where is your address? A: Ain't got one), the officer cut to the chase with a key question:

Q: Where is the knife that you had along with this (showing the
       respondent the CO_2 gun found in the car) when you ripped off
       the Mac's Milk on Wilson Avenue?

Manninen saw it was a trick question, but apparently missed the real trick:

A: He's lying. When I was in the store I only had the gun. The knife was in the tool box.

As far as exculpatory statements go, most defence lawyers would rate this one a bummer.

A few moments later, Officer McIver showed Manninen two knives that he found in the car:

Q: What are these for?

A: What the fuck do you think they are for? Are you fucking stupid?

The police officer thought about that second question for a minute, but then carried on without answering it:

Q: You tell me what they are for, and is this yours? (showing the grey sweatshirt)

A: Of course, it's mine. You fuckers are really stupid. Don't bother me anymore. I'm not saying anything until I see my lawyer. Just fuck off. You fuckers have to prove it.

Now, prior to the *Charter*, that would seem to have been that. As a former prosecutor, I used to like such statements from suspects as, "When I was in the store I only had the gun"; they tend to give you a modicum of confidence in your case. I also liked statements that had a lot of "f-words" in them because they do not flatter the accused when you have the officer repeat the statement for the jury. The problem for the prosecutor in this case, though, was that the Supreme Court of Canada told him he would have to try Ronald Charles Manninen without the benefit of these statements. It's not that they were unreliable. They obviously were. It's just that once Manninen said he was not saying anything until he spoke to his lawyer (even though he apparently didn't mean it very much), the police had to back off. If a detained suspect wants to enjoy his constitutional right to "retain and instruct counsel without delay," you simply have to let him do it.

The same rule applies where, part-way through an interrogation, an accused person says, "I'm not saying anything more. I would like to speak to my lawyer." At that moment the interrogation is supposed to stop until the suspect has been given a reasonable opportunity to do so. On numerous occasions Terry Burlingham said words to that effect, but the officers kept rolling on.

There was more. Remember those bits where the police tried to convince Burlingham that his lawyer was not interested in him, was useless to him, and was concerned only with money? They also violated

Burlingham's constitutional rights. I guess you could say that people have a constitutional right not to have the police insult their lawyers. This restriction is not because we want to protect the reputation of the profession, which is probably somewhat like trying to put the top back on Mount St. Helens. The reason we keep the police from insulting those of us at the bar is that many accused persons are vulnerable. They are isolated, locked up, and usually afraid. Many do not have the wherewithal to appreciate the importance of counsel, and they are susceptible to the psychological games that get played in an effort to have them forgo their rights. If the police can go around attempting to undermine the confidence of a person such as Burlingham in his relationship with his lawyer, they could defeat the right to counsel. If the accused loses faith in his lawyer, he will not talk to him, he will not receive advice on what his rights are or how to act, and it will be easy to manipulate him into losing his rights. As any lawyer will tell you, the retainer is not only the document in which the client promises the lawyer that he or she will be paid, it is a bond that is to be respected, a constitutionally protected relationship. It is not something to be poked fun at, and it is not just about "money, money, money." It is also about access to rights and liberties.

Finally, there was one other problem — a major one. When a client talks to a lawyer, the advice he or she receives is based on the factual context at the time. For example, if you are charged with an assault, the advice you receive from a lawyer may be different than if you are charged with murder. If during the course of an investigation the nature of the investigation changes, you are entitled to be readvised of the right to counsel so you can obtain relevant advice. The police learned about this one after a confession was thrown out by the Supreme Court of Canada in a Halifax case back in 1989.[5]

A woman named Black, while extremely intoxicated, got into a fight with Deborah Lynn Tufts. Tufts bit Black a number of times during the fight, until Black ultimately plunged a knife into Tufts' neck. When the police arrested Black, Tufts was still alive. Black was arrested for assault with a weapon, advised of her right to counsel, and then allowed to call a lawyer. She made the mistake of calling a non-criminal lawyer, who was awakened by the call. He gave her only thirty to forty seconds of his time. The police, satisfied that she had had her right to counsel, then began to question her. An hour and a half later, while the investigation was still under way, they learned that Tufts had died and they told Black this information. They broke it to her that she was now facing a first-degree murder charge. She requested to speak to her lawyer again, but when the officer tried to reach him, the phone was busy. So the police gave up and returned to questioning Black. After a time, she admitted the stabbing and led the police to the knife.

The Supreme Court of Canada ruled that even though she had spoken to a lawyer when first arrested, her rights to counsel were breached, in part because there had been a material change in circumstance when the nature of her jeopardy changed from assault with a weapon to murder. She should have been readvised of her right to counsel and given a reasonable opportunity to exercise it. The attempts to get her that advice had been inadequate: there was no urgency in continuing with the questioning, and the officers should have waited until the next day when the lawyer was back in his office before continuing in their efforts to obtain a statement. They had violated her constitutional rights.

Although this is not exactly what happened with Terry Burlingham, it is close. Burlingham was presented with a deal by the police. They knew he had a lawyer. The deal was a material change in circumstance that had occurred since Burlingham had last spoken to his lawyer. The police understood the importance of his obtaining legal advice on such a crucial matter, but instead of assisting him in getting it, they set about to force him to make a decision before he could speak to his counsel. Even though he had been allowed ultimately to call another lawyer, that happened only after he promised them he would give them a statement if they let him do so. More important, within reason, accused persons have a right to counsel of their choice. There was no urgency here. There was no reason why the offer could not have been left open until Monday when Burlingham's lawyer returned. The police actions were designed to cut this lawyer out and to obtain, behind his back, what they knew they could not get if he was in the picture.

By the standards of the 1950s, or even the 1970s, it might seem that the officers did a fine job. They solved the crime, outsmarted the criminal, and even got their murder weapon. But by the standards of the 1980s and 1990s, they behaved shamelessly. They violated Burlingham's constitutional rights. After all, the *Charter* is not just the law in this country; it is the highest order of law. It is part of the Constitution of Canada, a document that constitutes a promise by the governments of Canada about how the state and its agents will treat private citizens. As the *Magna Carta* was to early England, it is the supreme law of the land. It is not intended simply to provide ordinary rights and freedoms, but rather to preserve fundamental rights and freedoms, those values we consider fundamental to a free and democratic society. This is the law that the officers investigating Burlingham, officers who swore to uphold the law of the land, chose to break. They ignored his stated desire not to speak to them

until he consulted counsel further, they sought to undermine his relationship with counsel, and they used a promised deal on a plea bargain in
an effort to cut out his counsel. In the process, they deprived him of his
constitutional rights. Whether they knew they were violating the
Constitution or not does not matter. Ignorance of the law is no excuse to
the rest of us. That is the last thing it should be for police officers.

I know there will not be much public sympathy for Burlingham, and
that many Canadians will applaud the police in this case. Those of you
who feel this way will do so because Burlingham's claim to his constitutional rights rings hollow, given that he did not give a wit for the right to
dignity and the right to life of Denean Worms and Brenda Hughes. But
this *Charter* right is not so much about Terry Burlingham. It is about you
and me and about the kind of society we want to live in. I suspect none
of us want to live in a society where the police can conspire to keep us
from learning about our legal rights and how best to enjoy them. I suspect none of us want to live in a society where the police could take you
into custody and keep you from getting access to a lawyer.

Do not be seduced by the idea that the case of Terry Burlingham is
different because he was truly guilty, and that if you were arrested you
would not be. Do not be misled by this "ends justify the means" thinking
because, fortunately, we live in a country where the police do not arrest
people they think are innocent. They arrest people they think are guilty.
If all it takes for them to deign it appropriate to fiddle with the law is a
belief in the guilt of the suspect, then no one who is arrested, guilty or
innocent, can count on rights. Nor is this just about the right to counsel.
The same holds true with the right to be free from unreasonable search
and seizure, the right not to be arbitrarily detained, and the right to a fair
trial. Loosen those rights when it is convenient to catch the bad guy, and
they do none of us any good. Still, this leaves unanswered the most
important question here. How should we deal with a case where the
police do violate the constitutional rights of suspects? Should we throw
perfectly valuable evidence away?

Sacrificing the Truth When the Constable Has Blundered: Excluding Unconstitutional Evidence

Proponents of throwing out evidence that the police obtain by breaching
the constitutional rights of suspects do not confine themselves to a single
argument. They claim there are a number of reasons to do so — reasons
that are not without merit.

A RIGHT WITHOUT A REMEDY IS NO RIGHT AT ALL: THE REMEDIAL RATIONALE

First, there is the idea that if we do not exclude unconstitutionally obtained evidence, the Constitution will become meaningless. A right without a remedy is a useless thing. If we are going to do nothing where the police deprive a suspect like Terry Burlingham of his right, then why bother giving him that right in the first place? According to this view, we exclude the evidence so we can put accused persons back in the same position they would have been in if their constitutional rights had been respected. This solution is sometimes called the "remedial rationale" — we exclude to remedy the breach.

Opponents of exclusion criticize this mode of remedying constitutional violations because it is available only if the police discover evidence. If the police broke into my house, they would find nothing, so this remedy would do me no good. It advantages only those persons whom there is evidence against. Critics argue that the use of exclusion as the remedy for violations discourages the development of more effective and generally available remedies, such as tort actions against the individual officers, or the prosecution of constitutional violations as police misconduct.

I think this latter point is true. It is extremely rare for police officers, all of whom have sworn to uphold the law, to be prosecuted under their disciplinary statutes for violating the Constitution. When evidence is thrown out, the response of police chiefs is more likely to be to criticize the courts for letting a criminal go than it is to hold the officers to account. As for lawsuits by citizens against the police for violation of their *Charter* rights, they too are rare because it is difficult to show real damages. "My damages, Your Honour, are that the police caught me" is not a legal submission calculated to win significant monetary restitution from the courts. This is unfortunate because arguments in favour of the exclusionary remedy are largely driven by the fact that if the evidence is not thrown out, nothing will be done. In both Canada and the United States, the attraction of an exclusionary rule lies, in no small measure, in the failure of police administrators and politicians to get serious about holding the police to the law. In the absence of the political will to deal with this lapse, we have fallen into the habit of looking to exclusion as a remedy for unconstitutional violations.

A related point can be made in favour of the remedial rationale, something that its critics tend to overlook. Whenever we limit the powers of the police to investigate, we are in a sense excluding evidence; we are throwing away valuable information. When we tell accused persons they have the right to remain silent, we are preventing the police from getting information from them. When we restrict powers of police search, we are preventing the police from finding evidence that may well exist. If we had effective remedies that would bring about full respect for constitutional limits, the police would never discover much of the evidence that is excluded as unconstitutionally obtained. What the remedial rationale has going for it is that it seeks to put the accused in the same position he or she would have been in had the police respected the Constitution. Where the evidence would not have been discovered without the constitutional violation, this is a strong argument for exclusion.

The only counter-argument, and it is not without force, is that we can never truly turn the clock back. Once the breach occurs and the evidence is out, we have learned something, and where truth is given appropriate premium it will be asking too much in some cases to try to put the genie back in the bottle. It is one thing to live with the fact that we may never catch a murderer. It is quite another to catch him and then have to let him go.

PUNISHING THE POLICE: THE DETERRENCE RATIONALE

The second argument in favour of excluding evidence is known as the "deterrence rationale." Excluding evidence, it is believed, can deter police officers from violating the Constitution. If they know they are not going to gain anything by doing it, then they will not bother. The two rationales differ in that the remedial rationale is aimed at fixing the wrong done to the suspect whose rights have been breached, and the deterrence rationale is aimed at discouraging new violations.

The main problem with the deterrence rationale is that its effectiveness cannot be established empirically. We are therefore left to accept the effectiveness of deterrence as a matter of faith. But as in the case of deterrence as a principle of sentencing, that faith may be misplaced. I expect for a variety of reasons that the deterrent effect of intimidating officers into not violating the Constitution is likely to be modest. My own view is that officers who respect constitutional limits do so because they believe that is the right thing to do. Trying to intimidate those who do not feel this way by excluding evidence strikes me as a useless exercise. First, evidence is excluded only if the constitutional violation is detected. Often it will come down to the word of a suspect, who will most often be a convicted criminal, against the word of the police. Like doctors and perhaps even lawyers, police officers do not enjoy telling on one another. While there are many officers who perceive their highest duty to be upholding the law and who would never perjure themselves to save an arrest or to protect the reputation of a colleague, there are others who are jaded with "the system." These officers see themselves as being in a war against crime, a war to be fought not only against criminals but also against slippery defence lawyers and what they perceive to be mindless technicalities that obstruct their ability to keep the streets safe. They see the risks of doing what it takes to catch a criminal to be worth it, and they take solace in the likelihood that if evidence is excluded and a case lost, the public will blame the judges, not them. To the extent that this ideology exists in segments of the police subculture, and it does, it can counter deterrence as peer support effectively reinforces improper police behaviour.

Critics of the deterrence rationale also suggest that the consequence of exclusion is too remote from the officers to deter them effectively. The only consequence is that the case is lost, and they go for a beer with their colleagues and curse the judge. If you really want to deter them, the argument goes, they must be disciplined or suffer personally when they cross constitutional lines during an investigation. As things now stand, in cases where the evidence would not be discovered without the breach, they have nothing to lose by violating the Constitution. If they respect the Constitution, they do not have the evidence. If they violate it, they will have the evidence, unless they are caught and that evidence is ultimately rejected. The only risk they take by breaching the Constitution, then, is that their case might be better off. Worse, even if the evidence is excluded, there may still be other collateral advantages secured by violating the Constitution, such as recovering stolen goods, getting drugs or weapons off the street, confirming suspicions, or, in some cases, inducing guilty pleas.

I'll give you an example of a collateral benefit from the pages of my past. Someone was breaking into houses in my neighbourhood — dozens of them. The neighbourhood was up in arms. Then the police got a break. After responding to a suspicious person's call, the officers apprehended a young man hiding in the bushes behind a store. As it happened, the young man had been sprayed by a skunk while skulking through the backyards. The police arrested him and some reporter dubbed it the case of the "pungent bandit." The police even managed to get the bandit to confess, after violating his right to counsel and conducting a questionable but non-violent interrogation. He owned up to all the break and enters. He was denied bail and was waiting in jail for his trial. I ended up with the case to prosecute. When I saw the police report it was obvious that the case was going to be thrown out. I asked the officer, an experienced policeman, why he had broken so many basic rules about proper interrogation.

He replied: "I know this case isn't going anywhere and the confession is going to be thrown out, but we had nothing. What were we going to do? Pinch him for smelling like a skunk? Now we've wrapped up over fifty B & E's, he got to spend ten days in jail waiting for trial, and when he gets out, he won't be back in that neighbourhood." That made sense to me, save for two things. First, these benefits were obtained at the cost of depriving this young man of his rights. Second, it meant that I was going to lose the prosecution. As I feared at the time, my neighbours now think I am a lousy lawyer because I failed to get the man sent to Alcatraz.

I ended up making a plea bargain with his lawyer that he would get time served for a plea to possessing burglary tools — a screwdriver and crowbar he had hidden in a nearby field and which he showed the officers. The moral of the story is that losing evidence does not always mean that the police lose.

One of the most important impediments to effective deterrence is the sheer complexity of the law. People can respond only to clear messages. Members of the Supreme Court of Canada are often in disagreement over whether there has been a *Charter* violation in a particular case, and they are almost never unanimous over whether evidence should be excluded. How can we expect the police to sort out the limits of their powers? And even if the message the Court sends is clear, it must be communicated effectively to the officers on the street. In truth, this rarely happens. Although they understand the broad rules, many officers are woefully uninformed about many of the requirements of the *Charter*. Anyone who spends time in the provincial courts in this country can tell you that.

In short, while the theory of deterrence is solid, practice tends to weaken it substantially. The essentials of effective deterrence — a sanction that is strong enough to induce compliance, a clear appreciation of the scope of the law, and the expectation of being caught if the law is contravened — are all missing.

PROTECTING JUDICIAL INTEGRITY AND REPUTE: REASONS OF PRINCIPLE

Advocates of exclusion also rely on the "judicial integrity rationale." This has become the catch-phrase for at least two separate but closely related theories. First, in theory, excluding evidence enables courts to maintain the respect of the public. If courts were to accept the fruits of unlawful behaviour by state agents, they would be seen to be condoning illegal behaviour and would lose public support. Second, the exclusion of unconstitutionally obtained evidence preserves judicial integrity by enabling courts to distance themselves from the wrongful breach. According to this view, even if the public would disapprove, courts must apply appropriate principles. It is not the job of courts to be popular. It is their job to uphold the law and to do what is right. While there is hope that the values demonstrated by courts who act to preserve their integrity will ultimately trickle down to the community, unconstitutionally obtained evidence is excluded simply because it is the right thing to do.

To the extent that the judicial integrity arguments are based on preserving the respect of the public for the administration of justice by enabling courts to avoid the taint of lawlessness, they have serious problems. First, if receiving unconstitutionally obtained evidence is seen to be condoning constitutional violations, then all unconstitutionally obtained evidence should be excluded, for when could it be appropriate to condone breaches of the Constitution? Presumably never. But no system, including that in the United States, excludes all unconstitutionally obtained evidence.

The second problem is with the accuracy of the assumption that we can enhance the repute of the administration of justice by throwing out useful evidence. Consider the actual impact of excluding important evidence in a high-profile case. Does the public send letters of congratulations to the editors of newspapers and call open-line shows extolling the virtues of having courts with integrity? Anyone who lives in this country knows the opposite to be true. Excluding evidence because of *Charter* breaches has probably done more to undermine faith in the justice system than any other single activity that our courts engage in, with the possible exception of sentencing and maybe "mollycoddling" young offenders. If we are truly concerned about the impact of our decisions on the reputation of the administration of justice, it may be worth worrying about the observations of an American judge:

> [I]n the real world, the integrity of the justice system has been far more greatly undermined by its current penchant for releasing the obviously guilty, by permitting juries to be misled by incomplete evidence, and by its tolerance of false testimony of defence witnesses who cannot be impeached on cross-examination by suppressed evidence. The devastating impact of . . . the release of violent criminals is the real cause of the contemporary decline in respect for the American justice system.[6]

The only rationale that cannot be challenged using competing logic is the second branch of the judicial integrity rationale: courts have to protect their own integrity by doing the right thing and upholding the law through the exclusion of evidence, even if it damages them in the eyes of a public that is not learned in the importance of constitutional rules. Others can disagree and say that the right thing to do is to give priority to crime fighting, but they cannot show this belief to be invalid or wrong. It is entirely a matter of values. As an argument of pure principle, it is secure from empirical attack. Whether you give priority to sending messages about crime or sending messages about constitutional values is entirely a matter of choice. Advocates of a vital exclusionary rule simply claim that sending messages about constitutional values is more important.

This was the view in the Burlingham case of Chief Justice McEachern of the British Columbia Court of Appeal:

> I am deeply conscious that [the exclusion of evidence in this case] will understandably be a highly unpopular decision.... Our function, however, is to apply the law to the cases that come before us, and we must always be mindful that popular decisions will sometimes make bad law. The principled administration of justice can only be served by deciding cases according to law as we understand the law to be at the time of decision.[7]

Twenty years ago the idea that a judge would be opting to exclude valuable evidence because the police have broken the law would have struck most Canadian lawyers as bizarre. Our common law rules, the ones we inherited from England and which applied before the adoption of the *Charter* in 1982, required courts to admit evidence even where it was illegally obtained, so long as it would help determine what happened. If the accused felt that the police had broken the law, he could always sue them or complain to some police complaints commission, but what the police had done did not distract from the real issue at a criminal trial: what the accused had done. The relevant question, it was believed, was not whether the evidence was obtained illegally, but whether it was relevant, useful proof.

One of the leading pre-*Charter* cases in this area is *R. v. Wray*,[8] decided in 1971. Wray was the suspect in a robbery turned murder. The police arrested him and obtained a confession from him after improper questioning and treatment. In the end he brought the police to the gun. The confession was thrown out, not because it was illegally obtained, but because it was unreliable. The existence of the gun, in contrast, was perfectly reliable because it was there in court. The fact that Wray knew where to find it was also reliable because a number of witnesses saw him lead the police to it. While we may have been left with some insecurity about the reliability of the unconfirmed parts of his confession because it was induced

by threatening police behaviour, we had no such concerns about the reliability of the gun and about Wray's knowledge of where it was. So, according to the law at the time, the judge let these facts be proved.

Wray appealed to the Supreme Court of Canada, saying his trial
was unfair. The police were profiting from illegally obtained evidence.
The Court disagreed. The evidence was relevant to his guilt, and it was
not being given exaggerated importance. Its admission in no way distorted the outcome of the case. The trial, which had been conducted
properly, was about Wray's guilt, and the evidence showed him to be
guilty. While this illegally obtained evidence may have operated unfortunately for Wray, it did not operate unfairly. If he was upset with the
officers, then sue them or complain to their superiors, but do not ask to
get away with murder.

The Road to Exclusion and Disrepute

Things had been rolling along in this way for generations. Then came
Pierre Elliott Trudeau with his constitutional vision for Canada. When it
was decided to try to repatriate the Constitution of Canada from Great
Britain, the federal government and the provinces negotiated at length on
the form of the new Canadian Constitution. The decision was made to
attempt to include a charter of rights and freedoms, which would serve as
a blueprint for a just society. Once this was agreed and legal rights relating to police investigation were being debated, the issue of excluding evidence as a constitutional remedy came to be hotly contested. Based on
the American experience, in which "the criminal goes free because the
constable has blundered," a number of provinces insisted that a charter, if
passed, should not allow courts to exclude evidence because of constitutional violations. In late 1980, the draft charter therefore provided
expressly that judges did not have the power to exclude evidence to remedy charter breaches.

When public submissions were invited on the draft, this clause
served as a red flag for those who believed that courts should be excluding unconstitutionally obtained evidence. Its effect was to attract repre-
sentations in support of an explicit exclusionary clause.[9] In the end, it was
decided to reach a compromise, in typically Canadian fashion. While persuaded by the arguments in favour of an exclusionary rule, the framers of
the *Charter* wanted to avoid an absolute rule, or even a rule that was as
aggressive as the American one, which, at the time, was perceived to be
causing the loss of a great deal of unconstitutionally obtained evidence.
That rule was being criticized in its own country because it often caused

the loss of important evidence through relatively minor constitutional breaches. We apparently wanted a rule that would maintain some proportionality between the seriousness of the breach and the costs of excluding the evidence. Hence, section 24(2) of our *Charter* was born. It requires courts to exclude unconstitutionally obtained evidence where "having regard to all of the circumstances, the admission of it in the proceedings would bring the administration of justice into disrepute."

Of course, when a statute is passed, including a constitutional one like the *Charter*, courts have to interpret it. Section 24(2) proved to be something of a challenge in that regard. If we were to take its language literally, we would probably exclude very little unconstitutionally obtained evidence. "Disrepute" is about reputation, and reputation has to do with what others think of you, not what you think of yourself. In effect, the section seems to tell Canadian courts to exclude unconstitutionally obtained evidence not where they think it is the right thing to do, but only where the Canadian public would lose respect for the courts if those courts were to admit it. One might expect that this would rarely be so, given that the public is more apt to lose respect for courts that exclude valuable evidence. Indeed, we had been applying the rule used in *Wray* for many years and there was no sign that the credibility of the courts was in jeopardy.

This approach to section 24(2) was quickly rejected by the Supreme Court of Canada as an inappropriate way to read the section. To read it that way would largely gut the exclusionary remedy, which was part of a fundamental document designed for the unremitting protection of fundamental rights and freedoms. Instead, the Supreme Court of Canada took the view that we are to judge the impact of the exclusion of evidence not from the perspective of the average Canadian, but from the perspective of the reasonable Canadian who appreciates fully the importance of constitutional rights. The decision whether to exclude evidence, the Court decided, cannot be left to the judgment of the majority, since the whole point behind the *Charter* is to protect unpopular minorities, such as those persons who are charged with offences, from a majority that may be caught up in the shifting winds of public passion. When this decision was taken, exclusion of evidence became the Achilles' heel of the credibility of the administration of justice.

In the end, the Supreme Court of Canada crafted a very technical and, in some contexts, aggressive approach to exclusion. The current approach, the one used in the *Burlingham* case but described more clearly in *R. v. Stillman*,[10] involves drawing a distinction between "conscriptive" and "non-conscriptive" evidence.

Self-Incrimination, Conscription,
and a Fair Trial

Conscriptive evidence, broadly speaking, is evidence that the police obtain by compelling the suspect to incriminate him- or herself by means of a statement, the use of the body, or the production of bodily samples. For example, statements made by the accused will be conscriptive. So too will blood samples, breath samples, pulled hairs, re-enactments of the crime, or even the act of standing in an identification lineup. Derivative evidence, evidence found as the result of conscriptive evidence, is also treated much like conscriptive evidence. For example, a gun that was found only because of a statement made by the suspect is effectively considered to be conscriptive. All other evidence is non-conscriptive. Things found during a search, such as drugs, clothing, or a weapon found in a car or in a home, will generally be non-conscriptive.

The two kinds of evidence, conscriptive and non-conscriptive, are treated differently for the purposes of exclusion. A court is required to throw out conscriptive evidence if it was obtained in violation of the *Charter* unless the prosecutor can prove that it would have been found even without the breach. By contrast, non-conscriptive evidence, and conscriptive evidence that would have been found without the breach, may or may not be excluded. That depends on the balance between the seriousness of the violation and the degree to which excluding the evidence would harm the reputation of the administration of justice. In effect, the court engages in an assessment of the proportional evils between the constitutional violation and the loss of the evidence. The more serious the breach, the more likely the evidence will be excluded. The more serious the case, the less likely that is to happen.

The Supreme Court of Canada chose to treat conscriptive evidence this way because of an important principle that has long been of central importance in our criminal justice system. One of the things that most repulsed English society about the procedures of the Courts of Star Chamber and High Commission was that they forced people to incriminate themselves. Without proof of crime being demonstrated, they compelled individuals to answer to the state, on pain of punishment. Since that time, a seminally important principle in our system has been that no one should be forced to be his own accuser. In a free and democratic society, if the state wants to call on you to answer for your alleged conduct, it must first present its case before a neutral judge. We would consider a trial to be unfair if the Crown could simply do as was done in the Star Chamber and prove its case by forcing the accused to testify. For this reason, accused persons are non-compellable as witnesses at their own trial. They can testify if they choose to do so, but they cannot be made to. If the Crown cannot prove its case without the accused, then the accused is entitled to be left alone.

It should be readily apparent that the right to refuse to testify would be pointless if the police could make accused persons speak before court and then simply introduce their own words as evidence against them. That would be tantamount to forcing them to testify, since they would effectively be witnesses against themselves. For this reason, suspects are given the right to remain silent, even during the investigation of the crime. Although it is ill-advised, if the police begin to question you, you are entitled to paraphrase (but not quote) Ronald Charles Manninen and say, "Don't bother me anymore. I'm not saying anything . . . Just jump in the lake. You boys in blue have to prove it." A response I more strongly recommend, and which the more courteous among you may prefer, is to say, "I needn't even dignify that allegation with a response." While human experience may suggest that silence is the refuge of the scoundrel, in our system we see it as the prerogative of the free.

Sometimes the police do not see it that way. Susan Nelles, the nurse who was wrongly charged with the Toronto Sick Children's Hospital baby deaths in the early 1980s, became firm as a suspect in the eyes of the police because she told them she had a right to remain silent and would not answer their questions. To them, that meant she had something to hide. While, in practice, refusing to tell your story can be unwise for this reason, it is also generally unwise for a suspect to give a statement. Remember in that great American film, *My Cousin Vinnie*, when the cousin was confronted with the preposterous allegation that he had shot the store clerk at the Sack-o'-Suds convenience store, he exclaimed in absolute disbelief, "I killed him? I killed him?" That, of course, made it into the officer's notes as "I killed him. I killed him," and the case for the prosecutor was on its way. This can happen to you. If you are a suspect, and you need to talk to the police to clear yourself, let a lawyer do it.

What does this have to do with conscriptive evidence? Since conscriptive evidence originates with the accused in the form of statements, bodily samples, or participation in lineups and re-enactments, it is, in a broad sense, self-incriminatory. Our courts have come to accept that if this self-incriminatory evidence has been obtained from you in violation of the *Charter*, its admission would render your trial unfair. To use you as the source of unconstitutionally obtained information is tantamount to calling you as a witness against yourself. There is no public interest in having an unfair trial, so this kind of evidence must be excluded to preserve the fairness of the trial.

This, of course, is what happened when Terry Burlingham was prosecuted for the murder of Denean Worms. His confession, obtained in violation of his right to counsel, had to be excluded according to this rule. Its admission would have rendered his trial unfair, so it had to go. As for the gun, it was found only because of the confession. It was sunk at the bottom of the frozen Kootenay River, where it would have stayed for all eternity had Burlingham not shown the police where it was. It, too, was therefore conscriptive, and had to be thrown out lest its admission render the trial unfair. The same was true of the conversation Burlingham had with his girlfriend. The Supreme Court of Canada reasoned that had Burlingham not confessed and shown the police where the gun was, he would not have told his girlfriend that he knew something about the killing and that he had helped the police find the gun. This statement was also the fruit of his confession. As such, it too was conscriptive. It did not matter how serious the offence was, or how trivial the *Charter* breach may have been. Once the evidence was determined to be conscriptive, it was gone.

Had this evidence been non-conscriptive, a very different approach would have been taken. The Court would have determined how serious the constitutional violations were, and how costly exclusion might have been to the case and the public perception. The decision in *R. v. Evans*[11] illustrates how non-conscriptive evidence is analysed. Unlike Terry Burlingham, Robert Evans did not kill anyone. He committed the unpardonable sin of growing *cannabis sativa*, that leafy green substance that, when dried, rolled, and smoked, can produce a mildly narcotic effect. It is the same substance that American president Bill Clinton put to his lips but never inhaled, and that our former prime minister, Kim Campbell, helped pass around at a party once.

The police, acting on an anonymous tip that Evans had been cultivating marijuana, went to the door of Evans' house incognito so they could, quite literally, "sniff around" when the door was answered. They smelled marijuana, inhaled as deeply as they could, and floated back to the cruiser, a condition now known in Canada as the Ross Rebagliatti effect. This clever police tactic was actually a contravention of Evans' constitutional right to be free from unreasonable searches because it interfered with his reasonable expectation of privacy. It is not that he had a right to be able to grow marijuana in private. It is that he had a right to expect that the police would not approach his home to investigate him unless they had a proper basis for doing so.

I can understand that. I, for one, would not want the police sniffing under my front door, even if all they are likely to smell is a pot of spaghetti sauce. Nor would I want them posing as Fuller Brush people and going from door to door in my neighbourhood trying to peak inside the houses. If the police have reasonable and probable grounds to suspect that I am committing a crime, then come on down. Otherwise, leave me alone. Since the police did not have reasonable and probable grounds to believe that the anonymous tip about Evans was accurate, their olfactory observations violated the *Charter*. They had sniffed, contrary to Evans' constitutional right that they not sniff.

The police obtained a search warrant to enter Evans' house and, on their return, they found his crop. The police can get a search warrant only where they have reasonable and probable grounds to believe that a crime has been committed and that there will be evidence in the place to be searched. The warrant they used when they entered Evans' home was defective because the reasonable and probable grounds arose from their prior illegal, olfactory search. For obvious reasons, you cannot rely on a prior illegal search to make a later search legal. So, when the police entered and found the marijuana plants, they broke the law. They had breached the *Charter*. The Court nonetheless let the evidence stand. In the course of ruling this non-conscriptive evidence to be admissible, it said:

> I would note that the exclusion of the evidence in this case would tarnish the image of the administration of justice to a much greater extent than would its admission. The cultivation of marijuana is a serious offence, often leading to other social evils. The evidence obtained in violation of s. 8 is necessary to substantiate the charges against the appellants: simply put, if the evidence is excluded, the perpetrators of a very serious crime will go unpunished. As a result, I would hold that the evidence obtained by the *Charter* violation in this case must not be excluded pursuant to section 24(2). To hold otherwise would certainly lessen the esteem in which the public holds the administration of justice.[12]

I trust the irony here was not lost on you. The esteem in which the public holds the administration of justice would be lessened if we excluded marijuana plants, thereby allowing Evans to go free and unpunished for his serious crime of facilitating "reefer madness." We therefore forget about the *Charter* breach and let the evidence in. For Terry Burlingham, in contrast, we feel that the entire reputation of the administration of justice would be hurt if we did not throw out the evidence, even though it could have the effect of allowing him to go free and unpunished for the crime of raping and killing a young woman. What happened to the idea that there should be some proportionality between the breach and the effect of potentially compromising the truth by throwing out evidence?

While we appropriately cling to the principle of proportionality when dealing with non-conscriptive evidence, it has been abandoned as irrelevant for conscriptive evidence. No matter how reliable or important the evidence is, or how serious the offence is, or how trivial the *Charter* breach is, if the evidence is conscriptive, under the current law it is gone.

This decision to exclude automatically conscriptive evidence is wrong in principle. It is based on the questionable assumption that to admit conscriptive evidence is the same thing as forcing accused persons to testify at their trials. But it is not the same. When an accused person is forced to testify at his trial, it is the court that is breaching his rights; of course that would render his trial unfair. When the police violate the *Charter*, they are the ones who have broken the law, not the courts. When an accused is forced to testify, he is being made to do so against his will in the full sense of the term. He is told he will be jailed by law if he does not. By contrast, while some conscriptive evidence is obtained against the will of an accused, not all of it is. Take Terry Burlingham, for example. He knew his rights and he had been given advice on how to use them. He just did not use them wisely. He made an improvident decision to cooperate with the police in return for a lesser charge. While that is an inducement, it is a far cry from being told by a judge, "Testify, or you are going to jail." To equate conscriptive evidence with being compelled to be a witness against yourself at your trial is simplistic.

There is no getting around it. The Supreme Court of Canada's decision to characterize the admission of conscriptive evidence as rendering the trial unfair is entirely a matter of choice, not legal imperative. Remember *Wray*. When it was decided in 1971, our view was that admitting reliable conscriptive evidence had no impact on the fairness of the trial. What has changed since then? Only our characterization. Even with the elevation of some rules to constitutional status, we are not now compelled by the force of unshakeable logic or legal principle to throw out all conscriptive evidence. We have chosen to do so and it is an unwise choice, both from the point of view of contextual justice and, as important, from the perspective of the public perception about the integrity of the administration of justice.

The truth is, we do not really believe that the admission of conscriptive evidence makes a trial unfair. We allow breath samples to be admitted in drinking and driving cases. We now permit DNA samples, obtained against the consent of accused persons by warrant, to be admitted into evidence. Why is this not tantamount to calling these people as witnesses at their trials? Why does the admission of this proof not render their trials unfair? The Supreme Court of Canada would have to say,

"Because it is obtained lawfully, not unconstitutionally." Of course that is correct, but what this means is that our concern is not really with the conscriptive nature of the evidence. It is with the fact that it has been obtained unconstitutionally. That being so, it should be treated like all other unconstitutionally obtained evidence.

On a simple view of things, even if we accept the questionable condonation theory, or the notion that the courts should not sit idly by and ignore illegal conduct, the fact is that a criminal court judge who learns during the criminal trial that the police have broken the law by violating the constitutional rights of the accused is faced with one actual and one potential breach of the law — the one shown to have been committed by the officers, and the one alleged against the accused. The court is therefore placed in a difficult position. If it allows the evidence in, it is turning a blind eye to a constitutional violation and condoning it. If it throws the evidence out, it may be turning a blind eye to the truth about the crime of the accused and effectively condoning the acquittal of the guilty. Obviously, a choice has to be made. That choice should be based on a contextual evaluation of the seriousness of the constitutional violation and the potential costs of excluding the evidence. The long-term interests of the administration of justice should be considered, and so, too, should the public interest in calling criminals to justice, as well as the potential danger to the community. In this way we can arrive at proportional responses to the competing claims of illegal conduct. Is it more important in the present case to reaffirm values about the importance of the *Charter*, or is it more important to come to an accurate decision on the criminal charge, given the nature of the allegation? This is effectively what we do for non-conscriptive evidence. It is what we should be doing for all unconstitutionally obtained evidence.

This approach can be explained to the Canadian public. They can even accept it grudgingly, I think. Automatic exclusion of conscriptive evidence will never be accepted, and never should be. It is an unwarranted *mea culpa* and, in truth, a collective act of self-immolation.

What, then, of Terry Burlingham? How should he have fared? To be sure, the police conduct in his case was reprehensible. It was a wilful and flagrant effort to keep him from enjoying the full benefits of his rights to counsel, and the officers should have been disciplined for it. On the other hand, Burlingham was in no way abused. He was allowed to speak to his lawyer and did so on two occasions. He had also spoken to another lawyer, the man who ultimately represented him at his trial, immediately before he took the officers on their ghastly field trip. He was fully aware of his right to silence and he chose to speak, albeit improvidently. In my world view at least, it was simply asking too much for him to insist on having the Court throw out perfectly valuable evidence that might well enable it to arrive at the truth — that Terry Burlingham is a serial rapist and a serial killer of young women. Applying an exclusionary remedy in response to the police misconduct was, in my view, disproportional. If the Court felt the need to send signals to the community about illicit behaviour, it was far more important on this occasion to send the signal that it would address the serious allegation against Burlingham with full information than it was to send signals about police misconduct.

This does not mean that all the evidence against Burlingham should have been admitted. The Court should have done as it did in the *Wray* case some twenty-five years before. The confession had to be excluded for the simple reason that it violated the confession rule. While not being extracted completely against his will, it was obtained through hope of advantage. There was a sufficient inducement that it could have been untrue. But the gun, and so much of that confession as was confirmed to be true and reliable, including that Burlingham knew where the gun was, where Denean Worms had been shot, and where the body had been hidden, should have been admitted. So, too, should the conversation he had with his girlfriend. Excluding this evidence to prove our fidelity to the Constitution could well have proved too high a price to pay.

Fortunately, the Burlingham saga did not result in the release of a killer. By the time the appeal relating to the Worms killing made its way to the Supreme Court of Canada, Burlingham had already been convicted of first-degree murder in the Hughes case and his appeals from that conviction had been exhausted. He was serving a life sentence with no eligibility for parole for twenty-five years. As for the killing of Denean Worms, the Crown attempted to retry Burlingham on the evidence it had left. Faced with motions relating to allegations of further police misconduct, comforted by the life sentence Burlingham had already received for the Hughes killing, and insecure about the strength of its case absent the excluded evidence, the Crown settled for a plea of guilty to manslaughter and a ten-year sentence.

It is distasteful, but understandable, that the Crown felt it prudent to accept the lesser charge of manslaughter for what was no doubt a murder. I find some consolation in the fact that even if Burlingham had been retried through to a verdict on a murder charge, the administration of justice would still have suffered. It would have suffered because that trial would have been conducted under the pretence that there was no discovery of the gun and no tour of the killing field. The Canadian public would have been required to await the decision of a jury that would be called upon to decide the case without the benefit of full information. What happened to Burlingham during the investigation was very wrong, but as a matter of balance, even considering the long-term interests of the administration of justice, it does not come close to requiring us to search for the truth about the death of Denean Worms by blinding ourselves to what could well prove to be crucial information.

Privacy and Truth

Fortunately, although there are notable exceptions, in most other areas the law of evidence is evolving in a fashion that recognizes that truth is the indispensable handmaiden of justice. Consider the case of *R. v. Gruenke*.[13]

Adele Gruenke was a young woman in crisis. She had been practising "reflexology," a therapeutic technique not unlike "acupressure." One of her clients, an eighty-two-year-old man named Philip Barnett, decided to finance her business. She moved in with him, although platonically. He began to make unwelcome sexual advances, so she moved back in with her mother. Around that time Gruenke began to feel ill. She became convinced that she had leukemia, the dread disease her father had died from several years before. She began to attend the Victorious Faith Centre, a born-again Christian Church, to receive physical and emotional healing. The church pastor, Harmony Thiessen, and a lay counsellor, Janine Frovich, began to offer her counselling. On 30 November 1986 Gruenke must have made her counsellors' hair stand on end because she told them how two days before, she and her boyfriend, Jim Fosty, had beaten Barnett's head, leaving him dead in his car in a ditch on the outskirts of town. She allowed as to how she had been planning the killing for some time. He died because he had destroyed their relationship, becoming something she hated. He had once been her "surrogate father," and he had betrayed that, seeking to use her for sex. She also decided he had to die because she needed the money and she was the beneficiary of Barnett's will.

At her trial, Gruenke defended her case on the basis that she had little or nothing to do with the killing. Fosty had administered most of the blows while defending her from Barnett's sexual advances. This story, of course, did not look good against her confession to her pastor and spiritual counsellor, so she sought to keep the jury from learning about that little detail. She claimed the conversation was "privileged," on the basis that it was a religious communication.

In law, privileged conversations are kept confidential. A court of law cannot learn about them. The idea is that there are compelling reasons of public policy that make respecting the confidentiality of certain communications more important than giving a court access to information about the communication. But Gruenke lost in her bid to keep her pastor and the counsellor from testifying. They were legally compelled to testify about what they knew, and Adele Gruenke was convicted of first-degree murder.

In the course of denying her appeal, the Supreme Court of Canada refused to recognize a blanket privilege for all religious communications. It did not hold that the confidentiality of religious communications can never be protected. Where there is a strong expectation of confidence, and the public interest in supporting the confidential relationship is enough to outweigh the correct disposal of the litigation, private confidences might be respected. In this case, though, the claim failed because there was no solid evidence that Gruenke expected that what she had said would be kept between them. In the course of her decision, Justice L'Heureux-Dubé reaffirmed the central principle of the law of evidence, creating an unwelcome environment for future privilege claims:

> If the aim of the trial process is the search for the truth, the public and the judicial system must have the right to any and all relevant information in order that justice be rendered. Accordingly, relevant information is presumptively admissible.... [For this reason] the categories of privilege are . . . very limited — highly probative and reliable evidence is not excluded from scrutiny without compelling reasons.

The current trend is to resist rules that would exclude evidence because of competing policy interests. Still, there are rules that do impede the search for the truth in the pursuit of interests that have nothing to do with finding out what happened. The most notorious example is spousal incompetence. At common law, the husband or wife of an accused could not testify at the criminal trial of the accused, even if the spouse had relevant information. There were a number of reasons for this rule, including the legal fiction that husbands and wives are, in law, one person — namely, the husband. To allow the wife to testify against her husband would therefore be tantamount to making him testify against himself. Fortunately we are largely beyond such silliness, but, as a base rule, spousal incompetence still persists. It continues to find support in the belief that having spouses testify against each other would harm marital harmony, and that it is repugnant to use one spouse to bring harm to the other. These archaic beliefs, it seems, are more important than deciding a criminal case accurately.

The law has gradually whittled this rule back, allowing spouses to testify in the defence of each other and crafting specific exceptions where the

Crown can call spouses as witnesses. The first exception was recognized in *Lord Audley's Case*.[14] Upset with his wife, Lord Audley ordered one of his footmen to rape her, which he did. Lord Audley was charged. He sought to prevent his wife from testifying against him. The House of Lords created an exception to allow her to testify because, if she could not, men would be free to victimize their wives in private without any fear of prosecution. So the law now permits and even compels spouses to testify where they are the victims of the crime. We have created other exceptions by legislation. We now permit the Crown prosecutor to force a spouse to testify where the accused is charged with a sexual offence, or with crimes of violence against children, including murder. But as the law still stands, the Crown cannot call the spouse of the accused at a murder trial where the victim was an adult, even if the spouse wants to testify, unless the parties are separated and the relationship has hopelessly and irreconcilably broken down. The Crown recently ran into this ancient rule in the non-homicide case of *R. v. Hawkins*.[15]

Hawkins was a police constable assigned to gather intelligence against a Satan's Choice Motorcycle Club. He entered into a relationship with Cherie Graham, a night-club dancer. Hawkins confided in Graham that he had been receiving payoffs from Satan's Choice. For a time, the pair separated because of Hawkins' abuse and she ratted on him. The police began an investigation and ultimately charged Hawkins with obstruction of justice. Then the pair reconciled, and they approached a lawyer to find out what effect marriage would have on Graham's obligation to testify. They learned it would make her incompetent as a witness if she married him. Ultimately they broke up again, and Graham testified at his preliminary inquiry. During the first few days, her evidence sunk him deep. Then the love-bug bit again and, once more, they reconciled. She took the stand again and recanted all her testimony, blaming the police for pressuring her into giving false evidence. Hawkins was nonetheless committed to stand trial.

Before the trial could be held, however, the two married. At the trial, the trial judge held that the Crown could not make Cherie Graham testify. Indeed, so long as the two did not become hopelessly separated, Graham could not have testified even if she had wanted to.

Hawkins was convicted on the other evidence against him, but that does not remove the sting from this remarkably silly rule. Imagine if Hawkins had killed an adult and that Graham was an eye-witness. The spectacle of seeing one spouse harm another by testifying about what she knew, it would seem, would be so offensive to us that we would rather turn our back on her testimony. We would rather not know the truth. We would rather let a killer go. While it is entirely probable in some marriages that the spouse would not prove to be the best Crown witness, the current law would not even let the Crown try. It would permit her to refuse to take the stand.

We have other rules that, to my mind, are equally questionable in rejecting reliable evidence in the interests of competing policy, but this is not the place to describe them. Suffice it to say that a criminal trial should be about what happened. While we cannot always know the truth, we should strive for it with all resolve. With rare exception, the law should not close itself off to sources of useful reliable information that can help us get there. Unless there are compelling reasons to the contrary which are of overarching importance to the truth, we should have full access to relevant information. Without question, the reputation of the administration of justice would be best served if the law was to make this commitment.

Those who tire of seeing accused persons getting off on evidentiary technicalities will find this argument appealing. But be aware, the currency of truth is a coin with two sides. Above all else it is even more critical that we allow the accused complete access to relevant information in his or her defence. If we close our eyes to defence evidence because of competing policy considerations, we may well be making an innocent citizen bear the price of pursuing some public policy that has nothing to do with the question we are there to resolve — namely, guilt or innocence. Think both of your disgust at wasting evidence that will point the way to the truth for the Crown, and about the risk of convicting the innocent the next time you hear complainants in sexual offence cases seeking to shield their counselling records from the accused. Think about it the next time you hear about the Crown attempting to keep evidence from the accused, or Parliament proposing to limit the means that the accused might have to raise a doubt about his or her guilt.

Justice is meant to be blind so it will treat everyone the same. It is not meant, however, to be blind to the truth.

JUSTIFIABLE
HOMICIDE

Forgiving Human Weakness

The *Mignonette*, a private yacht, set sail from England on 19 May 1884. No sooner had the docks and the smoke of Southampton fallen out of sight than the sea became black, save for the froth that rolled and spat on the tops of its waves. Pelting rain streaked the white sails grey and cold. The cabin boy, Richard Parker, then seventeen years of age, decided whether to be afraid by watching the eyes of the crew of three that had charge of the vessel. It comforted him to see that Thomas Dudley, the thirty-one-year-old captain who had been commissioned to deliver the yacht to Henry M. Want, in Sydney, Australia, smiled broadly as he yelled orders to Edward Stephens, the mate, and to Edmond Brooks, the seaman. Even as the storm grew worse, these men were calm in their aspect, and calming in their effect on young Parker. By the time the weather cleared, the cabin boy had developed complete confidence in the crew who handled the craft so ably as it fell into deep troughs, always to climb again to the crest of the next wave as though this was the most natural thing in the world.

For Richard Parker, this was high adventure. The boat was to skirt the west coast of Africa before rounding the Cape of Good Hope for its passage across the great Pacific. As they approached the equator, Parker enjoyed standing on the deck while the sun, now more efficient than he had ever experienced it, warmed him and dried the sea spray almost as quickly as it bathed his face. All was well, if not idyllic, until the boat had the temerity to turn away from the coastal path it had been following into the teeth of the Atlantic.

On 5 July 1884 "the sea broke strange and dangerous."[1] It swelled, heavy and then violent. The waves, which rose high in front of the craft, blocking out the horizon, stood like some great black mass before collapsing from their height, lashing the boat with brine. Richard Parker, clutching his oilskin with one hand and the stair rail with the other, looked into the eyes of Thomas Dudley. He found no comfort. What he saw was naked terror.

It was too late to change the rigging. The four men were clinging to what they could as they heard the foresail rip. At that point, the boat, which had performed well until then, leaned as though she would roll, but held for a time. Then the sea stove in her side and all was panic. Parker, frozen by fear, closed his eyes and silently implored the crew to hurry as they made the 13-foot lifeboat ready. Thomas Dudley, not prepared to go down with his ship, managed to rescue the chronometer, sextant, and compass. As if by last-minute impulse, he also grabbed two one-pound tins of turnips. With these things and no more, the four clambered into the lifeboat just as the *Mignonette* pointed skyward, before leaving the roar of the storm for the eerie tranquillity of the sea-bed, hundreds of fathoms below. The last reading showed that she went down 27 degrees south, 10 degrees west, around 1600 miles from the "camelhump" of the coast of Africa, 2000 miles east and 500 miles north of Rio de Janeiro.[2]

In time, the sea quelled, leaving the four men leaning against the sides of the boat while their tiny craft bobbed towards Brazil at the agonizingly slow speed of $1^3/_4$ miles per hour under a makeshift sail they had fashioned from their clothing. If this held up, there was promise they might reach shore in about seventy-five days — a figure all of them understood to mean certain death. Their only hope was to find a sail breaking on the horizon.

On the third day, the turnips were opened. Until then, the men had survived on the rain water they had gathered in their oilskins, which they draped over their laps while they scanned the sea around them. On the fourth day a sea turtle happened too close to the boat and was caught. The crew forced it from its shell, pulled the grey-white flesh from its leathered crust, and ate reasonably well on it for eight days. That was the last they would consume until five days later, when, in the non-hospitable sense, the other three had Richard Parker for dinner.

The day after the turtle was caught, the men had broached the possibility of having ultimately to draw lots to see who might be consumed to save the others. If history is any guide, it is a dangerous business to be the one to make this proposal. A Dutch writer, Nicolaus Tulpius, recorded in Amsterdam in 1641 how seven Englishmen had found themselves in similar circumstances in the Caribbean. In the second week, one of them proposed they should "cast lots to settle on whose body they should assuage their ravenous hunger."[3] It is not clear if the men cast dice, broke matches, drew straws, or played "rock, paper, scissors," but, in the end, the one who proposed the idea lost the contest and was eaten, no doubt over his protests that he had just been kidding. With the lesser odds of one in four for the intrepid crew of the fated *Mignonette*, Edmond Brooks would have none of it. The matter was dropped when he, always the spoilsport, protested that "he did not wish to kill anybody and did not wish anybody to kill him."[4]

Some days later, Richard Parker, parched and beyond sound advice, could stand his thirst no more. He cupped his hands with seawater and drank heartily. Shortly thereafter, he was curled in the bottom of the boat, sick, weak, and helpless, drifting in and out of consciousness and lucidity. By the eighteenth day, the fifth without food, it was once again proposed that lots be drawn, but again Brooks would not agree. In the meantime, young Parker began to look more appetizing. The next day, Dudley and Stephens agreed between themselves that if they were not rescued by the next morning, Parker would be killed. After all, they had families and he did not, and he was the weakest and the most likely to die first.

As dawn broke, Stephens took the tiller from Brooks, who crawled to the bow of the boat to rest. Stephens' and Dudley's eyes met. It was time. Dudley drew out a 2-inch penknife, prayed that their souls might be saved, and told Parker that his time had come. Parker was too weak to resist or protest. Thus, on the twentieth day, Dudley pressed the dulled knife into Parker's throat, and there the cabin boy's adventure ended. The bailer was filled with his blood, which Dudley and Stephens drank. Dudley then cut open Parker's belly to expose the liver, which they ate. Brooks, who claimed to have fainted just before the killing, resisted temptation for a time, but ultimately he too partook of the cabin boy. For the next four days, the three survivors fed on Richard Parker's body and blood.

On 29 July 1884, while the men lay weakened and ill in the bottom of the boat, it was boarded by rescuers from the German barque *Montezuma*. One of the sailors, Julius Erich Marten Weise, would later describe the scene:

> They were all very weak, Dudley and Stephens being the worst. He saw in the boat small pieces of flesh, one piece of a rib, some old clothes, a chronometer, a sextant, and a compass. . . . At the moment he could not tell what sort of flesh or bone they were. They were all too excited. When the men came on board, none of them said what the remains were.[5]

After regaining their strength, and believing that they had acted justifiably, the men agreed to tell their story, ultimately sharing it with the customs officials when they arrived in Cornwall. Much to the surprise of the men, they were promptly arrested by the harbour police. Dudley, obviously the sentimental type, was reported to have asked the officials if he could hold onto his penknife "as a keepsake."

Without the aid of television or radio, word of the bizarre killing spread rapidly through England. On 8 September 1884, two days after their arrival home, the men were taken to Falmouth Police Court and charged with murder. The matter was adjourned for three days before a packed courtroom. When the three reappeared on the third day, their counsel asked for bail to be set. Although all but unheard of in homicide cases, it was granted. A *Times* reporter related that this decision "was received with applause in a crowded court."[6] The people on the street understood the cruel dilemma the men had been under, and there was widespread sympathy for them.

Even though everyone knew that Dudley, with Stephens' approval and encouragement, had killed Richard Parker intentionally, the prosecutors still had a difficult case to prove. They needed the testimony of at least one of the three men, yet all were charged, and, at the time, accused persons were not allowed to appear as witnesses. Brooks' status therefore changed from that of an accused to a witness for the Crown. It was a reasonable choice. He had not participated in planning the killing, or in carrying it out, nor had he even encouraged it. In the eyes of the law, he was innocent and should not have been charged in the first place. Then, as now, it was not a crime to witness a crime, or to fail to intercede to prevent one.

At their trial, Dudley and Stephens tried to justify the killing of Richard Parker on the basis that it was necessary in all the circumstances. The accused argued "that in order to satisfy your own life, you may lawfully take away the life of another."[7] That being so, they contended that their act of intentionally killing the cabin boy was not criminal.

The idea that people can choose to disregard the law where it is somehow "necessary" to do so is, in some respects, a frightening prospect. As Lord Edmund-Davies of the English Court of Appeal was to say close to a century later, "necessity can very easily become simply a mask for anarchy."[8] Still, the idea has undeniable appeal. The rules of law are by their nature rules of general application, and there will be unforeseeable situations where the application of the law makes little sense. Jonathan Swift's Gulliver discovered as much when he was in Lilliput. After he had gained their trust enough to be untied and to roam the kingdom, mindful always to avoid stepping on Lilliputians, horses, houses, and the like, he happened upon the royal palace after fire had broken out in its rear towers. He could stomp the fire out, but that would do little for the palace, so, thinking quickly, he chose to "make water," as Swift so delicately put it, to extinguish the flames. The king was happy to overlook the strict ordinance against relieving oneself in a public place because this breach of the law saved the palace.⁹ Things would have been worse had Gulliver been bashful about it, or intimidated by the law.

Unfortunately for Dudley and Stephens, the imagined adventures of Gulliver in Lilliput could not stand as a precedent, and the court was interested in what English law had to say on the matter. Lord Coleridge, the chief justice, writing for a bench of five judges, analysed the law and concluded that the only authority to support a proposition that necessity can be a defence to a crime, including homicide, was Lord Bacon. The irony of a man named after cured meat endorsing a doctrine that would allow Englishmen to select persons for victuals was lost on Lord Coleridge, or he at least had the good taste to avoid making a point of it. Instead, he rested content to observe that even as great a lawyer as Lord Bacon had erred in principle. "If Lord Bacon meant to lay down the broad proposition that a man may save his life by killing, if necessary, an innocent and unoffending neighbour, it certainly is not the law of the present day."¹⁰

The chief justice had numerous reasons for rejecting the defence. First, was what happened on the lifeboat really a case of necessity at all?

> Who is to be the judge of this sort of necessity? By what measure is the comparative value of lives to be measured? . . . In this case the weakest, the youngest, the most unresisting, was chosen. Was it more necessary to kill him than one of the grown men?¹¹

Of course not. Any of the men could have served equally well as "filet *Mignonette*." More important were the implications of recognizing such actions as justifiable. Taking the life of another in self-preservation is not always a morally acceptable choice. There are times when self-preservation is not the highest duty. Indeed, the "plainest and highest duty may be to sacrifice [one's life]," such as in war, or in the case of a shipwreck where the captain and crew must perish to give passengers room on the lifeboats, or as it is with "soldiers [who should save] women and children" ahead of themselves:

> [T]hese duties impose on men the moral necessity, not of preservation, but of the sacrifice of their lives for others, from which no country, least of all, it is to be hoped in England, will men ever shrink, as indeed, they have not shrunk.¹²

Now, it may be that not being a soldier or a sailor or even an Englishman, I do not have the appropriate ethic, but I know myself well enough to be confident that I would not have piped up "Oh, eat me, please, I insist," at the first sign of impending starvation. Like Dudley and Stephens and most other humans, I believe I am conditioned to shrink to survive. To most contemporary people, self-sacrifice is a noble thing, but it is hardly a universal legal principle that guides the criminal law.

Lord Coleridge was worried not only about honour and higher duty but about the precedent that would be set. It was not that he was troubled by the precise fear that if this killing was held to be justified, in the future the menu on cruise ships could be expected to express the caveat that management reserves the right to substitute "pâté de foie de cabin boy" for "pâté de foie gras." His concern was the much more general one that to recognize a broad necessity-based justification for homicide would diminish intolerably the degree of respect the law accords to human life. He was therefore at pains to confine the circumstances in which the killing of another can be justified as necessary. He held that the only form of necessity he would countenance as justifying the killing of another is self-defence against an assailant.[13] The killing of Richard Parker had nothing to do with self-defence because the cabin boy posed no threat to the men. The law therefore needed to set its face against this kind of self-serving conduct, however harsh the result might seem:[14]

> It must not be supposed that in refusing to admit temptation to be an excuse for crime it is forgotten how terrible the temptation was; how awful the suffering; how hard in such trials to keep the judgment straight and the conduct pure. We are often compelled to set up standards we cannot reach ourselves, and to lay down rules which we could not ourselves satisfy. But a man has no legal right to declare temptation to be an excuse, though he might himself have yielded to it, nor allow compassion for the criminal to change or weaken in any manner the legal definition of the crime. It is therefore our duty to declare that the prisoners' act in this case was wilful murder, that the facts as stated in the verdict are no legal justification for homicide.

The men were guilty, and the sentence was death.

To leave this story there would be to mislead. The weight of the predicament facing Dudley and Stephens, and the natural human weakness that impelled them to choose life over honour, was not lost on Victorian society. It was tacitly agreed by all concerned that while the court must stoutly denounce the conduct and sentence without sympathy, a reprieve would be granted by the Home Secretary, who in modern times held the king's power to pardon offenders. The usual drama was therefore decidedly absent from the courtroom that 9 December 1884 when the death sentence was pronounced. Indeed, so as not to scare the two men too badly, Lord Coleridge chose not to don the black cap that was customarily worn when sentencing prisoners to death. Shortly afterwards, the sentence of death was commuted to six months in prison. In fact, it is doubted that Dudley and Stephens ever served any of that time.[15] These men "got away with murder" not by legal excuse, but through executive clemency, as a concession to human weakness.

Whatever one might think about the merits of the case, the *Dudley and Stephens* saga is the kind of story that can discredit the law. The trial was a charade. The justices were able to make hard and clear pronouncements about the law without having to be concerned about any injustice to the defendants. What would they have done if there had been no power to pardon convicted offenders, or if it was clear that no pardon would be forthcoming? Would these men have died for failing to reach standards that "we could not ourselves satisfy"? Where is the justice in that, and what is the point in punishing it? In the end, the rule of law sustained more damage when the court imposed a sentence that it knew would not be carried out than it would have if the court had recognized a defence that would allow the law to be avoided in appropriate cases.

Victims of Circumstance: The Defence of Necessity

The law in Canada has since come to recognize a general defence of necessity, albeit an extremely limited one. It happened in a case[16] involving another ship, the *Samarkanda*. This fine vessel, which left port in Tumaco, Colombia, bound for Alaska, carrying 634 bales of cannabis, began to experience more mechanical problems than the Mir space station. Then, when the weather whipped up off the coast of Canada, the crew became endangered. The ship was forced to move into a sheltered cove on the west coast of Vancouver Island for repairs. The boat got caught on a rock because the depth sounder was not working. Then the tide ran out, causing the vessel to list to starboard. The crew was forced to off-load the cargo, bringing the marijuana ashore in the process.

The men never intended to import this narcotic into Canada. They were not lily-white, since they were intending to import it into the United States, but they had not planned to bring it into Canadian waters. They therefore argued that they should not be convicted of importing the narcotic into Canada. They landed along with their cargo solely because it had become necessary. A west-coast jury accepted this argument and acquitted the men. The Crown appealed. The Supreme Court of Canada had to decide whether "necessity" was an acceptable legal defence, and, if so, whether the trial judge got it right when he told the jury about it.

Justice Dickson, later to become the Chief Justice of Canada, went through much the same process as Lord Coleridge had many years before him, referring to the views of philosophers, ethicists, legal authorities, and to prior decisions. In the end, he held that there is a defence of necessity, but that the trial judge had it wrong when he explained it to the jury, so there had to be a retrial of the men. He did not say that the men had a valid defence. What he said was that they had the right to have their case decided correctly according to law. In other words, let's get the law right and *then* convict them.

Unfortunately, Canadians will never know whether the defence would have worked for the crew of the *Samarkanda*. After their first trial ended in the acquittal, the accused men all left the country, as they were entitled to do, returning to their lives and their jobs in the United States. After its successful appeal, the Crown sought to have the men extradicted so they could be retried. The men urged the American courts to refuse to extradict them, arguing that forcing them to be retried was unjust. Their argument was based on the fact that in the United States, jury verdicts of acquittal are considered to be final. In the American system, the prosecutors would not have been allowed to appeal, so an American court should not send them to Canada to allow a Canadian court to do that. In the end, the men did return for their retrial, but so much time had passed that they applied to a Canadian court to have the charges thrown out for unreasonable delay. In a decision that would not be decided the same way on the current law, the trial judge held that their right to be tried within a reasonable time had indeed been breached. When this happens, a court has no choice but to stop the prosecution because, if it allowed it to continue, a court would be permitting a trial to be held after a reasonable time for doing so had passed. So the charges against the crew of the *Samarkanda* were dismissed. The legacy of the case was not prison terms for the men. It was an authoritative pronouncement by the Supreme Court of Canada on the nature and scope of the defence of necessity.

In developing the defence, Justice Dickson explained that there are two different but related ideas behind the concept of necessity. The first is the "utilitarian" notion that there are cases, like Gulliver's, where it is justifiable to break the letter of the law because doing so will avoid greater harm than obeying it. The second is a "humanitarian" principle. In emergencies, it may be that obeying the law imposes an intolerable burden on the accused, and, where this is so, the law should not punish the conduct. He then embarked on a discussion that has bedevilled Canadian lawyers ever since. He drew a distinction between defences that are "justifications" and defences that are "excuses." As he explained, some con-

duct is not criminal because it is justifiable. We applaud it. This is generally true of self-defence, where we recognize that conduct that is normally against the law is morally right. Such acts are "justifiable." Other
conduct is not criminal, even though we may deplore it and it is not right,
because we realize that it is not politic or fair to punish it. In such cases
we "excuse" the crime. He then explained that it is best to consider
"necessity" to be an excuse:

> It rests on a realistic assessment of human weakness, recognizing that
> a liberal and humane criminal law cannot hold people to strict obe-
> dience of laws in emergency situations where normal human
> instincts, whether of self-preservation or altruism, overwhelmingly
> impel disobedience. The objectivity of the criminal law is preserved:
> such acts are still wrongful, but in the circumstances they are excus-
> able. Praise is indeed not bestowed, but pardon is, when one does a
> wrongful act under pressure which, in the words of Aristotle . . .
> "overstrains human nature and which no one could withstand."[17]

As he explained it, the "choice" to break the law is not realistically a "voluntary one." It is "remorselessly compelled by normal human instincts." It
constitutes "moral or normative involuntariness,"[18] and it is therefore as
wrong to punish it as if the action had been unintentional.

On the face of it, this theory would seem to fit the actions of
Dudley and Stephens quite nicely. Lord Coleridge said that the "prisoners were subject to terrible temptation, to sufferings that might break
down the bodily power of the strongest man, and try the conscience of
the best."[19] Yet there is often a gulf between legal theory and the legal
rules that emerge. Justice Dickson was afraid that this defence could
"become the last resort of scoundrels,"[20] so he developed a legal rule that
has strict limits — limits so strict, in fact, that they would have denied
even Dudley and Stephens of a defence. First, there must be a situation of
"imminent risk" where the action is taken to avoid a direct and immediate peril. Second, there can be no alternative, legal way of avoiding that
peril. Third, the harm inflicted must be less than the harm sought to be
avoided. And fourth, the peril cannot be a foreseeable consequence of the
accused's own actions. Dudley and Stephens would likely have foundered
on the first, second, and third criteria. Was there really an "immediate and
direct peril" or did they kill the boy too soon? Perhaps they could have
waited one more day, or two, or even three. It appeared that he was going
to die before them in any event. Should they not have waited for the legal
alternative of letting God decide? And can it be said that the harm
inflicted, the death of one, is less than the harm sought to be avoided, the

starvation of all four? Perhaps, but can we measure such things numerically? And was it necessary to choose the youngest and weakest rather than, say, Brooks, who was being thoroughly uncooperative about the plan in any event? The great jurist, Oliver Wendell Holmes, argued that the law should have excused the men if they had drawn "lots" to make the selection process fair. In Holmes' remarkable legal mind, Parker's ground for complaint was not that he was eaten, but that he was eaten without a fair selection process.

This necessity defence has worked in Canada before, but only for relatively minor charges. It has been used successfully in speeding cases where drivers have exceeded speed limits to avoid tailgaters. It has even been employed in spousal assault cases, where self-defence was not available. One night when a couple named Morris were returning from an evening at a pub that they patronized regularly, things got ugly. Mrs. Morris was inebriated and agitated because a friend of hers, who had been banned from the pub "for life," was arrested for coming to the pub and causing a disturbance. She and other supporters of the woman had been making a ruckus, demanding that the woman be served, while an opposing camp were telling her to leave. Mrs. Morris was most distraught over what she perceived to be the maltreatment of this woman by the police, who were ultimately called. After thinking about it for a while during the drive home, she demanded that Mr. Morris turn the car around and go to the police station. What happened after he refused can best be told in Mr. Morris' own words:

Q: Did your wife do anything that would cause you to have concern for her safety?

A: Well she said if I wouldn't do anything she wanted to get out of the truck and go back. Now my wife was quite drunk, it was approximately 2 miles out of town by then which is a long run for a drunk person. She wouldn't have done any good and I couldn't see her being drunk and going up to argue with the policeman anyways, its not exactly what I thought was right. She then reached for the door to jump out.

Q: And at this time the vehicle is in motion?

A: Yes, the vehicle was in motion. I grabbed her around the neck and made the corner.[21]

Not guilty. Apparently a half-nelson by the driver of a moving vehicle, normally an offence and almost always an ill-advised manoeuvre, can, in some circumstances, be prudent, wise, and "necessary." After all, Mr. Morris not only saved her from harm but he made the corner.

More recently, a man named Manning used the same defence. His "common law" was also drunk and she was pregnant. During a dispute, she had grabbed a large rock and was threatening to hit her own abdomen with it:

> The accused reacted immediately to this perceived threat of injury to the foetus by slapping the complainant once in her face, with sufficient force to cause a black eye to develop. This was the end of the incident.[22]

Manning was lucky he did not get the rock in the head. It would have no doubt been better had he simply grabbed it and restrained his partner. On the other hand, his chosen tactic, although crude, was effective. More important, the saga engendered enough sympathy in the judge that he acquitted the man, finding the slap to be necessary in the circumstances to prevent a greater evil.

It is one thing to allow the defence of necessity for lesser charges, even when there may be technical problems with its application, but what about serious offences like homicide? The Law Reform Commission of Canada has suggested that a law be passed so that the defence of necessity should not be available to anyone who "purposely kills or seriously harms another person."[23] As the application of the defence to the facts of *Dudley and Stephen* shows, this is probably unnecessary on the current state of the law, even if it is considered appropriate to limit the defence in this way. When will an intentional killing ever satisfy the defence's rigid criteria? The only reported effort to use the necessity defence to excuse the intentional killing of a human being in Canada was by Saskatchewan farmer Robert Latimer. He killed his daughter Tracy because medical science was incapable of alleviating her excruciating pain, and the only way to end her suffering was to "see her put to sleep." The trial judge refused to allow the jury even to consider this defence. There was no "imminent and direct peril"; the problem was with Tracy's quality of life, not with any immediate emergency. Nor was it a situation of "normative voluntariness." Many people are visited with similar misfortune and they are not dispatched by their loved ones. Ending Tracy's life was not the only choice. As the trial judge put it:

> [T]here was an option, albeit not a particularly happy one. The option was to persevere in the attempts to make Tracy comfortable in her life, however disagreeable and heart wrenching those attempts might have been.[24]

The general "excuse" of necessity does not, therefore, provide a serious basis for defending homicide charges.

A Concession to Cowardice:
The Defence of Duress

There are other defences, closely related to necessity, that can arise in homicide cases. One is the defence of duress. It came before the Supreme Court of Canada in the recent case of *R. v. Hibbert*,[25] a case involving the ambush and non-fatal shooting of Fitzroy Cohen.

Lawrence Hibbert, or "Pigeon" to his friends, was Fitzroy Cohen's best friend, at least until he set Cohen up. Both young men were acquaintances of a drug dealer named Mark Bailey, better known on the streets of Toronto as "Dogheart" or "Quasi." Hibbert made it a point to avoid Quasi. He had stiffed Quasi for $100 worth of drugs and thought it best not to be in his company. His friend Cohen had even greater reason to avoid Bailey. He had made the mistake of laughing at Bailey while Bailey was being robbed by a rival drug dealer named Andrew Reid. When Reid was later found dead and another young man who had been involved in the robbery was fired on by Bailey, Cohen knew full well that he had best stay clear. He had "dissed" the wrong guy. He managed to avoid Bailey quite effectively until the evening his friend Hibbert led Bailey to his apartment and lured him into a trap.

It happened one evening in November 1991. Hibbert had been visiting another friend at an Etobicoke apartment. He swaggered into the lobby. His runners no doubt squeaked to a halt on the tile floor when he saw Bailey standing there. "Hey, Pigeon," Bailey said. After this brief salutation, which was missing the friendly inflection that Hibbert would have hoped for, Bailey grabbed him. Without observing the niceties of the Queen's English, Bailey managed to communicate to Hibbert that he had a chore for him, and a gun to see that he did it. Hibbert was going to take Bailey to find Cohen. At first Hibbert played tough and refused. After being dragged into the basement and punched in the face a few times, his resolve weakened. He was sure that he would be shot if he did not cooperate, and came to recognize that discretion is the better part of valour, friend or no friend.

Bailey led him to his car and made him get in. He then raced through the city streets, before screeching to a halt next to a phone booth. He told Hibbert to call Cohen to arrange a meeting in the lobby of Cohen's apartment building. He crowded the phone box to listen to the conversation: "Hey Fitzroy. It's Pigeon. Listen, man. I have something for you. Meet me in the lobby at your place in twenty minutes." He hung up.

A half an hour later, the two men arrived at Cohen's apartment building. As they got out of the car, Bailey took out his pistol and trained it on Hibbert. They made their way to the doors at the front of the building, where Hibbert called Cohen's apartment on the intercom: "Come on down, Fitzroy. It's me." He did not ask Cohen to buzz the door open, hoping that Cohen would come down and see Bailey through the locked glass and flee. But, as he put down the intercom phone, Hibbert heard the obnoxious growl of the automatic door lock being held open, and he was walked into the lobby by Bailey. Meanwhile, Cohen jogged down the stairs from his second-floor apartment and strode into the lobby to greet his friend. Before he knew what was happening, Bailey grabbed him. Pulling Cohen towards him, Bailey pushed the gun into his chest saying, "You're dead now, pussy." He ordered Hibbert, who by now was "all sweating," to "stay some place where I see you." He then turned his undivided attention to Cohen. The two had a hurried discussion before Bailey pushed him away and opened fire. Four shots struck Cohen, in the groin, legs, and buttocks. Cohen lay bleeding on the floor. Bailey turned to Hibbert and said, "Come, Pigeon." When they got to the car he calmly explained to Hibbert that he would kill him if he went to the police. He then drove him to Etobicoke and dropped him off.

Hibbert debated with himself about what to do. After some reflection, he called Cohen's brother and told him what had happened. He then called Cohen's mother. He even tried calling Cohen's apartment in the hope that maybe he was all right. The next day he turned himself into police and was charged with attempted murder. Bailey, the shooter, managed to avoid capture, leaving Hibbert holding the bag.

Hibbert, of course, had not done the shooting. In our law, anyone who aids or abets in the commission of a criminal offence is as guilty as the perpetrator. Aiding involves giving assistance, while abetting is encouraging or promoting the criminal act. Whereas Stephens "abetted" Dudley by agreeing with him that Parker would be killed for the benefit of both of them, Hibbert had "aided" Bailey by leading him to his prey and by helping him lure Cohen into the line of fire. For this, he was convicted of aggravated assault and sentenced to four years in jail. He appealed all the way to the Supreme Court of Canada. The issue was whether the jury members, who had rejected the defence of duress, had properly understood it. Their understanding depended on whether the judge described it correctly when he explained it to them.

The defence of duress is spelled out in section 17 of the *Criminal Code of Canada*. That provision gives a complete defence to an accused person who acts under compulsion by threats of immediate death or bodily harm from a person who is present, provided the accused believes that the threat will be carried out. The defence is based, of course, on the recognition that it would be unjust to punish people for being human enough to behave as others might well do if found in the same situation. Still, it has long been felt by some that there should be limits to when we excuse criminal conduct "as a concession to human weakness" because the crime was committed under duress. Since 1893, when section 17 was drafted, this excuse has not been available for particularly serious offences like murder, attempted murder, robbery, sexual assault, and aggravated assault. The sentiment that limits the defence was captured by Lord Hailsham in comments he made in 1987:

> I do not believe that as a "concession to human frailty" [murderers] should be exempt from liability to criminal sanctions. . . . I have known in my lifetime of too many acts of heroism by ordinary human beings of no more than ordinary fortitude to regard a law as either "just or humane" which withdraws the protection of the criminal law from the innocent victim and casts the cloak of its protection upon the coward and the poltroon in the name of a "concession to human frailty."[26]

As Sir James Stephen said almost one hundred years before:

> Surely it is at the moment when temptation to crime is strongest that the law should speak most clearly and emphatically to the contrary. It is, of course, a misfortune for a man that he should be placed between two fires, but it would be a much greater misfortune for society at large if criminals could confer immunity upon their agents by threatening them with death or violence if they refused to execute their commands.[27]

When faced with the muzzle of a gun in your mouth, then, you are legally obliged to spit it out and sputter, "Go ahead and kill me." If you are a coward or a poltroon who is not made of such stern stuff, and you kill to save yourself, you are to be convicted of the same offence as the thrill killer, the psychopathic killer, or the child killer. You are a murderer, and you chose to burn yourself on the wrong fire.

All this clearly rests on notions of honour. The law is not so preposterous as to presume that it can inspire individuals into accepting immediate death or injury out of fear of some potential lesser punishment. It therefore expresses a value judgment. It chooses to dub, as evil, the pitiable act of self-preservation that many, if not most, of us would undertake if caught between two fires.

This harsh policy is not without its detractors. In 1973 a man named Clermont asked Pacquette for a ride because his car had broken down.

Pacquette agreed. Clermont got into the car and told Pacquette they were going to do a robbery at the Pop Shoppe. When Pacquette declined the invitation, Clermont pulled a gun and changed Pacquette's mind. On instructions, Pacquette picked up another man, Simard, and then a rifle. Pacquette was told to wait outside while the other two went inside the shop. He panicked and drove around the block. In the meantime, Simard fired a shot, killing a bystander. He and Clermont ran out of the store and twice tried to climb into Pacquette's vehicle, but he kept driving and they were left behind. The lesson for robbers, of course, is never let a poltroon drive the get-away car.

The law of murder was particularly harsh at the time. Although unintentional killers were normally convicted only of manslaughter, in some cases the law treated people who did not intend to kill as murderers. When this happened, the accused was convicted of "constructive murder."[28] This occurred, for example, if someone died at the hands of a robber who was carrying a firearm, even if the firearm discharged by accident. The usual requirement for murder — that the killing be intentional — was waived because the intention by the robber to commit a robbery while armed with a gun was considered to be evil enough, and the act dangerous enough, to justify treating the killer as if he had actually intended to kill. Indeed, not only was the shooter guilty of murder but so too were those who aided and abetted him in the robbery. Simard and Clermont were therefore guilty of murder, whether or not Simard intended to kill the bystander. As for Pacquette, because he drove them to the robbery, he too was guilty of murder — unless he had a defence to the charge. The relevant defence, of course, was duress — but section 17 of the *Criminal Code* does not apply to the offence of murder.

Pacquette did not give in so easily, and, fortunately for him, the Supreme Court of Canada became creative. It used a technical argument to hold that the restricted defence of duress in section 17 of the *Criminal Code* did not apply to Pacquette. Instead, a more generous common law or judge-made defence of duress would apply, and this defence is available in murder cases. Section 17, the Court held, did not cover Pacquette because it applies only to "a person who commits . . . murder." Pacquette did not "commit murder." He aided murder, which is a different thing. He could therefore use the broader common law defence. As a result, he was found not guilty.

Pacquette's good fortune inured to the benefit of Lawrence Hibbert. Like Pacquette, Hibbert was not the shooter. He had only aided the shooter. He could therefore avoid section 17 and rely on the broader common law defence. Since the trial judge had not properly described the common law defence to Hibbert's jury, the Supreme Court of Canada held that he was entitled to a new trial. Apparently the Crown had had enough. It decided to withdraw the charges against Hibbert, content with the eighteen months he had served in custody awaiting his appeal.

Unquestionably, the Pacquette decision to dodge the restrictions of section 17 by clever interpretation and to make a duress defence available was sparked by sympathy for Pacquette's predicament. What could he reasonably have been expected to do? The Court did not like the absolute bar on using duress as a defence to murder and therefore got creative, as a concession to human weakness and out of a realization that it would be unjust to convict Pacquette of murder. What had he done? He had driven, at gunpoint, two armed men to a robbery. If you are not convinced that the Court should have gone out of its way to avoid convicting him of murder by relying on this "technicality," ask yourself how you would feel if the hijacked driver had been your grandmother. When the law becomes unduly harsh, it is often rendered irrelevant by creative compassion.

Just Following Orders: The Defence of Obedience to Authority

In recent years, the law has had to grapple with a necessity-based excuse in a remarkably different context. Imre Finta, a Hungarian national who had fled Hungary for Canada after the Second World War, was being prosecuted for offences that included robbery, kidnapping, and manslaughter. As part of the "final solution," Hungarian Jews were rounded up, dispossessed of their property, and detained before being taken off to concentration camps. The Crown said that Finta was in charge of a holding facility contained at a Hungarian brickyard, and that he was ultimately responsible for detaining hundreds of Jews in the kilns and drying sheds that had once fired and held hot bricks. He supervised the soldiers who pushed close to one hundred terrified human beings into each boxcar, even though those cars would have been crowded with half that number. Many had to stand for the long journey. Conditions were so unspeakable and deplorable, so dehumanizing, that many, particularly the elderly, died in transport.

When the evidence in the case was done, the trial judge described the law to the jury. One of the things he told them distressed the Crown. He said that they should consider whether the defence of "obedience to military orders" applied to Imre Finta. When the jury acquitted him, the Crown appealed to the Supreme Court of Canada, arguing that this defence could not be used in a war crimes prosecution. The Supreme

Court disagreed. It held that the defence of obedience to superior orders is available to members of the military or police officers in two situations, including war crimes prosecutions. First, if the orders in question are not "manifestly illegal" according to international law, it is a defence to obey them. Second, even if the orders in question are "manifestly illegal" because they are obviously and flagrantly wrong, there will be a defence where the accused "has no moral choice as to whether to follow those orders." The Court explained the absence of moral choice in more detail:

> That is to say, there was such an air of compulsion and threat to the accused that the accused had no alternative but to obey the orders. As an example, the accused could be found to have been compelled to carry out the manifestly unlawful order in circumstances where the accused would be shot if he or she failed to carry out the orders.[29]

In short, while the honourable thing to do may be to throw oneself on one's own bayonet rather than to defile and degrade others, natural human weakness, the survival instinct, the compulsion of self-preservation, can nonetheless remove the evil from acts of great atrocity.

The irony of this interpretation will not, I trust, be lost. As the law now stands, soldiers, our bravest and strongest, those who are trained to put life and limb at risk for God and country, are given a defence that is denied to peacetime cowards and poltroons. A soldier who is ordered to do so can kidnap, rape, pillage, kill, and torture with impunity, so long as those acts are done because he fears he will be killed or tortured if he refuses. Soldiers can set huts on fire, drop grenades into dugout shelters filled with women and children, and fire revolvers into the necks of civilians. In the meantime, civilians who commit murder with a gun to their head are treated much more harshly. Those who aid and abet murders can shelter under the clever technicality of the *Pacquette* decision, but those who pull the trigger or plant the bomb have no defence. Worse, they are subject to conviction for an offence that has a minimum penalty of life in prison without eligibility for parole for between ten and twenty-five years. There is no room for them even to use their horrendous dilemma to mitigate their sentences.

In this state of affairs, it is not difficult to predict that the law will change. It cannot go on as it is. Does it make any sense to convict Dudley and Stephens for their acts of self-preservation while exonerating soldiers who have aided genocide to preserve themselves? Does it make any sense to tell Hibbert he is innocent because he only lured Cohen into firing range, but he would have been guilty had he been forced to pull the trigger? The law is currently in this state not because there is no vision about what constitutes sufficient moral fault to warrant punishment, but because it is the lot of the common law to develop on a case-by-case basis. When appropriate facts present themselves, the courts will use the *Charter* to remove the restrictions in section 17 to allowing the defence of duress for serious offences like murder and aggravated assault. They will allow accused persons to exonerate themselves where they had no choice but to kill, maim, or kidnap. They will do so because it is both pointless and contrary to basic principles of moral fault to punish those who do evil things without having any real choice in the matter. When this happens, Canada will not be rendered less safe than it is now. A moment's reflection should reveal that any law that purports to encourage people to sacrifice themselves now to avoid future punishment is only so much wasted paper. Canada will not be rendered less safe, but it will become more sympathetic to the realities of the human condition. There is a natural tendency to want to punish despicable acts, but the fact is that some despicable acts are done under intolerable pressure. Where this is so, the law must excuse, even if it means that some will get away with murder.

CHAPTER 12

Kill or Be Killed: The Law of Self-Defence

J oe Pintar stirred in his bed.[1] He had been awakened by noises outside his bedroom door. "Must be Stephanie and her boyfriend," he thought, "but what the hell are they doing?" A splinter of early morning light was leaking through the crack between the curtains. He could just make out the time on the old alarm clock beside the bed. Six forty-five. Seven hours before, his daughter and her boyfriend had gone to bed in her upstairs room after the three of them sat up talking. Pintar pulled himself up and took the morning's first shuffling steps, stiff and unsteady. Still squinting, he entered the hall to see what was going on. What he saw drove him from the loosening grip of sleep. Standing menacingly in front of him was Alan Ross, a man who had a big bone to pick with Pintar. His face was ruddy and his eyes were heavy.

"What are you doing in here, Alan? Get the hell out."

"Bullshit. I'm here to finish this off."

Ross, turned strong by years of farming, advanced, taking a swing at Pintar. Pintar's instincts took over. He ducked and countered, catching Ross with a punch to the face. Ross reeled backwards. The screen door flew open as Ross fell against it, then sprawled onto the porch outside. Pintar slammed the door and threw the bolt. He hurried into his bedroom and jumped into his clothes, sure that the fracas was not yet over. Ross, who had regained his feet, pressed his face against the broken window frame and shouted: "Let's get this over with. Come outside. Get the fuck out here. Joe, I want to talk to you. You sonofabitch, I killed your cock-sucking dog and I'm going to kill you."

Joe Pintar had no need to wonder why Ross was after him. Neither did Stephanie, who had been awakened by the commotion. Pintar half-expected this moment to arrive. He had known Alan Ross and his wife, Rose, for more than two decades, ever since they had purchased neighbouring farms at Pass Lake near Thunder Bay, Ontario. He knew Ross as the bully he was, a man who abused Rose and his children. Many times Pintar had been the peace-maker, taking it upon himself to walk across the field to Ross' house to talk him down when things got out of hand. After twenty years of just being neighbours though, things changed. Pintar became Rose Ross' lover. When she finally left Alan Ross in early 1990 and went to Winnipeg, Pintar fancied her enough to follow her into the bite of a prairie winter, and the two developed a relationship. Soon after, Rose had a change of heart and returned to Ross. Yet she and Pintar did not end their affair. While they remained with their spouses and children, they never stopped seeing each other, not after she returned, and certainly not after she walked out on Ross for good in July 1992. Not surprisingly, Ross had not accepted this breakup well.

Word was out that Ross would like to kill Pintar, whom he blamed for the loss of his wife. He had once even asked his son, Ron, if he could help him find a hitman to do the job. Ron warned Pintar, and later told him of another threat Ross had made. In the summer of 1993 Ross continued with his threatening behaviour, telling Rose he would rather kill her and Pintar than pay the money she was seeking in the divorce settlement. Once, when he bumped into Pintar, Ross told him that he and Rose would pay for what they had done. Pintar tried to put these threats off as naked bravado or drunken talk, but he could not help worrying that the volatile Ross might try to make good. As Pintar rushed to finish dressing, he was certain it was now more than talk. Ross was trying to hurt him.

Alan Ross did not decide calmly that early morning of 15 August 1993 that now it was time to get his pound of flesh. His long-simmering anger was turned into a half-cocked plan of action through the lethal combination of copious amounts of alcohol and the flooding testosterone of the young male animal. Not Ross' flooding testosterone — he was forty-seven — but Jason Gill's. Gill, a 210-pound twenty-year-old had been helping Ross at the riding stable. After going to a community dance the night before, the two met at Ross' place with other friends and drank the night away. Ross began to curse Pintar and allowed as to how he would like to give him "one good punch." Gill, pumped up by the thought of watching someone get hurt, or maybe even helping to hurt someone himself, egged Ross on: "Yes. He messed with your wife. He deserves to be hit. He deserves it." By 4:30 Gill was not only affirming the validity of Ross' desire for payback. He was prompting Ross into action and offering his help: "Let's go. Let's do it."

Ross, loaded with 246 milligrams of alcohol per 100 millilitres of blood, enough to pickle eggs with their shells still on, "drove" the half-ton.

Gill, whose autopsy would later reveal that his reading was a close second at 232 milligrams, "rode shotgun." The stage had been set: two drunken bullies, bouncing on the bench seat of a pickup as it ploughed through the potholes of a country road, riding off to meet their maker.

At the sound of her father and Ross fighting, Stephanie ran downstairs. She could hear Ross continuing to scream at the door. She told her father to stay where he was and went outside, thinking she could convince Ross to leave. When she opened the door, she noticed Gill sitting in the truck. Ross ignored her and continued to taunt Joe Pintar into coming out. Pintar, unwilling to leave his daughter out there alone with the enraged Ross, stepped outside. Ross threatened him again: "I killed your dog and now I am going to kill you. You fucked up my life. Nobody is getting a penny out of me." Gill, seeing things heat up, jumped out of the truck so he could contribute his own thoughts on justice and wrongdoing. Through the stench of heavy beer breath he bellowed: "You've been fucking around with his woman and now you're going to pay."

Stephanie pleaded with both men to leave. Gill then moved towards Stephanie, telling her to shut her mouth or he would do it for her. Pintar decided he needed the great equalizer. He ran inside and grabbed his rifle. At first he asked Stephanie's boyfriend to take the gun and fire a warning shot, but then thought the better of it and decided to handle things himself. He stepped outside, holding the gun across his chest. This did not have the desired effect. It just made Gill mad. He moved slightly towards Pintar, testing his resolve: "Come on, shoot me, shoot me, chicken shit. Why don't you put the gun down and fight us like a man."

At the risk of being rude, Pintar declined both invitations. He ordered the men to leave. Eventually, they both climbed into the truck. Ross started the engine. Then he shut off the key, turned to Gill, and made the worst decision of his life: "Fuck this. That fucking gun doesn't work anyway." Pintar told the rest of the story at his trial:

> They both got out of the truck. [Gill] said something: Nobody pulls a gun on me and gets away with it. Alan Ross yelled: You cocksuckers, you're all going to die. And, as he's walking around the front of the truck, he changes his tone of voice. He ain't yelling anymore. He's just talking to me. Now you're all going to die — you, Karen, Stephanie, Joey, Jannine and Rose. When he gets to the word Rose, he's standing right next to me and grabs the rifle and we're fighting for the rifle. [Gill's] coming. I hit Ross with the rifle. [Gill's] back. He turns around and says: I'm going to kill you, fucker. Boom, the gun went off. I turned, Ross is u[p]. Boom, the gun went off again.

> I don't remember the exact events. All I remember is myself say-
> ing, "never," when I was fighting with those two guys. There was no
> way they were going to get that gun from me.[2]

Gill died when one of the bullets tore through his neck, having been fired
from close range at a horizontal trajectory. Ross took the other bullet to
his face, just below his left eye.

Complicating Basic Instinct:
The Defence of Self-Defence

It is probably evident to all, even those who are not legally trained, that
this is a case that should turn on the law of self-defence. There are times
when people simply have no choice but to assault or even kill to preserve
themselves. No doubt since the beginning of recorded human history and
probably even before that, humans of all stripes have recognized the jus-
tifiability of using force to repel wrongful force. Self-defence is a timeless
and completely understandable notion, and it is indispensable to any
practical concept of justice. As much as we would like to discourage violence and self-help, think about the armed intruder who broke into the
prime minister's residence while the RCMP guards in the security hut
were daydreaming about the musical ride. Imagine a law that would have
thrown the street-fighter from Shawinigan in jail if he had managed to
cream the man with four pounds of soapstone.

Self-defence is a simple idea, but as with many things simple, it is
an idea that lawyers have managed to complicate. We have complicated
it so badly, in fact, that I am not sure I can explain the law of self-defence
to you in a logical fashion. Even the Chief Justice of Canada despaired at
trying to make sense of the tangle of rules, admitting that any attempt to
do so would produce some undesirable or illogical results.[3] In its treatment of self-defence, as Dickens' Mr. Bumble said in *Oliver Twist*, "the law
is a ass, a idiot." It is so technical that it is impossible to believe that many
judges, let alone jurors, understand it. In the end, self-defence cases are
probably decided more according to human instinct than law. Its complexity leaves the application of the law prone to manipulation, politics,
and emotion. How did this happen? As with many such stories, this one
begins a long time ago.

When we first began to consider homicide to be an offence against
the king's peace, the only chance of avoiding capital punishment for
killing another person was to obtain a pardon. Initially, pardons could be
granted at the king's discretion. Like all unbridled power, this one was

prone to abuse. Those who were well connected or wealthy were able to get preferred treatment. So, in 1328, a statute was passed limiting the Crown prerogative to pardon killers to cases of self-defence or accident.[4] It was in this way that self-defence became a formal legal concept.

At the time, self-defence was a narrow notion. The killing had to be an absolutely necessary act of self-preservation. The killer therefore had to retreat as far as he could safely go before he would be forgiven for killing the aggressor.[5] If he did not at least try to run to avoid the violence, he could not claim that the killing was necessary. Similarly, if a man provoked the attack on himself in some way, or if he agreed to fight, he could not kill in self-defence even if the opponent had escalated the level of violence to the point where his life fell into danger. He could not claim, in such a case, that he had to kill in self-defence because the whole mess could have been avoided had he not provoked the attack or had he declined the invitation to brawl.

Over time, "as men ceased to go about armed and manners became calmer [and] the sudden clashes of the past became less common," the law also became less strict.[6] First, the retreat requirement was abandoned for those who had not provoked the attack they defended against. Why should gentlemen have to run like cowards if attacked by a wrongdoer? Honour required that they be allowed to stand their ground. Second, while those who provoked the attack still had to try to flee when things got out of hand, if they could not get away and they had to kill in self-defence, they would be convicted of manslaughter instead of murder.

The law was complex enough, with its distinction between provoked self-defence and unprovoked self-defence and with its variable retreat criteria, even before lawyers began to flesh out the concept of necessity that buttressed the justification. First, lawyers tried to make firm rules about when fatal or extreme force, as opposed to lesser force, could be used in self-defence. It was concluded that fatal force would only be needed where the accused was at risk of death or grievous bodily harm. In other cases, a lesser degree of force should be used to fend off the assault. So, different rules developed depending on the degree of harm that the defender intended or caused. Next, an equation was drawn between imminence and necessity; self-defence could not be used to justify defending against future harm. Unless the assault was under way and the harm imminent, self-defence could not be said to be necessary. The appropriate response would be to leave or seek help, not to strike a pre-emptive blow.

As the criminal law matured, it began to pay increased attention to the state of mind of the defender. If an accused was attacked and then struck back, not in self-defence but rather in anger or with vengeance, the defence would not apply because the violence was not used for the morally innocent purpose of self-defence. In this way the state of the mind of the accused took on central importance. It was immediately appreciated, though, that more was required to justify self-defence than the belief by the accused that self-defence was needed; some persons might unreasonably come to believe that force was needed in self-defence when it was not. Would it be justifiable for them to kill or assault? Not unless their mistake was a reasonable one. This could be tested by asking whether a reasonable person, in the position of the accused, would have come to the same conclusion and would have acted in the same way.

The result of the effort to reconcile and systematize all these ideas was that the law of self-defence became a remarkably twisted body of rules. The simple idea that people should be allowed to defend them-selves from force became complex and confusing, a problem that was aggravated by some horrendous legislative drafting when the defence was put in the *Criminal Code*. The legacy is that we now have one rule of self-defence applicable to unprovoked assaults where the accused does not intend to cause death or grievous bodily harm. We have a different rule for cases where the accused causes death or grievous bodily harm, whether he intends to or not and whether he is provoked or not. This rule does not require retreat even if the accused provoked the assault he has to defend against. We have yet a third rule for self-defence by an aggres-sor, which covers the same ground as the prior rule. This rule is rarely used because, unlike the previous one, it requires retreat. And for good measure we have a fourth rule relating to self-defence designed to pre-vent an assault. On its face, this rule appears to apply to both provoked and unprovoked assaults, regardless of the consequences. Even though it seems to cover all possible permutations and combinations, making the other more specific rules redundant, the Supreme Court of Canada has told us not to use this last rule unless none of the other rules apply.

This complexity is silly. The four different self-defence sections that are currently in the *Criminal Code* cannot be reconciled with one another either technically or as statements of policy. They are the most confusing tangle of sections known to law. They are enough to drive lawyers to dis-traction. Imagine how confusing they are for juries. As Justice Moldaver said with appropriate judicial reserve when the *Pintar* case made it to the Ontario Court of Appeal: "The self-defence provisions of the *Criminal Code* are complex and confusing. They continue to plague and frustrate trial judges in their efforts to instruct juries in a meaningful and compre-hensible fashion." Without appropriate judicial reserve, it would be equally accurate to say that the law of self-defence is equine excrement. It is a breeding ground for legal error. Even when the judge gets it right, jurors sit there with confused looks on their faces, wondering whether the law makes no sense or whether it is just them. Despite consistent cries for law reform by judges, academics, and law reform bodies, the law of self-defence remains a mess because there is no political mileage in changing it. By streamlining it, the government might appear to be soft on violence. Better to leave the law a mess.

It is not surprising that the trial judge messed up when directing the jury about the law of self-defence in Joe Pintar's first trial. Indeed, even though a capable jurist, the judge made three distinct errors in what he said. These mistakes made it necessary to give Pintar a second trial, for he was entitled to have his guilt decided according to law, not according to the jury's misunderstanding of the law. We, the taxpayers, paid for the first trial, which proved a waste of time because the complexity of the law was beyond the expert comprehension of the judge.

In some respects, it may be a good thing for justice that the Pintar trial had to be redone. The jury at the first trial had somehow managed to convict Joe Pintar of manslaughter. The basis for that verdict is perplexing. To arrive at it according to law, the jury had to reject entirely the defence of self-defence, since where self-defence applies, the correct verdict is an acquittal. In law and on these facts, the jury could reach its manslaughter verdict in only two ways. Even though it seems unlikely on the facts, it could have had a doubt about whether Pintar intended to kill when he fired his high-powered rifle into the heads of the two men; Pintar talked in his testimony about how it was an unintended reflex, albeit a well-aimed one that included injecting each of the two shells into the chamber of the rifle before firing. Alternatively, the jury could have given Pintar the benefit of the partial defence of provocation, a defence that does not lead to an acquittal but does reduce the offence from murder to manslaughter. To do this, it would have had to find that Pintar acted "on the sudden" as the result of an act or insult that would have caused an ordinary person to lose the power of self-control. Although the killing of a farm dog may qualify as a sufficiently provocative act, the evidence here does not support the suggestion of a loss of control. Even after he knew his dog had been killed, Pintar was trying to avoid fatal force by scaring the men into leaving. His decision to fire the gun was not an impulsive act of vengeance, but a response to an ongoing attack. The first verdict, then, does not appear to be a case where manslaughter was chosen on the basis of law. Rather, it looks like a case where the aura of self-defence percolated through the mind-numbing legal technicality making murder convictions seem unduly harsh, but in circumstances where the jury may have felt that Pintar's actions might make a total acquittal improper. Be that as it may, at his second trial, Joe Pintar was luckier. Pintar walked away a free man because of the law of self-defence. He spent a couple of months in jail pending his appeal, but he was ultimately cleared of any criminal wrongdoing.

Was the decision right and justifiable? When you separate the wheat from the chaff, the *Criminal Code* section that was most relevant to his defence was section 34(2), the main provision that applies where death has been caused. Its requirements, like those of the other self-defence sections, are intended to ensure that self-defence is justified solely where it was reasonable for the accused to believe that the force used in self-defence was necessary.

The first prerequisite is that the accused is being, or reasonably believes he is being, "unlawfully assaulted." Most think of assaults as occurring only when the actor strikes the victim. Many do not realize that it is an assault to threaten to make such contact in circumstances where there are reasonable grounds for believing that the person making the threat has the present ability to carry it out. Both Ross and Gill were threatening force and were advancing on Pintar when he shot them. They had come to his farm for the express purpose of assaulting him and seemed more than able to do so. Without question, this first requirement was met.

The second prerequisite is that the accused believes he is at risk of death or grievous bodily harm, and it is reasonable for him to have this belief. It is relevant in such cases to consider the context of the attack and the history of the parties. The two attackers, both of whom were described in the evidence as very strong, were threatening to kill Pintar. Pintar knew Ross as a violent man who had ample motive to want him dead. Ross had been talking about killing him for some time and had even considered hiring a hitman. Ross had gone into Pintar's house looking for him while Pintar was asleep and Ross attacked him there. Ross hated Pintar's guts and had brought along a young muscle-man to back him up. What else could Pintar believe but that he was at risk of at least grievous bodily harm? Not only was it reasonable for Pintar to believe this in all of the circumstances but it was inevitable that he would.

The third prerequisite that is needed for this defence to work is that the accused must reasonably believe at the time of the assault that it is not possible to preserve himself from harm except by the infliction of death or grievous bodily harm. Here there was some question. It is apparent that the trial judge who presided at the first trial had concerns about whether this criterion could be met. He appeared to be unimpressed with Pintar's response to the events of that morning. He told the jury:

> Although we live in the Northwest, this is not the wild west of the nineteenth century. Carrying a rifle with a clip in it, even though it is unchambered and carried across the chest pointing skyward, is a very serious and drastic show of force. It is for you to decide whether, in the circumstances of the case, this force was more than necessary.[7]

Yes, it was a very serious and drastic show of force, even if it didn't work all that well. Grabbing a rifle and using it to evict trespassers may, and did in the events, prove to be a provocative act, but it is important to remember that section 34(2) does not disentitle those who have provoked the assault from relying on the section. Even if Pintar had provoked the ultimate assault that occurred after Ross turned off the ignition, the question is whether, when Ross and Gill came at him and attempted to get the gun from him, he believed, and reasonably believed, that he could not preserve himself from death or grievous bodily harm except by shooting them. Of course he believed this — he would have been a fool to think otherwise. These men, who promised to kill him with as many uncreative but attention-grabbing adverbs and adjectives as they could conjure, were trying to take a loaded gun away from him. I say it was a reasonable guess that his life was in danger at that point. A drunken man whose wife you have been sleeping with is coming at you saying, "Now you're all going to die." What would a reasonable person think? "Ah, get out, you kidder you. You're foolin', right?"

Yes, after knocking Ross onto the porch, Pintar could have tried calling the police instead of taking the matter into his own hands, but he did not, perhaps because they were more than forty minutes away and he had an irate man scratching at his door trying to get at him. Yes, he could have stayed in the house, but he did not. No doubt Pintar blew it by getting the gun and standing like GI Joe on his front stoop, but having done that with the evident intention of ending the confrontation with a mere show of force, the man's life fell into deep and immediate danger and he had no choice but to shoot. Some people get away with murder, and others just get away with self-defence. While he no doubt made matters worse by getting the gun, if there is anything to this self-defence notion, and the events of that fateful morning were anything like those depicted here, Pintar got away with self-defence, not with murder.

Although Joe Pintar had a good case for self-defence, there are occasionally even better examples. One is the recent Ottawa acquittal of James Morrow. Morrow, it seems, had been in the business of selling home-made wine. One night Morrow's wine received a higher compliment than if all of the medals in the Napa Valley were pinned to his chest after the wine-tasters refused to spit it out. "Chico," a former customer, was apparently so intent on obtaining a bottle of Morrow's nectar that he kicked in the glass door in the front lobby to Morrow's apartment after being denied entry. He then burst into Morrow's apartment, after threatening to shoot him through the door, by kicking in three locks, including a $3^1/_2$-inch deadbolt. As an added touch, he was wearing Outlaws motorcycle garb. He would be a frightening sight, even for a vintner. Morrow was ultimately excused for having shot the man four times, killing him dead as they say. It helped his case enormously that Morrow was on the phone at the time with a 911 operator who taped the whole thing. It was so obviously a case of self-defence that the judge effectively stopped the trial by confronting the Crown after the evidence went in: "He's having his life threatened. What are you going to do, jump off the balcony?"[8] He asked the prosecutor whether she would not have shot the intruder. She replied she would not have. "Then, Ms. Parfett, we would have been attending your funeral," the judge said. "The answer is so obvious." The defence lawyer was told to stay in his chair and the charges were thrown out. James Morrow, for his part, is reported to have stopped selling wine.

The intentional killing of another human being is always a tragedy, but it is not always the wrong thing to do. Indeed, there are times when it is the only thing to do and, when it is, or when there is a reasonable doubt about it, the killer has to go free. Any system of law that attempted to require people to give of their own life and limb to remain law-abiding would be worse than useless. It would be an abomination.

CHAPTER 13

Losing Control: Provocation and Excusing the Inexcusable

The private life of Norman and Joan Thibert remains largely closed to those of us who use law books to peer through private windows. The pages of those books do not tell us what kind of wedding they had. The case reports do not tell us how excited they were when they bought their home in Edmonton, Alberta, or whether they had been good friends to each other before the spring of 1991. Those pages do not even tell us whether Norma and Joan Thibert had been wonderful parents to the two daughters they raised together into early adulthood. We know very little about the early lives of the Thiberts other than the unsavoury detail that Norman had a series of extramarital affairs early in their marriage. We do know, however, more than we should about their lives in the spring of 1991. We had to find out about Norman and Joan during this period because it was then that Norman shot Joan's lover, Alan Sherren, to death. Our criminal justice system had to find out how and why this happened so we would know how best to punish Norman Thibert. Their pitiable story is as follows.

In April 1991 Norman Thibert experienced the anguish that his wife had doubtlessly suffered when she first learned of his extramarital affairs. It was then that Joan told him that, for several months, she had taken her co-worker, Alan Sherren, as her lover. She wanted out of the marriage. Despite his anger at being betrayed, Norman did not want to break up. He was desperate to keep Joan. He made the usual promises that things would be different, that the marriage would work, and that they would grow old together and be happy. Joan agreed to give it one more try but after little more than two months it became evident to her that the marriage was truly over. On 2 July 1991, when Norman was out, she packed her bags, preferring to stay in a hotel room to returning home with him.

Norman was distraught when he noticed that she had cleaned out her drawers. His first reaction was the understandable, rational one. He went looking for Joan so they could talk things out. After all, he had talked her into staying with him once before. He drove around the city, even combing through the hotel where she was staying, but he did not find her. As he wandered around their empty home waiting to hear from her, his grip on constructive thinking loosened. His mind became a cauldron of horrifying thoughts — images of him blasting his own brains out, vignettes in which his wife was under him being strangled or stabbed, Sherren on his knees with a gun to his head about to die. For a time the stars seemed to be aligned and fixed so that a violent end was unavoidable. In preparation, Norman had pounced down the stairs, flush with twisted resolve, and grabbed his rifle and a shotgun from the basement of his house. He dragged the weapons into the garage, loading the rifle. It was as though he was watching someone else's hands opening the magazine, inserting the cartridge. He paused and let out a wail. His resolve wilted into confusion. He tossed the guns into the corner and walked away, afraid of them, afraid of himself. He was unsure both of what he should do next and of what he would do next.

He was sobbing loudly, holding his head in his hands, when his nineteen-year-old daughter Catrina came home. "Your mother's gone," he blurted out. "She's been cheating on me." He wiped his hot, contorted face with his sleeve, hoping to clear the blurred image of his daughter standing before him. She made him a cup of coffee and they talked.

At 11:00 that evening the phone rang — Joan — calling to tell Norman herself that she was leaving him, that their marriage was over.

"Just talk to me first, Joan," he pleaded. "Just let me talk to you. Talk to Catrina."

They set up a breakfast meeting the next day: Smitty's Restaurant on Albert Street, 7 o'clock. Norman Thibert sat up all night, waiting. Minutes ticked by, one second at a time, then those minutes collected slowly into hours, until, mercifully, morning broke. An eternity. A nighttime of semi-lucid fantasies, of dark thoughts, of abject agony. A night spent alone with the demons.

At their meeting, Norman, Joan, and Catrina talked for an hour. When Joan spoke, Norman stared at her, wondering if he loved her or hated her for what she was doing to him, but when he spoke, the words that came out were imploring her to come home. He could not risk anger. It would drive her away. As waitresses brushed by with pancakes and steaming pots of coffee, as men rustled through newspapers checking the market or the box-scores, as the city of Edmonton awoke to the warm breeze of the prairie summer, Norman Thibert sat there feeling as though he was begging for his life, and maybe for Joan's life as well, and probably even for Alan Sherren's.

Believing she was bargaining from strength, Joan promised that if he did not bother her at work, she would think about coming home. She needed time to think. As the meeting broke up and Joan was speaking to Catrina, Norman stepped out of the restaurant. He glanced nervously around, waiting for his daughter, and then he saw him. Sherren! He had brought Joan to the meeting! The whole time he was talking to his wife, Sherren lurked outside waiting to talk her out of returning home, waiting to steal her away. The demon that had climbed into Norman's soul the day before reared up. He walked up to Sherren and said: "I hope you intend on moving back east or living under assumed names . . . Because as long as I have got breath in my body I am not going to give up trying to get my wife back from you, and I will find you wherever you go."

To a prosecutor those are words of threat. To a defence lawyer, they exhibit a non-violent intent by Thibert to win his wife back, maybe even with boxed candy, bouquets of flowers, or poems. All would agree, though, that they were the words of desperation.

Norman made his way into the garage when he got home. After his arrest later that day, the police would search his home and they would find that he had passed some of his time that morning sawing the barrel from the shotgun. Norman would later testify at trial that he was only preparing to kill himself when he sawed the barrel, but that he abandoned his plan because the firing pin was broken. The story, like many of the tales told by accused people trying to wish away damning evidence, made no sense. People who are going to kill themselves are not generally concerned about the length of the gun. People who want to hide the gun under their coat so they can "get the drop" on others want to have a short barrel.

After he finished sawing the gun down, Norman went into the house, leaving the gun behind. He stared at the phone, willing it to ring, willing it to be Joan saying she was coming home. He paced. He sat. He paced. His head ached. The bile in his stomach rose each time his gut knotted. He pulled his palms along his temples and ran his hands through his hair. He couldn't stand it anymore. He picked up the phone and called Joan at work. She protested that she could not talk, and then cut the call short by telling him she had to go. He phoned again, and then again. Each time she told him to stop calling her there. He pictured Sherren beside her, telling her to hang up. He kept calling into the early afternoon, whenever his will to resist broke down. During the last call Joan told Norman not to call back as she would not be there anyway. She was going to the bank to make a deposit. He hung up. Good, he thought. If I meet her at the bank, Sherren won't be there and maybe we can talk. He threw his rifle into the back of the car, just in case it became necessary — just in case he had to kill the bastard. At his trial he would testify that, a few miles from home, he decided that, whatever happened, he was not going to kill anyone, but that, with the gun, he could get Joan to see how serious he was, how desperate he was in his need for her. Maybe she would take pity on him if it looked as though he was going to shoot himself and she would come back.

Norman wheeled his car into the parking lot across from her work. It was 2:45 p.m. She pushed open the heavy glass office door, not noticing him there, and began walking swiftly towards the bank. His car pulled out and crawled along beside her, the window down. "Joan. Joan. Get in. Please come and talk to me." She walked on, staring ahead, but stealing the odd glance over her shoulder to see what he was up to. Her heart raced. Her legs felt light, her mind sharp. This was getting dangerous. He rolled beside her all the way to the bank and then he threw the car in park and scurried out.

"Please. Let's go someplace private where we can talk."

To placate him, Joan agreed. "I'll meet you in that vacant lot. Just let me get the banking done first."

Good, he thought. They would talk. He would convince her.

He waited. Instead, when she came out of the bank, she walked briskly towards her office. He followed her, choosing to intercept her in the parking lot: "Talk to me, Joan. Stop Joan. I have a gun." Her face blanched. "It's not loaded, but I brought the gun. Talk to me or I'll have to bring the gun into the office. Please, Joan."

Sherren could see the two through the window. It was as though he was watching some bizarre dance. Norman moving forward, hands open in supplication. Joan standing, turning her shoulder towards the door and taking a small step, never taking her eyes off Norman, then stopping, turning back, saying something, moving forward, turning back, looking scared, looking as if she needed him. Sherren went outside. Norman could not believe it. Here is the man who won't give me a half-hour alone with my wife after twenty-one years, he thought, and he has had her for the last twenty-four hours. Sherren tried to take charge. He grabbed Joan around the waist and began to usher her back into the office, telling Norman to leave her alone and go home.

Norman threw open the back door of his car, reached in, and pulled out the rifle. Sherren stopped when he saw it. Perhaps Joan told him that Norman had said the gun was unloaded, but, for whatever reason, instead of running or seeking refuge in the building, or making promises to Thibert in order to calm him, Sherren decided to call what he was sure was a bluff. He put his hands on Joan's shoulders and turned her between him and Thibert. Sherren began swinging her from side to side, laughing and grinning, advancing towards him. "Come on, big fellow, shoot me," he taunted. "You want to shoot me? Go ahead and shoot me."

Those were ill-chosen words. They are the kind of words that seem too fanciful for fiction, but appear to get spoken with astounding regularity in real life by many men who are looking down the barrel of a gun. The last words spoken in real gun cases are only rarely the stuff of Hollywood, things like "Take care of my children," or even "Win one for the Gipper." No. They are more often the stupidest words that can be imagined — "Go ahead and shoot me." A cautious person, if he felt compelled to use the phrase "Go ahead and shoot" in such a situation, might be tempted to try, "Go ahead and shoot yourself," but for some reason these words appear never to have been spoken under such circumstances, not in the annals of recorded forensic history. So there it is. Sherren saying "Go ahead and shoot me" and advancing on Thibert, tauntingly waving Thibert's wife of twenty-one years in front of him, sticking her in the face of her distraught husband, handling her as possessively as a human can be handled, coming at Thibert, coming quickly.

Norman backed up, telling Sherren to stay back. But Sherren didn't. He kept coming. Norman closed his eyes, trying to retreat into himself, as he would later describe it in his evidence. He allowed that he wanted to scream. At some point in those racing seconds, as Sherren bulled forward, Joan either moved or was moved aside. Then the gun went off. The affair between Alan Sherren and Joan Thibert had ended. It stopped when Sherren crumpled in the parking lot, dead. A casualty of emotion, killed by a man who in thirty-four short hours had become a stranger to reason, a creature of passion.

Joan turned and this time ran into the office building. Norman laid the gun down and walked into the building. "I want to talk to my wife," he said calmly. Just as suddenly he wheeled around and left, but not before putting more ammunition in the gun. "I am not going to hurt anyone," he called out. He climbed into the car with the gun and drove away. Within minutes a police car was behind his vehicle. Norman pulled over, opened the door, raised his hands and got out, surrendering to the police: "It's out of me now. He was fooling around with my wife. For what it's worth, I was just after him. For what it's worth, it's out of me now. He was fooling around with my wife."

At his first-degree murder trial, the window into the private lives of the Thiberts during the spring of 1991 was pried open and recorded in the law books. Mother and daughter testified as Crown witnesses. Then Norman Thibert told his story to the jury. He told them that he did not mean to fire. He described how the gun accidentally discharged while his eyes were closed. The jury did not believe him. Although it had a doubt about whether the killing was premeditated, the jury had no doubt that it was an intentional killing. They convicted him of murder in the second degree. He was to go to jail for life, with no eligibility for parole for ten years.

To a lay person, that might seem to be the end of that. Not so to a lawyer, and here is why. The defence put forward alternative theories. It said that Norman Thibert did not intend to kill Alan Sherren, but that if he did intend to kill him, he was provoked into doing so. When the judge described the law of provocation to the jury he made a significant mistake, so the defence appealed. It appealed all the way to the Supreme Court of Canada and won Thibert a new trial.

Before discussing the judge's error and exploring the defence of provocation in more detail, it is probably necessary to say a few words about alternative defences. They no doubt sound suspect. How much faith can you put in the claim of a man who says, "I didn't intend to kill, but if I did intend to kill it was because I was provoked"? It is like an accused going to the jury, as he is entitled to in our system, saying, "It was not me, but if it was, it was an accident, and if it was not an accident, I was insane at the time." A lay person listening to this kind of a defence might be tempted to say, "I don't know whether you were insane then, Buddy, but you sure are now if you expect me to believe a word you're saying." Lawyers, however, have an easier time understanding alternative pleas like this, not because they, too, are insane, but because they appreciate that the jury is entitled to believe some of the evidence, or all of the evidence, or none of it. It is up to the jury to decide what happened. In the opinion of a majority of the Supreme Court of Canada, a juror listening to the evidence in the Thibert case could quite understandably say, "Look. I have no doubt he meant to pull that trigger. I do not believe him for a minute when he says it was an accidental discharge. But I do think that he may have been provoked into the shooting by the way Sherren acted."

The most notorious example of an alternative, inherently contradictory defence being led was during Guy Paul Morin's first trial. His lawyer, Clayton Ruby, defended the case on the basis that the killer of Christine Jessop was not Guy Paul Morin, who had an alibi, but that if it was Morin, he was insane at the time. As things turned out, the insanity defence proved to be unnecessary because the jury disregarded it and acquitted Morin because of a reasonable doubt about whether he was the killer. After the Crown won a retrial in the Morin case, it prosecuted him with a vengeance, mistakenly assuming that the alternative defence of insanity by Morin's defence team was tantamount to an admission by Morin that they were prosecuting the right man. As we have since learned, they were not. Guy Paul Morin, an innocent man who was wrongly convicted after his second trial, served several months in prison before he was released on bail pending appeal. He was ultimately exonerated by DNA testing.

Although we appreciate it is a dangerous tactic that can cause others to assume guilt,[1] lawyers have learned to indulge the apparently preposterous spectacle of an accused person presenting alternative, conflicting defences. Until a jury has spoken, it is never clear how it will see the case. And so it was in the Thibert prosecution.

Given the possibility of a successful provocation defence arising on the evidence, the trial judge had a duty to tell the jury about the law of provocation, and he had to get it right when he explained it to them. Sadly, he made an error, an all too common one. He failed to tell the jury that it was not up to Thibert to prove that he was provoked. According to the law, as is true of most defences, including self-defence, Thibert was entitled to the provocation defence unless the Crown could disprove it beyond a reasonable doubt. If, at the end of the evidence, the jury believed that Thibert was *probably* not provoked, but it could not rule out the *possibility* that he was provoked beyond a reasonable doubt, it would have to acquit him. Since the jury was not told this, it might have convicted Thibert of murder even though it still had a doubt about whether he was provoked. Accordingly, Thibert was entitled to a new trial.

The Law and Losing It: The Defence of Provocation

What, then, is this defence of provocation that enabled Thibert to get his new trial? In a nutshell, it is the defence that applies where an accused person kills the deceased immediately on losing control because of some wrongful act or insult by the deceased, where that wrongful act or insult is so extreme that it could have caused an ordinary person to lose control. Leaving aside the technicalities of the defence for a moment, the bottom line is that whereas self-defence is a justifiable act of self-preservation, provoked homicides are nothing more than acts of "understandable" but extreme anger. This definition at once marks provocation as a somewhat bizarre and controversial defence. Why should anger be an excuse? I will attempt to explain in a moment, but it is important to appreciate at the outset that provoked homicides are not justified homicides. While those who kill in self-defence are let off entirely because they have acted with justification, provoked killers are not. They are found guilty, although they are convicted of manslaughter instead of murder. In other words, the effect of a provocation defence is to reduce the conviction for an intentional killing from murder, which carries a minimum penalty of life imprisonment, to manslaughter, which has no minimum penalty. This verdict enables the trial judge to take into account, when sentencing, that the killer acted suddenly as the result of some wrongful act or insult by the deceased, and to adjust the sentence that will be imposed to take this factor into account.

The defence of provocation has been performing its role of sentence reduction for a long time. Aristotle spoke about it in *Nichomachean Ethics*.[2] Still, it was not until the seventeenth century that English law came to recognize the defence. When it came to be accepted in England, its function was not to absolve the killer of all responsibility, but to reduce the sentence that would be imposed for the killing. At the time, a successful defence of provocation would spare the accused the gallows, but not the jail. In later years, it came to perform its current role of reducing the conviction from murder to manslaughter.

Because its sole effect is to remove the harsh penalties for murder, provocation is not a defence to assault, wounding, vandalism, or any other offence. It is not needed for those offences because, unlike murder, they do not have minimum penalties. The judge is already free to consider all the relevant circumstances, including the existence of provocation, when coming to an appropriate sentence.

This defence raises a question that has so far been avoided: Why should we reduce the sentence at all simply because the killer has lost control? The answer lies in our belief that criminals are punished because of their moral fault, which is determined largely by their mental state at the time. Just as there are various frames of mind, so there are various levels of moral fault. The worst killer is the killer who murders after planning and deliberating. He is the first-degree murderer. His evil is extreme because he has made a fully considered decision to kill. He has reflected and has decided that the "pros" of killing outweigh the "cons." He is worse than the killer who takes a life intentionally, but impulsively, because his was a reflective and fully considered decision.

Even among impulsive killers, there are degrees of moral fault. The killer who is in his normal frame of mind and who has resort to his full faculties of reason when making an impulsive decision to kill is the second-degree murderer. He has chosen to kill after employing his normal faculties of reason, which tells us something about his innate cruelty or evil. This kind of killer has demonstrated greater moral fault than the provoked killer. His violence is the instantaneous act of a mind that is not controlled. His decision to kill is not at all reasoned. His crime is, in the purest sense, a crime of passion, and he may well regret his actions when his passions have had time to cool. He lost his head. He acted out of character.

This description, on its own, is incredibly simplistic and probably quite unconvincing. From a public protection point of view (for those who believe that the law can discourage crimes like homicide), the impulsive, ill-tempered clod whose reason is supplanted by dangerous emotion could well pose more of a threat on a day-to-day basis than the clever, discriminating criminal who will kill only when it is seen to be economically advantageous to do so. The world is full of frustrations and disappointments. They are the common lot of most. Coddling those who are apt to fly off the handle and to use violence and cause mayhem hardly sounds like good public policy.

Rest assured, this reservation did not escape those who were responsible for developing the law of homicide. To exclude the dangerous, unthinking, impulsive, mean-tempered clod, the law set out to limit the defence to those acts of provocation which not only deprive the accused of his powers of self-control but which would also have been extreme enough to have deprived "ordinary" people of their powers of self-control. It is not enough for the accused to become unglued. The defence is available only if an ordinary person might have reacted just as the accused did if they were put into the accused's position.

The technique that was initially used to identify such cases was to create a list of situations where the provocation defence could work, and a separate list of situations where it could not.[3] According to that list, striking an accused person could be provocation. So too could angry words followed by a minor assault such as pulling someone's nose, which was considered at the time to be a symbolic challenge to one's honour rather than simply an unsanitary and ill-advised practice. The sight of a friend or relative being beaten would qualify, although, at the time, you were supposed to stay cool if the victim was an acquaintance or a co-worker or someone else's child or partner. The sight of a citizen being unlawfully deprived of his liberty was considered provocative as well, probably to take into account that the act of homicide would be done in aid of enforcing the law. Finally, in those unforgivably sexist days, the sight of a man in adultery with the accused's wife would ground a provocation defence. But affronting gestures, trespass to property, misconduct by a child or a servant, breach of contract, and words alone did not qualify.

In explaining the general rule that words alone will not suffice, Viscount Simon made use of the proverb "hard words break no bones,"[4] which in its more familiar form is uttered on the playgrounds of North America with mocking inflection as "sticks and stones may break my bones but names will never hurt me." The problem with using this rhyme, in my experience, is that the rhyme itself normally provokes the other to fetch sticks and stones, making the whole issue about who provoked what rather complicated. Be that as it may, for a time this was both a rhyme and a legal principle.

As frequently happens as the law develops and matures, it breaks away from strict and arbitrary categories of case and becomes more general, focusing instead on the reason behind the rule. So it happened with the law of provocation. It was decided that instead of relying on a predetermined list of sufficiently provocative acts, a court should simply ask whether, given the nature of the act or insult, an ordinary person would have lost self-control. By the time provocation was included in the *Criminal Code*, therefore, this partial defence was extended to any "wrongful act or . . . insult that is of such a nature as to be sufficient to deprive an ordinary person of the power of self-control," an issue that is to be decided on the specific facts of the case. In some cases, words alone might be enough. In other cases, they might not. It all depends on the facts.

The law also built in other prerequisites to its partial defence. The wrongful act or insult must not only be sufficient to deprive an ordinary person of self-control but must have caused the accused to have lost self-control. Moreover, the accused must act impulsively, before his passions cool. If the accused was able to maintain composure even though an ordinary person might not have, and the accused kills, his homicide is not provoked. It is simply a murder.

What, then, of Norman Thibert? How did this reasoning apply in his case? First, as described, for the defence to be available to him, there must have been some evidence of a wrongful act or insult that would have deprived an ordinary person of self-control. This requirement has two components. There must have been a wrongful act or insult, and it must have been such as to have deprived an ordinary person of self-control.

It was clear going into the case that Thibert could not claim that Sherren's adulterous affair with his wife was a sufficiently provocative, wrongful act or insult. As Justice Cory said (falling perhaps into the old habit of listing appropriate and inappropriate grounds of provocation), "events leading up to the break-up of the marriage can never warrant taking the life of another. Affairs cannot justify murder."[5] This is not to say that catching one's spouse making the "beast with two backs" with another can never be sufficiently provocative, but the law insists on what Baron Parke referred to as "the condition of ocular observation."[6] As Viscount Simon said in *Holmes* v. *D.P.P.*, where the accused sought to defend his act of bludgeoning his wife with a coal hammer and then strangling her after she told him that she had been unfaithful, "Even if Iago's insinuations against Desdemona's virtue had been true, Othello's crime was murder and nothing else."[7] Othello would have had to have caught Desdemona *in flagrante delicto* to have any chance before a modern court. Of course he did not; while Shakespeare was quick with the naughty quip, this would have been too bawdy a scene to have staged, leaving poor Othello without his partial defence.

Thibert's lawyer had to think fast. He had to find something other than the mere adulterous relationship to constitute the wrongful act or insult. He convinced the majority of the Supreme Court of Canada that the wrongful act in the case was Sherren's taunting behaviour in swinging Joan back and forth, laughing and heckling and humiliating him. It did not matter that there was no law against it. Conduct can be wrongful without being unlawful, since not everything that is legal is right to do. Or, as it has been expressed elsewhere, "the law does not approve of [every]thing it does not forbid."[8]

The more difficult legal question was the second one. Would this wrongful act or insult have deprived an ordinary person of self-control? This kind of question is, on close examination, really quite peculiar. The entire criminal law is premised on the assumption that ordinary people can maintain their self-control and remain law-abiding. Ordinary people certainly do not kill every time their choler rises. For example, one would suspect that for every *in flagrante delicto* killing, there are probably thousands of lovers who suffer only the indignity of having to hop down the hall while they are pulling on their pants on the way out the door while the offended spouse vents verbal spleen or sulks away in humiliation. Still, the idea is that humans are weak, and if a provocative act is extreme enough, it may be understandable that an otherwise reasonable person's passions have overtaken reason, even if the overwhelming majority of us would have reacted with far less drama and with far less deadly consequence.

Who, then, gets to make the decision about whether an act is sufficiently provocative that a reasonable person's reason may be overtaken by passion? Of course, it is the jury, but since the rule of law does not want the result to vary from jury to jury, we do not simply ask jurors, "Might you have lost your powers of self-control in this case?" Instead, we go through the legal fiction of having them construct in their minds an imagined person, an ordinary person. We then have the jury ask whether that imagined "ordinary" person might have lost the power of self-control had he or she been in the shoes of the accused.

This intellectual device for injecting objectivity into what are, in truth, hopelessly subjective decisions is as familiar to lawyers as it is bizarre to non-lawyers. We use it all the time in law. Even though we have been employing it for generations, there remains controversy about how this technique is to be done. Feminists are naturally troubled about history's habit of conceiving of the reasonable person as a "reasonable man." Women and men probably think differently. Critical race theorists are naturally troubled about history's habit of conceiving of the ordinary person as "the reasonable man on the Clapham omnibus," the erstwhile London public conveyance on which it was believed one could find the "common man." We, in Canada, inherited this bloke as our prototypical model of reason when we adopted the English common law, even though the image of your well-mannered but ordinary Anglo-Saxon Protestant, reading the *Times* while clutching an umbrella, is a far cry from your typical Canadian. Even lawyers and judges are uncomfortable with their task of conjuring up an ordinary person who will be used to test the reasonableness of the homicidal fury of the accused. They are unsure about how far they should go in imbuing this reasonable person with the characteristics and circumstances of the accused. If the accused is young and black and female, should the ordinary person be conceptualized as young and black and female, or do we stick with the chap on the Clapham omnibus?

This is an important issue, for the characterization of the ordinary person can make a difference. For example, in 1954 an eighteen year-old man, known in the reports only as Bedder, was with a prostitute. To skirt the indelicacies, suffice it to say that he was not performing well. This was not entirely unexpected since he had been having a problem in that department and was deeply troubled by it. The prostitute began to jeer at him. Her behaviour set off a struggle in which he grabbed her and was ultimately kicked in the privates. His response (no doubt after doubling over and squealing like a market pig) was to pull out a pocket knife and stab her fatally. The issue that preoccupied the court was whether the imaginary ordinary person who was going to be used as the gauge was to be impotent like Bedder. His lawyer argued that unless the reasonable man was also impotent, the jeering would not have the same impact. Asking how a virile reasonable man would react to the mocking of his sexual performance would hardly answer the question as to whether it was understandable for Bedder to have lost his cool. Alas, neither Bedder nor his argument could stand up. Lord Simonds relied on an earlier case which said that you are not to assume that the reasonable person has the same personality as the accused, since to do so would allow different people to live up to different standards of self-control. This the law could not do. He then remarked how it would be illogical and confusing to recognize that the ordinary person is to be imbued with the unusual physical characteristics of the accused, such as impotence, but not with the unusual temperament of the accused, such as unusual excitability or pugnacity. Hence, the ordinary person was to receive neither Bedder's temperament nor his affliction. Unlike Bedder, the ordinary person was to be both upstanding and erect. Bedder was a murderer even if every impotent man in those pre-Viagra days would have reacted the way he did.

The law has since moved away from this rigid and preposterous position. Some insults are meaningless if hurled at the ordinary person, but may be particularly stinging if hurled at the accused. To make the point poignantly, as Justice Cory did in *Thibert*, "obviously the effect of calling a black person a 'two bit nigger punk' . . . would be far greater than if the same demeaning epithet was applied to a white man."[9] We have moved beyond *Bedder* and now judge the reasonableness of the loss of self-control (as preposterous as that sounds) by imagining how an ordinary person, imbued with those personal characteristics of the accused which make the insult relevant and which are necessary to give the wrongful act or insult context, would have reacted in the same position as the accused. What is not to be considered are those personal characteristics, like unusual excitability or pugnacity, that might lower the reasonable and responsible behaviour that the criminal law is intended to promote.

For the *Thibert* court, this meant that the question was whether a married man, faced with the breakup of his marriage, who had succeeded in convincing his wife to return to him on an earlier occasion, and who had not slept in thirty-four hours, could have lost the power of self-control when his wife's lover prevented him from having a private conversation with her and then held her in a proprietary and possessive manner while mocking and taunting the accused to shoot him? In the majority's view, a jury might well answer that question yes.

Still, this argument did not get Thibert home. Even if a reasonable person might have lost the powers of self-control under those circumstances, it would have to be decided whether Thibert lost control. The evidence on this question was extremely problematic for him. On his own testimony, when he retrieved the guns on 2 July 1991, he did so thinking that he might shoot Sherren. He had also cut the shotgun barrel, suggestive of a plan to conceal the weapon. When he initially put the rifle into the car on his way to the shooting, he did so in case events played out such that he had to shoot Sherren. After the shooting, he told the officers that "it was out" of him, and that he was "just after" Sherren, who had been fooling around with his wife.

Thibert nonetheless testified that he abandoned all intent to shoot Sherren before he arrived at the scene, and the circumstances as they actually played out were potentially provocative in nature and unexpected. For the majority of the Supreme Court of Canada, this meant that even though he claimed that the gun discharged accidentally, a jury might disbelieve this testimony but still infer that he did not intend to shoot Sherren until he lost control because of Sherren's conduct.

The final requirement of the provocation defence, that the accused act on the sudden before the passions have had a chance to cool, did not pose a problem. As is evident, this requirement is intended to ensure that provocation applies solely where the killing is an act of immediate, non-reflective emotion. On the facts, if Thibert was reacting to the wrongful act of Sherren's mocking him, the shooting was clearly "on the sudden." The insulting act was still happening when Thibert shot.

Thus, on the evidence, a bare majority of three out of five Supreme Court of Canada judges concluded that there was a possibility that the defence of provocation might be accepted by a jury. Since the judge had not properly directed the jury at the first trial, Thibert was entitled to be tried again. By the time Thibert's retrial had arrived, the man had served two years and eleven months in jail. On 1 November 1996 the prosecutors evaluated their case and decided it should be resolved by way of a guilty plea to manslaughter. After the plea was entered, Thibert received a sentence, not of life in prison as the jury at his first trial had decided, but of four years.

The defence of provocation, around which the Thibert case revolved, is a troubling one. It is problematic for many reasons. Both its recognition of violent anger, seen to be a predominantly male reaction, and its history, steeped as it is in decisions excusing provocation relating to female infidelity or recognizing provocation by homosexual advance, make the defence unpopular with some feminist legal theorists. They believe that it indulges and even promotes sexist and homophobic rage. Its historical resort to the ordinary white male as the standard for judging the reasonableness of losing control does not help its image either. But its public relations problems do not end with politically incorrect optics. It is easy to miss the fact that the partial defence is available only when you kill the very person who has done the wrongful act or authored the insult. It is implicit in the defence, therefore, that the victim must share some measure of the responsibility for what happened. To a degree, he or she has been the cause of his own demise,[10] even though the act of fatal violence by the accused is almost invariably the worst of the relative indiscretions. It is troubling to draw on this reasoning as a partial basis for even a partial defence. In Canada the state does not capitally punish killers and rapists. Why should the law allow mere insults to provide a restricted licence to private individuals to kill?

Perhaps the most trenchant criticism of the defence is that the concept of provocation rewards anger, giving it priority over other emotions. As has been aptly pointed out: "It is crucial to ask . . . how homicidal rage can be excused on the grounds of provocation when there is no defence if the motivating emotion is compassion or pity as in the case of euthanasia?"[11] Without question, the defence is arbitrary in its limits.

Like all technical rules, provocation also has the potential to fail to reach cases that it should reach. If its purpose is to remove the minimum penalties for murder because the moral fault for killing can vary according to the circumstances, consider whether the following case might not provide a dramatic example of its shortcomings.[12] A young woman had a relationship with a man, an abusive man, a man who, with good reason, she suspected of sexually assaulting her daughter. Her daughter had told her that the man had "licked her yuppy." This woman was afraid to leave the man because of his violence, but, finally, she came to be free of him when he was jailed for assaulting her. Some time later she unexpectedly saw him in a bar. He should still have been in jail, she thought, but there he was. She expressed fear of him to her friends, so one of them gave her a knife in case she needed to protect herself. He saw her and came over. In the course of his conversation, in which he was abusive and threatening, he told her that her daughter tasted better than she did. He left her on that note and went back to his own table. Some time later, he left the bar. She followed him outside and, in a rage, stabbed him to death. Why does she not get the benefit of the defence of provocation, given the monstrous and vile statement he had made? Because she did not act "on the sudden." There had been time for her passions to cool. She killed out of hatred, not spontaneous impulse. She was, in law, a murderer. The trial judge was unable to take these horrendous facts into account when sentencing her. She was a murderer plain and simple. Life, with no eligibility for parole for ten years.

Technically, it is probably not possible to quibble with the result. Too much time had passed for the attack to be characterized as the sudden kind of flareup addressed by the law of provocation. This was not an instantaneous explosion. Instead, it was a deeply smouldering burn that was fanned because she could not exorcize the images and emotions caused by his obscene and contemptible behaviour. Too much time had passed for the law, but not enough time had passed, nor has enough time yet passed, to make it appropriate to sentence this woman for murder without any opportunity to take into account the horrendous emotional pressure she was under. The defence of provocation failed her and so did the law.

Provocation is, in my estimation, an unacceptable concession to human weakness because it is a formal rule that overtly privileges anger and loss of reason over other emotional, mitigating factors. It assumes that sudden anger is so materially different in kind that it should be excusing, but that festering anger should not, even where ordinary people might brood and work themselves up. It forces lawyers and jurors into intellectual gymnastics as they strive to imagine what the ordinary person is like, and what this person would have done in similar circumstances. It complicates jury charges and murder trials. It provides a rationalization by which murders can be sold through plea bargains as mere manslaughters. Without question, it should be abolished as a defence, but not before its *raison d'être* is remedied. You see, the real culprit is not the assumption underlying the defence of provocation that impulsive acts of anger should be allowed to reduce the penalty. In some cases they should, and in others they should not. The real culprit is the minimum sentence for murder. Abolish that, and we will not need a formal provocation defence, with its chequered and offensive history, its tortured analysis, and its message that it is somehow acceptable in law to lose control.

There is strong reason to believe that the law of provocation will, in fact, be amended in the near future, but not as I suggest, and not because of the problems I have identified. Instead, it will be amended to make the law tougher. The outrageous case of Bert Stone, who received a sentence of four years in prison for killing his wife by stabbing her forty-seven times before leaving for a para-sailing vacation in Mexico, has galvanized public support for the abolition of the partial defence of provocation, at least in cases where it is relied on by men who kill. Stone, it seems, "snapped" when his wife launched into a tirade about his poor sexual performance and cast doubts on his paternity of his two sons from a former marriage.[13] What is easy to miss in the Stone case is that the law of provocation, even with its many problems, did not require such a light sentence. The law permitted the judge who sentenced Stone to give the man a far longer sentence than he did, and he should have done so. In spite of this, it is the defence that is being blamed.

The minister of justice, Anne McLellan, has announced, even while the Stone sentence is on appeal before the Supreme Court of Canada, that she will conduct a review of the law of provocation.[14] A review, of course, is a positive thing, because the law needs to be changed. The problem is that since the review is inspired by "get tough" lobbying, it is unlikely to solve the relevant problems. It would take an act of great political courage to respond by removing the minimum penalty for murder, along with the defence. That will almost certainly not happen. Instead, the defence is likely to be removed, leaving courts with no authority to respond to mitigating circumstances in murder cases. I am not asking anyone to cry for the Bert Stones of the world. Think about the young woman who killed the man who had tormented her and sexually abused her daughter. There are murders, and then there are murders. Making the law even more rigid will do little for justice, and nothing to reduce violence, domestic or otherwise. If Bert Stone really did snap, do you think he would have kept his head if the defence of provocation did not exist? Forget it. We should change the law for the right reasons and in the right way, or we should leave it alone before we make matters worse.

CHAPTER 14

The Abuse Excuse: "Psychobabble" and the Protection of Basic Values

"Rooster" to his friends, he was known as Kevin Rust on official documents like birth certificates and driver's licences. One of the last official documents to bear his name was typed on 31 August 1986. It was a coroner's certificate, verifying his cause of death to be a gunshot wound to the head. That date is a vital statistic not only in the brief life of Kevin Rust but also for Lyn Lavallee, his common-law wife. That was the day he stopped beating her.

Angelique Lyn Lavallee was still a teenager when she first moved in with Kevin. They lived together, although not without interruption, for the next three or four summers, but no one was keeping careful track. The time just passed. One day melted into the next. Bruises simply faded and disappeared while new ones took their place. From time to time she would leave him, but then return. That was just the way it was. By the summer of 1986, at the age of twenty-two, Lyn was already a veteran of a domestic war that had marked her time with Kevin, a war in which she had lost all the battles. A broken nose, black eyes, cuts, bruises — eight separate trips to the emergency wards of two different hospitals. These were the wages of love for young Lyn. As for Kevin, he had felt her fists, but, not surprisingly, she always got the worst of it. It seemed the only times that she managed to hold her own were the two occasions when she stuck the barrel of a gun in his face. The last time it was a loaded .303 calibre rifle. "If you ever touch me again," she had said, "I'll kill you."

But that was before. This day, 30 August, looked as though it might be one of the good ones. The summer of 1986 was closing down, they had just returned on their bikes from the Tourist Hotel, where they had shared some beers with friends, and Keith and Joanne were now planning to stay over. An impromptu party was breaking out at their residence. They had fetched some wine, hefted the "ball of beer" out of the fridge, grabbed a pump to coax it out with, and made their way to the picnic table outside. Together they drew back the foam that filled the first few mugs, and then got down to some serious drinking.

At first things were fine. Kevin had showered when they got back, and Lyn had even offered to wash his jeans for him. As if out of kindness, he told her not to bother. The pair he had would be OK. Then Lyn broke a wine glass. The tinkling sound of glass skipping around the sink had not even stopped before Kevin fell into character: "You clumsy slut. Be careful. Who the fuck is going to pay for that?"[1] Without apologizing, he stomped back out.

The festive mood and the weather seemed to mollify Kevin and, within minutes, it was as though nothing had happened. More friends arrived and they partied on. Within an hour or two, the stale ice cubes that had been cracked from the plastic freezer trays had melted into a pool at the bottom of the cooler. The beer was getting warm. Kevin decided to go to get more ice. He also planned to stop at the Canadian Tire to pick up some wire so they could drag the speakers outside to keep the party going. He and two of his buddies piled into a car and squealed away. Distracted by their own company and dulled from quaffing beer in the hot sun, they returned a short time later, having forgotten the ice. Embarrassed, Kevin resented the criticism that Lyn levelled at him. Words were exchanged. He refused to go back out, so Lyn and Joanne decided to go. As she was leaving, Kevin told her to drive out to his grandmother's to pick up some corn for the guests. Lyn refused, and they argued about that as well. The women left for the 7-11.

When Lyn and Joanne returned from their errand, they dropped the "munchies" and the ice on the picnic table and settled inside to watch television. The party carried on outside in the failing light, a dozen flushed faces lit as much by the red band that still hung on the horizon as by the bare bulb over the patio door. The familiar sound of drunk talk and uninhibited laughter carried through the still evening air into neighbouring windows, but Kevin was laughing less than he had been before. He was becoming sombre, quiet, brooding.

"Why is she avoiding me?" he thought to himself. Without leaving his seat, Kevin summoned Lyn through the open door. "Lyn. Lyn. Get the hell out here. You anti-social? The party's out here. Come on, get the hell out here."

Annoyed but knowing that it was easier just to do as she was told, Lyn obliged, taking a place at the picnic table. Herb came over and sat down beside her. The two friends started talking and laughing while Kevin looked on. He didn't like what he was seeing. Why had she not come to sit with him? "Come here, come here," he barked. "Get your ass over here." And so, as the daylight failed, so too did Kevin's temper. A familiar pattern was playing itself out as trivial incidents were being treated as if they were egregious, punishable failings. The mellow, numbing flush that had washed over Kevin with the first few beers was turning into a cruel, brooding edge, as it almost always did. A familiar, dangerous edge. It was evident when Kevin pushed his way out of the lawn chair, his mouth hanging snarly and mean, and brushed into the house. Lyn, hoping to defuse the situation, followed him in. He went to change the record, but Lyn stopped him.

"You're too drunk, Kevin. I'll do it."

"Fuck off. I can do it."

Keith, for his part, did not hear them exchange these words. He had passed out on the couch, a human barometer that would have signalled to a more tempered crowd that the night was done. But not here. The drinking continued and things turned worse. Lives were about to change.

Kevin made his way downstairs into the recreation room and vomited on the carpet. Lyn, who had followed him down to check on him, led him into the laundry room so he could be sick in the sewer. She rubbed his back, trying to comfort him, trying to reclaim his human side, but he kept pushing her away. He swayed as he made his way to the couch, clumsy and heavy. There he sat down hard, bowed his head, and nodded off. Lyn willed him to sleep long and deep and went back up to join the guests. The party carried on.

Lyn had never been fond of Kevin's sister, Wendy, and the feeling was mutual. Wendy had come over earlier that evening with three guys and another girl. Maybe it was just because she had been mellow from the several beers and the glasses of wine she had consumed, but at first Lyn did not seem to mind them being there. It had been fun to hear Herb ribbing the losers Wendy had brought with her about the white pants they wore, but now it bothered her to see them drinking her beer. One of the losers was filling glasses out of the ball of beer as if it was his own. Lyn decided that it was late and she didn't want them around.

"Who invited you?" she said to Wendy's girlfriend.

"Kevin did," Wendy piped in.

"Well. Kevin's passed out. I think it's fine to leave."

Muttering "bitch" under her breath, Wendy moved quickly in response, but not for the door. Instead, she went downstairs and shook

Kevin. She woke him from the sleep of bears. Egged on by Wendy's complaints, he ambled up the stairs and stepped outside, ready to take charge. He would settle things. Lyn took one look at Kevin's face and saw the danger. She started to make her case by arguing with Wendy, hoping that Kevin would see it her way. Either out of the loyalty of blood, or just because it was easier to take control by keying on Lyn, Kevin sided with his sister. He gave Lyn a fierce push. The line had been crossed. It was time to retreat.

Lyn scurried into the house, locked the door, and sought refuge upstairs. She paused at the top of the stairs. Nothing. He was not coming after her, at least not yet. She called down to Herb, whose voice she could hear in the kitchen: "Herb, come up here, please."

Herb went up. Lyn was crying, quaking, her eyes wide, her chest heaving: "Kevin is going to hit me, Herb. He is going to beat on me."

"I know. If you were my old lady, things would be different." Herb gave her a hug and went out to see if he could talk sense into Kevin. He unlocked the door and stepped outside.

As she huddled in the closet of their room, Lyn could hear Kevin's voice carrying through the window screen, asking about her. What was she doing? Where was she? She listened, picking up those sounds that were not drowned out by her pounding heart — the patio door sliding open — five seconds of silence — then leaden footsteps on the stairs, slow but purposeful. Then nothing but a presence in the room. "Wench. Where are you?" Not a yell, but a taunting, teasing, singing whisper, the "I'm going to get you" voice you learn as a child. Only this was no game. Then the light. "You left your purse on the floor." That same taunting, condescending voice. Then silence. One quiet, still, pregnant second where everything seemed to hang in pause. Then, "whack." The purse flew across the room as Kevin kicked it full force, its contents skittering across the floor like frightened mice. His game. His theatre of force. A message coded with power and impending violence: "Get the fuck out of there."

The taunting voice was gone, replaced by a bull command, echoing, hanging, foreboding. She froze, her eyes closed, waiting for what was next. The tips of his fingers sank in the flesh of her arm. A yank, and she was out. A tug, and she was up. He pushed her, the push of the aggressor, the kind meant to provoke a response. The universal signal that the pusher wants to fight. Lyn obliged, pushing him back, trying to assert herself as she had before, knowing that she would lose but somehow feeling she had no choice. Then two loud smacks. The sting — two quick explosions of light under closed lids as the blows rattled her head. She was down, shaking as the adrenalin pulsed through her veins — scared, deadly scared, fallen back on the bed, her legs drawn up to shield her in a turtlelike, pointless pose of self-defence. Whimpering.

What happened next is the subject of some dispute, but only with respect to matters of detail. Lyn claims that Kevin gave her a gun. "He must have gone into the other bedroom where the guns were kept to get it." she told the police. "He must have loaded it." In any event, the stakes had been raised. She lifted the gun. The barrel wobbled in her trembling hands. Through her tears, she aimed it as best she could. "Bang." The bullet tore through the window screen, whistling over neighbouring rooftops.

At the trial, four guests testified that Rust was downstairs when that shot was fired and that he then went back up. In her statement to the police, Lyn disagreed. Kevin was in the room at the time, she said. He had gone to get the gun and was still there when she fired it. Maybe Lyn was right, maybe not. It did not matter. What matters is that Kevin was in the bedroom for the final act as the drama unfolded. Whether he had come back or had never left at all, it is clear that he had taken the time to go into the other room to reload the gun and that he returned and gave it to her once again. This time she pointed it at herself. Better to be dead, she thought.

Kevin looked at her with derision. A contemptuous look, an expression reflecting his certainty that she did not have the guts to waste herself. He smirked: "I'm going downstairs." Then he drew himself to his full height and pointed his finger at her as if there might be some doubt about whom he was addressing: "You or me," he taunted. "You or me."

She lay back on the bed, holding the gun up on an angle towards him. He was committing the ultimate act of bravado, giving her a rifle, loading it, and daring her to shoot him. In her failure to do so, she had affirmed his complete domination over her. She was his. He was the master. "You're my old lady and you do as you're told. Wait till everybody leaves, you'll get it then." A parting smirk, a signal that he would enjoy putting her in her place. He turned his back on her and began to walk away, the sound of his threat still ringing in her ears. But it was a promise that he was not to keep. Lyn was the first to realize this as she watched a chunk of his head spin away from his body as the rifle kicked in her arms and its explosion rang in her ears. His body vaulted forward and he flew onto his face. "He just went just like in the movies, just down and he was lying there."[2]

It was a scene of abject horror, surreal, like slow motion. A piece of his head had been blown away, but he was there on the floor. A growing circle of dark blood, almost black, appeared around his head. His enfeebled voice, shocked, haunting, pleading, called her name. A piece of his head was gone, but he was calling her name! Panic. Escape from this.

Pounding down the stairs. Retreat onto the front lawn — confusion. Pounding up the stairs, shrieking: "Got to go back to see him. I didn't mean to hit him. I was aiming above him. I was aiming above him." Kevin talking — no, mumbling. Kevin dying. Someone calling the police. Someone saying: "Stay out, Lyn. Stay out of here." Sirens. Flashing lights. Cops all over the place. Handcuffs. This is somebody else, Lyn feels. This is not real.

But it was real. Imagine. On 31 August 1986 it was Kevin Rust, not Lyn Lavallee, who left their home feet first. Imagine. It was Lyn Lavallee, not Kevin Rust, who would stand trial for murder.

◆　　◆　　◆

Cases like Lyn Lavallee's present incredibly sympathetic facts. The real victim is the killer, while the dead man is a villain who got what was coming to him. It is tempting to consider these facts to be enough to justify such killings. Men like Kevin Rust seem no better than animals. They demonstrate no compassion, no conscience, no humanity. If the word retains any meaning today, such men are evil. In their brutality, they ask for brutality. Had Kevin Rust lived, he would have had no moral right to complain on his own behalf that Lyn Lavallee had injured him after claiming it as his right to injure her. Why should we raise such complaints on his behalf now that he has died from a situation he himself created?

This conception of justice, which converts violence against a villain into suitable punishment, may be simplistic and brutal, but it is also timeless and enticing. It is primal and deep, and we all carry it with us. How many among us did not say to ourselves, "Good," when we heard that Paul Bernardo got his nose punched in by a fellow inmate? How many of us cried when we heard that Jeffrey Dahlmer, the cannibal sex killer, or Joseph Fredericks, the pedophile who murdered an eleven-year-old boy while on parole, had been killed in prison? I didn't. The only vestige of civilization I could muster in response was to chide myself for thinking that perhaps they got what they deserved. I knew I should be better than that, but I wasn't.

Those who deny that this blunt and plain notion of desert lies whole beneath the veneer that is our refined, modern ideal of justice refuse to know humanity, and they do so at their peril. It is this impulse that defence lawyers exploit when they work to change the focus of a trial from what the accused did to the villain/victim into what the villain/victim did to the accused. It is the Menendes brothers trying to dull the report of their shotgun blasts with their own cries of sexual abuse at the hands of their father; it is Lorena Bobbit obscuring the image of her blade, slicing through her husband's penis, by recounting stories about his abusive conduct; it is

Bernard Goetz hiding the viciousness of his subway hunt with images of urban crime by young black men; and it is Colin Ferguson's lawyer trying to make faint the images of his subway shooting spree behind the fog of centuries of racism against African Americans. Nor should we forget its most infamous success. Before laws were passed to stop it, defence counsel exploited this sentiment by showing the sexual offence victim to be a whore who really lost nothing of value when ravished. Indeed, the tactic of deflecting evil is not even confined to defence lawyers. This nation had to endure the pathetic effort by the attorney general of Ontario to justify the plea bargain that gave Karla Homolka a twelve-year sentence for manslaughter arising from the kidnapping, sexual degradation, torture, and killing of two innocent children on the basis that she was a "victim" who had helped her sexual-psychopath husband only because he had broken her spirit by abusing her. These are spectacular examples of what Alan M. Dershowitz has coined "the abuse excuse."[3]

To be sure, these cases are the exception. They are extreme, infuriating illustrations that do not begin to reflect the reality of what goes on regularly in courts in this country, or even in the United States. But it is important to recognize that these examples exist because it is an easy thing to exploit the natural human tendency to measure the quality of justice according to the quality of the victim. It is equally important to recognize that unless the law exercises great caution, this same phenomenon can turn what is nominally a self-defence claim by a battered woman into what is, in fact, a "justified extermination" defence.

Traditionally, the law of self-defence relied on rigid, general rules to assist it in distinguishing true cases of self-defence from killings inspired by payback. These traditional, general rules presented serious problems for Lyn Lavallee, problems that were readily apparent to her lawyer, Greg Brodsky, QC. The first difficulty was that Lavallee was under no *immediate* threat of death or grievous bodily harm when she shot her partner. Rust was walking away from her. He had uttered a threat to get her later, but he was done with her for the time being. That she shot him while he was walking away after that assault had ended made it look as though she was striking back rather than defending herself.

There was yet another problem. Self-defence is justified only where it is necessary. According to then-established conceptions of self-defence, it is not at all evident that Lavallee had to resort to force to defend herself against the promised future assault. Presumably she could have called the police and had him charged with the assault he had committed or with threatening her. Arguably she could have left the house, sneaking out if need be. That she shot him rather than trying these apparent options made it look as though she was striking back instead of truly trying to prevent the anticipated assault.

A moment's reflection reveals that it would not be rare for the concepts of imminent threat and pure necessity to present problems for many women who kill. Women who are easily overpowered may die if they wait for the attack to begin. A rigid imminence requirement has the potential to leave them in the position where they will become statistics if they do not strike first, or criminals if they do. So, too, would a rigidly applied concept of necessity. Some women have been stalked and savaged for trying to escape or for calling the police. To such women, summoning help or attempting to escape may not be a realistic option to using preemptive force. The fact is that what can be a viable alternative under normal circumstances can be a self-signed death warrant in some cases. It is obvious that the law of self-defence that Lyn Lavallee faced was not crafted with battered women in mind. On classic legal principles, her defence was wanting.

Yet that is the law that Greg Brodsky had to deal with when he defended Lyn Lavallee. Even with these legal impediments, though, he had an extremely sympathetic case to defend. So long as he could get out the evidence about the history of the relationship, a jury might refuse to convict, legal technicalities be damned. He needed a bridge between the established law and that evidence, and he found it in the expert testimony of Dr. Fredrick Shane, psychiatrist, who came to court armed with a script that had been developed by an American psychologist, Dr. Lenore Walker. It was the script of "battered woman syndrome," a template that could be fit over the life of Lyn Lavallee to enable the expert to explain that she actually and reasonably believed that she had no choice but to kill or be killed.

Misusing Battered Woman Syndrome

As explained in chapter 3, "battered woman syndrome" is a collection of common characteristics that battered women tend to exhibit. Like all theories that purport to reduce the complex array of possible human behaviours into a digestible model, there are variations on the theme, but the basic text goes something like this. Battered women — those who have experienced two or more "cycles of violence" — tend to share particular characteristics. First, they develop the ability to predict the onset of extreme violence. This ability develops because the violence in a battering relationship is not random. There are three distinct phases in the battering cycle: tension building, the acute battering incident, and loving contrition. The first phase is marked by a gradual escalation of tension starting with things like name-calling, other mean intentional behaviour, and then physical abuse. Despite the efforts of the woman to placate the batterer, he becomes more oppressive and the woman begins to withdraw. Then the "inevitable explosion" occurs and the "acute battering incident" takes place. This is the phase in which the woman is normally injured. Next comes the third stage, the "loving contrition" episode in which the batterer, having vented his frustration and anger, now seeks to show kindness and remorse. This phase provides the positive re-enforcement for the relationship which deludes the woman into thinking that she can help him change, thereby encouraging her to stay in the relationship. This three-stage process has been dubbed the Walker Cycle Theory of Violence.

A second feature of the battered woman syndrome, most often termed "learned helplessness," explains why women do not leave the battering relationship. As Dr. Shane said in the Lavallee trial:

> [T]he spouse gets beaten so badly — so badly — that he or she loses the motivation to react and becomes helpless and becomes powerless. And it's also been shown sometimes . . . not that you can compare animals to human beings, but in laboratories, what you do if you shock an animal, after a while it cannot respond to a threat on its life. It becomes helpless and lies there in an amotivational state, if you will, where it feels there's no power and there's no energy to do anything.
>
> So, in a sense it happens in human beings as well. It's almost like a concentration camp, if you will. You get paralysed with fear.[4]

As this last passage suggests, this condition of learned helplessness has also been explained as an application of the "traumatic bonding," typically referred to as the Stockholm syndrome, that has been observed between "hostages and captors, battered children and parents [and] concentration camp prisoners and guards."[5] The domination of the less powerful causes the oppressed persons to become negative in their self-appraisal, incapable of fending for themselves and therefore more in need of the person in power. They become too dependent to break away. A well-known example is Patty Hearst, who became the collaborator Tanya in the Simbionese Liberation Army after its members kidnapped her.

What do these two theories, the cycle of violence and learned helplessness, do for self-defence cases? They build a bridge between the acts of violence of battered women and the traditional rules of law. The cycle of violence theory helps get over the imminence requirement. It explains how a woman can be acting reasonably in responding to the threat of grievous bodily harm even though the batterer is walking away at the time or sleeping; she knows better than those who are not in the relationship what is coming down the pipe. Because it is cyclical, the woman is able to predict accurately the onset of violence.

The learned helplessness theory, in turn, explains why women who see what is coming do not try what may seem to be more conventional and more acceptable avoidance strategies, such as leaving or calling the police. According to the theory, these women have lost the ability to respond in a rational way because they are psychologically traumatized. As Dr. Shane said of Lyn Lavallee, "She couldn't leave psychologically because there were steel fences in her mind and she was tyrannized psychologically."[6]

In the end, this battered woman syndrome evidence made the relationship of Lyn Lavallee and Kevin Rust relevant, enabling defence counsel to unveil the entire, infuriating history of abuse. Not surprisingly, the jury acquitted her. But the expert evidence was not done with spinning its magic. It even persuaded the Supreme Court of Canada to change the law of self-defence. The expert testimony revealed that force can be reasonably necessary even against non-imminent attack, and it showed that it can, in fact, be reasonable for some women to resort to force without trying what at first blush might appear to be available avoidance strategies, such as running away or calling the police. The Court developed a more flexible conception of self-defence in which the focus is not so much on the strict chronology of events as on whether the accused truly and reasonably believed in all the circumstances that she had no real choice but to use extreme force in self-defence. Without question, the battered woman syndrome evidence performed a valuable service. It tore us from our rigid patterns of thinking, placing the legal focus where it should be. It is simplistic to think that self-defence can be necessary only at the moment your life is at risk.

Having paid the battered woman syndrome theory the high compliment of crediting it with generating sage changes in the law, I nonetheless feel impelled to trash it. I feel that need because it is a prime illustration of what is known in the literature as "junk science." Indeed, it flatters the theory to call it "science" at all, even with the appellation "junk" attached. In truth, it is little more than public interest advocacy dressed in the imposing garb of "study," experimentation, and psychobabble. It is a pious fraud, permitting "scientists" to come before courts as experts who claim the exclusive ability to divine what battered women who kill are really thinking. It is a theory constructed on a flawed edifice, and continued resort to it in our courts is imperilling justice.

Although the theory, as a prototype applicable to battered women generally, suffers from many shortcomings, its soft underbelly is its concept of learned helplessness. This theory was borrowed by Walker from experiments that had been conducted by Martin Seligman at the

University of Pennsylvania on dogs — a methodological quirk that critics of the theory are quick to exploit. In Seligman's study, caged dogs, who were electrocuted without any opportunity to escape, stopped looking for a way out. They learned to lie there and take it. When fairly obvious means of escape where presented, the dogs failed to find them. Hence, learned helplessness. But dogs and women? What an insult. I would like to see how seriously a theory would be taken if it was based on the premise that women can be expected to react the same way as dogs when you scratch their bellies. But even leaving the problem of optics and cross-species generalizations aside, Seligman's dogs were locked in cages. How does the caged-dog experience help explain why abused women do not leave their abusers or choose to call the police? "She was treated like a caged animal" may be good rhetoric, but it hardly supports a cross-species generalization that battered women have the same low resolve and loss of self-control as caged, electrocuted canines.[7] Not surprisingly, "according to the scholars who identified learned helplessness, domestic violence is not an appropriate example of the condition."[8]

In fairness to her work, Walker does not rely solely on this specious theoretical link between the behaviour of women and of dogs. For her and her disciples, the dog thing provides a helpful, theoretical analogy, a way to explain what she claims to be a similar, observed phenomenon among battered women. Yet the problems with learned helplessness do not end where they begin. First, there is inherent idiocy in the idea that the battered woman who kills has learned to be helpless in the face of her abuse. How can a helpless woman suddenly rear up and take charge on a particular occasion by firing a bullet into her partner's head? That does not sound helpless to me, or to the many other critics of the theory. Even if there are parallels between electrocuted dogs and beaten women, how does this idea of learned helplessness begin to explain the material event, the homicide? As one critic has observed, "the animal studies Walker cites do not appear to report any incidents in which one of the experimental dogs suddenly attacked the experimenter who was doling out the electrical shocks."[9] Learned helplessness seems to be a better theoretical basis for explaining why most battered women do *not* kill.

In addition, recent research suggests that most women, rather than becoming passive, increase their help-seeking strategies in an effort to avoid violence.[10] There are also some data suggesting that women may be more likely to be subject to violence after leaving a relationship. Given all this evidence, the prototypical woman who is being attacked may not be the one who is trapped in a relationship by her learned helplessness; she is just as likely, if not more so, to be a woman who is trying to get away.

Even some defenders of battered woman syndrome evidence recognize the problems with learned helplessness. "[L]eading feminist legal scholars on violence against women and battered women's syndrome have criticized the original learned helplessness model for years."[11]

What then of the Walker cycle of violence theory, the second arrow in the "battered woman syndrome" quiver? It, too, is a much duller projectile than its proponents would have us believe. The theory is based on psychological experimentation that suffers from serious methodological flaws, some of which have been listed by an American researcher, David L. Faigman,[12] including the use of leading questions, evaluator bias in data interpretation, the disregard of inconsistent data, overgeneralization, the failure to examine non-battered women in discordant relationships for similar phenomena, and the melange of statistics from separate cases into a general three-phase theory. Social science is, by nature, soft science, and the battered woman syndrome is weak social science.

The real problem, though, is oversimplification in any effort to develop models for human behaviour. It is a problem endemic to social science. Researchers in the social sciences can describe generalizations, but people do not act according to script. No doubt all the phenomena identified by Walker, much of which is observed in subsequent research projects, can, in fact, be found in many battering cases. No doubt women often do stay with their abusive men. But none of this evidence enables us to forge a cookie-cutter theory that can explain the actions, beliefs, and perceptions of particular women who kill. There are numerous reasons why some women stay with abusive idiots, ranging from love, to utilitarian motives of food and shelter, to misshapen notions about what is best for the children, to a misguided sense of what is normal within a relationship, to the fear that they will be hunted down if they try to run. And no doubt women who have been beaten can often see that their partner's mood, disposition, demeanour, or actions are sending off danger signals that others, unaware of the battering relationship, might miss. It is fanciful to suggest, however, that, as a class of persons, battered women come equipped with some special sense that can be relied on to divine the onset of potentially fatal violence that the rest of us would not be able to see if we were only told about the history of the relationship and the circumstances of the event. You do not have to be Lyn Lavallee to recognize that it was reasonable in the circumstances for her to fear that she would subsequently be hurt or even killed by Kevin Rust. Anyone who looks at the facts knows that he was going to try to punish her later.

As a model for deciding what happened in a given case, the battered woman syndrome is nothing more than a stereotype. Indeed, it is a stereotype designed for the purpose of giving women who kill a defence.[13] It is a chameleon, able to explain both why Francine Hughes was temporarily insane when she lit the "burning bed," setting her husband on fire, and why women who kill are acting reasonably in self-defence. It is malleable enough to do that because the research that supported it was not designed to discover whether women who kill are morally responsible. It was constructed to prove that they are not. Battered woman syndrome is a theoretical model intended to support the assumption, reputedly mouthed by Lenore Walker, that "only men kill in anger."[14] It should go without saying that instrumental science should immediately be suspect. If you pay someone to prove that smoking does not cause cancer, do not be surprised when the research proves what you want it to. When you seek out a theory to explain why women who kill are not blameworthy, do not be surprised if you find one.

As with all stereotypes, it is dangerous to rely on this one. It can distort the truth. First, it has the potential to give a self-defence claim to battered women who kill, even though they have not truly killed in self-defence. The focus becomes whether the woman suffers from the syndrome rather than whether she killed out of anger or in reasonable self-defence. This shift is particularly dangerous, given that it is not at all difficult to find "experts" who are prepared to diagnose virtually any woman who kills her abusive spouse as suffering from battered woman syndrome. Take Lavallee, for example. How helpless was she when she pointed a gun at Rust's face on two prior occasions? Where were the steel fences when she left him on earlier occasions, as she had done? How helpless was she when she provoked some of the fights with him, as she had done? And how helpless was she when she chose to trade blows with him on other occasions, as she had also done? Yet the expert said she suffered from battered woman syndrome. In the process, the expert testimony obscured the real question of whether it was reasonable for her to have shot Kevin Rust without even trying to flee or without even calling the police. All the talk about the steel fences of learned helplessness made secondary what should have been the critical questions of whether Rust had dragged her back in the past when she had left, or whether he had pursued her and beat her for leaving, or whether he had stalked her, or whether she had ever even sought help. The expert testimony even protected her from having to testify and to explain, if it was so, that she was simply too scared to risk leaving that night for fear that he would catch her and kill her before she could escape. These critical questions became so incidental, in fact, that they do not even gain mention in the appellate court decisions. They are simply bowled over by the power of "expert" diagnosis. It is not even possible to know on the record whether Lavallee even turned her mind to her options before blasting him. I would not begin to suggest that Lavallee did not deserve access to the defence. I suspect she did. The point, though, is that we do not know whether she did because the important questions of fact got buried in the pomposity of battered woman syndrome evidence. Where this happens, you simply cannot count on getting the facts right.

The flip side plays no better. Indeed, it plays much worse. Reliance on a stereotypical conception of the mental state of women who kill in self-defence can result in wrongful convictions. There are women who have no choice but to kill, yet do not fit the stereotypical model of the battered woman. Many women who kill have been toughened by the harsh lives they have led. Frequently they are alcohol or drug abusers, have committed crimes themselves, or have initiated violence against the batterer on other occasions or maybe even on the occasion in question. The fact is that you need not be a wilting flower to stare death in the face and resort to extreme force to preserve yourself, nor does the one who poses a threat to your life have to have a track record of horrendous abuse. Yet the myth of the battered woman, carefully crafted to evoke sympathy for the woman and the vilification of the dead man, paints the prototypical battered woman as passive, helpless, retreating, and wholly victim. In this tableau, the man becomes a monster. What happens when these stereotypes do not meet the evidence in a case? What happens is that a legitimate case of self-defence can be lost.[15]

The stereotype of the battered woman also threatens the fairness of applying the law of self-defence to men who kill their partners. While commendably decrying the use of stereotype to limit access to self-defence in the case of women who kill, Justices L'Heureux-Dubé and McLachlin, the only two women on the Supreme Court of Canada, fell into the trap of stereotyping men who kill:

> My focus [said Justice L'Heureux-Dubé] on women as victims of battering and as the subjects of "battered woman syndrome" is not intended to exclude from consideration those men who find themselves in abusive relationships. However, the reality in our society is that typically, it is women who are the victims of domestic violence, at the hands of their male intimate partners. To assume that men who are victims of spousal abuse are affected by the abuse in the same way, without benefit of the research and expert opinion evidence which has informed the courts of the existence and details of "battered woman syndrome" would be imprudent.[16]

In other words, unless we hear otherwise from an expert, we are to apply different stereotypes to men. Instead of judging on the basis of the specific circumstances as revealed by the evidence in the particular case, we are not to conclude that a particular man may reasonably have felt compelled to make a pre-emptive strike in self-defence to protect himself from his abusive partner's anticipated violence unless we hear it from some hired gun who can lace the account with mystifying jargon. Our dependence on psychiatry has torn us from a contextual examination of the facts and invited us to apply its deceptively simple and unscientific paradigms and models.

If the battered woman syndrome is such a meddlesome and weak concept, why was it accepted so readily in the case of battered women? The simple answer is because it was so appealing. It gave the illusion of science, structure, and law to the laudable impulse to support women living the nightmare of domestic violence who, in turn, resort to violence of their own. In a phrase, it was politically correct, so much so that many of us felt silenced against challenging it for fear we would be branded as sexist morons for doubting its orthodoxy. To a large degree, its political allure has sustained it these several years, especially in the United States. In California, for example, a place that has generated more legal lunacy than any other Western legal system, a law has now been passed effectively deeming battered woman syndrome evidence to have scientific integrity. Why? Because there is great political mileage in siding with battered women, and there is an unfortunate perception that the best way to do so is to endorse the myth of battered woman syndrome. George Fletcher, after citing examples of polls supporting this defence, and mass grants of clemency by governors in the United States of women who killed their partners, despaired: "In this political mood no one is going to pay much attention to scholarly critiques of learned helplessness and its extension to self-defence cases."[17]

Paradoxically, it may well be the forces of political correctness that ultimately return to destroy the syndrome. Many feminist scholars want it banished, not just because the stereotype can cause meritorious self-defence cases to become lost, but because of the messages that the syndrome model perpetuates. As Anne M. Coughlin observed in a leading American law review article: "The [battered woman syndrome] defense itself defines the woman as a collection of mental symptoms, motivational deficits, and behavioural abnormalities; indeed, the fundamental premise of the defense is that women lack the psychological capacity to choose lawful means to extricate themselves from abusive mates."[18] It removes criminal liability by suggesting that these women do not possess "the human capacity for self-governance on which the norm of responsibility is founded."[19] In short, it perpetuates stereotypes about female helplessness, irrationality, and the dependence of women on men, not a good thing for the image of women generally, and it does so by painting the specific woman as unstable or mentally disordered.

PMS and the Politics of Justice

This is not the first time that feminist theorists have turned on a female criminal defence because of optics. In February 1987 Marsali Edwards, a Canadian Armed Forces corporal, drove 13 kilometres to her husband's home and plunged a butcher knife twice into his back, puncturing his lung. She tried to defend the case on the basis that she was suffering from PMS, or premenstrual syndrome. This syndrome, defined as "the recurrence of symptoms in the premenstruum with complete absence of the symptom in the postmenstruum," is said to have the capacity to produce numerous unflattering symptoms in its sufferers, such as irritability, anxiety, depression, hostility, mood swings, indecision, as well, apparently, as more than 140 other complaints.[20] Edwards, like a number of American and British accused women before her, suggested that she was not in control of her actions when she stabbed her husband because she was in the throes of the unrelenting grasp of PMS at the time. She really did not intend to do what she did. The jury did not buy it, convicting her of aggravated assault, perhaps because of the unhelpful and unsympathetic comment that this condition forced from her mouth after she stuck the man: "I hope you die, you . . . wife beater." The judge, however, did buy it. He gave her three years' probation, ordering her to get treatment from a doctor "other than a psychiatrist." When this happened, causing something of a media sensation, women's groups did not rally to her defence. Instead, many women decried the defence because it perpetuated stereotypes about what women are like when their periods are coming. I remember thinking that if there really was something to this PMS business, it would be somewhat unfair to deprive poor Marsali of her defence simply because of optics.

Without in any way being taken to accept the legitimacy of the PMS defence, the point of this vignette is to demonstrate how easily truth and justice can become challenged by the demands of politics, particularly sexual politics. When that happens, it is an obscenity. For this reason I would not support the deconstruction of the battered woman syndrome evidence simply because it perpetuates damaging stereotypes. Instead, I would relegate it to the junk heap because that is where it belongs. It is an opportunistically constructed, instrumental, distracting, and unscientific generalization that is being relied on to answer basic questions about intention when it lacks the tools for discriminating between particular women on relevant matters. Coming as it does out of the mouths of "experts," battered woman syndrome evidence threatens to mislead juries and even judges into thinking that self-defence applies where, and only where, stereotypes are met.[21] Having said that, if it does get ploughed under because it proves to be a politically incorrect theory, it would only be fitting. After all, it was accepted as readily as it was because at one time it seemed so politically attractive.

Manufacturing Victims and Cultural Excuses

One of the problems with accepting doctrine or science because of legal expedience is that, once accepted, it is difficult to control. Exculpatory syndrome evidence cannot be confined to battered women. Recently, Lorne McConnell and his friend Peter Letendre killed a fellow inmate at the Drumheller Penitentiary, McConnell pounding his head with a knuckle-duster and Letendre stabbing him in the heart with an "ugly knife." The victim, Casey, was the enforcer in a rival gang. He was also walking away when he was dragged down by the two men and killed "in self-defence." If the defence evidence that was presented is true, Casey and his numerous and well-armed associates were poised to attack McConnell and possibly Letendre. McConnell believed it was a "kill or be killed" scenario, and that if he did not make a pre-emptive attack when he had the advantage, he would be the man to die. Ask for the help of the guards? To get protective custody, the men had to walk down a breeze-way filled with rival gang members who were holding home-made knives, some even "uglier" than the one Letendre carried. A new trial was therefore ordered for the men because the trial judge had failed to direct the jury accurately that the apprehended attack need not be imminent to support a self-defence claim.[22] The real issue was whether these men, living in the prison environment and knowing what they did of prison culture and the dynamics of the institution, could reasonably have believed that they were left with no choice but to attack first. This is the issue that the post-*Lavallee* law of self-defence now allows to be left to the jury.

Apart from the fact that it is difficult to appreciate how killing Casey could somehow reasonably be seen by these men to lessen the threat posed by the rival gang, it may well be that this is an appropriate case of self-defence. No doubt the occasion for self-defence, including pre-emptive strikes, will be greater in prison than on the street. What is so intriguing about it, however, is that the defence evidence about the kill or be killed environment in a penitentiary fell not out of the mouth of inmates or guards or penologists who could describe the lawlessness of prison culture, but was supplied by a defence psychiatrist who could not resist describing the mental state of the inmates by comparing it to the mind-set of the battered woman. Indeed, Madam Justice Conrad, the only judge who came to the right decision in the Alberta Court of Appeal, could not restrain herself from describing the perceptions of the accused men as exhibiting "prison environment syndrome." It is as though we are incapable of making decisions about moral fault without the contribution of jargon and professional mind-benders.

The problem of the syndrome contagion is not confined to Canada. Indeed, it is much worse in the United States. George Fletcher describes how Americans are "witnessing the beginning of a transformation of the battered woman's syndrome into a general defence of abuse as a justification for retaliation."[23] Courts have become acclimatized to its psychobabble, welcoming in other species of "syndrome" evidence which purport to explain away moral culpability. Professor Alan Dershowitz notes of the concept of learned helplessness that,

> [s]ince this condition was first diagnosed in the early 1980's, thousands of defendants [in the United States] have invoked battered persons syndrome [a modified version of battered woman syndrome] as an excuse for murdering their abusive spouses, boyfriends, girlfriends, and even parents. Recent examples include the case of a seventeen-year-old Andrew Janes, who ambushed and shotgunned his abusive stepfather, and the killing of a forty-one year old woman by her thirty-seven-year-old husband, a city fire department captain in Hickory, North Carolina, allegedly out of fear for his safety.[24]

In truth, it is probably simplistic to blame this proliferation on Lenore Walker and her battered woman syndrome. There is undoubtedly a more complex chicken-and-egg phenomenon at work here in which battered woman syndrome is not the chicken that is laying these eggs. Instead, battered woman syndrome is itself one of the scrambled progeny that has been laid by the same chicken that is squeezing out these other orbs. Where, then, is the abuse-excuse chicken? In the United States, resort to abuse excuses is unquestionably a development that has emerged through the stunning combination of a public obsession with "psycho-science," the allure that victimhood has in popular culture, and the fear of being politically incorrect by rejecting defences that justify themselves as responses to gender stereotype or, in some cases, systemic racial or cultural discrimination. Before we Canadians become too smug, we have to appreciate that each of these conditions pertains in this country as well.

The American, indeed North American, cultural obsession with psychoscience is easy to observe. Take a glance through the "pop" psychology shelves in any respectable bookstore. Self-healing books abound. "Therapists" of all stripes do a booming business. Our current generation, with its postmodern stresses and the loss for many of the traditional support systems once found in religion, family, and small communities, is one in search of belonging and healing. Both individually and as a society, we reach out for explanations and for affirmation. Therapists and behaviourists are prepared to answer the call, for a fee. This ready supply of "experts" provides a resource for courts that crave help in answering hard questions. Courts are becoming increasingly comfortable with behaviourists and with the therapeutic expert. Margaret Hagen, in a book tellingly entitled *Whores of the Court: The Fraud of Psychiatric Testimony and the Rape of American Justice*, explains the attraction to a legal system:

> That the courts accept expertise on the expert's own valuation of it reflects desperation as much as acceptance. Our courts — we, the people — need help to understand past behaviour, to control present actions, and to predict who's going to do what kinds of awful things in the future. . . .
>
> We want more certainty than that provided by rules of thumb, and we want more safety than that provided by our own experience. Thus modern Americans will embrace almost any psycholegal theory or claim that highly paid and highly arrogant experts spin on the witness stand. We and our judges are blinded by jargon, fancy-sounding credentials, and fancy degrees.[25]

At the same time that our trust in behavioural experts is increasing, the work of many behaviourists is undermining traditional concepts of responsibility. Behaviourists, while trying to dole out self-esteem and affirmation, have created a society of victims. The fast lane to healing is to absolve people of responsibility. Whereas religion once absolved by pronouncing forgiveness for acts that the actor bore and admitted responsibility for, popular culture denies blame, even for the decisions we take, by finding ways to blame others, or by blaming circumstance, or by constructing notions of powerlessness. In the salty, if not inflammatory prose of Hagen: "The witness bearers expend their energy attempting to bind up the psychic wounds of their clients while absolving them of any responsibility at all for the conduct of their own lives, while their paralytic fix on abuse and powerlessness guarantees endless wound licking."[26]

Stephen J. Schulhofer, in a provocative article about why the American legal system seems fascinated with the abuse excuse, makes the following more tempered observation: "Tales of extreme victimization resonate for an ever wider audience and more easily gain credence — sometimes justifiably so. The victims, once pitied or despised for what was seen as weakness or masochism, are now survivors with status that brings respect."[27]

Many abuse excuses also exploit politically sacrosanct ideals. The battered woman syndrome wedged its way into our courtrooms for fear that, to disbelieve it, would be to admit that you were labouring under sexist and stereotypical notions. It was said to express women's reality. Deny it, and be branded, at the very least, insensitive to your own sexism, or, at the worst, a misogynist. The easy thing, the safe thing, for judges, academics, politicians, and even prosecutors is to buy it and stay quiet.

In the United States some of the abuse excuses that have been tried are building on other politically sensitive foundations. According to a list compiled by Dershowitz, these excuses include the "black rage defence," which suggests that anger over racial injustice can be a catalyst for violence by American blacks. This, apparently, should excuse criminal conduct, at least where the actor has a predisposing, serious mental illness.[28] He also describes the "urban survival syndrome" defence in which the experiences of the inner city are said to heighten perceptions of danger, thereby enabling self-defence to be pleaded for actions that otherwise would not qualify. This syndrome exploits both race and poverty.[29] He includes, as well, the "cultural norms defence," which is intended to allow cultural background to explain away, or significantly mitigate, one's actions. He provides the example of Fumiko Kimura, a Japanese woman living in Los Angeles who walked with her two children into the ocean in what was reported to be a ritualistic, traditional Japanese method of suicide, the parent-child suicide, called *oyako-shinju*. She survived, her children did not. Despite her intentional killing of the children, she was eventually allowed to plead guilty to manslaughter, receiving a one-year jail sentence.[30]

While courts are becoming far more accustomed to hearing from experts on such matters, it has been pointed out that, even in the United States, the impact of the abuse-excuse phenomenon is easy to exaggerate. By and large, these designer defences are not working. As Professor Peter Arenella, who gained popular notoriety as one of the many O.J. Simpson commentators, has observed, "if the media paid attention to ordinary criminal cases, they would find very few examples of successful abuse-related defenses that negated the defendant's criminal responsibility."[31] Although Lorena Bobbitt got away with tossing her husband's severed penis over her shoulder as she drove by a field, the black rage defence failed, and so too did the urban survival syndrome plea. As Arenella points out, American prisons, like our own, are filled with killers who have grown mean through early abuse and victimization, yet they are not forgiven, nor is their culpability reduced.

It is also easy to exaggerate the impact of the battered woman's defence. Under the banner "Canadian Justice System Takes a Beating," a *Globe and Mail* editorial responding to the release of a report by the federal government reviewing the convictions of woman who are under sentence for having killed decried the decision to alter four sentences that had been meted out by courts. Apart from principled objections to undertaking a *post facto* review of settled convictions, particularly those of women alone while many men remain under sentence for offences that have since been repealed, the *Globe*'s editorial said: "In any case, battered-woman syndrome or black rage, or blighted childhood or any one of the dozens of medical or sociological excuses for violent acts are given far too much in today's courts."[32] George Jonas decried the use of the battering defence under the headline "Jane Doe licensed to kill."[33] In fact, very few Canadian women who have killed their partners have been acquitted on the grounds of self-defence, even with the aid of battered woman syndrome evidence.

The report that the *Globe and Mail* was criticizing, conducted by Judge Lynn Ratushny on behalf of the minister of justice and the solicitor general, involved the review of the convictions of all women in Canada who were under sentence for homicide and who had accepted her invitation to have their cases reviewed to see whether their act qualified as self-defence. When she was done, Judge Ratushny had not opened the prison gates. In fact, she found that in only three of the ninety-eight cases reviewed was the defence satisfied.[34] A study by University of Toronto Professor Martha Shaffer disclosed that of the sixteen cases that she could find of women who have tried to use a battered woman defence after *Lavallee* on charges of spousal homicide, only three were ultimately acquitted, while, in two other cases, the Crown chose to drop the charges.[35] If we judge by the acquittals alone, most men need not sleep in fear.

While these meagre statistics do not show a wave of acquittals, they do give cause for concern. In her study, Shaffer also discovered that of the eleven women who were convicted, every one of them was found guilty of manslaughter. There was not a single murder conviction in the bunch.[36] Of the eleven, nine had plead guilty.[37] In those nine cases, prosecutors either charged manslaughter at the outset or agreed to take manslaughter pleas to murder charges as part of a negotiated plea bargain. Shaffer concludes, with appropriate reserve given for the size of the sample, that one of the main effects of *Lavallee* in cases in which a woman killed a batterer may be a greater willingness on the part of the Crown to accept a guilty plea to manslaughter.[38] But is that a good thing?

One cannot help but suspect that at least some of these cases are not legitimate manslaughter offences. Judge Ratushny in her report expressed concern that some women who have actually killed in self-defence may be pleading guilty to manslaughter solely to avoid risking life imprisonment with lengthy parole ineligibility should their self-defence claim not work.[39] It is also likely that some of these eleven cases were, in fact, murders in which the Crown agreed to take manslaughter pleas, either because of fear that the history of abuse would cause jurors to refuse to convict at all or because of an appreciation that the penalties for murder are simply too rigid to allow sufficiently for mitigation. Without doubt, the minimum penalty for murder is distorting the application of the law where there has been a history of abuse.

What happens, then, when these manslaughter convictions are registered? Shaffer tells us: "In 6 of the 11 cases in which the women were convicted of manslaughter, the sentencing judge declined to impose a term of incarceration, imposing probation with terms instead."[40] Six dead men, none of whom was killed in self-defence according to the verdicts, and not a day in jail to show for it. In four of the remaining five cases, the maximum sentence was two years less a day. The last woman, Marilyn Howard, received a sentence of five and a half years at trial, but when battered woman syndrome evidence was presented on appeal, the sentence was reduced to two years.

It is difficult to draw many conclusions from eleven cases. What is certain, though, is that no random sample selecting eleven men convicted of homicide in the death of their spouses, even if restricted to manslaughter cases, would produce results like this one. If it did, alarm bells would be ringing. The American experience has been similar:

> Wives who kill their husbands were acquitted in 12.9 percent of the cases studied while husbands who kill their wives were acquitted in only 1.4 percent of the cases. Women who were convicted of killing their husbands were sentenced to an average of six years in prison, while men received an average of seventeen years for killing their wives. Sixteen percent of female spousal killers get probation, compared to 1.6 percent for males.[41]

Quoting similar statistics, Patricia Pearson, lamenting the stereotype that woman who kill are not necessarily as evil as men who do, observes in her book *When She Was Bad* that "chivalry justice," as she calls it, "will continue to operate as long as the justice system has a host of exonerative excuses for female behaviour and a highly sophisticated vocabulary for motive."[42] Her point is that some women kill out of anger, jealousy, for money, or even through meanness, and they should be sentenced accordingly.

It is not only in homicide cases that "chivalry justice" — can be seen. In chapter 3, I introduced the case of Kim Tran, the woman who received a conditional sentence for separating her husband from his penis with a meat cleaver while he slept.[43] The victim, Vi Hoc Phong, earned little sympathy when it was learned that he insisted that his wife continue to have children until she bore him a son, even though it endangered her life to do so. Nor was the revelation that he told his wife he had fallen in love with a younger woman, before telling her to be quiet so he could sleep, likely to endear him to the court. He was a most unsympathetic victim. The fact remains, though, that he was permanently and profoundly damaged, both physically and mentally by a brutal assault. No one can, in good conscience, lobby against lenient sentences for men who kill while provoked, but seek to defend this kind of decision. Regardless of the circumstances or the provocation, had it been a man who had sexually mutilated a woman in anger, you would be hard-pressed to find a defence lawyer with the *chutzpa* or indiscretion even to ask for a conditional sentence. The man would not be studying English as a second language and receiving life-skills classes. He would be trying to find a way to grow accustomed to his prison garb, for he would doubtlessly be wearing it for many years. Without question, sexual politics and the myth that only men are violent has had a distorting effect on criminal sentencing.

The sentencing patterns that have emerged in this country and in the United States are disconcerting, to say the least. It may be too precipitate to make firm conclusions based on the post-*Lavallee* decisions, but it is not too soon to wonder whether the climate of moral panic about spousal abuse that swept battered woman syndrome in the door has caused judges to give too much weight to the battering history as a mitigating factor. When one sees sentencing patterns like the one described above, it is difficult to resist the conclusion that we are indirectly recognizing that there are indeed "some people who just need killin'," or at least maiming, and that those people are abusive men. The concern is not that light sentences and the occasional acquittal will lead to open season on men. While it is true that there are far more women killing their partners than society is generally prepared to admit, with an average of one in four spousal homicide victims being men, there is no sign that this number has risen since *Lavallee*.[44] The concern is that giving token sentences where self-defence does not apply, to express sympathy for the plight of the woman or indignation with the life the abuser has led, fails to express adequately societal disapproval for extreme violence.

Is our record in Canada any better when it comes to other politically attractive excuses? So far, notwithstanding our genuine fervour to promote multiculturalism and to be an open and inclusory society, we have generally been prepared to say no to those cultural-based excuses that threaten to challenge established standards of behaviour.

According to the defence of provocation, if the accused loses control because of an act or insult and kills while in the throes of passion, he or she is not guilty of murder but only of manslaughter. This partial defence applies so long as an ordinary person in the position of the accused might also have lost control, given the nature of the act or insult. But who is this ordinary person that we are to use as the measure of excusable loss of self-control? Mr. Ly found out. He is a Vietnamese immigrant who killed his unfaithful wife. His claim to provocation was not based on the suggestion that other Canadian men would have perceived adultery to be a shocking enough event to cause loss of control and a murderous response. His claim was that to a Vietnamese Canadian, raised in a culture which gives a premium to honour and saving face and which invests much of that honour in female marital fidelity, adultery by one's wife would be sufficient to provoke the ordinary person. He therefore wanted the ordinary person by whose standards he would be judged to be a Vietnamese Canadian. He failed, and for good reason. Even if Ly was correct about how a Vietnamese male might react to adultery, considerations of culture cannot be allowed to compromise those standards of behaviour ordained by criminal law.

A similar claim to Ly's was made in Australia by a Turkish Muslim immigrant named Dincer, who killed his daughter because she had married without his consent. While this might not set off your ordinary Australian, it was said to be an unbearable insult in Dincer's culture, so he claimed the right to be excused of murder.[45] Unlike Ly, Dincer succeeded, but mercifully the legal principle established in his case has since been overruled. In the future, the degree of self-control expected of all accused persons in Australia is not to be determined by the culture of the accused. Rather, all persons must exhibit that modicum of self-control that is exercised by your average Aussie.

In a British Columbia case[46] a Cambodian immigrant attacked a family with a 3-foot machete, striking the father repeatedly and severing his hand. His lawyers tried to ante up his insanity defence by calling a witness to testify that the attack was a manifestation of "amok syndrome" — "a cultural phenomenon observed in South East Asia" in which the individual, with a history of depression, broods over a trivial insult and then, with little or no provocation, suddenly and unexpectedly erupts into an indiscriminate assault on those around him. The judge did not buy it.

There is no doubt that we would also punish someone like the Iraqi father who unlawfully confined his thirteen- and fourteen-year-old daughters in Lincoln, Nebraska, so they would have to marry men their father had chosen. We would also punish the bridegrooms who whisked these girls away, consummating the marriages against their wishes.[47] Nor did the government of Canada restrain itself in criminalizing female circumcision. Although this was a cultural practice of some new Canadians, it is, to Canadian sensibilities, a degrading and disfiguring practice, having its roots in attitudes about the subjugation of women. For that reason, it simply cannot be tolerated.

Neil Bissoondath, no fan of the multiculturalism practices in this country, has expressed real concern, though, about the extent of our resolve to keep on this track. He describes a Muslim group in Toronto "who recently demanded, in the name of respect for . . . its culture," the right to opt out of the Canadian legal system in favour of Islamic law. He remarked:

> [O]ne awaits with bated breath calls for public performance of the ancient Hindu rite of suttee in which widows are cremated alive on their husband's funeral pyres.
>
> There is a certain logic to all of this, but a logic that indicates a certain disdain for the legal and ethical values that shape, and are shaped by, Canadian society — and therefore Canadian society itself.[48]

Well, there it is, then — the tension. The criminal law is about establishing and enforcing basic values within a society, including values that identify when conduct can be excusing or justifying, when actions are reasonable, and by whose standards reasonableness is to be judged. The politics of accommodation, in contrast, is about accepting other values. While the line has generally been held so far, normally because cultural tolerance tends to make victims of women who have a more powerful political claim to accommodation, the avoidance of cultural relativity in criminal law standards cannot be taken for granted. There are harsh critics of *Ly* who argue that in judging Vietnamese Canadians, we should test provocation and the standards of resistance that society expects through the eyes of Vietnamese Canadians, and they urge that *Dincer* was right. Judge Ratushny, in her recommendations to the Department of Justice on reform of the law of self-defence, calls for "race" to be a relevant consideration in deciding whether an accused person acted reasonably in self-defence. Finally, culture has been allowed to mitigate sentences, most notoriously in two Quebec cases. In one, the failure of two Haitian men to demonstrate remorse for raping a woman was disregarded because of the judge's perception that this response was related to their culture, "particularly with regard to relations with women."[49] In another, a judge gave a lower sentence to a Muslim who raped his stepdaughter, since, given his cultural respect for virginity, he restrained himself from penetrating her vaginally. He claimed cultural credit for having only sodomized her. These are shocking illustrations of how attempts at cultural sensitivity can perpetuate stereotypes. They also demonstrate how attention to culture can produce injustice. The most significant demonstration may well be the case of Leon Jacko.

Jacko, a shy, mild-mannered nineteen-year-old, bludgeoned Ron Thompson, another resident of the Shegiuanda Reserve, to death with a walrus bone. He pleaded self-defence to a manslaughter charge. Mr. Thompson's assault? He was reputed to be a Bearwalker — a spirit that uses medicines to curse and even kill its enemies. Young Jacko, who had been learning traditional aboriginal medicines and witchcraft, believed Thompson when he claimed to have the Bearwalker's power. In killing him, Jacko was found to have been defending himself as well as others from that risk, so he was acquitted. The trial judge said, "I accept the evidence on native spirituality as being a sincerely held belief."[50]

This is an incredibly sensitive, some would say enlightened, acceptance by the judge of native spirituality. To claim that Jacko's belief was an unreasonable one would be tantamount to rejecting an important part of aboriginal culture, and so the decision was applauded as a breakthrough by some. Yet, once we begin to go down this road, how far will it take us? A report out of Dakar suggests that lynch mobs in Senegal are burning and beating to death sorcerers suspected of having the power to cause a man's penis to vanish or shrink.[51] Apparently, scores of people have died in similar bouts of hysteria in Ghana and the Ivory Coast over the past year. What would we do if a new Canadian rehearsed in the spirituality of one of those regions beat to death a suspected genital thief in downtown Toronto? While I am sure the loss of a penis counts as grievous bodily harm, one has to wonder how much sympathy a claim of self-defence would or should generate. And that is as it should be. For good reason Canadian law has always insisted that reasonableness has to be based on the actual, temporal conditions, not on the subjective cultural or spiritual beliefs of the accused.[52] When it fails to do so, it produces indefensible results. In New Zealand, recently, a Maori forced a crucifix up a woman's nose until it entered her brain. Miraculously, she survived. He nonetheless escaped jail with a two-year suspended sentence, even though he did not qualify for an insanity defence, because Maori Christian priests testified that they believed he was possessed by an evil spirit, or makutu.[53] Apparently, the devil made him do it. Until the devil is captured, it seems no one will have to do the time.

The criminal law is not being unduly harsh when it requires everyone to meet generally accepted standards of behaviour and pushes minority cultural values and spiritual beliefs aside. It is merely accomplishing what it is meant to, by reinforcing acceptable standards of behaviour. If the law in this country is going to continue to serve that function, the allure of accommodation has to be resisted when it comes to the definition and enforcement of crime. So, too, must we resist the attractive psychobabble of the expert witness who claims a window into the minds and motivations of those whose plight can claim our sympathy.

One way to keep some control is to inject sufficient flexibility into the law to allow these kinds of considerations, where relevant, to mitigate sentence. This accommodation should not be in the excessively sympathetic fashion that seems to be happening with the sentences imposed on battered women who do not kill in self-defence, but in a more measured fashion, taking into consideration all the circumstances, including the fact that a human being has died. We can do so by removing the mandatory sentences for first- and second-degree murder.

Not only will removal of the minimum sentence for murder produce more justice but it may also reduce our temptation to accept abuse and cultural excuses. Stephen J. Schulhofer, who spoke about the allure of victimization in modern North American culture and of its threat to measured justice, noted a significant paradox. American culture, much like our own, is conflicted, although more so. The current mood in each country is "law and order." People are calling for harsher penalties, less technicality, and for aggressive prosecutions, and they are getting them in the United States: increased use of capital punishment, sentences of hundreds of years for people who expect to live eighty, three strikes and you're out. American criminals are getting hammered, at least when they are getting convicted. Yet Americans, and to a lesser extent Canadians, are at the same time being seduced by claims of abuse intoned by pitiable defendants. How does this work? Schulhofer explains that if we are going to be harsh with criminals, if we are going to declare war on them, we feel the need to personify them as evil or subhuman. We have to demonize those whom we punish:

> The sticking point for the scorched-earth conception of criminal justice comes when the defense gets its turn at trial. Cultural demo-

nization of the criminal offender provides the emotional energy to condemn without remorse and eventually to pull the lethal switch, but it also leaves a large opening for defense counsel, because the picture of the generic Mobster or Mugger seldom corresponds to the facts of the particular case. If a guilty criminal is defined as a moral monster who deserves execution or isolation from human society forever, then the individual on trial . . . probably will not fit the picture.[54]

The law becomes receptive to abuse excuses and sob stories. As he puts it, "the co-existence of a punitive blame game with increasing receptivity to the abuse excuse is therefore less paradoxical than symbiotic; each reinforces the other." It is a lesson long understood in law. If we allow the law to become too harsh, we become too soft so that we can prevent it from operating.

So far in Canada we have done reasonably well in holding the line. There is no open season on men (although the penalty for poaching is too low). At the same time, we have kept a modicum of control on the expert charlatan, and we have resisted the full logical force of our politics of inclusion. People are not getting away with murder, and the abuse excuse is, in the main, a source of bemusement as we watch the courts of our American neighbours. For now, with some regrettable exceptions, we are doing fine, but we best not close our eyes and rest. The abuse excuse is being hatched in the laboratories of spin-doctors with impressive credentials. In the meantime, the bullying force of political correctness is purveying the politics of accommodation. Together, these are anxious beasts, ready to exploit the laudable human capacity for compassion, sympathy, and tolerance, all in aid of the despicable human capacity for violence and cruelty.

CHAPTER 15

Disordered Minds: Insanity, Automatism, and Intoxication

E ven if we conquer all other worlds, the dimension of sleep will
remain our ultimate last frontier. We will never know it well
because we cannot be its conscious witness. When we sleep, volition is paralyzed. Reflexes are not only dulled but unplugged. When we
sleep, we are without defence, without control. That is why it is so outrageous for someone to be attacked in bed, a crime that is universally recognized as heinous, unforgivable, unspeakable. And that is why we are not
responsible for what we do when we sleep.

On 24 May 1987 Denis and Barbara Woods climbed into their bed
in Scarborough, Ontario. Like any other night, they let sleep come to
them. And there they lay, their thoughts stilled, their arms and legs
pinned by the swaddling of their blankets, their bodies all but motionless.

Meanwhile, 23 kilometres away, their son-in-law Ken Parks prayed
for sleep to come to him. Dressed in track pants and a T-shirt, his large
body lay on the couch in his Pickering home while the television strobed
light around the darkened room. Its volume was low so as not to wake his
wife, who slept in their bedroom above. He was not welcome in the marital bed, but there would have been no sense in going up there even if he
was. His mind was overloaded, a scrambled network of torturous
thoughts that were speaking so loudly and incessantly that they were
bound to keep him awake. His problems, difficult enough to bear in the
light of day, had undergone the nocturnal transformation that converts
even niggling trouble into matters of urgency. When your problems are of
great urgency to start with, as Ken's were, the night time has a way of

turning them into pending calamity. Ken Parks lay there, pondering his pending calamity.

It seemed that things could not have been worse for the twenty-three-year-old. His recent addiction to the horses had cost him his self-respect, his job, and was threatening his marriage. His savings were gone. And while his wife seemed ready to forgive him for it, he had gambled away her money as well. But worst of all, he had embezzled $30,000 from his employer and had been arrested. He had felt the pinch of handcuffs on his wrists, and he faced fraud and theft charges. He was a criminal. He would probably be going to jail. How could he possibly sleep? He lay there staring blankly at the television, his eyes burning, his mind racing. If sleep was to come, it would have to pull him in when he least expected it.

Sometime after 2:00 a.m., Parks got off the couch. He grabbed his car keys and pulled on a jacket. Then he took his wife's keys and headed out, leaving the front door open. Opening the garage door, he climbed into his car and eased it onto the road. Some twenty minutes, six turns, eight sets of traffic lights, and a stretch down the 401 later, he arrived at the Woods' townhouse complex in Scarborough. He rolled the car into a tight parking space. There he reached under his seat, taking his tire iron in hand. Dangling it at his side, he walked past the other townhouse doors and slipped a key into his in-laws' front lock, entering into the dark and sleeping refuge of Denis and Barbara Woods and their youngest children.

Denis Woods was wrapped in the protective mantle of sleep when he was suddenly torn awake by the sound of his own rattling and gasping. Someone was on him! He instinctively grabbed at the large wrists of the man whose hands were encircling his neck. Those huge hands pressed ferociously, collapsing his windpipe and closing off the blood to his brain. Denis could feel his face growing hot, his eyes bulging, and he could sense his head pulling uselessly from side to side. Through the cloud of tears, he could make out some hulking, unrecognized form straddling him. Before long, the blurred image gave way to blackness as Denis slipped back into unconsciousness. This time it was not the gentle slide of sleep that took him there; rather, his brain could not do its job without blood and air.

Perhaps mercifully, Denis was unconscious when his son-in-law, whom he had always liked, thrust a kitchen knife into his chest and then tried to stab him several times in the head. And he was unconscious when the man who slept with his daughter and gave him his only grandchild brutally murdered his wife, Barbara. At some point while Denis lay help-less, Ken drove his tire iron against Barbara's skull with sufficient force to fracture it and to cause enough bleeding into her brain to end her life. He plunged a kitchen knife deep into her right chest, slicing her lungs, her heart, her diaphragm, her stomach, and her spleen. Another stab went right through her. Three more punctured her back. In the frenzied attack, Parks fractured her ribs. Her son-in-law, whom Barbara used to call the "gentle giant," brutalized her with repulsive savagery, although she bore him no ill-will. In the sparse tableau that his memory kept of the events of that horrid night, Ken recalled how she looked up at him with her eyes and her mouth open in what he would later describe as "a help-me face, a sad face."

The Woods children awakened with the mêlée. Through the pandemonium, Parks could hear them crying out. He tore up the stairs where their bedrooms were, trying to yell for them, "Kids, kids, kids." But they did not recognize the words or the voice. What they heard was an intruder, banging down the hall like an animal, panting and running, grunting loudly, making deep, seemingly communicative but meaningless sounds. Next they heard footsteps pounding down the stairs and the slam of the door. Then all was quiet — far too quiet.

A short time later, the routine quiet of front-desk duty on the graveyard shift at the police station was suddenly shattered. Ken Parks burst in. Blood was oozing from deep cuts in each of his hands. His voice was hoarse and plaintive as he strode in circles around the foyer, crying in apparent disbelief:

> I just killed someone with my bare hands. Oh my God, I just killed someone. I've just killed two people. My God, I've just killed two people with my hands. My God, I've just killed two people. My hands — I just killed two people. I killed them. I just killed two people. I've just killed my mother- and father-in-law. I stabbed and beat them to death. It's all my fault.

But Ken Parks was wrong on two counts. Although he had killed his mother-in-law, his father-in-law had not died. Mercifully, he would survive. And while Parks was no doubt the one who had attacked them, it was not his fault. That is why he was found not guilty. It was not his fault because you can't blame someone for what he does when he is asleep.

Do you find it difficult to believe that Parks was sleepwalking when he performed all the complex actions he did during that strange and fateful night? I do. Intuitively, it seems nonsense to suggest he could organize himself the way he did, drive all the way from Pickering to Scarborough, find his in-laws' home, select a kitchen knife, undertake his attack, and then find his way to the police station, all the while being asleep. My image of a sleepwalker is Homer Simpson walking out the front door with his eyes closed and his arms held out in front of him, mumbling "Duff Beer, Duff Beer." On the other hand, it makes no sense that Parks would go out in the middle of the night and intentionally, without any motive, kill two people who had showed him nothing but kindness. When matters are as unusual as this case, intuition is an uncertain guide. So consider the evidence. Does it help you in believing Parks' story to know that the defence called four different expert witnesses from across North America, including psychiatrists and neurologists with experience in sleep disorders, who, after extensive testing, all agreed he was sleepwalking at the time? Does it help you to know that the Crown had found no experts who would contradict this theory with sufficient conviction to make it worth calling them as witnesses? Would it help you to learn that sleepwalking tends to run in families, and that there was a substantial history of sleep disorders in Ken Parks' family?

In the sleepwalking department, Parks' grandfather took the prize. He was a notorious and persistent sleepwalker. He would routinely rise from his bed in the middle of the night and cook himself a meal — fried potatoes, or scrambled eggs, or even steak — which he never ate, leaving his wife to clean up his bizarre mess. The next day the old man would have no recall of his culinary exploits.

Parks had his own more modest history of sleep disorders, including the common phenomenon of bedwetting and sleep-talking as a child, and he had experienced at least one episode of actual sleepwalking as an adolescent. Sleepwalking is apparently a common thing among children. Some children rise from their beds without truly waking and relieve themselves in strange places — garbage cans, flower pots, or on tables. To my horror I witnessed such an incident myself as a young teen when one of my friends, whom I could not wake after a movie, rose from his seat and wandered into the manager's office, where he relieved himself in the trash can. And the movie wasn't even that bad. Apparently slightly over 2 percent of adults never outgrow the predilection to wander nocturnally.

But the Parks case was of a whole different order. Ken Parks had not simply been drawn from his bed by the urge to water the geraniums. He engaged in sustained, complex, and violent behaviour. Even the experts were sceptical at first. But their neurological tests and their examination of his background and family history satisfied them that Parks was walking through a dream when he killed his in-laws. Even Parks' wife, Karen, believed it. Knowing the man, she simply could not accept that he would have willingly attacked her parents.[1] Most important, a jury of twelve ordinary people, no doubt imbued with the same degree of scepticism as the rest of us, could not disbelieve it.

Whether you believe Parks' defence or not, his bizarre case is a useful entrée into those legal defences that turn on abnormalities of the mind. To understand the legal significance of sleepwalking, a form of involuntary behaviour, and the loosely related but distinct defences of automatism, insanity, and intoxication that will be discussed in this chapter, it is necessary to begin with the most basic propositions about criminal responsibility.

Volition, Moral Fault, and Ken Parks

In defining criminal conduct, criminal lawyers draw a distinction between the accused's actions and the accused's state of mind. Although, as a general rule, a crime cannot be committed without a wrongful act, the mental state of the accused tends to play the more significant role in marking conduct as criminal. For example, if a woman leaning against the rail at Niagara Falls intentionally drops her child over the edge into the gorge, she is guilty either of murder or infanticide, and the law says she should be punished. But if she becomes dizzy from watching the stirring water in the falls and unintentionally drops the infant over the edge, both she and the child are the victims of a tragic accident. The woman is not to be punished, but rather pitied, because she did not intend to kill her child.[2] And that is as it should be. It is the state of mind with which an act is done that typically separates evil, or criminality, from misadventure, or accident. We generally do not brand people as criminals simply because their actions have produced horrendous consequences.

The most basic requirement of moral fault is that the actions of the accused must always be voluntary to be blameworthy. For example, if an epileptic was to thrash out during the throes of a seizure, striking someone, it would not be an assault. This is not simply because the act of striking the other was unintended but because the act of throwing out the arm is not even volitional. It is an involuntary spasm. It therefore seems inaccurate, even harsh, to describe it as an act of the accused. To be a physical action that the law will attribute to the accused, it must be willed. It must be thought-directed action, an act controlled by the accused. This distinction should be perfectly comprehensible. Criminal law is about blame. How can we blame someone for an action, even a devastating action, if the act was entirely out of his or her control?

According to basic criminal law principles, while acts must be voluntary to be blameworthy, mere volition is not always enough to justify punishment. Generally a criminal offence will spell out some further mental state that the offender must have before guilt can be proclaimed. Precisely what that mental requirement will be is determined by the nature of the crime and through an appraisal of what is needed to make someone morally blameworthy. For example, you cannot be convicted of arson if the fire you light gets out of control and accidentally burns down a nearby cottage. Even though you have done the act of destroying that cottage by fire and are likely to be sued for it, to be guilty of the crime of arson you must either intend to destroy the cottage or be reckless in the sense that you know there is a substantial risk that your fire would endanger that cottage, but you go ahead anyway.

Murder, for its part, is considered the most serious and stigmatizing offence, possessing the most severe and inflexible punishment known to Canadian law. The law therefore recognizes that it requires the most extreme form of moral fault. While a person can be convicted of the less serious offence of manslaughter without intending to cause death, murder requires that the accused intend either to end the life of another, or, alternatively, to cause serious bodily harm to another which he knows is likely to cause death. The crime of murder takes its essence, therefore, not from the fact that another has died at the hands of the accused, but from the state of mind of the accused at the time he killed. According to the rule of law, you cannot convict someone of murder, or of any offence for that matter, unless each and every one of the elements of the offence defined by law is present. Without volition, or without the necessary intention, there may be a killing, but there is no murder.

What then of Ken Parks? Were his actions truly volitional? On the evidence, no. While Parks' actions were undoubtedly directed by his brain, they were not voluntary. He was in a state of unconsciousness or disassociation at the time. His conscious mind, the state of which enables us to distinguish good from evil, was simply not functioning. In his state, Parks had no control over what he would do. He was every bit as vulnerable as the Woods, only his vulnerability was of a different order. He was vulnerable because his brain could take his body on a frolic of its own, one over which he could exercise no conscious choice. He was without reasoned intention. How then can we condemn him for the quality of his reason?

According to the scientific evidence:

> During a state of sleep-walking there is a durable, "very intense confusional state during which quite elaborate automatic behaviour can occur." A sleep-walker has no conscious awareness of his or her behaviour and usually has no recollection of it. A sleep-walker's ability to control voluntary even complex behaviour is severely limited or not available. The state of the sleep-walker might appear to an observer to be wakeful but, in fact, the person is asleep.[3]

Just as it would be a pointless act of abject cruelty to punish a sleep-walking child for unconsciously engaging in the socially unacceptable behaviour of peeing on the carpet, it would be pointless and cruel to punish Ken Parks. On the evidence, his acts were not volitional. As horrendous as the consequences were, one can no more blame him for what he did than one can censure the morality of an adolescent for having a wet dream. One can no more blame Parks for attacking his in-laws than one could blame his grandfather for overcooking the steak. Without volition, there can be no blame and there can be no criminal fault.

Because there is no moral fault for non-volitional behaviour, those who commit crimes without volition will have a defence. Normally that defence will be what is known in law as the defence of automatism. In a nutshell, "automatism is the [general] term used to describe unconscious, involuntary behaviour, the state of a person who, though capable of action, is not conscious of what he is doing. It means an unconscious, involuntary behaviour where the mind does not go with what is being done."[4] There have been numerous examples of automatistic behaviour over the years. Automatistic episodes have been brought about by blows to the head, poisoning (including carbon monoxide poisoning), infection, hypoglycemia drug or perhaps even alcohol intoxication, and physical disorders such as brain tumours and epilepsy. Automatism can also be induced by diseases of the mind such as schizophrenia or hysterical neurosis.

In every case of automatism, volition is suspended, but, for policy reasons, not all cases are treated the same. Cases tend to be divided according to whether they involve "sane automatism" or "insane automatism."[5] Where the automatism is "sane," the defence is simple automatism. Where, however, it is the product of a disease of the mind, the defence of "mental disorder," more commonly known as the "insanity defence," applies. The reason has to do with the consequences of each defence. The simple automatism defence results in a complete acquittal of the offender. Because the Crown cannot prove its case where the actions of the accused are not volitional, the accused walks out the door a free person; the law has no claim on that person, no matter how horrendous the actions were. The mental disorder defence is not quite so generous. Those found "not responsible on account of mental disorder" are subject to a disposition hearing. If they are shown to pose a danger to the public, they may be ordered into indeterminate custody, subject to periodic review. Even if released, they are most often released on strict conditions. Society tries to keep control over the criminally insane as long as necessary to protect itself. Where the automatistic episode is the result of a disease of the mind, then, the right of society to protect itself in spite of legal innocence kicks in.

By the time his case got to the appeal courts, there was no question that the Crown could not prove that Parks had acted with volition. It was therefore clear that he could not be convicted of murder or attempted murder, or even manslaughter. The sole remaining legal issue, and it was a significant one, was whether, technically, his defence would be automatism or insanity. That would depend on whether his somnambulism or sleep-walking was the product of a disease of the mind. If it was not, Parks would be free to go. If it was, as the law stood at the time, he would have to rely on the insanity defence, and he would be taken into custody and held in a secure psychiatric facility "at the pleasure of the Lieutenant Governor," until such time as it was considered he no longer posed a public danger.

Pleading Insanity: The Defence of Mental Disorder

The insanity defence has been with us for generations, although it has changed substantially. Until only 150 years ago, psychiatry was so rudimentary that lunatics were considered to be a special class of people, comparable with brutes or wild beasts. They were seen to possess no more capacity than infants, and, like young children, were considered to be incapable of evil and therefore incapable of crime.[6] By the mid-nineteenth century, both the medical conception of diseases of the mind and the legal notions of how to deal with crimes by the insane were maturing. The evolution of knowledge culminated in a profound change to the law during the case of Daniel M'Naughten. Even though much has happened in psychiatry since then, that decision remains the foundation for our modern defence of mental disorder.[7]

M'Naughten was an eccentric character, gloomy and unsociable. In the late 1830s he began to believe that he was being persecuted by the police. So significant was his fixation that he fled to France to escape. Finding no refuge there, he made his way to Scotland, believing that he was still being followed. While in Scotland, he began to fixate his persecution complex on the Tories. He made his way ultimately to London, where he began to stalk the Tory prime minister, Sir Robert Peel, by hanging around his office. In those pre-television days, however, he did not know what Peel looked like. He had observed Drummond, Peel's private secretary, coming and going from Whitehall and believed him to be Peel. On 20 January 1843 M'Naughten lay in wait and, when Drummond was returning from his bank, M'Naughten discharged a flintlock pistol at him, striking him in the back. He was preparing his second pistol when a police constable threw his arms around M'Naughten. The constable's heroic act was too late to save Drummond, who died five days later in great pain. M'Naughten believed he had acted justifiably, and he told the police so:

The Tories in my native city have compelled me to do this. They follow and persecute me wherever I go, and have entirely destroyed my peace of mind. . . . They have accused me of crimes of which I am not guilty; in fact they wish to murder me. It can be proved by evidence. That's all I have to say.

M'Naughten's case was tried before a jury of his peers in March of that year. It was evident from the start that he would be relying on an insanity defence. His problem, however, was that he was not prone to spectacular and bizarre behaviour. He was hard-working and intelligent. He did not think he was Napoleon or prattle to himself. Apart from hanging around Whitehall, the most daft thing he had done was to choose to leave France for Scotland. Even this did not make him a lunatic of the ilk who inhabited the infamous Victorian asylums. A conviction and a subsequent execution were widely anticipated.

Unfortunately for the many members of the public who lusted for his hanging, a clever lawyer got in the way. Alexander Cockburn, QC, later to become the Lord Chief Justice, did a masterful job, arguing that although he seemed sane in other respects, M'Naughten's fixation "takes away from him all powers of self-control." The only expert evidence called, the testimony of two "alienists," supported that claim. Chief Justice Tindal told the jury that the issue for them was whether M'Naughten had been "sensible that it had been a violation of God or of man" to shoot Drummond. The jury retired and returned a short time later with a verdict of not guilty by reason of insanity. M'Naughten was spared the gallows, but he was not released. He was dragged away, an innocent man, to a prison for the criminally insane. Ultimately becoming one of the first inmates of the infamous Broadmoor Prison, he was later to die there of tuberculosis amid the screaming of wretched souls and the clanging of steel doors. Perhaps the most curious aspect of the case is that it would go down in history as a victory for the defence.

Even though it hardly improved the quality of his life, M'Naughten's acquittal scandalized the nation. It was not enough to lock him away in some horrid building. Justice requires blame, and this murderer was absolved of blame. Those words "not guilty by reason of insanity" rankled the public. Calls for the abolition of the insanity defence were heard in each of the government houses, with the upper chamber, the House of Lords, ultimately taking the unprecedented step of summoning the judges who had presided over M'Naughten's case to come before them to explain the verdict. The statement of law that would influence the development of the insanity defence throughout the Commonwealth, and in the United

States, was uttered by Chief Justice Tindal not during M'Naughten's trial, but rather during his own appearance before the House to explain the law. When asked what jurors should be told about the insanity defence, he said:

> [J]urors ought to be told in all cases that every man is presumed to be sane, and to possess a sufficient degree of reason to be responsible for his crimes, until the contrary is proved to their satisfaction; and that to establish a defence of insanity, it must be clearly proved that, at the time of committing the act, the party accused was labouring under such a defect of reason, from disease of the mind, as not to know the nature and quality of the act he was doing; or, if he did know it, that he did not know he was doing what was wrong.

The *M'Naughten* test has been controversial since its inception. Its precise meaning has never been entirely free from debate. Leaving aside the finer points for a moment, it means that you do not get access to the defence of insanity simply because you suffer from a mental illness. The inquiry is not into your status as a "lunatic," as it once was. To qualify for the defence you must not only have a mental illness but that mental illness must prevent you from knowing the nature and quality of the act you are doing. Alternatively, that illness must deprive you of the ability to know that what you did was wrong. In other words, there are two different insanity tests. The first focuses on the accused's capacity to know the circumstances, and the second focuses on his ability to evaluate the rightness or wrongness of what he is doing. If you do not meet either test, you will not have a defence, even if you suffer from a serious mental disorder.

This is precisely what happened in Ottawa's infamous crossbow murder of a few years ago. Patricia Allen, a brilliant young government lawyer, was murdered at the age of thirty-one by her estranged husband, Colin McGregor. He stalked her and then shot her through the heart on a public street with a crossbow he had secreted in a garbage bag. It was an act of horror that traumatized a city, if not a nation. Even though both defence and Crown psychiatrists agreed that McGregor suffered from a serious mental illness at the time and that he would likely not have committed the atrocity had he been psychologically well, he was nonetheless convicted. While his illness warped his thinking and in a real sense caused him to murder his wife, it had not prevented him from appreciating the nature and consequences of his act or from knowing that what he was about to do was wrong.

In the 150 years since the *M'Naughten* case, most of the jurisdictions to adopt its test have either abandoned it or made significant changes to it. In Canada we continue to adhere closely to the test. We have made but one change to its text: we have altered the first insanity test by substituting the word "appreciate" for the word "know." We did this because simple knowledge of the circumstances may not be enough to justify imposing blame. Whereas "knowledge" is the mere possession of information, "appreciation" requires both knowledge and some degree of intellectual awareness of the significance of one's conduct.[8] For example, in the late 1950s the defence was used successfully by a woman who killed three of her children by hanging them. Just after it happened, a neighbour had asked her where her children were. She told her they were dead. The incredulous neighbour said, "You must be mistaken," whereupon the woman said, "Oh, but it is [true], I have hanged them." She then excused herself so she could return home to babysit them. Four children were soon found hanged by the neck in the laundry room. Only one survived. On the evidence, while the mother knew what hanging was and that the children would die if she hanged them, she "lacked any real understanding of the nature, character and consequences of her act."[9] It was evident that she did not appreciate the finality of death.

While "appreciates" involves an intellectual awareness of the consequences, it does not require that accused persons have an appropriate emotional response to the consequences they create. You can appreciate the consequences of your acts without feeling guilt, remorse, or even sympathy. The defence is not therefore available to "sociopaths" or "psychopaths," those whom psychiatry identifies as suffering from what is sometimes known as "antisocial personality disorder."[10] People with antisocial personality disorder are locked in a self-centred, aggressive, impulsive search for pleasure. They feel little, if any, guilt or remorse and are frequently in conflict with their culture and its laws. Their actions are untempered by compassion or empathy, and they are unamenable to either reason or law. In a word, they are predators, and their prey is the rest of us. They are often the ones with the page-long criminal records that cover an astounding variety of offences, frequently including acts of senseless brutality. Although they can be bright, their psyches show no more light than the black, lifeless eyes of a shark as it rolls to savage its quarry. They count among their numbers such stalwart citizens as Paul Bernardo and Clifford Olson. For the good of society, even though their minds are diseased in the sense that their psychological state liberates them from what society accepts as normal behaviour, they are denied the insanity defence. Why? Because they appreciate the nature and consequences of their acts. They just don't care.

The second, alternative test, relating to whether mental disorder has deprived the accused of the capacity to know that his conduct is wrong, continues to apply in the form it was described in *M'Naughten*. Although it was unclear whether Lord Tindal meant "legal"or "moral" wrong when he pronounced the *M'Naughten* test, it is now settled in Canada that "wrong" refers to the capacity of the accused to identify whether his specific conduct in the particular case "is wrong according to the ordinary moral standards of reasonable members of society."[11] Mathew Oommen[12] was acquitted of murder on this basis after killing Gina Lynn Beaton. He had fired between nine and thirteen shots at her as she lay sleeping on a mattress in his apartment. At the time he shot her he was labouring under a psychotic, paranoid delusion that members of a local union were attempting to kill him. He believed they had recruited Beaton and had just given her the signal to finish him off. In those circumstances, he believed he was justified in killing her. Like M'Naughten before him, from his demented perspective he was justified by ordinary moral standards in doing what he did. Society would, in his mind, approve of his actions.

The insanity or mental disorder defence has been controversial since its inception and remains so. In two Ontario cases, *R. v. McGregor* (the crossbow murder) and *R. v. Théberge*, polls conducted by the defence revealed that "13% and 19% of respondents, respectively, indicated that they would reject an insanity defense for any defendant regardless of the strength of the evidence."[13] This attitude caused the trial judge in the *McGregor* case to deny the public its normal right to a jury trial in murder cases and to try the case herself.[14] She did not have faith that, in the emotional and angry public mood at the time, the jury would follow the law.

It is easy to see why the defence is despised by the public. Recognizing mental disorder as the cause of devastating behaviour deprives society of its moral right to assign blame. When abject horror occurs, most of us want to make somebody pay. It is infuriating when those who may well be society's most dangerous citizens are absolved for atrocious actions that we know they did. A number of the respondents in the *McGregor* and *Théberge* polls expressed their belief that even the mentally ill should be punished for their actions.

In an effort to dull the symbolic insult of a "not guilty" verdict in such cases, we now declare these offenders to "have committed the act," but to be "not responsible on account of mental disorder." But the mollifying placebo of euphemism does not do enough to remove the disquiet. The defence remains hated. And, because the defence is distrusted, it is infamous even among those who accept that the mentally ill are not always morally blameworthy. At bottom, that distrust is closely tied to the distrust of the psychiatric profession.

Many of us do not trust psychiatry to identify those who should be absolved and those who should not. It is precisely when crimes are most unspeakable, incomprehensible, or depraved that the spectre of mental illness gets raised. The last thing society wants to hear when citizens are being pushed onto subway tracks is some guy named Sigmund telling us not to blame the monster because his cat died when he was four. Of all our criminals, the deranged are the ones who scare us the most. Many people want them locked up forever, illness or not, to protect society. The best way to accomplish this goal is by convicting them and putting them in maximum security jails. The worst thing we can do from the point of view of protecting society is to find them "not responsible" and then hand them over to white coats who will take them on outings, give them pills, talk to them about their problems, and pronounce them cured even though they are still dangerous. When the J.P. Goodmurphys of the world ask to get out ["Me and the boys just want to go fishing"], the truth is that many of us would rather they didn't. And we feel safer when it is a jailer, and not Nurse Ratchet, who holds the keys.

The distrust of psychiatry is not a new phenomenon. Even after M'Naughten's case, much of the anger centred on the unreliability of the psychiatric testimony. John Haslan, the first medic to publish on the law of insanity, once said during cross-examination, "I never saw any human being who was of sound mind."[15] This quote was brought up in the English House of Commons after M'Naughten's case as evidence that the insanity defence would open the floodgates. Distrust persists to this day. Recently New Mexico's Republican state senator, Duncan Scott, proposed an amendment relating to the expert evidence of psychologists and psychiatrists in insanity cases. Had the amendment become law, it would have required psychologists and psychiatrists, when testifying, to dress like wizards with cone-shaped star-bedecked hats and long white beards. They were to be required by law to stab the air with a wand to punctuate critical elements of their testimony. And on the amendment went, requiring other deprecating rituals such as the banging of gongs. The Scott amendment, reflecting a widespread belief that at worst, these professionals are charlatans and, at best, hired guns who will tailor their views to what the case requires, actually passed the Senate before being defeated in the House of Representatives.

I would not begin to deny that psychiatry has its shortcomings as a forensic science, but neither would most psychiatrists. In frustration after a gruelling cross-examination in the *McGregor* case, Dr. Sawer-Foner, a defence psychiatrist, was challenged: "Doctor, I suggest to you, you have no way of knowing what state of mind [McGregor] was in when he killed his wife." A flustered Dr. Sawer-Foner responded: "Sir, I'm a doctor of medicine. I'm not a god."[16] That statement was both an acknowledgment that he did not know and an apology for the state of his science.

The *McGregor* case was a showcase for the shortcomings of the profession. Different defence psychiatrists diagnosed McGregor as suffering variously from "schizophrenia," a "delusional disorder," and "psychotic depression, peppered with severe hypochondria." For a moment, one psychiatrist found retreat from the insecurity of his technical diagnosis by simply saying of McGregor, "he's nuts."[17]

Although their expertise is fallible and the state of their science is uncertain, we need medical professionals to assist us in understanding medical disorders. But fear not. We have not handed the psychiatric profession the power to decide the fate of mentally disordered offenders. Perhaps, to some, it will seem a bit like Alexander Haig mistakenly claiming he was in charge after President Reagan was shot by a mentally disordered John Hinckley Jr., but I feel obliged to say: "Do not worry about the psychiatrists. When it comes to mentally disordered offenders, we lawyers are in charge." Lawyers and politicians, not psychiatrists, decide when the law will allow mentally disordered offenders to be exonerated. Judges and juries decide whether they are guilty. Judges, or review boards staffed by medical personnel but also by lay people and lawyers, decide whether mentally disordered offenders will be released and on what terms, and these boards will most often make their decisions based on information presented by lawyers. No. The defence of mental disorder is not a tool for psychiatrists to protect their patients. It is a lawyer's idea, one that few psychiatrists even understand. A survey by the Clarke Institute of Psychiatry revealed that only one in two hundred psychiatrists fully understand the defence.[18] If the survey is accurate, it is a good thing that lawyers have more influence than psychiatrists over when the defence applies. After all, although no studies have been done on the question, I would guess that the ratio of lawyers who understand the insanity defence fully could be twice as high.

In truth, it hardly seems fair to blame psychiatry for all the public distress over the mental disorder defence, given that most psychiatrists hate it. They see its concepts as bizarre and primitive, failing to reflect the state of psychiatric knowledge. In this regard I am sure they are right. The mental disorder defence is probably an abomination in the eyes of medical science, in no small measure because it allows for the conviction of people like Colin McGregor who would not have committed their atrocities had they not been mentally ill. The thing that the medical profession must keep in mind, though, is that the law relating to the defence of mental disorder is not about mental health and healing. It is about societal protection and justice, and about when, as decent people, we should assign blame for indecent acts. These are questions that the legal system must answer.

Why, then, do we in the legal system feel the need to find some mentally disordered offenders not responsible for acts they have unquestionably done? When the two tests we use to exculpate medically disordered offenders are examined, our thinking becomes reasonably clear.

Of the two, the second branch of the mental disorder defence is the easier to explain. It is what is known in law as an "excuse." Those who are incapable of knowing that their conduct is morally wrong are "exempted from criminal responsibility because a mental disorder at the time of the act deprive[s them] of the capacity for rational perception and hence rational choice about the rightness or wrongness of the act."[19] As a matter of basic human decency and understanding, we excuse these people because we simply cannot justify punishing them. As much as we might like to see a day of atonement for horrendous behaviour, we cannot, in all conscience, blame someone for failing to choose to do right where, because of illness, they are not even capable of recognizing what right is. It is not only the soft-headed liberals of today who believe this to be right. Philosophers and lawyers have recognized for centuries that if we punish someone who kills when she is too sick to know that it is wrong to do so, we are effectively punishing her for being sick. As a just society, we simply cannot afford to act in this way.

Like this second branch, the first branch of the mental disorder test also has an element of "excuse" to it. The law no doubt takes pity on those who do not appreciate the nature and consequences of what they do. It therefore chooses to excuse them as a concession to their illness. In most cases, however, there is a more compelling reason for not convicting those who lack the ability to appreciate the nature and quality of their acts. It has to do with the rule of law and the requirement that, in order to convict, the Crown must prove each and every one of the elements of a criminal offence. Frequently, those who do not appreciate the nature and consequences of their acts will generally not have the intention or knowledge that the criminal law requires before a finding of guilt can be made. For this reason, where the first branch of the defence is met, the accused could not have been convicted of the offence charged, altogether apart from the mental disorder defence. For example, the woman who hanged her children in the laundry room did not mean to kill them in the legally relevant sense because she did not intend to end their lives. Given her absence of intention to kill, she could no more be convicted of murder than the sane woman who accidentally dropped her child over the Niagara Falls. Similarly, those who suffer insane automatism would not be guilty of crimes even if there was no mental disorder defence, since every criminal offence requires that before an actor is guilty, his acts must be volitional.

The fact that most of the people who qualify under the first branch of the mental disorder test would not be guilty of crimes, even if the mental disorder defence did not exist, reveals how misleading it can be to refer to it as a defence at all. A "defence" is typically understood to be something that enables you to walk away free. But not the mental disorder defence. It can have the opposite effect. Through its operation, those mentally disordered people who do not have the necessary intention or knowledge to be guilty in law are nonetheless denied their acquittal. Instead, they are found "not responsible by reason of mental disorder" and are almost invariably detained or subjected to rigid conditions that restrict their liberty. It should be evident that, for such people, the mental disorder defence is hardly a boon. It is not some technicality for getting away with it. Rather, it is the law's way of keeping control over dangerous people, even though they have not committed a criminal offence. Those who rail against the insanity defence should understand that it is less a defence than a means to maintain control of offenders. The mental disorder defence often does more to protect society than to endanger it. It creates a legal limbo in which innocent people can be exonerated but not freed.

As for Ken Parks, which of the two defences was to be his, mental disorder or automatism? The answer depended on whether his sleepwalking episode was the product of a disease of the mind.

Although the term "disease" has a definite medical ring to it, we lawyers do not ask the medical profession to decide whether a particular mental condition is a disease of the mind. Psychiatrists are probably thankful for this because the term "disease of the mind" is not a term of art used by their profession. It means different things to different psychiatrists. If we were to defer to the opinion of psychiatrists as to whether a given condition was a disease of the mind, the answer in each case would vary, depending on who the expert witness happened to be. The result, and therefore the scope of the defence, would depend not on law but on unguided opinion, and the rule of law cannot tolerate this inconsistency.

It is important to remember that the concept of a disease of the mind, like the mental disorder defence itself, is a lawyer's idea designed to identify those who should avoid conviction. It therefore performs a public policy function that differs in kind from the function of psychiatry. The concept of a disease of the mind has little to do with treatment or healing and everything to do with moral guilt, punishment, and public protection. These are legal, not medical, questions. If you want to know what qualifies as a disease of the mind, you'll have to ask a lawyer, not a doctor.

To serve its function of protecting society from dangerous people, the law once attempted to use fixed tests for identifying whether a given condition was a disease of the mind. One such test focused on whether the disorder was prone to recur. If it was, then the insanity defence would apply so that the accused person, even if legally innocent, could be detained so as to protect the public from the possibility of a recurrence. This test was problematic because it failed to catch cases of "temporary insanity," those rare instances where a transient condition of unquestionable mental origin deprives someone of the capacity to appreciate the nature and consequences of what they are doing. An alternative test turned on whether the disorder had an internal or an external cause. The thinking was that if the cause was internal, it was likely to be repeated. So, for example, whereas confused behaviour resulting from carbon monoxide poisoning would not be a disease of the mind, confused behaviour resulting from schizophrenia would be. People are usually lucky enough not to lose their mind from carbon monoxide poisoning more than once, but schizophrenia is an omnipresent condition that can become florid from time to time.

On its face, the internal/external concept was attractive, but it, too, was imperfect. It is often controversial whether it is best to characterize something as having an internal cause or an external one. To take a modern *en vogue* example, what of "post-traumatic stress disorder"? If an accident victim becomes dysfunctional, is the origin of that dysfunction the accident or the victim's inability to cope with the stress that the accident caused? Given this, the Supreme Court of Canada in *Parks* rejected the internal/external dichotomy as *the* way to identify diseases of the mind and instead developed a more holistic approach. Whether a particular condition is a disease of the mind should be decided by a general, functional inquiry designed to identify those cases where public protection is required. That inquiry is informed, but not determined, by whether the condition is prone to recur or whether it is internal or external in nature. It is also to be influenced by policy considerations. For example, where the condition is automatistic in nature, its categorization can be influenced by how easy it is to fake, or by the prospect that the way it is characterized might open the floodgates so that it becomes a common way of evading responsibility. In such cases, it may be in the interests of public safety for the law to regard the condition as "insane automatism" so that the less attractive "mental disorder" defence would have to be used. This, it is believed, would discourage manipulation. It was this holistic approach, then, that applied to decide whether Parks was to be acquitted or to be subjected to a mental disorder review.

Based on this test, the Supreme Court of Canada decided that Ken Parks did not have a disease of the mind. First, the internal/external cause inquiry provided no real guidance. Although there is a strong genetic and therefore internal predisposition to sleep disorders, particular sleepwalking episodes are usually triggered by externally generated factors such as stress, sleeplessness, or high levels of exercise. Given this, should Parks' sleepwalking episode be identified as having an internal or an external cause? It was hard to say. The "recurring danger test," for its part, suggested that a mental disorder defence would be inappropriate. It was "clear from the evidence that there [was] almost no likelihood of recurrent violent somnambulism."[20] What, then, of the general policy considerations: Did they support a finding that insane automatism was the best characterization? Not in the view of the Supreme Court of Canada. Sleepwalking is not something that is easy to fake, said the Court. Anyone who thinks they can exterminate their enemies with impunity by pretending to snore and by holding out their arms while walking over to fetch the gun should know that there are precise symptoms and medical histories that must be present, and batteries of tests that must be undertaken. This investigation significantly reduces the chance of a false diagnosis. As for fear of opening the floodgates by recognizing this defence, the Court observed that the law had accepted somnambulism as a basis for acquittal for generations, yet Parks was the first person in Canada to use the defence successfully. In the end, the Court held that Parks was not mentally disordered. It was not simply a case of his not being responsible for his act. It was a case of his being not guilty. His acquittal was therefore upheld.

Speaking of the decision in *Parks*, Justice La Forest said:

> It may be that some will regard the exoneration of an accused through the defence of somnambulism as an impairment of the credibility of our justice system. Those who hold this view would also reject insane automatism [or the mental disorder defence] as an excuse from criminal responsibility. However, these views are contrary to certain fundamental precepts of our criminal law: only those who act voluntarily with the requisite intent to commit an offence should be punished by criminal sanction. The concerns of those who reject these underlying values of our system of criminal justice must accordingly be discounted.[21]

In other words, if you think we should punish those who, because of mental disorder, do not appreciate the nature and quality of their acts, or do not know right from wrong, or unconsciously cause harm, then your views have to be ignored. They have to be ignored because your instinct for self-preservation and your fear of harm is stronger than your instinct for justice and your commitment to human decency.

Those, of course, are tough words, and they are not calculated to make the law popular. They reflect the firm conviction, however, that the law must do the right thing, even when it is not the popular thing. Inherent in that sentiment is the firm belief that if the law chooses to do the right thing over the popular thing, it will be respected by reasonable people. Perhaps nowhere in modern Canadian judicial history has this proposition been more severely tested than it was in the case of Henri Daviault, a man who did not steal a life, but whose act of attempted rape stole the dignity of an infirm and elderly woman.

Pleading Gluttony: The Defence of Drunkenness

Like Ken Parks before him, Henri Daviault sought to use a variation of the defence of automatism to exculpate himself. Unlike Parks, if Daviault was automatistic at all, he caused the condition himself by drinking like a pig. He guzzled his way from heavy-eyed, to pie-eyed, to wall-eyed, to shit-faced, and then asked the law to protect him from his sodden actions. If acquittals based on automatism are hard to take when the condition occurs through no fault of the accused, they are next to impossible to accept where the accused brings the condition on himself through debauchery.

It happened on 30 May 1989. Henri Daviault poured back seven or eight bottles of beer before making his way to the home of Rita Dumas, a sixty-five-year-old friend of his wife. Daviault's wife helped Ms. Dumas from time to time as she was partially paralyzed and used a wheelchair. When Daviault arrived at Rita Dumas' house, he was carrying a 40-ounce bottle of brandy. Ms. Dumas took one glass of the brandy while they chatted, then fell asleep. When she awoke some time later, Daviault grabbed her chair, wheeled it into the bedroom, hoisted her up, threw her on the bed, and then tried to have sex with her. On her evidence, she not only protested but, in the only moment of justice in the whole episode, squeezed his testicles with all the strength she could muster. Either because of the pain, or because of his condition, he was unsuccessful in having his way with her. After he left her place at 4:00 the next morning, she found the bottle of brandy, empty, on the kitchen table. When the police came calling, Daviault sought to excuse himself on the basis of his intoxicated condition. He sought to avoid responsibility by relying on a self-induced condition that made him dangerous.

The notion that over-indulgence can somehow exculpate harmful behaviour is intuitively offensive. For this reason, many Canadians detest the defence. Much of the hatred for it, though, is based on a misunderstanding of how the defence works. This misunderstanding is caused, in no small measure, by the term itself. To speak of the "defence of intoxication" is thoroughly misleading. We do not acquit people simply because they are drunk or stoned. Nor do we acquit them simply because alcohol or drugs may have loosened their inhibitions and caused them to act in ways they would not have if sober. These are popular misconceptions that do much to discredit the law. In fact, we acquit drunken or stoned offenders only where all the evidence, including proof of their intoxication, casts doubt on whether they had the mental state required by the offence charged. For example, in a murder trial, if the judge or jury decides that the accused intended to kill even though he was drunk or stoned, he will be convicted in spite of his intoxication. If the judge or jury decides that he killed intentionally because the drink or drugs made him aggressive, or affected him "so that he more readily gave way to some violent passion,"[22] he will be convicted anyway. However, if the judge or jury believes that he did not intend to kill because he was so drunk or stoned that he did not realize the implications of what he was doing, he will be acquitted of murder. Instead, he will be convicted of manslaughter, which does not require the same degree of intention.

If you find this distinction offensive, recognize this more common application. It is the legal system's readiness to consider the effect of intoxication on the mental state of accused persons that precludes you from being convicted of theft after you leave the office party wearing the wrong toe-rubbers, or after grabbing the wrong purse, or after forgetting to take the lampshade off your head. The law recognizes that you did not intend to steal these things; you were simply too "happy" to recognize that the property was not yours.

It should therefore be understood that the law's readiness to allow proof of intoxication to reveal the actual mental state of the accused is not based on any notion that intoxication excuses behaviour. Rather, it is based on the rule of law. If we were to convict intoxicated offenders of offences even where they do not have the intent required by the offence charged, we would be convicting them contrary to law. The defence of intoxication simply allows the judge or jury to consider the actual mental state of the accused. Where, on all the evidence including their intoxication, it cannot be proved that they had the mental state required by the crime, these offenders are acquitted of the offence charged because no crime has occurred.

Primarily because of the way it operates, the law does not allow evidence of intoxication to be considered for all offences. It is believed that, for some offences, the mental state required for guilt is so basic, so elementary, so low, that drink or drugs could not possibly prevent the accused from having the necessary intent. Where this is the case, there is no point in allowing the intoxication of the accused to be proved, for it could make no difference. For example, evidence of drunkenness cannot be considered in an assault case or in a prosecution for damaging property. Even the drunkest person, the law believes, will be able to decide whether to swing away at someone who is troubling him or to smash a window, so there is no need to consider the state of sobriety of the accused. We call such offences "general intent offences," to describe the fact that the mental state required for guilt is so basic that even intoxicated offenders will be able to form the necessary intent.

By contrast, there are offences that require a more sophisticated mental state. One form of first-degree murder, for example, requires planning and premeditation. It is entirely conceivable that a reasonable judge or jury, learning that the accused was intoxicated, may have a doubt as to whether she planned or premeditated a killing. Even second-degree murder requires an intention to kill, which is a more complete and precise mental state than merely swatting out at someone. We therefore allow evidence of intoxication to be considered in murder cases, just as we do for other offences requiring more precise mental discrimination, such as robbery, passing counterfeit money, or even theft. It is only in cases where the intention required is "specific" as opposed to "general" that the law has traditionally allowed the effect of intoxication on the mental processes to be considered.

If it were true that the mental element in all general intent offences was so low that it could not be cast into doubt by intoxication, the law would be entirely coherent and defensible. In fact, it is not. It probably takes no more mental sophistication to understand that an act will cause death than it does to appreciate that an act may cause damage to property, yet murder is a specific intent offence, and mischief to property is a general intent offence. It is entirely conceivable that a man may be too drunk to realize that if he pounds in anger on a window it will break. In such a case it cannot be said that he intends to break the window, but if he is charged, because mischief is a general intent offence, the law will not allow him to rely on his intoxication to establish his absence of intent.

Indeed, the law has not even insisted in every case that an offence must provide for only some rudimentary mental state before it is deemed a general intent offence to which the offence of intoxication does not apply. Policy undoubtedly has influenced the way offences are characterized. The clearest example is the now repealed offence of rape. It was a general intent offence for which proof of intoxication by the accused was deemed irrelevant, even though the offence required the accused to intend to have intercourse with a woman he knew was not consenting,[23] a mental state every bit as complex as that required to intend to kill. It was dubbed a general intent offence because it was perceived to be the kind of thing that drunk men may well do. The perceived need of societal protection inspired the law to deem it to be a general intent offence for which proof of intoxication could not be considered.[24] The law was happy, in the interests of law and order, to proceed on the assumption that intoxication could not undermine the basic intent required by the offence.

Understanding this reasoning should presumably reduce opposition to the defence of intoxication. As is sometimes true of the mental disorder offence, this defence gives the accused nothing that she would not have had even if there was no such defence. It works only where the accused does not have the mental state that the Crown is already required by law to prove. Even then, the defence of intoxication is not allowed to be used for all offences. For general intent offences it actually permits the Crown to prosecute an offender who was stoned or drunk at the time, on the artificial assumption he was not. Even though the law assumes otherwise, the reality is that in some general intent cases this permission will enable the Crown to prove intention or knowledge, even though, at the time, the accused did not actually have that intent or that knowledge because he was so stoned. It has the effect of broadening rather than narrowing criminal liability.

Henri Daviault was trying to use his intoxication as a defence to a charge of sexual assault. Like its predecessor offence, rape, sexual assault is a general intent offence. The "defence of intoxication" does not apply. Simple analysis would seem to require the trial judge to disregard Daviault's intoxication and convict the man. Simple analysis was complicated, however, by two things — the degree of Daviault's intoxication, and the demands of the *Canadian Charter of Rights and Freedoms*.

According to the puffed-up but uncontradicted defence evidence, Henri Daviault was not simply intoxicated. His intoxication was so extreme that he was on autopilot. He was an automaton. In his testimony, Daviault described the beer he quaffed and how he recalled arriving at Ms. Dumas' place and having a glass of brandy. After that point, he claims to remember nothing. The defence called a pharmacologist, who testified that if an ordinary person drank as much alcohol as Daviault did, he would have died or become comatose. Because he was a chronic alcoholic, however, this booze-bath did not cause Daviault to black out. Instead, it caused him to lose contact with reality. His brain temporarily disassociated from its normal function. This meant that he had no awareness of his actions, and it explained why he had no memory of his actions the next day. If this was true, it meant, of course, that Daviault could not have intended his actions. He was as unconscious as Parks was. While physically he was the one degrading Ms. Dumas, his offensive actions were not even volitional.

The suggestion that Daviault was not acting voluntarily complicated an otherwise simple case. In the end, it meant that the Crown could not rely on the simple rule that intoxication is not a defence to a general intent offence such as sexual assault. Why not? Because of the *Charter*. The *Charter*, of course, is a constitutional commitment by the government of Canada, and hence the Crown, to respect fundamental principles of justice. The same fundamental constitutional principle that assisted Ken Parks[25] was available to Henri Daviault: "only those who act voluntarily with the requisite intent to commit an offence should be punished by criminal sanction." While in cases of simple intoxication the law might be able to turn a blind eye and persist in its fictitious assumption that no one can fail to have the basic mental state needed to commit a general intent offence like a sexual assault, in cases where the intoxication is so extreme that the accused is akin to automatistic it is obvious that there will be neither intention nor volition. That being so, there can be no conviction without violating the *Charter*.

As a result of the *Charter*, then, a majority of the Supreme Court of Canada agreed that a person who is so extremely intoxicated as to be akin to automatistic cannot be convicted. However, the Court did not order Henri Daviault's acquittal. Instead, it ordered a new trial. Mindful of the need to ensure that the administration of justice would be protected from trumped-up claims of intoxicated automatism, it took the exceptional step of ruling that anyone who wants to rely on a defence of extreme intoxication must do more than simply cast doubt on whether he acted voluntarily or had the intent required to commit the offence. He must go further and prove on the balance of probabilities that he was so intoxicated that he was akin to automatistic. Since the judge who acquitted Daviault had not applied this high standard of proof, the trial would have to be redone. This time, it would not be enough for Daviault to leave the judge in some doubt about whether he acted voluntarily. He would be convicted unless he could convince a court that when he assaulted Ms. Dumas, he was more probably than not automatistic.

The Crown was confident it could convict Daviault the second time around. It would be much more prepared. This time it would be armed with expert evidence that would claim that it is impossible for someone to become automatistic from alcohol consumption alone. Since alcohol depresses central nervous system activity, including both motor ability and cognitive ability, it is highly unlikely to induce an automatistic state. Alcohol-induced automatism could occur only if alcohol could somehow drastically impair cognitive capacities so as to induce an unconscious mental state, while at the same time leaving motor function sufficiently unimpaired that complex actions like wheeling wheelchairs into bedrooms, or lifting crippled women and overpowering them, could still be performed. The problem for experts who claim that this can happen is that there is simply no scientific evidence on their side. There is nothing that proves that alcohol alone can have this uneven, bifurcated effect on volition and motor-functioning.[26] Since the burden would be on Daviault to establish that he was automatistic when he plucked Rita Dumas from her chair, given the state of scientific evidence about alcohol-induced automatism, he was bound to fail.

Sadly for justice, Canadians were never given the opportunity to see Daviault tried again. Rita Dumas died before the retrial could be held, leaving the Crown with no evidence of the assault. Daviault walked away a free man.

◆   ◆   ◆

The legacy of the *Daviault* decision is a sad one, but not only because Rita Dumas did not live long enough to see justice done. It is particularly sad because of the negative effect it has had on the long-term interests of justice and on the repute of the Supreme Court of Canada. The Canadian people simply could not see past a sodden boor and a crippled victim to the larger issues at stake. The Court was pilloried for affirming the basic proposition that the Crown should not be able to convict people who act involuntarily. It was denounced for accepting that where Parliament creates an offence that requires intention, if the Crown cannot prove intention its prosecution should fail. Instead of applauding the Court's commitment to basic propositions relating to the decent treatment of citizens by the state, the Canadian public criticized the Court for its gullibility and its insensitivity to women and to victims.

The mantra of victim/women, with all its political force, resounded in the halls of Parliament. With astounding pace, the government of Canada set about to change the law so that the Henri Daviaults of the world will be convicted, even if the evidence can show beyond all doubt that they acted involuntarily or without the intention required by the offence charged. Section 33.1 of the *Criminal Code* was passed to accomplish this change. It now prevents anyone from relying on the defence of extreme intoxication for offences involving violence or the threat of violence.

While many, if not most, Canadians will say "bully for Parliament," we would do well to pause and think. We would do well to think about the long-term interests of justice and how fragile our basic principles of justice can be when the public mood is offended. What Parliament has done in the name of the Canadian people is to reject basic promises it has made to the people of Canada about how it will treat them. In the name of Canadians it has claimed the right to punish Canadians for their involuntary acts. It has claimed the right to convict them of offences which purport to require intention, even where that intention was not present at the time. In doing so it has run roughshod over basic principles of criminal law. Parliament in its politicking, and we in our encouragement of it, have forgotten that these principles are there for the protection of us all. We have forgotten that they are the tools that allow us to assess moral blame, and to choose when and how to punish. While it is easy to vilify Henri Daviault and wish him the worst, it is easy to forget that not all accused persons are Henri Daviault. Ask Nicole Lafleur.

Nicole Lafleur was tried for manslaughter because her abusive husband died after she stabbed him in the leg. She, too, claimed to be extremely intoxicated, although on the more credible foundation of a combination of alcohol and prescription drugs. Her attack, she said, was not an intentional or volitional one. Because the attack occurred before section 33.1 was passed into law, she was allowed to raise extreme intoxication in her defence.[27] Had she stabbed him a few weeks later, though, she would have been denied the right to defend herself based on her absence of intent or volition. Section 33.1 would have taken that defence away from her by preventing her from proving her intoxicated condition. She would have been tried on the assumption that she was not blotto, even though she was. Even if the evidence could have established conclusively that she did not intend to stab him, or was acting involuntarily at the time, it would have been too bad for her. We would have been required to convict her anyway. Section 33.1 would effectively have culled the moral fault needed to find her blameworthy and to punish her for manslaughter, not from any desire she had to harm her husband, but rather from her decision to drink while on medication. As the law stands now, we would convict her, contrary to fundamental principles of justice.

In pandering to the public outcry in the way it did, Parliament, with our complicity, has diminished and devalued the basic principles that protect the mentally disordered, the automatistic, and those of us who take the wrong toe-rubbers after the Christmas party. Fundamental principles are intended to guide our choices so that we do the right thing, and so that our system remains coherent. Without them, we do not have a system at all, but, rather, a series of opportunistic rules.

The temptation to ignore fundamental principles when they produce results we do not like is strong. But principles are, by their nature, meddlesome. Their role is, simply, to keep us from doing what is convenient or popular, so that we will do right. If we disregard them when they are inconvenient or unpopular, we may as well not have principles, for that is precisely when they are supposed to do their work. If we use them only when we like the results they produce, they are useless. When we use them like that, they are not guiding us at all. Instead, they are doing no more than allowing us to create the illusion that our system is committed to ideals of justice, morality, and fairness.

Among our fundamental principles, the principles of fault are particularly important. They tell us when there is sufficient moral fault to punish. As difficult as it is to refrain from assigning blame for the devastation of the mentally disordered, the automatistic, or even the extremely intoxicated, if we, as a society, choose to disregard these principles in order to strike back with convictions for offences that require volition or intention that is, on the facts, absent, we will be ripping the fabric of the law. More important, we will be punishing without moral authority.

THE ROLE
OF THE
VICTIM

The Sad Truth about Victims' Rights

The Coelhos lost their son. He died because Marty Stoltz drove dangerously. The young man was not claimed by some inherent vulnerability that left him susceptible to terminal disease, nor was he torn down by some "act of God." He did not die as most of us would want, through the gradual and slow process in which our bodies are so well used that they ultimately fail in the final years of a long and full life. He died young, leaving a fiancée behind. He also left behind his terminally ill mother and his father, who would now have to cope with his mother's death alone. He died pointlessly, tragically, and traumatically, and Marty Stoltz was to blame.

Jose Coelho and his wife planned to be there for the sentencing, so they could experience closure and see justice done. They also wanted to participate, even hiring their own lawyer to speak for them during the sentencing hearing. A "victim impact statement" prepared by Mrs. Coelho was filed with the sentencing judge. She wanted to speak personally, but became too ill from her cancer and was unable to remain at court. The lawyer whom the Coelhos had hired stood up during the sentencing process and asked to address the court. He wanted to provide more information about the dead man. The judge, in the absence of objection by the accused, agreed to listen, but not before imposing strict limits on what the lawyer could say: "I will allow [Mr. Azevedo, the Coelhos' lawyer] to speak only about the victim. No submissions about anything else. I would expect to be told about the relationship with he and his family only."

Mr. Azevedo said his piece, telling the judge about the great source of support the dead man had been to his family, particularly to his mother, whom he cared for in her illness. When this was done, the judge handed down a sentence that bitterly disappointed the Coelhos. Marty

Stoltz was to be jailed for six months and placed on two years' probation. In the meantime, their son was gone forever, denied the right to dance at his wedding, to have children of his own, to cradle his mother as she passed from this life, and to prop his father up when they buried her.

Unlike most victims, Jose Coelho did not simply give a helpless shrug and walk away, one more person who had lost faith in the justice system. The process by which he lost faith in the system was dragged on a bit first. He instructed his lawyer to complain to the British Columbia Supreme Court. He wanted a higher-level judge to set aside the sentence and to direct the trial judge to let him make submissions about the kind of sentence that Stoltz should get. As a victim of the crime, he wanted the full right to participate in the process. He argued that by preventing him from participating more fully than he did, the judge had denied him his freedom of expression under the *Charter*. The Supreme Court judge, Justice Saunders, ruled against him. He explained:

> [T]he contest in criminal proceedings is between the state and the accused. . . . [T]he keen personal interest of a victim must be pursued through other lawful forums, such as the civil process, that may be available.
>
> I find that Mr. Coelho's rights to fully express his strongly held views by all lawful means does not give him the right to audience in a court of law. While he is a victim of this crime, neither the *Criminal Code* nor the *Charter of Rights and Freedoms* requires that he be permitted to speak, in addition to Crown counsel, on the severity of the penalty to be imposed.[1]

Think about that. Mr. and Mrs. Coelho, the surviving victims of this crime, had no right to make submissions about the sentence of the man who had killed their beloved son — no voice, no standing, no part in the process other than to describe their pain and to sit on the hard benches of the courtroom like any other spectator. They were told, in effect, to bring their own civil suit if they wanted more. This was a criminal case, and it was a matter for the Crown and the accused alone. They were told that the criminal trial into responsibility for the death of their son was not really about them.

The Victim's Blood but the King's Peace

Jose Coelho's bid for greater involvement in the criminal process was destined to fail. It ran headlong into what may be the most controversial, yet least understood, of the founding principles of our current criminal justice system: criminal conduct is treated in our system not as an offence against the crime victim, but rather as an offence against the state. When a criminal case is being prosecuted, it is not the victim who is the "plaintiff" or prosecutor. It is Her Majesty the Queen, as the figurehead of the state. The victim has no place at the prosecutor's table. The lawyer who prosecutes the case, the Crown attorney, is not the victim's lawyer. The crown attorney represents "the people" in the name of Her Majesty the Queen. It is she who, in our system, is the conceptual crime victim.

As in more ancient times, criminal acts are considered to be breaches of the "king's peace," and therein lies their criminality. It is as if Her Majesty, while stepping around the broken body of one of her subjects lying on the street, was to say of the assailant, "How dare he do this to me?" The prostrate subject, if he regained consciousness long enough, would no doubt look up and say, "Do this t' who'? It's my blinkin' 'ead that's ringin'." Her Majesty would then calmly explain that the real criminal wrong done by the assailant was in offending her peace by attacking one of her subjects. It would be much the same, she would say, as if someone were to poach one of Her Majesty's deer, or if a neighbour, tired of her pet corgis' barking, were to feed them dogfood laced with antifreeze. As offensive as it sounds, we, as the queen's subjects, have value in criminal law theory, but only, it seems, as the chattels of Her Majesty — our right to protection from crime is enjoyed only in her name.

Among the many mysterious notions in the criminal law, this is one of the most difficult to sell. Try convincing crime victims that the crime was against the state, not against them, and that it is being prosecuted not on their behalf, but on behalf of the queen. Victims are the ones whose blood has been shed, whose property has been taken, or whose dignity has been left in tatters, and the queen is unlikely even to know about it. As one critic has said:

> Our notion that a "crime" is a wrong against the state (even though it is my throat that was cut, my jaw punched, my horse stolen) is a complicated notion, at once mystical, self-deceptive and abstract. It is a Chaplinesque sort of dream world in which we pretend that when you club my head, the "state" feels the pain.[2]

Although this theory has ancient lineage, it did not always hold sway. In the beginning, the victim was the critical player in the criminal process, such as it was. Initially the law of the jungle applied. If you killed another, you could expect the family of the dead man to attempt to avenge his death. The best-case scenario was that only the wrongdoer would be killed in retribution. Primitive law facilitated this process by developing the concept of "outlawry" for the worst offences — murder, for instance. An outlaw had only the rights of a wild beast and could be slain justifiably by anyone. He ceased to be a member of the community and therefore lost its protection. It would normally be the family or clan of the victim who took advantage of this declaration by slaying the wrongdoer. In the worst case, however, a vendetta or feud would break out. Hatfield would kill McCoy and McCoy would kill Hatfield.

When the law began to intercede, its objectives were simple but ignoble. It had to stop, or at least regulate, this kind of behaviour, not so much to protect the Hatfields and McCoys but, rather, to protect the power of the king. It is impossible to rule or govern in a state of anarchy. It is necessary in the interests of those in power to ensure that society is as peaceful and law-abiding as possible. So the Anglo-Saxon kings sought to end the blood feud and tried to restore order to society. Initially they did so by compelling the wrongdoer to offer compensation to the injured party. The duty of the wrongdoer was to pay *wer*, the money value of a person varying with rank, as well as *bot*, or compensation for the effects of the wrong done. This system was arrived at because the only way to satiate the natural craving for vengeance and to prevent further breaches of the king's peace was to buy off the offended party. If the compensation was not paid, the blood feud would be allowed to occur, although the law would regulate how many lives or limbs could be taken, quantified according to the social status of the victim.

This first effort to establish some form of proportionality between the harm done and the "sentence" was accomplished with rude calculus. For example, "the death of six ceorls was in early law the authorized retribution for the killing of a thegn."[3] I cannot claim to know what a "ceorl" or a "thegn" were, but I can tell you this much — in such a system I would rather be a thegn than a ceorl.

Over time, the regulated feud gave way to a moderately more civilized form of victim-based justice, the "Appeal of Felony." An appeal was not, as we currently understand it, a plea to a higher court to correct an error made by an inferior court. You appealed the offender by calling him to justice. This meant, in contemporary jargon, that you were effectively "calling him out"; as the victim or a member of the victim's family, you could challenge the offender to combat in a trial by battle. It was a process steeped in both complex legal procedure and superstition. At first, faith was placed in God to give the victim the strength to win if the offender was truly guilty. It was much like the contemporary American football huddle where each team prays before a game, certain that God is cheering for it. When it became apparent that physically powerful accused persons were rarely, if ever, guilty in the eyes of God, the law of the marketplace took over. If you were a noodle-armed ceorl who had been wronged and you could hardly lift the broadsword, you could always hire a "champion" to fight on your behalf. Champions were, it seems, the first lawyers — those who would represent others in settling disputes for a fee. The main difference between the champion and the contemporary lawyer, however, is that whereas lawyers tend to be small people with glasses mounted on large heads, champions were large people with small heads. Oh yes, another difference. Whereas a losing champion was slain, a losing lawyer now gets paid, a corollary of the march towards civilization that we, at the bar, applaud.

By the end of the thirteenth century, this form of crime prevention had become rare. As society became more civilized, it was appreciated that this was not the best way to promote peace and harmony. Interestingly, the procedures were not formally abolished. As late as 1818 a man named Thornton was tried and acquitted on a charge of killing William Ashford's sister. Ashford, who was not at all impressed with the verdict, sought to use the ancient procedure of bringing a private appeal of murder to a court. This process would effectively allow Thornton to be prosecuted again. While he had been acquitted of the offence against the Crown, he had not yet been acquitted of an offence against the victim. This strategy had worked twice in the eighteenth century and resulted in death sentences for the retried offenders. After sizing Ashford up, Thornton "countered one archaism with another."[4] If prosecution by the victim's family through an appeal of murder still existed in law, then so, too, did the right to trial by battle. "Thornton threw down his glove in a 19th century court challenging Ashford to combat."[5] The court agreed that the procedure was still available.[6] With the prospect of a fight to the finish hanging over their heads, the two decided it might be best just to drop the whole thing, and Thornton walked away a free man. The next year the English Parliament abolished both the appeal of felony and trial by battle.[7]

In the days of outlawry, of the regulated blood feud, and of trial by battle, the legal system, such as it was, did little more than allow for "self-redress governed by rules."[8] It was a victims' system. Slowly, though, the state became involved in prosecuting crime. When compensation was being ordered as the price for avoiding the regulated feud, the state, too, would extract a fine, known as the *wite*. Historians differ over whether this was the first sign that the offence was considered to be a wrong against the king, or whether the *wite* was simply paid as compensation to the monarch for the trouble involved in regulating the whole mess.[9] Before the end of the Anglo-Saxon period, however, unmistakable strains of the current theory can be seen. The law had come to recognize certain "unemendable offences," also known as *botleas*. These crimes were considered too serious to be compensated for through payment of *bot* or *wer*. Those who committed such serious offences had demonstrated an anti-social attitude. They represented a threat to public order and required corporal or even capital punishment, not to compensate the victim, but to protect the state. These offences were therefore prosecuted as Pleas of the Crown. Since the acts were believed to "evince an incurable vice, not capable of reformation,"[10] limbs would be lopped off, heads would roll, and, if the Crown was upset enough by the conduct, the offender's property would be forfeited, disentitling his dependants of its use.

Initially, unemendable offences were obvious crimes against the state, such as treason or cowardice in battle. Over the years the concept of the king's peace grew so that his right to peace was seen to apply throughout the entire realm, "at all times and in all seasons,[11] whether the king was there or not. In time, acts seen to be breaching that peace came to include many of the victimizing acts currently recognized as our prototypical crimes, including robbery, theft, rape, arson, aggravated assault, and forcible entry.[12] Murder was included, but only if the killing was done in secret, a characteristic that would make the deed particularly dastardly; honourable people, it seems to have been believed, would murder in public.

Since the object of Pleas of the Crown was to enable the state to rid the community of its worst offenders, those found guilty of felonies would be punished capitally. Accused felons who survived the trial by ordeal would be spared, but would be made to quit the realm by taking the shortest road to the nearest port, "on pain of death if they strayed from the path."[13] The victims would get no compensation from the procedure because they were not the complainants before the court; the king was. While victims could still seek redress if they did so before the Crown executed or banished the offender, they would have to obtain it on their own through non-criminal law suits, alleging trespasses to their persons or their property. The law of tort, which regulates lawsuits brought to obtain compensation for personal wrongs, and the law of crimes, two branches of the law that were once blended in early procedure, now ran in different channels, each pursuing different objects. Crime was to punish and protect society; tort was to compensate. By this process, contemporary criminal law theory was born. It is the state, not the victim, that is the injured party in a criminal prosecution. Crime threatens the state and is therefore an offence against the Crown, and only the Crown can punish or pardon the offender.

◆ ◆ ◆

The practice of prosecuting offences in the name of the queen is not simply some anachronistic, offensive symbolism. It is a central principle that has enabled the law to develop in a just, humane, and effective way. Who would be less able to decide on a just sentence for Marty Stoltz than the Coelhos? We have learned that a neutral, dispassionate judge is required. Understandably, Mrs. Coelho wrote in her victim impact statement that she wanted the maximum sentence for Stoltz because his crime had irrevocably damaged her life. Mr. Coelho spoke of how he, himself, had died with his son; in his eyes, Stoltz' crime had rent his very soul. These victims were not in a frame of mind where they could recognize justice, save in terms of their own profound loss.

The other side of the coin is that there are victims who do not want to see due punishment imposed. For some it is because they have been blessed with the gift of forgiveness. In other cases there are more pragmatic reasons. Take the case of Michael Friginette. He beat his partner of four years viciously. He came home drunk and began striking her. He punched her in the face with a closed fist, he slapped her many times, he grabbed her throat, he bit her face, and screamed at her at the top of his lungs, threatening her, telling her he was going to knock all her teeth out, and that he hated her. After more than an hour it ended, leaving her with a blackened eye and what may have been a broken nose. He was released on bail after his arrest, on condition that he not contact her. He contacted her anyway, long enough to threaten that he would kill her if she called the police again and that he wished her dead. After all this abuse, she took him back in.

At his sentencing hearing, Friginette received a sentence of eight months in jail. Even though substantial by sentencing standards in such cases, it was not a sentence applauded by his victim. She was, after all, his partner and the mother of their twenty-month-old child. Instead, she stood with him as he appealed his sentence, supporting his request that he not be jailed. The appeal court was told of her desire to resume the relationship, in the hope that he could "continue as a loving spouse and father." She simply wanted him to have counselling. The appeal court declined. Justice Lambert noted that she was not the only victim of this crime. "[W]e have to account to other women in vulnerable positions in our society," he said.[14] Justice Ryan agreed: "When the state intervenes and an accused's conduct is deemed criminal, his conduct is a crime against society and it is therefore the public, not the private interest which must be served by the sentencing process."[15] Where conduct is criminal, it poses a public danger, and it is not up to the victim either to punish or to forgive. In the interests of both public peace and public protection, that role falls to the state.

It would not be an overstatement to say that the theory that crimes are offences against the state is the spinal column of our law of crimes — snap it, and the whole body of law becomes lifeless and limp. Consider the way the law was developing before compensation was separated from punishment. When the focus is on compensation and on satisfying the victim, concepts of *mens rea*, or intention, do not matter. What is important is that the victim has been injured, the accused caused that injury, and the victim needs to be compensated. We need not trouble ourselves with whether the accused deserves punishment, since the issue is not whether to punish. It is whether to compensate. In Anglo-Saxon times, "[t]he question was who was hurt and how badly, not who did what and how and why did he do it."[16] Even if harm was done accidentally, in self-defence, or by an insane person or by a child, compensation was still payable to the victim or his kin,[17] backed up by the threat of the regulated, court-sanctioned blood feud or outlawry. It was only when the state became involved with the express purpose of punishing rather than compensating that the law developed the basic principle that, to warrant punishment, there must be a "vicious will." The only felonies punishable by death and forfeiture, therefore, were intentional killings or assaults. Other killings or assaults would be compensable, but they were not felonies. As early as 1508 Justice Rede, speaking of the liability of archers and errant arrows, said: "As where if a man is shooting at the butts and kills a man it is not a felony and it shall be as if he had no intent to kill him — but where a man shoots at the butts and wounds a man although it is against his will it will be called trespass."[18]

It is important in understanding this illustration to distinguish "buts" from "butts." A "butt" in 1508 referred to the mound behind an archer's target, not the mound that is the behind of the victim. In the example, the archer is attempting to strike the target, not to make it considerably more difficult for the victim to sit comfortably in church. It is an illustration of an accident. It is no felony because there is no evil mind or intention, but because there is injury, the archer is still liable for damages. So, in 1629, a man who shot his servant at night, believing she was a burglar, was not guilty of murder.[19] He did not intend to kill unjustifiably. If compensation was the sole or even the main issue in these cases, it would not matter where the arrow was aimed to strike, or whom the shooter thought he was striking. The consequences were the same regardless of the actor's intention, and compensation redressed consequences. However, if punishing acts in proportion to their evil is the purpose of the law, the existence of an evil, rather than an innocent intention means everything.

It was therefore the movement away from victim-centred justice which enabled the development of the bedrock principle of our criminal law that, to be blameworthy, the acts of the offender must be intentional, or the actor must at least foresee that his conduct is dangerous. It was only in the late fifteenth and sixteenth centuries, when it came to be believed that the explicit purpose of the criminal law was to punish sin rather than to compensate and satiate victims, that moral culpability, as measured through the vicious intent of the actor, came to play the central role that it now holds.[20] This concept of moral fault allows us to distinguish the clumsy from the evil, the insane from the sane, the acts of children from those of adults, manslaughter from murder, and accident from manslaughter. It also enables us to prosecute so that we can punish, censure, and attempt to protect future victims, even where past victims just want to forget about it.

As compared with a victim-based, compensatory system, this has both a liberating and a repressive impact on the punishment of offenders. Those who are morally innocent are not to be punished, whereas those who are not morally innocent can be punished more extensively than they could be in a compensation-based system. Their long-range danger to the community as exhibited by their actions can be taken into account, and the degree of their wickedness can warrant punishment that is far more severe than could be extracted in the name of compensation. Focusing on moral fault rather than compensation even justifies imposing liability for victimless crimes, or for mere attempted crimes that produce no loss to the victim. In short, the movement towards state-based punishment and away from a victim-based system that occurred some four or five hundred years ago has enabled the law to focus on deserved punishment rather than solely on the degree of harm done, making it at once more forgiving yet more flexible in addressing wrongful conduct and future threat.

The movement towards a state-based punitive system has also permitted the development of rules of criminal procedure that have more regard for innocence. There is no presumption of innocence in a civil case, and the standard of proof on the civil plaintiff is lower. In a civil case, the plaintiff wins if the case presented is probably true. In a criminal case, the Crown must prove guilt beyond a reasonable doubt. Why? Because we perceive the stakes to be higher in a criminal case, and the moral right of the state to punish depends on being sure about guilt. We need not be as guarded where the issue is whether an innocent, injured party should gain restitution from the party who is probably responsible for the loss. Similarly, the rules of evidence are more restrictive in criminal cases than in civil cases.

For this reason, it is not always pointless to sue civilly after the acquittal of an accused. In Windsor, Ontario, the family of Robert Lord, like the Goldmans and Browns in the O.J. Simpson case, commenced a wrongful death suit against two young men who were charged with, but not convicted of, the shooting death of their son. Differences in the standard of proof and the admissibility of evidence could well produce a different result than was arrived at in the criminal prosecution. While the deceased's father may not recover even the costs of the litigation if successful, he is bringing the lawsuit primarily to right the wrongs that he believes the justice system did not correct. "I lost my son," he said, "and I'd hoped the justice system would have taken care of it. Two men are walking free today and it has upset our family greatly."[21] So he has sued civilly. He will not gain the punishment of the defendants, but he may gain a symbolic victory and possibly some compensation.

Naturally, the conception that our system of criminal justice is redressing wrongs against the state has significant consequences not just in the way criminal principles develop, but also in the way criminal cases are prosecuted. We have all watched American television shows in which the offender walks free because the victim will not "press charges." In Canada, there is no such thing as victims "pressing charges." Although, in the United States, crimes are also offences against the state, we take that idea more seriously here. Since the crime is against the state, not the victim, it is not up to the victim to decide whether to "press charges." It is up to the Crown attorney. While the prosecutor will normally consider the wishes of the victim as well as the impact that an unwilling victim can have on the success of the prosecution, the decision whether to proceed is based on the prosecutor's perception of the greater public interest. This view often conflicts with the wishes of the victim, and in some cases can even conflict with the victim's best interests.

I recall standing in the ante-room to a provincial courtroom with my stack of prosecutor's files, maybe fifteen cases in all, each of which was set to be tried that day in that courtroom. I was meeting with investigators and witnesses in that breathless frenzy that occurs outside provincial courtrooms across this country shortly before court begins. As often happened, I was approached by a woman who had been assaulted by her partner and who wanted the charges dropped. I leafed through the file as she spoke, refreshing my memory about the facts. I flipped through the photographs of her bruised face. Her eyes were red and swollen, bearing the crude marks that had been left after her partner had ground his thumbs into her eyes once he had finished pulling her hair. "He was drunk. It was my fault. I hit him first. I started it," she pleaded. "This has never happened before." I unfolded his criminal record. The details escape my memory, but he had been to court before. I looked up and gave her my prosecutor's speech about how we could not drop the charges, about how what he did was a crime, and about how it was in the public interest, and perhaps even in her interest as well, that we proceed. I knew I would ask for jail as well as probation, and told her so. I can still see her desperate face, flushed with frustration and anger, her eyes welling with tears. I can still feel the spray from her anguished mouth as she cried in disbelief: "It's my life. Why are you doing this? It's my life." I thought I was supposed to be the guy in the white hat. Instead, I was the one she was convinced was ruining her life, in the name of Her Majesty the Queen. I was the enemy, not the man who ground his thumbs into her eyes. The prosecution degenerated into an unseemly spectacle in which she "forgot" everything about that night because she was "too drunk." She walked out of court with her tormentor when he was acquitted for lack of evidence.

As they walked away I asked myself, "Why did I do that?" Separated from the frustration by several years, I now know at least what the official answer is: I did it in the public interest. My obligation was to prosecute criminal conduct, not to bury it because the victim was too afraid, too confused, too dominated, too much in love, or too forgiving to proceed. She might have told the truth, or he might have pleaded guilty once it became clear I would not withdraw the charges and been held accountable. The crime from which she felt the pain was a crime against all of us, and I simply could not disregard it, even to please her or to satisfy her best interests.

The obligation of the Crown to refrain from taking directions from a victim goes far beyond deciding whether to proceed with a charge, largely because of the peculiar role of the Crown attorney in our system. The prosecutor is not the victim's lawyer. The prosecutor represents the state, so each of the many significant decisions the prosecutor must make are to be based on the public interest, not on the directions or even the interests of a private "client." Prosecutors have incredible power in our system. They can decide whether charges should be laid and, if so, what the charges will be. They can decide whether charges should be withdrawn. In many offences they can elect whether the charges should be treated as "indictable offences," exposing the accused to a more expensive and protracted trial and the risk of increased punishment. They can decide what sentences to seek and, while their recommendations are not binding on the judge, they are influential. They can also plea bargain, a detested but indispensable part of the process. Because of the power the office holds, a central feature of our system is that the Crown is not just the lawyer who represents one side of the case. The Crown is a minister of justice. Those powers must be exercised in the interests of justice, not in the interests of trial tactics or to please victims. In a classic passage quoted time and again in Canadian case law dealing with the role of the prosecutor, Justice Rand said some forty years ago:

> It cannot be over-emphasized that the purpose of a criminal prose-
> cution is not to obtain a conviction, it is to lay before a jury what the
> Crown considers to be credible evidence relevant to what is alleged
> to be a crime. Counsel have a duty to see that all available legal proof
> of facts is presented; it should be done firmly and pressed to its legit-
> imate strength but it must be done fairly. The role of the prosecutor
> excludes any notion of winning or losing; his function is a matter of
> public duty than which in civil life there can be none charged with
> greater personal responsibility.[22]

On more than one occasion as a prosecutor I tried an entire case, only to join the defence lawyer in asking the trial judge not to convict. In each case I could not find credible submissions to support guilt, given the way the evidence had come out. I could not, consistent with my obliga-tions as a prosecutor, seek to obtain a conviction of someone whom I believed might be innocent. In at least one of those cases, it meant that the victim would not receive compensation. Yet that was not my concern. My duties lay with the interests of justice, not with winning the case, even if it was in the interests of the victim to have done so.

Imagine a private lawyer saying to her client, "I am not really inter-ested in winning your case. I have to seek justice, and I have to worry about being fair to the other side. You understand that, don't you?" That lawyer would soon be doing what many other failed legal practitioners do — trying to write a book. Prosecutors are not private lawyers. They are most certainly not the lawyers for the victim. They are public officials. While some no doubt fancy themselves as victims' lawyers, they are fail-ing in their obligations if they allow this perception to influence the way they discharge their function.

Who, then, represents the victim? The blunt answer is that no one represents the victim at a criminal trial because the criminal trial is not the victim's day in court. It is the people's day in court. The victim's day in court occurs when he appears before a Criminal Injuries Compensation Board for public compensation, or when she sues the accused for damages for injuries sustained. While this remains true both in theory and in practice on most issues, it is too harsh to be a politically acceptable response. Victims have been lobbying effectively for change. One of the demands is for a greater role in the criminal justice process. And politicians have been listening.

The most extreme suggestion for increased victim participation to come from a credible source of late has been American law professor George P. Fletcher's call that crime victims be allowed to participate in the guilt phase of the trial. Pointing out that continental European trials permit the victim or the victim's family to appear as a party to the proceeding, Fletcher urges that victims should be allowed to have their own lawyers ask questions of witnesses. He argues this because the trial has greater positive meaning for the victim than anyone else. Yet, for reasons of strategy, or because of perceptions about the public interest, the prosecutor may feel justified in downplaying the importance of those who have suffered the most, in some cases even keeping them from the witness box.[23]

Not even the most ardent victims' rights advocates in Canada appear to be going this far. Fletcher's views have been criticized justifiably in the United States because his opinion is based on his theory that the purpose of the criminal process is to stand by the victim. While I share Fletcher's view that we prosecute crime in part to show that society supports crime victims and that we will punish in their stead, it is simply wrong to suggest that this is the purpose of the guilt phase of the criminal trial. The sole issue at this stage is whether the accused has violated the state's criminal rules. It is for the state to prove this fact, unencumbered by any strategically untimely or ill-advised interjections by the lawyer for the victim.[24] Even where victim's counsel is "in synch" with the prosecutor and making a meaningful contribution, is it fair to force the accused to face two opposing lawyers, including one whose victim-oriented agenda might be more evocative than informative? From an equality perspective, is it fair to give this advantage to "those victims wealthy enough to hire counsel?"[25] Trials are already complex and expensive enough. This suggestion is impractical and inconsistent with our basic criminal law model.

The Case against Giving Victims a Say in Plea Bargaining

Fletcher would also give victims a significant role in the plea bargaining process, those pretrial discussions in which the Crown and counsel for the accused often agree on a mutually acceptable sentence or on the charges that guilty pleas will be received on. Fletcher would give victims the right to veto any plea-bargained deals. In Fletcher's view, this right would improve restorative justice by enhancing the goal of reconciliation between offender and victim. "By gaining control over the wrong that has occurred to him, the victim would have a greater hope of reestablishing his position as a person secure in his rights, and from this position of strength he could approach the offender with a less compelling need for vengeance."[26] Perhaps, although American studies suggest this conclusion is wrong. While some victims are more satisfied with the result after participating in the process, others are more frustrated for having been involved.[27] But even if Fletcher is correct, at what cost? When properly done, plea bargains are arrived at based on a sober, dispassionate appraisal of the relative strengths of the case, and are often undertaken in the public interest, including the realistic allocation of resources. What would any of that mean to a victim? As one commentator has said, "Why should a person who would be instantly disqualified from serving on the defendant's jury be granted a veto over the terms of a disposition by plea?"[28] And as another notes, "the proposal for a veto power over plea bargains places the state's penal resources in the hands of individuals, again making criminal convictions more a matter of private, rather than public, law."[29]

The public nature of a criminal prosecution cannot be expected to have much significance for the victims or their families. For them, it will always be their pain, their grief, and their call for justice that is being negotiated away during the plea bargaining process, or that is being traded off against the interests of the accused and the community during the sentencing process. They will always cry out for a voice, a say, for some chance to play a vital part in the process. Few understand this more than Karen Vanscoy.

It was 8:45 in the evening, a crisp, clear evening in the early fall, when Karen pulled onto her residential street in St. Catharines, Ontario. The street was not its usual quiet "self." There was no chance to watch the first felled leaves scurry along the curbs on the sides of the road. Instead, all focus was drawn to the red lights that seemed to stir the air near the tiny home she had scrimped to buy so her children would have a stable, safe environment. A crowd had gathered around her front door. A sense of panic washed over her. "Please God. Don't let it be one of us." She jumped out of the vehicle and ran to the nearest police officer to ask what had happened. The words she received in reply made no sense: her fourteen-year-old daughter had been shot.

Karen Vanscoy, after a frantic drive to the St. Catharine's hospital, would learn that the bullet had entered Jasmine's forehead. She would later learn that half of Jasmine's brain had been shattered. She would stand at the side of the bed while Jasmine's young body was clinging to life by some irrepressible instinct to survive, even though the brain stem had been extensively damaged. She would watch while life support machines pumped blood pointlessly through Jasmine's body, pushing her chest up as oxygen was forced through a hideous tube. Karen, single mother, friend, and confidante, had to declare it was over by directing the doctors to disconnect her child so her body could follow the spirit that was already gone.

Over time, Karen Vanscoy learned that the shooter was a seventeen-year-old boy who had come to the Vanscoys' house to visit a friend of Jasmine. He was a troubled young man on the edge of serious calamity. Before he left his home that night, he had lifted a .45-calibre pistol from his stepfather's arsenal. During his visit, he had taken the gun out of his pants on a few occasions, and it had been passed around by the young people present. He had the power. At one point, he and Jasmine were left alone. Shortly after, a male voice could be heard saying, "You're lucky I didn't pull the trigger. I had it pointed at you." About thirty seconds later a loud bang was heard. Pandemonium. The panicked words "I shot Jasmine!" jolted the air while the smell of gunpowder lingered.

Only the "shooter," whose name has been suppressed because he was a young offender at the time, will ever know what really happened. Was it a thrill killing? An act of impulse? Or was he clowning around with a gun that accidentally discharged? All the police had was an apparently senseless shooting, vague information that Jasmine had expressed fear of the young man (information that seemed inconsistent with the events of that evening), the fact that he may have spoken about killing another boy that night, and the statement by the shooter himself. In the sterile space of a police interrogation room, with its metal chairs and dirty white walls, he acted out what he said had happened:

> And I grabbed it and, like, say, you're her, right, I aimed it past her, you know, cause I wanted to see and then I don't even re — I didn't even really pull. I don't even remember pullin' the trigger and then all of a sudden, okay, all's ya hear is "boom," and my hand moved, and it got her, like, she hit the ground.

"All's ya hear is 'boom,'" and she hit the ground. "All's ya hear is 'boom,'" and a young child is ripped from the world, a permanent shadow of loss and grief enveloping her mother and her family for the rest of their days. "All's ya hear is 'boom,'" and lives are ruined.

The Crown — an experienced and well-respected lawyer, Ray Houlahan, who had earlier prosecuted Paul Bernardo — was assigned the case. He poured over the evidence and came to two important decisions. First, he concluded that the defence would win in its efforts to keep the case in the Young Offenders' system.[30] Second, he decided that the Crown could not prove murder. Even with the suggestion of fear and threats, there was simply no evidence that would prove beyond a reasonable doubt that the boy intended to kill Jasmine. There was as much reason to believe it was a tragic accident as there was to believe it was an intentional killing, and no evidence available to the Crown would ever dispel that doubt. There was therefore no reasonable prospect of a murder conviction. Discussions with defence counsel ensued for a plea bargain. In the end, it was agreed that the youth would plead guilty to manslaughter and would be sentenced to two years in custody followed by one year of probation. It was a decision that would lead Karen Vanscoy to complain to the attorney general, the judicial officer ultimately responsible for the prosecution of crime in the province. At the centre of that complaint would be the "Victims' Bill of Rights," a statute that came into force in Ontario in June 1996.[31]

Among the bill's more important provisions is the right of victims to information. For too long, victims have been lost in the shuffle. They have often not been kept advised of court appearances, of the release of the offender on bail, of their right to apply for compensation to the Criminal Injuries Compensation Board, or of the services and remedies available to them. This statute, and similar statutes in other provinces, give victims the right to this information. The Ontario act also entitles them to have access to information about "any pretrial arrangements that are made that relate to a plea that may be entered by the accused at trial." This is the right that was to become the flash-point between Karen Vanscoy and the Crown. At issue was how far that right goes.

Within days of the shooting, the Crown met with Vanscoy for a half-hour to explain the process to her. He then spoke to her for an hour over the phone, outlining the difference between murder and manslaughter and the difference between Youth Court and adult court. This call was followed by a two-hour meeting in which the evidence was discussed with her. At that time, she was told that the Crown was going to be accepting a plea to the lesser charge of manslaughter, and was agreeing to the two-year sentence. The prosecutor explained his thinking. Not surprisingly, Vanscoy was not happy. Why not murder? Jasmine was afraid of the boy. He had threatened another boy. Why Youth Court? He was seventeen. Get him into adult court and try him for murder. Don't knuckle under so easily. At least try.

As a result of her protests, the plea was delayed so that an independent review could be done by another Crown. In the end, the propriety of the deal was endorsed by that Crown, by Houlahan's superior, and then by the trial judge, both during a pretrial and, ultimately, when the plea was accepted and the agreed-to sentence was imposed by the judge. Still, Vanscoy was dissatisfied. She was upset not only by the result but also with the process. Yes, everyone was courteous and sympathetic, and the Crown had kept her advised of what was happening. But she was not invited to participate in the prosecutor's decision. She did not expect to have the right to veto the Crown. She did expect, however, to have a say. She did expect to be in a position to influence the prosecutor by making meaningful suggestions and by expressing her views intelligently. She also wanted to be in a position, if necessary, to recognize if the Crown was screwing up so things could be corrected before the damage was done.

When Karen Vanscoy approached the attorney general to complain, she made the compelling point that victims cannot possibly participate in these ways without the necessary information. She claimed the right for victims to have access to the Crown's files. Only then will they have the information needed to make a contribution or to recognize whether what is happening is acceptable.

In one respect Vanscoy and her lawyer are entirely right. It is preposterous to expect victims to participate intelligently when they do not have full information. Yet her claim to have access to the Crown file begs a fundamental question. Does the victim even have the right to participate in decisions, or is the victim's right simply to be kept informed of the decisions that have been made? I say it has to be the latter. Although it is never easy or popular to say no to the innocent and the suffering, victims cannot be given the rights of participation that are implied by the demand for the Crown file. The answer has to be no, both as a practical matter and as one of principle.

Dealing first with the practical problems, prosecutors are overburdened as it is. Human understanding and compassion, if not real politics, demand that victims be kept advised and that decisions be explained. But how far should we take this consideration? Do we require prosecutors to spend time convincing victims of the wisdom of their decisions? Do we expect them to take victims through a tour of all the evidence and provide a crash course in law and trial strategy? Do we expect them to meet with victims' lawyers to discuss the case? Do we delay cases when prosecutors are second-guessed so that others can spend time reviewing their decisions? If we are going to have watch-dogs for our prosecutors, should victims, the people least able to exercise an impartial eye, be the ones who are to perform this role? Not in my opinion.

Far more important than the practical objections are the objections in principle. Is it even right to give the victim this kind of involvement? Without doubt, the more the victim is seen to be a player in the criminal process, the more the process comes to be about compensation or forgiveness. The more we require prosecutors to consult with victims and to work to leave them happy, the more compelling their claims for unduly harsh or unduly lenient sentences will be. In short, the more that Crown prosecutors take on the mantle of the victims' lawyers, or even the victims' partners, the more difficult it will be for them to act as ministers of justice instead of state-funded, private lawyers. As much as we would like to have a criminal justice process that is acceptable to victims, this desire has to be resisted when the involvement of victims threatens to compromise the proper discharge of the prosecutors' role. Giving victims a right of access to the files of the Crown so that they, or their advocates, can second-guess the wisdom and motives of prosecutors by engaging them in legal debate, or by undertaking over-the-head lobbying, is the point where the appropriate line has been crossed. If Crowns become inhibited by victims' "rights" to the point where they will not make decisions in the public interest, or with a view to the best interests of the accused, or in the interests of the efficient discharge of the administration of justice, they have lost their effectiveness. I can think of no better way to accomplish this than by pulling up a chair for the victim and saying, "Here is our file and here is what we are thinking. Are you happy with this?" Of course victims will not be happy with it. Because they are human, they will measure justice by their loss. In the process, many will fail to recognize how complex a concept justice really is. Trials will be run pointlessly, and unwise sentencing positions will be taken. When judges are forced to resist the excesses, they will become the problem. This process will do nothing for the administration of justice or for its reputation. We will simply have pushed the dirt uphill so that it can needlessly soil judicial robes rather than sully the hands of the prosecutor. Prosecutors cannot at the same time be the first line of defence against injustice, yet answerable for their decisions to crime victims. Victims have the right to know, in broad strokes, what is happening. They cannot, however, be given the right to help decide what will happen.

This lesson is being lost on some prosecutors who fancy themselves as representing victims, and their behaviour is harming the proper conduct of cases. It is understandable that some prosecutors will succumb to the temptation to act as victims' lawyers because victims are people in need. Natural human compassion tempts one to try to please. It is also personally rewarding to assume the role as champion for those who have been harmed and abused. Yet a prosecutor who handles his or her job professionally will do as Houlahan did and remember that prosecutors represent the public interest. That role will not always be the same as satisfying the victim.

Victims and Sentencing: The Victim Impact Statement

To the extent that we involve victims in the criminal justice process, we generally do so by giving them a modest role to play in sentencing. Still, our practices are not as extreme as those in Saudi Arabia, which seemed, for a time, to be prepared to leave it up to Australian Frank Gilford to decide whether Deborah Parry, the alleged murderer of his sister, Yvonne Gilford, should be executed.[32] Frank Gilford initially placed his thumb down, saying that Parry should die. He later had a change of heart, agreeing to receive cash compensation as the price for Deborah Parry's life.[33] Before Gilford could collect his money, King Fahd commuted Parry's sentence and she was released, so the money was never paid. Parry, who maintains her innocence, is now reportedly suing Gilford for mental anguish and for making false statements.[34]

This whole episode has made for high, international drama, and will no doubt be scooped up by some made-for-TV movie producer. Much of the story's immense intrigue lies in how different Saudi perspectives about crime and punishment are from those in the West. According to our traditions, it is unconscionable for the family of the victim to have the responsibility, or even the right, to determine the penalty; we prefer to let the state be the "executioner," so it can bear any guilt there may be for the harm it is inflicting on the convict, and so proportionate punishment can be achieved. Moreover, there is no way, in our view, that public policy is truly advanced by allowing a criminal sentence, imposed in the name of justice, to be bought for blood money. It privileges the rich defendant, and debases the victim's claim to the pursuit of justice. The role that we give to victims in Canada is therefore much more modest. We allow them to express themselves through victim impact statements, such as the one filed in the Coelho case, and then we require them to leave matters to the parties and the judge.

Victim impact statements are written accounts describing the harm that the crime has caused. Often they are read into the record by the victim. This can be a cathartic process, assisting in bringing some degree of closure. It can give victims a sense of participation, some small space within which to inject themselves into what is otherwise an impersonal process. It is also helpful to put a human face on the crime during the sentencing phase so that the evil that has been done does not become buried in an examination of the accused's deprived childhood. Finally, to the extent that offenders may be persons of conscience, it is even hoped that by learning of the damage and suffering they have caused, they will feel guilt that may enhance the prospect of their rehabilitation and their sense of accountability. There is much to be said, therefore, for victim impact statements. Still, they do not come without appreciable risks.

In terms of what they add to the sentencing process itself, the truth is that they fit that process in much the same way as a foot fits into a glove. They tend, on balance, to provide little constructive information, and they threaten to distort the process. They do so, in part, by inviting emotion to overtake reason. When crafted skilfully, they can be powerful, evocative documents which, in serious cases, turn the sentencing phase of a trial into a public display of emotion that resembles a eulogy or a testament to the courage or quality of the victim more than a dispassionate search for just punishment. I defy anyone with an ounce of compassion to hear, with a dry eye, the poems that had been written by Jasmine Vanscoy and that her mother read out in court. This was a bright, talented, and loving child who died, and the powerful statement read in by her mother made that point with resounding clarity. But what did it add to the ability of the judge to sentence? Technically, these statements are meant to enable the trial judge to identify the seriousness of the offence, but they invariably contain far more than is needed to enable the judge to do so. In most cases the judge can learn how serious the offence is simply by examining the medical evidence and the crime scene photos, or by learning about the conduct of the accused; she need not be emotionally bombarded by what is often, in substance, a funeral oration or a testimonial to family love, sacrifice, and suffering. Through their emotional content, these statements tax the ability of the best judges to decide sentence dispassionately.

At the same time, their focus on the loss to the private victim can skew the enterprise. As Justice Wood has put it:

> The dilemma facing the sentencing court [that is presented with a victim impact statement] is to balance a proper consideration of the consequences of the criminal act against the reality that the criminal justice system was never designed or intended to heal the suffering of the victims of crime.[35]

Sentencing is not about giving the victim satisfaction or doling out an equivalent portion of pain to that inflicted by the offender. Yet the victim impact statement can create the impression that this is what it is about, and it can undermine a more complete and balanced disposition. In short, increasing the role of victims in the sentencing process can create the impression that a criminal sentence is about giving remedies to victims, but this is precisely what it is not to be. We are to sentence in the public interest.

I am not simply expressing a fear that victim impact statements can cause unduly harsh sentences in those cases where they are filed. I am suggesting, as well, that the use of victim impact statements can skew the sentencing process generally, even in cases where they are not filed, and they can do so in a manner that is morally indefensible. George Fletcher, who would otherwise give victims an unprecedented involvement in the criminal process, laments the impact that victim impact statements can have on the equality of sentences and, symbolically, on the inherent dignity of crime victims:

> [I]n the traditional quest for a mode of punishment that fits the crime, the "crime" is always understood as a generalized wrong, not as a wrong to the particular victim. A theft is a theft, regardless of how rich or poor the deprived owner might be. A murder is a murder regardless of how large or small a family the decedent might have. The peculiarities of the victim count for everything in determining the proper amount of compensation for personal injury. But they should not count in determining the gravity and proper punishment of the criminal act.
>
> Raskolnikov kills an old woman to take her money. Should it matter that she has no friends, no family? She lives alone and no one notices that she is no longer there. The murder is just as heinous, as any man with conscience comes to discover. It is wrong . . . to punish a man more severely because the victim turns out to leave behind a little Nicholas who will miss him. The older law [in which such statements were not received] was right. But by confounding compensation and punishment, [we] have come to the unfortunate conclusion that the victim's sensibilities should influence the [sentence].[36]

Where the pain caused is small, the criminality of the conduct might be undervalued. Where it is monstrous, it can subjugate all other facts, supporting potentially harsh and inappropriate sentences. While there is too much that is good in victim impact statements to argue that they do not have a place, the fact is that judges have to use them with scrupulous care. So if you come to be involved in a case and the judge seems to be less influenced by a victim impact statement than seems appropriate, bear in mind that the judge is probably not just being insensitive. The judge may simply be trying to be just. Just as it would be unprofessional and dangerous for emergency room physicians to allow themselves the luxury of becoming distracted by their emotions in dealing with battered and broken patients, it would be unprofessional and dangerous for judges to allow this to happen when determining sentence.

The Clash between Restitution and Retribution

There is another area of victims' rights that has the potential to undermine the effective application of the criminal law. It is the emerging practice of using the criminal courts to compensate crime victims. As the result of effective lobbying, where quantifiable loss has occurred, we have embraced victim compensation as a central feature of the criminal justice process. Indeed, the purposes of sentencing now recorded in section 718 of the *Criminal Code* includes, along with other sentencing considerations, the goal of "provid[ing] reparations for harm done to victims." Recent amendments to the *Criminal Code* have made it easier for courts to order compensation to be paid to victims. Criminal courts can even order those convicted of spousal assault to pay victims the cost of moving and accommodation. Some of the provincial victims' bills of rights augment this trend. The Ontario Act, for example, allows civil courts to award damages for emotional distress and bodily harm against anyone who has been convicted, without having to prove the offence in court.

Like the use of victim impact statements, these are positive developments. Not long ago, the entire criminal allegation had to be relitigated during a civil trial before a crime victim could qualify for compensation. This was senseless duplication, and we have done well to be rid of it. Still, the compensatory spirit that is fostered by these measures, with their implicit message that the criminal prosecution is being undertaken in partnership with victims, poses a potential threat to the integrity of the criminal process. Cries for restorative justice, and victims' rights, increase our perception that the criminal process is a system for resolving disputes and providing compensation to victims. Whereas courts once threw out charges if they were inspired by a desire to enable a victim to gain compensation, it is now acceptable for Crowns, in deciding whether to prosecute, to take into account the prospect of obtaining compensation for victims.[37] This possibility raises the risk that prosecutions that may be in the interests of the victim, but not in the public interest, will be brought so as to facilitate recovery. Where this happens, the criminal process becomes a publicly funded private collection service in which the debtor is needlessly stigmatized by the use of the criminal process.

The creeping influence of compensatory principles is also being pushed along by simple pragmatics. We can no longer afford to prosecute what are perceived to be minor offences. We therefore remove them informally from the criminal process, not by taking them out of the *Criminal Code*, but by developing diversion programs, alternative measures, and by sending them to mediation. Where mediation occurs, the victim will have an effective veto over the disposition of the case, since the whole purpose of the process is to achieve reconciliation between the parties to the crime without having to use the formal criminal justice process. Often mediated settlements focus on compensation. While these alternative measures have the undeniable attraction of reducing the caseload in criminal courts, let us not be naive about their impact. In many cases, diversion and mediation without punishment amount to nothing more than the informal decriminalization of otherwise criminal behaviour. By process rather than legal amendment, we convert the actions from crimes to be punished into disputes that have to be resolved.

All these developments contribute to an environment in the criminal courts in which compensation and dispute settlement are seen to be central principles. The force of these principles reduces the impetus to sentence in order to impose just punishment. I have never considered an accused person to be punished, for example, for having to pay for what he has stolen. If the downside of getting caught is that you simply have to do what you should have done in the first place, then where is the punishment? Such arrangements often appeal to victims who fear the criminal process and would sooner see the criminal trial simply go away, and who are happy to leave court with something in their pocket. These arrangements are also attractive to many Crown prosecutors who are overburdened with other cases and who love to dispose of files on a "win-win" basis. The trouble is that the only people considered in this win-win calculus are the parties before the court, the victim and the accused, whereas the prosecution is supposed to be on behalf of the public. It has too much the aura of buying off the victim to be a just resolution.

The influence of the pragmatic use of compensation-based settlements is not confined to diversion programs and plea bargains. Judges, accustomed to endorsing compensatory plea bargains and inspired by the fresh focus on reparations as a sentencing principle, become comfortable crafting restitutionary sentences. These "sentences" can be little more than civil judgments masquerading as criminal sanctions.

Then there is the other side of the coin, which is much worse. If the wage of sin is simply to be compensation, we can become less cautious about convicting. Remember that, in the beginning, when the criminal justice system was a compensatory one, we worried little about the moral fault of the offender. If you caused harm by accident, the criminal justice system held you responsible because the system was concerned not with deserved punishment, but with compensation for harm. Culpability based on who should pay for loss is much wider in nature than culpability that is determined according to moral fault and just deserts. If we continue to move down the restorative justice road, we will feel comfortable identifying much more conduct as criminal than is now the case.

No doubt, the movement to criminal-based compensation is too politically attractive and pragmatic to reject. We had best be careful, though. If we become too comfortable thinking about criminal law and compensation in the same breath, we may make the mistake of thinking that justice and compensation for victims are synonymous, which they are not. The paradox is that the seductive call to pay increased regard to the wishes and interests of crime victims, who often decry the leniencies of the system, can in fact weaken our impulse to punish in the public interest. In other cases, it can cause the net of criminality to be cast too wide. It took our legal system hundreds of years to learn that criminal justice differs from victim-based compensation. Now that a few hundred more years have passed, we could be in danger of forgetting that distinction. As Hegel so engagingly put it, "what history teaches is that men have never learned anything from it."

The Bastardization of Victims' Rights

The biggest threat posed by the victims' rights movement to the integrity of the criminal justice system is not, however, in the increased role of victims in the sentencing process. It is not even the influence that victims have had in resurrecting compensation as a focus of criminal prosecution. The biggest threat is the claim made by some victims' rights advocates, echoed sadly by some politicians and even some judges, that the way we treat offenders within the system is a matter of victims' rights. They urge, in effect, that one way to improve victims' rights is to treat offenders more harshly. Indeed, in the unspoken assumption that all complainants are victims, and all persons charged are offenders, even changes to the laws of evidence and to criminal procedure are being advocated, and in some cases implemented, in the name of victims' rights. The most devilish examples are fortunately American. For example, California's Proposition 115, known as the "Crime Victims Justice Reform Act," was approved by voters in 1990. This bill has little if anything to do with victims. It is nothing more than an omnibus statute designed to make convictions easier to obtain. Among other things, it requires defence counsel to make broad disclosure to the prosecutor, allows hearsay testimony to be admitted at preliminary hearings, limits state-based constitutional protections for accused persons, and increases penalties. The Californian "victims' rights" initiatives have also modified the exclusionary rule to allow for the easier admission of unconstitutionally obtained evidence, have imposed limits on the mental disorder defences, and have provided for the unrestricted use of prior felony convictions to challenge the credibility of those accused persons who testify.

These may or may not be good law reform initiatives. In most cases I happen to think not, but that is a matter for debate. What is clear, though, is that none of them has anything to do with victims' justice or victims' rights. The changes do not relate to the treatment of the victim by the system, nor to the absence of a voice for victims. They are not about compensation or information, or even victim representation. They do nothing other than reduce the rights and protections given to accused persons, all in the name of victims.

There are only two ways that these changes can be perceived of as victims' rights initiatives. The first is in accordance with the theory that the victim has a right to be satisfied with the verdict and the sentence, such that any rule of law that makes it harder to obtain a conviction or to punish ferociously undermines that right. That, of course, is not so. We do not punish in the name of the victim or as agent for the victim. We punish on behalf of the state.

The second way to treat amendments to the general criminal law and procedure as victims' rights issues is to conceive of all successful prosecutions as increasing the rights of future victims to be free from crime. This theory depends, of course, on the belief that successful prosecutions reduce crime. For those crimes that victims most fear, it is doubtful that they do, but that is a practical objection. There is a more profound objection of principle: this way of thinking about victims' rights is, in truth, nothing more than a technique calculated to reduce human rights and liberties, not to enhance them. By treating all criminal law and procedure as implicating the rights of future victims, we are effectively legitimizing increased state power to investigate, prosecute, and punish its citizens. On the basis of this kind of thinking, allowing officers to barge into private homes without warrant is a victims' rights initiative, since it would make it easier to detect offenders. Allowing criminal convictions to be based on the probability of guilt, or even the possibility of guilt, would be a victims' rights initiative, since it, too, would reduce the number of potential offenders on the street. Denying accused persons the right to speak in court would even be a victims' rights measure, since it, too, would prevent some from gaining acquittal. As perverse as it sounds, even abolishing the battered woman's defence would be a victims' rights initiative, since it might protect the lives of men. To think of all criminal law as implicating victims' rights threatens to reduce the rights of all of us by converting the state powers of oppression, a thing that should be resisted in a decent society, into a human right, a thing that should be pursued vigilantly by a decent society. I can think of no greater perversion of the concept of rights than to use it to increase the powers of the state against its citizens.

The technique of wrapping pro-conviction law reform initiatives in the soft and appealing swaddling of victims' rights is not an uncommon one in the United States. As one American commentator has observed: "Based on a simplified concept of 'victim' and an unarticulated concept of 'rights,' the changes in the criminal process proposed or spawned by the victims' rights movement are the same changes that have long been advocated by conservatives."[38]

An unsettling development in Canada could, potentially, produce much the same result. The *Charter of Rights and Freedoms*, like any constitution, is a document that is intended to impose limits on the powers of government. Yet it is being used to confer constitutional rights on "victims" that can be exercised by the state against private citizens — in particular, against accused persons. This development is particularly disturbing, since the constitutional rights of victims are considered to have equal value to the constitutional rights of the accused. They can, at least in theory, be used to neutralize any and all constitutional rights possessed by those accused of crime in this country.

So far, this curious notion has produced little actual damage in court-based decisions. It was used by one member of the Supreme Court of Canada to support the view that young complainants in sexual offence cases can present their evidence through videotaped statements[39] or from behind screens,[40] but these initiatives could have been upheld without reference to the constitutional rights of victims. Constitutional language has also been used to explain why there must be restrictions on the access that accused persons can have to the psychiatric records of complainants in sexual offence cases,[41] why defence counsel cannot ask any questions they want about the sexual experiences of sexual offence victims,[42] and why judges should protect sexual offence victims from abusive cross-examination that pries needlessly into their private lives or their general character.[43] With the possible exception of the admissibility of videotaped testimony, a measure that is intended to improve the chances that the Crown allegation can be proved, these are all areas where victims have a legitimate interest that the criminal justice system must take into account in crafting its rules. An appropriate balance could have been struck in each case, however, without loading the discussion with the needless and dangerous reference to the constitutional rights of victims. While we are not yet in a free fall, we have started down a steep and dangerous slope.

The government, for its part, has also used the inviting language of constitutional victims' rights in an effort to justify passing criminal laws that reduce the rights of accused persons. Claims to vindicate the constitutional rights of victims salt law-and-order speeches by politicians, including government ministers, and constitutionalized victims' rights have found their way into legislative preambles that seek to explain controversial criminal legislation. To take but one example, in 1996 the government of Canada, by statute, abolished the defence of extreme intoxication. It justified the legislation on the basis that it would protect the constitutional equality rights of women. The theory, of course, is that this defence poses the risk of creating future victims whose rights must be considered, most of whom will be female. This change is a made-in-Canada example of the perverse thinking that led California into believing that increasing state powers of investigation and conviction is a matter of human rights. Whatever one thinks of this legislation, which arguably has much to commend it as a matter of policy, whether we recognize a defence of extreme intoxication or not has nothing to do with any acceptable conception of victims' rights.

The Painful Process of Identifying Victims

So far I have chosen to avoid raising a seminally important but highly sensitive matter. I have spoken generally about "victims' rights," even to describe interests that arise before a verdict has been rendered. The fact is that not all those who claim to have been victimized are actually victims. Some are liars, like Nina Shahravan, the woman who claimed that Michael Irvin, the bad-boy of the Dallas Cowboys football team, had helped rape her at gun-point. Given his reputation, it was an easy allegation for many to believe, at least until she admitted it was a lie and ultimately pleaded guilty to perjury.[44] There are other complainants who, while not lying, are confused, or are too bent with bias or self-interest to recognize where the real fault should lie. And there are others who are victims, but who are mistaken about the identity of the accused; these trials have two victims. The point, of course, is that when we think of "victims' rights," we conceptualize the innocent, injured, and vulnerable citizen, pitted against the self-indulgent and heartless cretin who authored her suffering. When asked whose "rights" we, as a society, should prefer, any thinking person would pick the victim. Unfortunately, not all "victims" are victims, and not all accused persons are criminals.

Of course, it is more common, probably vastly more common, for the complainant to be an actual victim and for the accused to be the actual offender. As George Jonas puts it, though: "We should be thankful that it's more frequent for genuine victims to be complainants than defendants in our system, but we shouldn't confuse frequency with importance."[45] His point, of course, is that, simply because most defendants are probably guilty, we cannot assume that each defendant is to blame. It is true that the system would be right far more frequently if we just skipped the trial and went straight to the sentence, but justice is not about percentages. The notion that we should sacrifice some who are innocent, simply to make the system easier on, and more pleasing to, those who are victims, or even to make it more efficient in catching criminals, has long been abhorrent to us and still is. Unfortunately, the earliest point at which we can know whether a complainant is a victim is when the verdict has been rendered. Before that, we cannot confer "rights" on "victims" without presuming guilt. Worse, we cannot confer rights on true victims without also conferring them on liars, perjurers, and those who, without malice, bring false witness. We have to realize this danger when speaking of victims' rights during the trial phase of a criminal prosecution, or we will lose the ability to separate the victims from the victimizers. We can give real victims only those rights that are compatible with the search for both real criminals and false victims.

When we want to deride the process by which we search to see who is really being wrongfully treated, we refer to it as "putting the victim on trial." Is the expression apt? Not in the sense that an accused person is on trial. No matter how unpleasant the task, the victim is not at risk of leaving the courtroom in handcuffs at the end of the day. In another sense, though, we undoubtedly do put victims on trial. Both real and false victims will have their memory, their ability to observe accurately in the circumstances of the case, and even their resolve and ability to tell the truth subjected to the crucible of cross-examination and challenge. Their word is put on trial, and often so, too, are their actions. It is difficult to resolve the controversy of "who did what to whom?" without looking at the actions and intentions of both parties. This cannot be helped. We can, and should, protect complainants, and all witnesses for that matter, from unproductive, abusive, and discourteous treatment by defence lawyers, judges, and police officers. If we reach the point, however, where we no longer allow the integrity of complainants to be challenged, or for their versions to be doubted, or for the defence to suggest that the complainant is the one who is to blame, we will be placing one form of kindness ahead of truth, and ahead of a more compelling kindness. It should be obvious that we cannot, at the same time, have a system that protects the innocent by presuming innocence, but which chooses to assume that everything a complainant says is accurate and true.

This means, of course, that a criminal prosecution will almost always be an unpleasant experience for victims. It will often be more than that. It can be offensive, frightening, and even demeaning. Do not blame the criminal justice system, though. Blame the human weakness of self-preservation, which prevents those who are truly guilty from admitting it. Blame the human frailty that enables witnesses to lie, or to be wrong; if they were always truthful and accurate we would not need to challenge them. Blame those human shortcomings that prevent our judges and juries from knowing where the truth lies simply by looking into the eyes of another. And if you must, blame that flame of human decency that keeps us from accepting the conviction of the innocent. The paradox is that if we become too aggressive in respecting "victims' rights," we will be increasing the number of victims.

Victims' rights rhetoric has undoubted appeal, and many criminal victims no doubt have much to complain about. They should be kept informed of the progress of the case and be treated with as much respect as can be afforded them in a system where their claims must inevitably be challenged to see if they can be relied on. In the interests of justice, however, we cannot give victims a full seat at counsel table or even conceive of the criminal trial as a proceeding that is intended to please, compensate, or even heal them. Nor can we spare them the indignity of being doubted. If we do so, we will weaken the system's ability to censure and punish effectively, while at the same time making it insensitive to questions of moral fault and proportionate sentencing. We will enmesh the law of crime with the law of tort, and the knots will become impossible to untangle. Both systems will be hurt in the process. We have to remember that when we toy with the theory that criminal conduct involves an offence against the state and not the victim, we are not simply playing with an offensive legal fiction. We are putting at risk the entire criminal justice system, with consequences that those who champion victims' rights would both like and abhor. Tragically, if our politicians and even some of our judges continue to be seduced by the siren cry of victims' rights, they will steer our criminal justice system into the shoals where it will be dashed and torn.

◆   ◆   ◆

Last year a reporter for the *Daily Telegraph* reported witnessing the public execution of a murderer in a soccer stadium before 10,000 spectators in Khandahar, Afghanistan. The judge arrived in a four-wheel-drive pickup equipped with a loudspeaker, while the convict, Abdullah Afghan, stood shackled on the pitch. The judge gave an hour-long lecture to the crowd about the evils of crime, read the death sentence, and then turned to the family of the victim and appealed to them to spare Afghan's life in exchange for money. They refused. The guards then made Afghan kneel on the ground with his face turned away from the crowd. They surrounded the field, holding their rifles at the ready, while it was announced that anyone attempting to interfere would be shot dead. One of them then handed a Kalashnikov rifle to a relative of the victim. Abdullah Afghan tensed his muscles as if they could somehow repel the shots. He closed his eyes and drew his head into his shoulders as if he could shield himself from witnessing his own demise. The victim's relative stepped forward and fired three shots into his back. The power of the first shot drove Afghan forward. He rolled over as he hit the ground, and then spun as the other bullets tore into his body. As his life ebbed from him, he was shot again, three times in the chest. A brand of justice, known only to our history books, had been done, and the crowd cheered.

There are no complaints in Afghanistan about excluding victims from the process. The complaints that are made are of another kind.

CONCLUSION

CHAPTER 17

Responding to the Credibility Crisis

I n Franz Kafka's novel *The Trial*, Joseph K is subjected to an investigation and prosecution that he does not understand. He meets a priest who belongs to the court. He is the first person from the court that Joseph K trusts. Hoping to unravel some of the mysteries being presented by the "system," Joseph K asks the priest to explain the law to him. The priest responds by telling him a story:

> [B]efore the Law stands a door-keeper. To this door-keeper comes a man from the country who begs admittance to the Law. But the door-keeper says that he cannot admit the man at that moment. . . . Since the door leading into the Law stands open as usual and the door-keeper steps to one side, the man bends down to peer through the entrance. When the door-keeper sees that, he laughs and says: "If you are so strongly tempted, try to get in without my permission. But note that I am powerful and I am the lowest door-keeper. From hall to hall, keepers stand at every door, one more powerful than the other. . . ." These are difficulties which the man from the country has not expected to meet, the Law, he thinks, should be accessible to every man and at all times.[1]

The priest's story is depressing enough to have been one of Kafka's own creations, but it was no doubt inspired by a passage in the New Testament of the Bible, in Luke 11:52: "Woe unto you, lawyers! for ye have taken away the key of knowledge; ye entered not in yourselves, and them that were entering in ye hindered."

I have to say that, as a lawyer, I do not like finding this passage in the Bible of all places. If I am a door-keeper, I want it known that I am only a lowly one. And I am quite certain that I do not hold the key to knowledge. What I do have, though, is access to the law, and I can tell you this much: it is something to behold. The last thing I want to do is bar the door to those who wish to enter. It is something I want to share. It is not because I do not want "woe" that I have tried to open the door a crack in these many pages. It is because I appreciate that the law belongs to all of us. The man from the country in the priest's story is absolutely correct. The law "should be accessible to every man and at all times."

In Kafka's novel, Joseph K needs access to the law because it is his only hope of salvation from arbitrary arrest, trial *in absentia*, and biased adjudication. The poor man never finds the law and, in the end, is summarily executed by having a knife plunged into his throat, without ever knowing what he was alleged to have done wrong. He cries out, but not for his lost life. He cries out about his loss of dignity at the hands of a system that held none of the safeguards that we have so carefully constructed. "Like a dog! he said: it was as if the shame of it must outlive him."[2] He would go down in infamy as a criminal, in spite of his innocence.

It is not only those who are accused who require access to the law. The Canadian public requires access as well. Of course, our courts are open, many of our judicial decisions are published, media stories give sound-bite versions of high-profile cases, and our Supreme Court of Canada hearings, televised on CPAC, are fighting head to head with *Dukes of Hazard* reruns in the Nielsen ratings race. But the demands of time and the sheer complexity of the law mean that most Canadians remain like the man from the country. They are doing nothing more than bending down to peer through the entrance to the Law to see what they can, without ever gaining admission, and what they see often disgusts them. But they are not seeing the whole picture. They are getting a distorted glimpse of what is there to be seen.

To me, this is a tragedy. It is a tragedy because, by simply standing at the door, the Canadian public has been deprived of what is truly the majesty of the law. Even Kafka sees the majesty of the law, and his books are so bleak and depressing that, in my estimation, they should not be sold in stores that carry razor blades. Kafka's appreciation of the majesty of the law is apparent from his parable of the man from the country. This man is so incredibly patient that he waits at the door to the Law even longer than it takes to get served at a Ministry of Transportation counter. In fact, he waits at the door so long that he grows old. His body withers and his sight fails him. Just before he dies, he sees something: "But in the darkness he can now perceive a radiance that streams inextinguishably from the Law."

As it always does, this metaphor of light signifies knowledge and wisdom, even salvation. Never one to allow a happy ending, Kafka does not permit the poor sod from the country to be saved by the law. Instead, the man is made even more blind by the light — and then he dies. That man died without ever knowing what those of us who have gained access to the criminal law know, and that is truly sad. We marvel at its knowledge and wisdom. But, mostly, we marvel at its promise of salvation for the innocent. We recognize that while our system is far from perfect, it being a system of human justice, it is nonetheless a monumental accomplishment in the march towards civilization.

Unfortunately, the majesty of law cannot always be seen by examining the outcome of particular cases, which is what the public most often gets to observe. Some will find no majesty in the fact that Anthony Goodchild received the sentence he did, and that he was convicted only of manslaughter. But if that case is understood as the unavoidable price of living in a society that presumes innocence and requires proof beyond a reasonable doubt, the long-term good that was done on the day that Goodchild was judged and sentenced can be seen. We can all have our suspicions, but I warrant that none of us want to be judged on the suspicions of others. It would be a wicked system that would have allowed Goodchild to have been treated in that way, and I am proud that our system refused to do so.

I know that many will find no majesty in a law that cannot punish Brenda Drummond for what might well be judged to be a callous and cruel act. But if her case is viewed through the lens of the rule of law, with its commitment to preventing the arbitrary, subjective, and abusive use of power in the persecution of citizens, it can be understood and accepted. Indeed, it can be applauded.

The majesty of the law will be obscured for many by the acquittal of Joseph Pintar for shooting two men to death, in the acquittal of Kenneth Parks for the vile attack on his in-laws, or perhaps even by the acquittal of Lyn Lavallee. But if we appreciate that these are the costs that we must ineluctably pay in a society in which, collectively, we vow not to punish and ruin those who do not have moral fault for their actions, the merit in the law comes through and so, too, does the decency that it holds.

If we think about how the system treats "victims," by being as solicitous as it is to the accused during the trial process while enduring challenges to the credibility of the "complainant," we will see nothing redeeming in the administration of justice. If we pause to remember, however, that we cannot presume to know who the victims really are until the trial is over, we can understand and accept what we do.

This is the "cultural gap" that I hoped to help close by writing this book. If we seek to define justice as the public tends to, according to whether, in individual cases, the result conforms to our instincts or sometimes even our absolute knowledge about guilt or innocence, we will often find it to be wanting and we will strive to change it. We will tug at the precious and fragile fabric of the criminal justice system until it unravels. But if we look for justice by remembering that what we have is a "system" of justice that is intended to do more good than harm in the long run, then I suspect we will be gentle and respectful when we try to improve it and we will endure it with dignity when it means that someone gets away with murder. We have to remember that ours is not a system that was drafted in one fell swoop to reflect a single architect's vision of what is right. The principles, rules, and practices that form the foundation for our current law come to us as the collected wisdom of generations of men and women, each striving in its own way to find the mark of decency while bringing order to disorder. Its principles have been forged on the anvil of experience, and they form an integral part of who we are. They connect us, in a seamless web, to our past, and they offer guidance for the future. They deserve respect, not disdain.

If this heritage is understood, it should be enough to inspire at least a grudging respect for the criminal justice system, even enough to endure what will doubtlessly be the continuation of misleading media reports and opportunistic politicking. But grudging respect is not enough if the criminal justice system is to succeed entirely in its mission of inculcating basic values, and in giving the public sufficient confidence that offenders are going to be held accountable. What is required is that the system be trusted. At a minimum, this will happen only if those of us within the system strive to be honest.

Honesty requires that we admit we cannot reduce most kinds of crime by punishing offenders or ordering their rehabilitation. This is especially true of violent crime. If we keep promising to reduce violence by punishing offenders, our promises, like those of political hucksters, will become meaningless and we will continue to lose credibility. This hurts not only those of us within the system, but the public as well. If the administration of criminal justice does not have public confidence, it cannot function. If we do not recover public confidence, we will leave the public with an enfeebled system.

There are other needless costs to perpetuating the myth that the punishment of offenders protects society. By claiming that punishing others will make us safer, we give an unwarranted aura of legitimacy to demands to make the system even tougher on criminals. As criminologists Julian Roberts and Loretta Stalans predict, "if the public are not made more aware of the true state of affairs in the area of punishment, the result will be the passage of more repressive legislation."[3] I take no pride in admitting that we, as a society, have yet to rise above our primitive instinct to strike back at those who have harmed us. I take considerable solace, however, in knowing that by admitting that we punish to hold criminals accountable, we will have a kinder system than the one we will end up with if we do not stop the charade now. Along with the need for retribution, humans also have the capacity for compassion, restraint, and in some cases even forgiveness, attributes that have little to do with the utility of rehabilitation and deterrence, but everything to do with justice.

Admitting that we cannot save society from violence by punishing offenders will even help to unmask the injustice of our minimum sentences for murder. Like all minimum sentences, these are part of a "get tough" message that is intended to protect us by scaring criminals into not killing. It does not work. All it does is to denude judges of the discretion they need to forge just sentences in exceptional cases. The ongoing saga of Robert Latimer proves it, as does the joke that is the law of provocation. Unjust, "hedge-your-bet" plea bargains to manslaughter that are inspired by the intimidation of a potential first-degree murder sentence prove it as well, and so, too, does the extension of full defences that give disproportionate credit to sympathetic defendants, like some battered women. If we admit that we cannot reduce murder by being inflexible, perhaps the public would accept a political party that had the courage to do the right thing, as has been done in the United Kingdom, by removing the minimum sentence for homicide.[4] Not just for second-degree murder, as has been mooted by the current government, but for first-degree murder as well. Without question, admitting that we punish because we feel the need to harm those who harm us can actually make us kinder.

I also take solace in knowing that by admitting that we punish to hold criminals accountable, we may even help build a better society. If we admit that we cannot reduce injurious behaviour by sentencing, society will be inspired to take proactive rather than reactive steps in fighting crime. So long as the public has the luxury of expecting the criminal justice system to make the streets safer by harming offenders, we, as a society, will be able to continue to ignore the real causes of crime and human suffering, and things will get no better.

So, honesty will help us build a better system, and it will give the system far more respect. But that is still not enough. Our system will not achieve the level of respect it requires to be as effective as it can be unless it reflects the long-term values of our society. For the most part it already does, in its commitment to liberty, equality, and the integrity of every individual which is reflected so clearly in many of its rules and principles. The rule of law, for example, requires a specific allegation, the presumption of innocence, that the Crown prove the case beyond a reasonable doubt, the right to silence, the right to counsel, and many of the other rights and freedoms that we have wisely chosen to develop and harbour. The one long-term value that we have not pursued with sufficient dedication, though, is accountability. Within the limits of its protective principles, the system must strive to hold offenders accountable. The public expects it, and rightfully so. Until that commitment is made clear, the public will never give the system its due.

First, we have to punish those criminals who are convicted. It is not enough to try to heal or reconcile with those who commit serious offences, particularly crimes of violence. We have to hold them accountable. We can do this adequately and credibly only by abolishing parole and statutory release, each of which are predicated on rehabilitation and reintegration, and each of which undermine the efficacy of the denunciatory role of sentencing. We would gain more public confidence by declaring shorter, real-time sentences than we inspire by exaggerating the length of incarceration, and by having a system of corrections that is functioning at cross-purposes with the system of justice. And we have to use our conditional sentences with greater circumspection for our worst offences than we have in the past.

Second, we have to continue to put a high premium on uncovering the truth when crafting and applying our rules of evidence. We have to avoid excluding reliable evidence unless it is absolutely necessary to promote a higher public good, and we should do so only where that public good is clearly more important than responding accurately to the criminal accusation. There can be few things that demand greater priority than truth when it comes to the prosecution of our citizens, particularly for serious offences. We can sacrifice truth in such cases only when the competing interest is both burning and palpable, and never if it could cost an innocent person his or her liberty.

Third, we have to resist the impulse to sacrifice accountability on the altar of diversity, cultural sensitivity, or sexual politics. We also have to be guarded against the temptation to treat crime as being pathological. Only a small percentage can be attributed to mental disorders that truly negate moral fault. The tendency of behavioural science to want to explain away crime as somehow outside the control of the offender requires that we be cautious, if not sceptical. Behavioural scientists do an invaluable service in helping us to understand human behaviour, in addressing the causes of crime, and in helping us to heal when we are harmed. But they are not in the justice business. If we fall too far under their influence and allow them to entice us into conferring defences on those who do not warrant them, we deprive ourselves of the ability to hold offenders accountable, and we tarnish our credibility in the public eye.

In all honesty, in terms of changes that need to be made to salvage public respect, there is not much that needs to be done. All we lawyers need to be is honest and committed to the pursuit of truth. Before you laugh too heartily at that suggestion, bear in mind what we lawyers have accomplished, as the trustees of your criminal justice system. While we may not have explained well what we have been up to, we have accomplished a great deal. Indeed, if it is true that "the quality of a nation's civilization can largely be determined by the methods it uses in the enforcement of its criminal law,"[5] you can thank us for crafting, with the assistance of our English forebears, including a Pilgrim or two, a system that demonstrates a profound decency. It is a system that Canadians should truly be proud of. It is grounded in respect for human dignity and liberty. And it strives, within the limit of always protecting the innocent and maintaining human dignity, to hold offenders accountable. Without doubt, ours is a system to be celebrated, even though we know it will sometimes give refuge to the guilty. In its commitment to the innocent and to the proper treatment of all citizens, it is truly a system of justice. But it is even much more than that. Because it reflects both who we are and where we have been, it is part of that elusive Canadian culture that we are always trying to define. If it is truly our institutions that help us to define who we are as a people, we should stand proud to be judged by the way we judge others. We should point with pride to our system of criminal justice when someone asks what a Canadian is. We should be thankful, for reasons that will be clear to those new Canadians who have come here from countries whose justice systems could well have provided the setting for Kafka's novel. If you cannot bring yourself to kiss a lawyer out of gratitude for all of this, then, by all means, kiss a Pilgrim.

NOTES

CHAPTER 1: **The Credibility Crisis**

1   See Julian V. Roberts and Loretta J. Stalans, *Public Opinion, Crime and Criminal Justice* (Boulder, Colo.: Westview Press, 1997).

2   Sheremeta Davis, "Call it a merciless killing: A man accused of murdering a euthanasia activist goes free," *Alberta Report - The Weekly News Magazine*, 9 June 1997, 25.

3   See John Fekete, *Moral Panic: Biopolitics Rising* (Montreal: Robert Davies Publishing, 1994), for a critique of victimization statistics and their penchant for overrepresenting the incidence of crime. Although the critique is vitriolic and animated, it is difficult to discount the general thesis. In a number of the studies, sexual victimization and family violence rates have been shown at preposterous levels. This exaggeration contributes to a crisis mentality in which fundamental change is both demanded and sympathized with.

4   "Victims politically exploited, says group," *Ottawa Citizen*, 11 April 1997, A3.

5   Roberts and Stalans, *Public Opinion* at 292–93.

6   *R. v. Parks*, [1992] 2 SCR 871 at 908.

7   *R. v. Collins*, [1987] 1 SCR 265 at 282.

8   *Ibid.*, quoting Dale Gibson, *The Law of the Charter: General Principles* (Calgary: Carswell, 1997) at 246.

9   *R. v. Collins*, [1987] 1 SCR 265 at 282.

10   Walter Schaeffer, "Federalism and State Criminal Procedure" (1956) 70 *Harvard Law Review* 1 at 26.

11   [1987] 1 SCR 265 at 282.

CHAPTER 2: **In Defence of the Need to Punish**

1   Canadian Sentencing Commission, *Sentencing Reform: A Canadian Approach* (Ottawa: Ministry of Supply and Services, 1987) at 145.

2   Negley K. Teeters, *The Cradle of the Penitentiary: The Walnut Street Jail at Philadelphia, 1773–1835* (Philadelphia: Temple University Press, 1955), cited in George B. Vold and Thomas J. Bernard, *Theoretical Criminology*, 3d ed. (Oxford: Oxford University Press, 1986) at 8.

3   Canadian Sentencing Commission, *Sentencing Reform* at 40–44, quotes six-teen Canadian government reports, dating back to 1831, which arrive at the same conclusion.

4   Home Office, *Crime, Justice and Protecting the Public*, Cm. 965 (1990) para. 2.7, cited in Andrew Ashworth and Michael Hough, "Sentencing in the Climate of Opinion" [1996] *Criminal Law Review* 776.

5   Solicitor General of Canada, "A Summary and Analysis of Some Major Inquiries on Corrections – 1938 to 1977," cited in *R. v. Wismayer* (1997), 115 CCC (3d) 18 (Ont. CA).

6   Le Dain Commission, *Final Report of the Commission of Inquiry into the Non-Medical Use of Drugs* (Ottawa: Information Canada, 1973) at 59.

7   Canadian Sentencing Commission, *Sentencing Reform* at 138–39.

8   Clemens Bartollas, *Correctional Treatment: Theory and Practice* (New York: Prentice Hall, 1985), reproduced in Ron Boostrom, *Enduring Issues in Criminology* (San Diego: Greenhaven Press, 1995), 229 at 234.

9   Daniel J. Curran and Claire M. Renzetti, *Theories of Crime* (Boston: Allyn and Bacon, 1994) at 135 et seq.

10 Neil Boyd, *The Last Dance: Murder in Canada* (Scarborough: Prentice Hall, 1988) at 8.

11 Falcon Baker, *Saving Our Kids from Delinquency, Drugs and Despair* (New York: HarperCollins, 1991), reproduced in Boostrom, *Enduring Issues in Criminology*, 237 at 246.

12 Curran and Renzetti, *Theories of Crime* at 40–41.

13 *Ibid.* at 42–45.

14 Vold and Bernard, *Theoretical Criminology* at 84–92.

15 Curran and Renzetti, *Theories of Crime* at 62.

16 *Ibid.* at 65.

17 Vold and Bernard, *Theoretical Criminology* at 95.

18 Curran and Renzetti, *Theories of Crime* at 68.

19 Vold and Bernard, *Theoretical Criminology* at 102.

20 Curran and Renzetti, *Theories of Crime* at 78.

21 Vold and Bernard, *Theoretical Criminology* at 99.

22 Curran and Renzetti, *Theories of Crime* at 91–99.

23 *Ibid.* at 99–103.

24 *Ibid.* at 114.

25 Boyd, *The Last Dance* at 9. New research is being touted, however, to sug-gest that criminal conduct is, in fact, much more prevalent among the mentally ill, specifically those with schizophrenia. Dr. James Beck of Harvard University claims that the prevailing practice of discounting the link between mental illness and crime "was a matter of kindness and polit-ical correctness." Jeannie Marshall, "Mentally ill often violent, research reveals," *Ottawa Citizen*, 3 June 1998, A5.

26 World Health Organization, *Mental Disorders: Glossary and Guide to Their Classifications in Accordance with the Ninth Revision of the International Classification of Diseases* (1978), cited in N.D. Walker, *Crime and Punishment in Britain*, rev. ed. (Edinburgh: Edinburgh University Press, 1968), 61–67.

27 Don C. Gibbons, *Talking About Crime and Criminals: Problems and Issues in Theory Development in Criminology* (Englewood Cliffs, NJ: Prentice Hall, 1994) at 136.

28 C.S. Lewis, "The Humanitarian Theory of Punishment" (1953–54) 6 *Res Judicatae* 224 at 226.

29 Boyd's statistics showed that 40 percent of the victims were family, and 40 percent were acquaintances. His book was published in 1988. In the ten-year period between 1985 and 1995, Statistics Canada shows that 37 percent of the homicide victims were the family of the accused, with 47 percent being "acquaintances." This difference may reflect, in part, the higher percentage of "common law" marriages in recent years. At the same time, the percentage of stranger murders declined slightly. Statistics Canada, Canadian Centre for Justice Statistics, *Homicide in Canada — 1995*, vol. 16, no. 11 (1996).

30 Boyd, *The Last Dance* at 4. Ten percent were killings for money (often involving illicit drugs), 5 percent for sex, and 5 percent by the emotionally disturbed (at 9).

31 Statistics Canada, *Homicide in Canada — 1995* at 7.

32 Boyd, *The Last Dance* at 47.

33 *Ibid.* at 1.

34 Statistics Canada, *Homicide in Canada — 1995*.

35 Canadian Sentencing Commission, *Sentencing Reform* at 135. Between 1975 and 1985, 60 percent of those released on mandatory supervision were readmitted to federal penitentiary, while 49 percent of those who had been released on parole were readmitted.

36 *Ibid.* at 136.

37 *Ibid.* at 136–37.

38 *Ibid.* at 138.

39 Statistics Canada, *Homicide in Canada — 1995* at 5.

40 Julian V. Roberts, "New Data on Sentencing Trends in Provincial Courts" (1994), 34 CR (4th) 181 at 194.

41 Canadian Sentencing Commission, *Sentencing Reform* at 137.

42 *R. v. Edwards* (1996), 28 OR (3d) 54 (CA).

43 Curran and Renzetti, *Theories of Crime* at 13.

44 H.R.S. Ryan, *The Theory of Punishment* (1970), Study Note, reproduced in Don Stuart and R.J. Delisle, *Learning Canadian Criminal Law*, 5th ed. (Carswell: Toronto, 1995) at 139.

45   Andrew Ashworth, *Sentencing and Criminal Justice* (London: Weidenfeld
     & Nicolson, 1992) at 23.

46   Canadian Sentencing Commission, *Sentencing Reform* at 148.

47   Richard A. Posner, *Overcoming Law* (Cambridge, Mass.: Harvard
     University Press, 1995) at 157.

48   Canadian Sentencing Commission, *Sentencing Reform* at 139.

49   Julian Roberts, *Empirical Research in Sentencing: Research Report of the
     Canadian Sentencing Commission,* published by the authority of the
     Minister of Justice and Attorney General of Canada (Ottawa: Ministry of
     Supply and Services, 1988) at 10.

50   *Ibid.* at 10.

51   Figure obtained from *R. v. Wismayer* (1997), 115 CCC (3d) 18 (Ont. CA).

52   Statistics Canada, Canadian Centre for Justice Statistics, *Adult
     Correctional Services in Canada, 1995–96,* vol. 17, no. 4 at 2.

53   Don Campbell, "Justice served: Police take credit for reduction in prop-
     erty crime," *Ottawa Citizen,* 1 August 1997, D1–2.

54   It has been reported that between 1963 and 1985, only three paroled
     murderers killed again. Without doubt, that is three too many, but it is
     an incredibly small percentage, making it difficult to use incapacitation to
     justify lengthy homicide sentences. Robert Silverman and Leslie Kennedy,
     Deadly Deeds: Murder in Canada (Scarborough: Nelson Canada, 1993)
     at 241.

55   Canadian Criminal Justice Association, "Parole: The Alternative" (1987) 4
     Justice Report 8–9.

56   Ernest Van Den Haag, *Punishing Criminals: Concerning a Very Old and
     Painful Question* (New York: Basic Books, 1975) at 52, reproduced in
     Boostrom, *Enduring Issues in Criminology* at 188.

57   Canadian Sentencing Commission, *Sentencing Reform* at 140.

58   See Kenneth R. Feinberg, "Selective Incapacitation and the Effort to
     Improve the Fairness of Existing Sentencing Practices" (1983–84) 12 *New
     York Review of Law and Social Change,* reproduced in Boostrom, *Enduring
     Issues in Criminology* at 205.

59   H.R.S. Ryan, "The Theory of Punishment" (1970), Study Note, repro-
     duced in Don Stuart and R.J. Delisle, *Learning Canadian Criminal Law,*
     5th ed. (Scarborough: Carswell, 1995) at 138.

60   *Ibid.*

61   *Ibid.* at 139.

62   *Ibid.*

63   H.L.A. Hart, *Punishment and Responsibility* (Oxford: Clarendon Press,
     1968) at 159.

64   Roberts, *Empirical Research on Sentencing* at 30.

65   George P. Fletcher, *With Justice for Some: Protecting Victims' Rights in Criminal Trials* (Reading, Mass.: Addison-Wesley, 1996) at 6.

66   Hermann Mannheim, ed., *Pioneers in Criminology*, 2d ed. (Montclair, NJ: Patterson Smith, 1972) at 392.

67   Curran and Renzetti, *Theories of Crime* at 147.

68   J.D. Morton, "The Function of the Criminal Law," reproduced in Stuart and Delisle, *Learning Canadian Criminal Law* at 142–43.

69   Boris Pasternak, *Doctor Zhivago* (London: Harvill Press, 1958) at 47.

70   Posner, *Overcoming Law* at 264.

71   J.W. Mohr, "Sentencing Revisited" (1990) 32 *Canadian Journal of Criminology* 531 at 534.

72   Lewis, "The Humanitarian Theory of Punishment" at 227–28.

73   Canadian Sentencing Commission, *Sentencing Reform* at 147.

74   *R. v. C.A.M.*, [1996] 1 SCR 500.

75   Roberts, "New Data on Sentencing Trends in Provincial Courts" at 195.

76   Ashworth and Hough, "Sentencing and the Climate of Opinion" at 780–81, citing, among others, A. Doob and J. Roberts, "Public Punitiveness and Public Knowledge of the Facts" in N. Walker and M. Hough, eds., *Public Attitudes to Sentencing: Surveys from Five Countries* (1988).

77   *Ratten v. R.*, [1972] AC 378 (PC).

78   *R. v. Lemky*, [1996] 1 SCR 757.

79   *R. v. Piche*, [1971] SCR 23.

CHAPTER 3 : Conditional Justice

1   For a critique of the theory, see chapter 14, "The Abuse Excuse: "Psychobabble" and the Protection of Basic Values."

2   *R. v. Lavallee*, [1990] 1 SCR 852.

3   George Fletcher, *With Justice for Some: Protecting Victims' Rights in Criminal Trials* (Reading, Mass.: Addison-Wesley, 1996) at 138.

4   *R. v. Tripodi*, [1955] SCR 438 at 443.

5   Canadian Centre for Justice Statistics, *Longitudinal Court Outcome Study of Individuals Accused of Homicide* (Ottawa, 1993).

6   Statistics Canada, Canadian Centre for Justice Statistics, *Homicide in Canada — 1995*, vol. 16, no. 11 (1996) at 11.

7   Stephen Bindman, "Judge: Let some murderers go free," *Ottawa Citizen*, 24 July 1997, F1, discussing the Self-Defence Review conducted by Judge Lynn Ratushny on behalf of the minister of justice. The review was established to inquire into the convictions and penalties of those women convicted of killing their spouses to determine whether the outcomes should

be different as a result of battered woman syndrome. Research conducted during the review disclosed that most battered woman syndrome cases end up with guilty pleas to manslaughter because the women fear the minimum penalties for murder and are therefore afraid to gamble on a full self-defence acquittal.

8   These statistics, taken from the sentencing database of Statistics Canada, are presented in this fashion in Julian V. Roberts, "New Data on Sentencing Trends in Provincial Courts" (1994), 34 CR (4th) 181 at 188, 192, and 193. They apply solely to sentences handed out in provincial level or lower level courts. Comparable statistics are not available for superior courts, such as the one that decided *R. v. Goodchild* (22 January 1996), (Ont. Gen. Div.) [unreported], where experience has suggested that sentences tend to be somewhat higher.

9   *R. v. Latimer* (1995), 41 CR (4th) 1 at 54 (Sask. CA).

10   Rick Block (*Montreal Gazette*), "Mom who drowned son, 6, not jailed," *Ottawa Citizen*, 3 July 1997, A3.

11   *Ibid.*

12   *R. v. Myers* (3 December 1994), (NSSC) [unreported].

13   *R. v. Mataya* (24 August 1992), (Ont. Gen. Div.) [unreported].

14   *R. v. de la Rocha* (2 April 1993), (Ont. Gen. Div.) [unreported], quoted from *R. v. Latimer* (1995), 41 CR (4th) 1 at 62 (Sask. CA), affirmed [1997] 2 SCR 217.

15   [1997] 1 SCR 217 at 240.

16   *R. v. Latimer* (1997), 121 CCC (3d) 326 (Sask. QB), and *R. v. Latimer,* [1997] SJ No. 849 (Sask. QB).

17   Murder is an indictable offence that is to be tried before a jury. Procedurally, this means that the Crown must bring the "information" (the document that contains the charge), before a provincial court judge and convince the judge that there is sufficient evidence to justify having a trial. The procedure is intended to ensure that people do not face pointless trials. The hearing where this is done is called a "preliminary hearing." If successful at the preliminary hearing, the Crown then has to prepare an "indictment," which from then on replaces the information. It contains the charges on which the case will ultimately be tried. This process meant that the police refusal to change the charge was pointless. Had Dr. Morrison been committed to stand trial, the Crown could have decided to indict her only on manslaughter. In this way, the Crown could ultimately have controlled the charge.

18   *R. v. Morrison*, [1998] NSJ No. 75 (NS Prov. Ct.).

19   Graeme Hamilton, "Doctor's criminal trial will go ahead," *Ottawa Citizen*, 3 July 1998, A5.

20 Roberts, "New Data on Sentencing Trends in Provincial Courts," 190, citing S. Mihorean and S. Lipinski, "International Incarceration Patterns, 1989–90" (1992) 12 *Juristat Service Bulletin* no. 12.

21 Statistics Canada, Canadian Centre for Justice Statistics, *Adult Correctional Services in Canada, 1995–96*, vol. 17, no. 4 (1997) at 1.

22 *R. v. Wismayer* (1997), 115 CCC (3d) 18 at 34 (Ont. CA).

23 Where a suspended sentence is ordered, the judge places the offender on probation, including terms much like those that a conditional sentence bears. At that time, the judge reserves the power to resentence the offender if he or she reoffends while on probation, but the judge does not describe the sentence that would be given. In practice, persons placed on suspended sentence were almost never resentenced for the suspended sentence, even when they did reoffend. They would be sentenced for the new offence, and sometimes sentenced for breach of probation, but it was impractical and considered redundant to attempt to get them before the sentencing judge again to be resentenced on the original charge.

24 Pauline Tam, "Conditional justice: Officials try to curb use of sentencing option," *Ottawa Citizen*, 12 May 1997, D1 and 2.

25 *Ibid.*

26 Neal Hall, "Woman who cut off husband's penis won't go to jail," *Ottawa Citizen*, 7 July 1998, A5.

27 P. Devlin, *The Judge* (1979), cited in Don Stuart and Ron Delisle, *Learning Canadian Criminal Law*, 5th ed. (Scarborough: Carswell, 1995) at 152.

28 *R. v. Latimer*, [1997] SJ No. 849 at paras. 91–92 (Sask. QB).

CHAPTER 4 : The Injustice of Parole

1 "Convicted killer on verge of full parole," *Globe and Mail*, 13 January 1997, A1, A6.

2 During the O.J. Simpson trial, police officers testified that Simpson was not a suspect when they entered his property shortly after his wife was killed. Had they admitted that they considered him a suspect, their warrantless entry would have been found illegal and the evidence excluded.

3 "Police officer jailed 10 years for slaying (Nicole Mattison case)," *Globe and Mail*, 12 June 1993, A5.

4 "Convicted killer on verge of full parole," A6.

5 Julian Roberts, "Early Release from Prison: What Do the Canadian Public Really Think?" (1988) 30 *Canadian Journal of Criminology* 231 at 245.

6 *Ibid.* at 234–36.

7 H.R.S. Ryan, Foreword to David P. Cole and Allan Manson, *Release from Imprisonment: The Law of Sentencing, Parole and Judicial Review* (Toronto, Carswell, 1990) at i.

8   Statistics Canada, Canadian Centre for Justice Statistics, *Adult Correction Services in Canada*, 1995–96, vol. 17, no. 4 (1997) at 11.

9   Report of the Auditor General of Canada to the House of Commons, *Correctional Service Canada — Reintegration of Offenders* (November 1996) at 30-7.

10 See, for example, Fred E. Gibson, chairman, National Parole Board, "The Renewal of Parole" (1990) 32 *Canadian Journal of Criminology* 487 at 488.

11 National Parole Board, Fact Sheet, *Judicial Review of Parole Ineligibility — Backgrounder*, January 1997.

12 *Corrections and Conditional Release Act*, Regulations, SOR 92-620, s.159.

13 *Corrections and Conditional Release Act*, RSC 1992, c. C-44.6, s.126(1).

14 Canada, House of Commons, *Taking Responsibility: Report of the Standing Committee on Justice and Solicitor General on Its Review of Sentencing, Conditional Release, and Related Aspects of Corrections* (Ottawa: Queen's Printer, 1988) at 195.

15 Report of the Auditor General of Canada to the House of Commons, *Correctional Service Canada* at 30-7.

16 Canadian Sentencing Commission, *Sentencing Reform: A Canadian Approach* (Ottawa: Minister of Supply and Services, 1987) at 239.

17 Neil Boyd, *The Last Dance: Murder in Canada* (Scarborough: Prentice Hall, 1988) at 7.

18 Report of the Auditor General of Canada to the House of Commons, *Correctional Service Canada* at 30-13, 30-15.

19 *Ibid.* at 30-12.

20 Statistics Canada, *Adult Correctional Services in Canada, 1995–96* at 6.

21 Canadian Sentencing Commission, *Sentencing Reform* at 250.

22 Statistics Canada, Canadian Centre for Justice Statistics, *Justice Spending in Canada*, vol. 17, no. 3 at 6.

23 Report of the Auditor General of Canada to the House of Commons, *Correctional Service Canada* at 30-19.

24 Canadian Sentencing Commission, *Sentencing Reform* at 251.

25 Report of the Auditor General of Canada to the House of Commons, *Correctional Service Canada* at 30-23.

26 *Ibid.* at 30-13.

27 Jean-Paul Brodeur, "The Attrition of Parole" (1990) 32 *Canadian Journal of Criminology* 503 at 505, quoting a 1987 National Parole Board publication entitled *Some People Say . . .*

28 Fred E. Gibson, "The Renewal of Parole" (1990) 32 *Canadian Journal of Criminology* 487 at 488.

29 *Ibid.*

30 Quoted in *R. v. Gardiner* (1982), 68 CCC (2d) 477 at 513 (SCC).

31 Canadian Sentencing Commission, *Sentencing Reform* at 242.

32 While the National Parole Board has been making commendable efforts to open the process up, by notifying victims and by making hearings public and granting observers permission to attend, it remains a mysterious process that is carried on "somewhere else" by "somebody else."

33 Brodeur, "The Attrition of Parole" at 507.

34 *Taking Responsibility* at 52.

35 Statistics Canada, *Adult Correctional Services in Canada, 1995–96* at 2.

36 *Corrections and Conditional Release Act*, RSC 1992, c. 20, s.116(b).

37 *Taking Responsibility* at 193–94.

38 Shereen Benzvy-Miller and David P. Cole, "Integrating Sentencing and Parole" (1990) 32 *Canadian Journal of Criminology* 493 at 496.

39 Alan Cairns, "Wife-killing cop granted parole," *Toronto Sun*, 28 November 1996, 7.

40 Allan Manson, "The Supreme Court Intervenes in Sentencing" (1996), 43 CR (4th) 306 at 309–10. The number of second-degree murderers in Ontario who are eligible to apply after ten years has dropped from the three-quarters reported by the Canadian Sentencing Commission to 43 percent. Slightly more than 30 percent received greater than fifteen years.

41 Thomas O'Reilly-Fleming, "The Injustice of Judicial Review: Vaillancourt reconsidered" (1991) 33 *Canadian Journal of Criminology* 163. The average is based on those prisoners released between 1968 and1974.

42 National Parole Board, *Judicial Review of Parole Ineligibility — Backgrounder.*

43 National Parole Board Pre-Release Decision Sheet, David Mattison, Day Parole and U.T.A. Pre-Release, 1996/03/13, p. 6; 1996/11/27, p. 4.

CHAPTER 5 : **Defining Crime**

1 *R. v. Sullivan* (1988), 65 CR (3d) 256 (BCCA), affirmed (1991), 63 CCC (3d) 97 (SCC).

2 *Keeler v. Superior Court of Amador County*, 87 Cal. Rptr. 481 (1970), (Sup. Ct. of Calif., In Bank).

3 *R. v. Prince*, (1988), 44 CCC (3d) 510 (Man. CA).

4 (1988), 62 CR (3d) 1 (SCC).

5 Andrew Coyne, "One second can mean a difference to a baby's rights," *Ottawa Citizen*, 27 December 1996, editorial page.

6 J.C. Smith and David N. Weisstub, *The Western Idea of Law* (London: Butterworths, 1983) at 396.

7 A.K.R. Kiralfy, *Potter's Historical Introduction to English Law*, 4th ed. (London: Sweet & Maxwell, 1958) at 9.

8 Harold J. Berman, "The Origins of Western Legal Science" (1977) 90 *Harvard Law Review* 894 at 895.

9 A.K.R. Kiralfy, *Potter's Historical Introduction to English Law* at 18.

10 *Ibid.* at 19.

11 J.D. Eusdon, *Puritans, Lawyers, and Politics in Early Seventeenth-Century England* (New Haven: Yale University Press, 1958) at 93.

12 Peter Stein, *Roman Law and English Jurisprudence Yesterday and Today* (Cambridge: University Press, 1969) at 8, quoting S.E. Thorne, *Sir Edward Coke, 1552–1952* (Seldon Society Lecture, 1952) at 4.

13 Sir Mathew Hale, *History of the Common Law of England*, 2d ed. (1716), cited in Smith and Weisstub, *The Western Idea of Law* at 417.

14 J.P. Kenyon, ed., *The Stuart Constitution, 1603–1688: Documents and Commentary* (Cambridge: Cambridge University Press, 1969), "James I on Monarchy: Speech to Parliament" at 13.

15 Sir William Holdsworth, *The History of Modern English Law*, vol. 1, (London: Methuen, 1903) at 485.

16 *Ibid.* at 487.

17 *Ibid.* at 486.

18 *Ibid.* at 490.

19 *Ibid.* at 491.

20 *Ibid.* at 479.

21 A.K.R. Kiralfy, *Origins of English History*, 5th ed. (London: Sweet & Maxwell, 1958) at 82.

22 Eusdon, *Puritans, Lawyers and Politics in Early Seventeenth-Century England* at 5–6.

23 Edward Greenspan, "In Defence of Lawyers," (1998) 9 (6) *The Law Times* at 8–9.

24 RSC 1953–54, c. 51, s. 8, provides that no person shall be convicted of an offence at common law.

25 J. Willis (1950) 28 *Canadian Bar Review* 1023 at 1025.

26 Jerome Frank, *Law and the Modern Mind* (New York: Coward-McCann, 1970) at 159–60.

27 Borowski went all the way to the Supreme Court of Canada arguing that the abortion laws did not go far enough in protecting the right of a foetus to life, as guaranteed by the *Charter*. Needless to say, he failed: *Borowski* v. *Canada (A.G.)*, [1989] 1 SCR 342.

28 Stephen Kloepfer, "The Status of Strict Construction in Canadian Criminal Law" (1983) 15 *Ottawa Law Review* 553 at 560.

29 Livingston Hall, "Strict or Liberal Construction of Penal Statutes" [1934–35] 48 *Harvard Law Review* 748 at 760.

30 (1974), 28 CRNS 331 (Ont. CA).

31 *Johnson* v. *R.* [1977] 2 SCR 646.

32 [1987] 2 SCR 618.

33 Ruth Sullivan, *Statutory Interpretation* (Concord, Ont.: Irwin Law, 1996) at 38.

34 Berman, "The Origins of Western Legal Science" at 916–17.

CHAPTER 6: Getting Off on Technicalities

1 *R.* v. *Clarkson*, [1986] 1 SCR 383.

2 *R.* v. *Feeney* (1997), 115 CCC (3d) 129 (SCC).

3 *R.* v. *Landry*, [1986] 1 SCR 145.

4 Even though *Landry* was decided in 1986, four years after the *Charter* was proclaimed in force, the events leading to the appeal had occurred prior to the *Charter*. The law used to resolve the issue in the case was therefore pre-*Charter* law.

5 The *Criminal Code* has since been amended to provide a procedure whereby warrants can be obtained to enter dwelling-houses for the purpose of effecting an arrest.

6 "The Privilege against Self-Incrimination Endangered" (1962) 5 *Canadian Bar Journal* 6 at 8.

7 David Mellinkoff, *The Conscience of a Lawyer* (St. Paul, Minn.: West Publishing Co., 1973) at 153–54.

8 *R.* v. *Demeter*, [1978] 1 SCR 538.

9 [1979] 2 SCR 381.

10 *Ibid.* at 395.

11 Alan M. Dershowitz, *Reasonable Doubts: The O.J. Simpson Case and the Criminal Justice System* (New York: Simon & Schuster, 1996) at 42–43.

12 *Ibid.* at 42.

13 [1997] BCJ No. 744 (BCCA).

14 Robert Bolt, *A Man for All Seasons: A Play in Two Acts* (New York: Random House, 1961) at 66.

15 [1987] 1 SCR 265 at 282.

16 L. Schapiro, "Prospects for the Rule of Law" in (1965) 14 *Problems of Communism* at 2, cited by Ed Ratushny, *Self-Incrimination in the Canadian Criminal Process* (Toronto: Carswell, 1979) at 46.

CHAPTER 7: The Specific Allegation

1 The facts surrounding this case were taken in part from Christopher Harder, *Mercy, Mistress, Mercy: The Plumley Walker Saga* (Auckland: HarperCollins, 1991).

2 *R. v. Thatcher* (1987), 57 CR (3d) 97 at 131 (SCC).

3 Leonard William Levy, *Origins of the Fifth Amendment: The Right against Self-Incrimination* (New York: Oxford University Press, 1968) at 28.

4 Ed Ratushny, *Self-Incrimination in the Canadian Criminal Process* (Toronto: Carswell, 1979) at 172.

5 Levy, *Origins of the Fifth Amendment* at 162.

6 The Honourable Roger E. Salhany, *The Origin of Rights* (Carswell: Toronto, 1986) at 93.

7 Ratushny, *Self-Incrimination in the Canadian Criminal Process* at 165.

8 Salhany, *The Origin of Rights* at 91–92.

9 E.M. Morgan, "The Privilege against Self-Incrimination" (1949) 34 *Minnesota Law Review* 1.

10 Ratushny, *Self-Incrimination in the Canadian Criminal Process* at 175.

11 8 Edw. 7, c. 45.

12 *R. v. Ball*, [1911] AC 47 (HL).

13 On 7 February 1985, as a result of intense lobbying, the government established a Commission of Inquiry on War Criminals (Deschênes Commission), to be headed by the Honourable Jules Deschênes. The Commission revealed that Canada had indeed become home to many former Nazi collaborators.

14 (1994), 28 CR (4th) 265 (SCC).

CHAPTER 8: **Presumed Innocent**

1 [1935] AC 462 (HL(E)).

2 Advisory Committee to the Attorney General on Screening of Criminal Charges, Resolution Discussions and Disclosure, *Charge Screening, Disclosure, and Resolution Discussions* (Toronto: Queen's Printer for Ontario, 1993) at 15.

3 *Ten Years a Police Judge* (1884), cited in 4 Wigmore, *Evidence* (Chad. Rev.), s. 2511.

4 The Honourable Fred Kaufman, *The Commission on Proceedings Involving Guy Paul Morin* (Toronto: Queen's Printer for Ontario, 1998), Recommendation 83 at 1167.

5 W. Blackstone, *Commentaries on the Laws of England*, 4th ed. (1770), Bk. IV, c. 27, p. 358.

6 Fortescue, *De Laudibus*, c. 28, p. 65 (S.B. Chrimes, ed. and transl. 1942, written c. 1460).

7 Thomas Starkie, *Evidence* 751 (1824), as quoted in *Schulp v. Delo*, 115 S. Ct. 851 at 865 (1995), and see Alan M. Dershowitz, *Reasonable Doubts:*

The O.J. Simpson Case and the Criminal Justice System (New York: Simon & Schuster, 1996) at 37–38.

8 K. Jaffary, "The Right to Remain Silent: A Reply" (1970) 4 *Law Society of Upper Canada Gazette* 150 at 152, replying to the Hon. Edson Haines, address delivered to Academy of Medicine at Toronto, 7 April 1970, subsequently published in (1970) 4 *Law Society of Upper Canada Gazette* 78. See Ed Ratushny, *Self-Incrimination in the Canadian Criminal Process* (Toronto: Carswell, 1979) at 7–11.

9 Law Reform Commission of Canada, *Burdens of Proof and Presumptions*, SP No. 8 (1973), 52–53.

10 *R. v. Lifchus* (1997), 118 CCC (3d) 1 (SCC).

11 *In re Winship*, 397 U.S. 358 at 371 (1970).

12 Dershowitz, *Reasonable Doubts* at 40.

13 (1968), 438 P.2d 33, discussed in Sir Richard Eggleston, *Evidence, Proof and Probability* (London: Weidenfeld & Nicholson, 1978) at 144–45.

14 *R. v. Riley* (1992), 11 OR (3d) 151 (CA).

15 *R. v. Marquard* (1995), OJ No. 3050 (Ont. Ct. of Justice (General Division)).

16 E.M. Forster, *A Passage to India* (London: Penguin Books, 1924) at 237.

CHAPTER 9 : **Closing Our Eyes to Find the Truth**

1 *Makin v. A.G.N.S.W.*, [1891–94] All ER 24 at 25–26 (PC).

2 The hearing resulted in Milgaard's release from prison because new information cast doubt on his guilt, but the Supreme Court of Canada stopped short of pronouncing him wrongfully convicted: *Reference re Milgaard*, [1992] 1 SCR 866. He would not be cleared for several more years, when DNA evidence demonstrated that Milgaard had spent twenty-three years in jail for a murder he did not commit.

3 DNA tests have since established that the semen found on the body of Gail Miller belonged to Larry Fisher.

4 *R. v. Morgan*, [1997] OJ No. 5478 (Ont. Gen. Div.).

5 (1996), 108 CCC (3d) 108 (Man. CA).

6 Khan was retried on each count separately and initially convicted. In each case, the law of evidence prevented the jury from learning of the other allegation. Indeed, even after Khan was convicted of the first murder, the second jury was not allowed to consider this in deciding whether he was guilty of the second murder. The legal saga is not yet over, though. Khan has succeeded in obtaining yet another retrial on one of the charges due to errors by each of the judge and prosecutor.

7 (1996), 108 CCC (3d) 108 at 121 (Man. CA).

8   *R. v. Nikolovski,* (1996), 3 CR (5th) 362 at paras. 13 and 18 (SCC).

9   Michael Grange, "Interrogation being given third degree," *Globe and Mail,* 28 November 1998, A10.

10   In fact, as the Honourable Fred Kaufman illustrates in his report into the wrongful conviction of Guy Paul Morin, a number of the points in the profile could not relate to Morin in any way. *The Commission of Proceedings Involving Guy Paul Morin: Report,* vol. 2 (Toronto: Queen's Printer, 1998) at 841.

11   *D.P.P. v. Boardman,* [1975] AC 421 at 454 (HL), Hailsham J.

12   [1891–94] All ER 24 at 25–26 (PC).

13   *R. v. Bedingfield* (1879), 14 Cox. C.C. 341.

14   *Ratten v. R.,* [1972] AC 378 at 391 (PC).

15   *R. v. Khan* (1990), 59 CCC (3d) 92 (SCC).

16   *R. v. Nikolovski* (1996), 3 CR (5th) 362 at 368 (SCC).

CHAPTER 10 : **Abandoning the Search for the Truth**

1   The names of the police officers are not disclosed in the reported cases. They are identified as AG and JM. I have chosen to call them Alan Green and John Morrison.

2   In fact, there was a "misunderstanding" by the officers. They had been authorized to agree to a plea of guilty to second-degree murder on the Denean Worms killing, not to offer to have him charged only with second-degree murder.

3   An exception is made for roadside breath tests. You must comply without the right to speak to counsel first, although the readings obtained cannot be used as evidence against you. Their purpose is solely to determine whether the officer's suspicions that you may be over the legal limit are sound enough to justify making you go to the station. Once there, you are entitled to speak to a lawyer before doing the breath test that will be used as evidence against you.

4   *R. v. Manninen* (1987), 34 CCC (3d) 385 (SCC).

5   *R. v. Black,* [1989] 2 SCR 138.

6   Stephen J. Markman, "Six Observations on the Exclusionary Rule" (1997) 20 *Harvard Journal of Law and Policy* 425 at 431.

7   *R. v. Burlingham* (1993), 85 CCC (3d) 343 at 383 (BCCA), in dissent.

8   [1971] SCR 272.

9   Dale Gibson, "Enforcement of the Canadian Charter of Rights and Freedoms" in Walter S. Tarnopolsky and Gérald-A. Beaudoin, eds., *Canadian Charter of Rights and Freedoms: Commentary* (Carswell: Toronto, 1982) 489 at 512.

10   (1997), 5 CR (5th) 1 (SCC).

11   [1996] 1 SCR 8.

12   *Ibid.* at 27.

13   [1991] 3 SCR 263.

14   (1631), 3 Howell's State Trials 401, 123 ER 1140 (HL).

15   (1996), 2 CR (5th) 245 (SCC).

CHAPTER 11: Forgiving Human Weakness

1   This expression was pilfered by Jonathan Swift for *Gulliver's Travels* from
    directions for handling a ship in a storm published by Samuel Sturmey's
    Mariners Magazine (1669). This makes me feel somewhat less guilty
    about stealing it, in turn, from Jonathan Swift, *Gulliver's Travels* (New
    York: Barnes & Noble Books, 1995) at 98.

2   Michael G. Mallin, "In Warm Blood: Some Historical and Procedural
    Aspects of *Regina* v. *Dudley and Stephens*" (1966–67) 34 *University of
    Chicago Law Review* 387 at 388.

3   *R. v. Dudley and Stephens* (1884), 14 QB 273 at 276, n. 5.

4   Mallin, "In Warm Blood" at 388.

5   *Ibid.* at 389.

6   *Ibid.* at 390.

7   *R. v. Dudley and Stephens* (1884), 14 QB 273 at 281.

8   *Southwark London Borough Council* v. *Williams*, [1971] Ch. 734, [1971] 2
    All ER 175 (CA).

9   The queen never got over the indignity, and when Gulliver's enemies con-
    spired to charge him with treason, she was happy to have this offence
    included in the list of charges.

10   *R. v. Dudley and Stephens* (1884), 14 QB 273 at 286.

11   *Ibid.* at 287–88.

12   *Ibid.* at 287.

13   *Ibid.* at 283.

14   *Ibid.* at 288.

15   Mallin, "In Warm Blood" at 407.

16   *R. v. Perka* (1984), 42 CR (3d) 113 (SCC).

17   *Ibid.* at 130 (SCC).

18   *Ibid.*

19   *R. v. Dudley and Stephens* (1884), 14 QB 273 at 279.

20   *R. v. Perka* (1984), 42 CR (3d) 113 at 130 (SCC).

21   *R. v. Morris* (1981), 61 CCC (2d) 163 at 164 (Alta. QB).

22   *R. v. Manning* (1994), 31 CR (4th) 54 at 56 (B.C. Prov. Ct.).

23   The Law Reform Commission of Canada, *Recodifying Criminal Law*
     (Ottawa, 1987), vol. 1 at 33.
24   *R. v. Latimer* (1995), 41 CR (4th) 1 at 38 (Sask. CA).
25   (1995), 40 CR (4th) 141 (SCC).
26   *R. v. Howe (H.L.(E))*, [1987] 2 WLR 568 at 579 (HL).
27   Sir James Fitzjames Stephen, *A History of the Criminal Law of England*,
     vol. 2 (New York: Burt Franklin, 1883) at 107–8, cited in *R. v. Abbott*,
     [1977] AC 755 (Stuart 427).
28   The Supreme Court of Canada has since removed constructive murder
     from the law as being unconstitutional, on the footing that no one should
     be guilty of the heinous offence of murder without actually intending to
     kill.
29   *R. v. Finta* (1994), 28 CR (4th) 265 at 323 (SCC).

CHAPTER 12 : **Kill or Be Killed**

1   The following facts are taken from the appellate decision in *R. v. Pintar*
    (1996), 110 CCC (3d) 402 (Ont. CA). In reciting them, Justice
    Moldaver cautioned that there were other facts that pointed away from
    self-defence, but that they need not be discussed for the purpose of
    describing the law of self-defence. Indeed, the Crown prosecutor con-
    tended that the evidence revealed that Pintar did not kill in self-defence.
    As is always the case when we seek to recreate events through evidence
    and testimony, only the witnesses to the event can know with certainty
    what truly happened, and even they may not have it right. What follows
    is a dramatization of the facts of the case, based on the evidence most
    favourable to Joe Pintar.
2   Pintar, who had not met Gill before, referred to him as LeClair during his
    testimony.
3   *R. v. McIntosh* (1995), 36 CR (4th) 171 at 180 (SCC).
4   A.K.R. Kiralfy, *Potter's Historical Introduction to English Law*, 4th ed.
    (London: Sweet & Maxwell, 1958) at 367, citing 2 Edw. 3, c. 2.
5   *Ibid.* at 367.
6   *Ibid.*
7   *R. v. Pintar* (1996), 110 CCC (3d) 402 at 412 (Ont. CA).
8   Patrick Dare, "Court frees man who killed 'wacko,'" *Ottawa Citizen*, 26
    June 1997, A1–2.

CHAPTER 13: **Losing Control: Provocation and Excusing the Inexcusable**

1   In commenting on the use by defence counsel of the alternative insanity defence during the first Morin trial, Commissioner Kaufman remarked:

> I accept that [the prosecutors] saw [the insanity defence] as confirmation of what they already knew (or thought they knew). . . . This was not unreasonable — the "insanity evidence," carefully scrutinized, may not have made Mr. Morin's guilt more likely, but the fact that such a defence would even be advanced had to impress itself on almost anybody.

The Honourable Fred Kaufman, *The Commission on Proceedings Involving Guy Paul Morin, Report*, vol. 2 (Toronto: Queen's Printer, 1998) at 1069.

2   Aristotle, *The Nichomachean Ethics*, with an English translation by H. Rackham (London: Heinemann, 1947), Bk. V, 8.

3   See A.J. Ashworth, "The Doctrine of Provocation" (1976) 35 *Cambridge Law Journal* 292.

4   *D.P.P. v. Holmes*, [1946] A.C. 588 at 598 (HL).

5   *R. v. Thibert* (1996), 45 CR (4th) 1 at 11 (SCC).

6   *Pearson's Case*, 2 Lewin CC 216, 168 ER 1133.

7   *Holmes v. D.P.P.*, [1946] AC 588 at 598 (HL).

8   *R. v. Haight* (1976), 30 CCC (2d) 168 (Ont. CA).

9   (1996), 45 CR (4th) 1 at 8 (SCC).

10 See Ashworth, "The Doctrine of Provocation" at 307–8.

11 Sheila Galloway and Joanne St. Lewis, *Reforming the Defence of Provocation* (Toronto: Ontario Women's Directorate, 1994) at 2, citing Isabel Grant, Dorothy Chunn, and Christine Boyle, *The Law of Homicide* (Toronto: Carswell, 1994) at 6.2.

12 The case remains unidentified because it was one of the cases examined, with promise of confidentiality, by the *Self-Defence Review — Final Report* (11 July 1997), appointed by the Government of Canada to review the convictions of women who killed and who are under sentence, to identify women who would have been entitled to rely on the defence of self-defence if the current law had applied at the time they were tried. The review, which made recommendations in some cases where the defence of provocation applied (all of which were rejected by the government), could not make a recommendation in this case for the reasons outlined below.

13   Stephen Bindman, "But she just wouldn't stop yelling at me," *Ottawa Citizen*, 22 June 1998, A1.

14   Stephen Bindman, "'Passion Killing' defence in review," *Ottawa Citizen*, 29 June 1998, A1.

CHAPTER 14: The Abuse Excuse: "Psychobabble" and the Protection of Basic Values

1   It is not in fact clear precisely what Kevin said, other than that he was profane and angry.

2   From the statement of Angelique Lyn Lavallee to the police, signed at 8:28 a.m., 31 August 1986.

3   Alan M. Dershowitz, *The Abuse Excuse: And Other Cop-outs, Sob Stories, and Evasions of Responsibility* (Boston: Little, Brown, 1994).

4   (1990), 55 CCC (3d) 97 at 121 (SCC).

5   *Ibid.* at 123.

6   *Ibid.* at 105.

7   Even if they do, Walker fails to reveal that not all the Seligman dogs demonstrated learned helplessness. Some of his dogs were given no prospect of escape and then shocked until they gave up trying to get away. Then they were placed in cages that presented an avenue of escape, if they could find it. These dogs did not even bother looking. Dogs who were zapped for the first time in a cage from which escape was possible had a very different reaction; they got the hell out at the first available opportunity.

8   Patricia Pearson, *When She Was Bad: Violent Women and the Myth of Innocence* (Toronto: Random House, 1997) at 51.

9   Anne M. Coughlin, "Excusing Women" (1994) 82 *California Law Review* 1 at 81.

10   Vidmar, Ellis, and Fischer, "The Culture of Battering and the Role of Mediation in Domestic Violence Cases" (1993) 46 *Southern Methodist University Law Review* 2117.

11   Lynne Henderson, "Whose Justice? Whose Victims?" (1996) 94 *Michigan Law Review* 1596 at 1618.

12   David L. Faigman, "The Battered Woman Syndrome and Self-Defence: A Legal and Empirical Dissent" (1986) 72 *Virginia Law Review* 619.

13   See the critique of Walker's theories in *Buhrle v. State*, 627 P.2d 1374 (Wyo. 1981).

14   Pearson, *When She Was Bad* at 50.

15   Fortunately, this fact has been recognized recently in the Supreme Court of Canada in the case of Margaret Ann Malott, a battered woman who

shot her abusive, drug-dealing husband and then drove to a trailer park and tried to kill his lover: (1998), 121 CCC (3d) 456 (SCC). Although Malott's defence ultimately failed, Justices L'Heureux-Dubé and McLachlin, the two female members of the Court, warned trial judges to be careful not to reject, out of hand, the self-defence claims of women who do not fit themselves within the stereotype of the battered woman. Unfortunately, the Court stopped short of criticizing the theory, re-enforcing the importance of this kind of evidence in the self-defence cases of battered women.

16 *R. v. Malott* (1998), 121 CCC (3d) 456 at 473 (SCC).

17 George P. Fletcher, *With Justice for Some: Protecting Victims' Rights in Criminal Trials* (Reading, Mass.: Addison-Wesley, 1996) at 140.

18 Coughlin, "Excusing Women" at 7.

19 *Ibid.* at 29.

20 Eugene Meehan and Katherine MacRae, "Legal Implications of Premenstrual Syndrome: A Canadian Perspective" (1986) 235 *Canadian Medical Association Journal* 601.

21 And this response is all happening unnecessarily. Recently, at the request of the attorney general of Canada and the solicitor general, Judge Lynn Ratushny, an Ontario Provincial Division judge, conducted a review of the convictions of those women who are currently under sentence for a homicide offence. The purpose was to identify those women who would have had access to the defence of self-defence had they been tried according to the more generous law of self-defence that now exists. In conducting that review, Judge Ratushny did not rely on expert evidence about battered woman syndrome in resolving the ninety-eight cases before her. Why not? Because she did not need it. An examination of the particular facts of the individual case, including learning about all the circumstances of the event and of the relationship of the parties, told her all she needed to know about whether the accused woman really believed she had no choice but to kill, and whether, given her experiences, that was a reasonable belief. She was absolutely right. These are matters that any intelligent and properly instructed juror can answer. See *Self-Defence Review — Final Report* (11 July 1997), submitted to the minister of justice of Canada and the solicitor general of Canada.

22 *R. v. McConnell* (1995), 109 AR 321 (Alta CA), overturned with the dissenting judgment of Conrad JA, approved of (1996), 48 CR (4th) 199 (SCC). In the end, Letendre was convicted of manslaughter and received a six-year sentence. McConnell was found guilty of aggravated assault and sentenced to four years in prison.

23 Fletcher, *With Justice for Some* at 140.

24   Dershowitz, *The Abuse Excuse* at 322–23.

25   Margaret A. Hagen, *Whores of the Court: The Fraud of Psychiatric Testimony and the Rape of American Justice* (New York: Regan Books - HarperCollins Publishers, 1997) at 10–11.

26   *Ibid.* at 69.

27   Stephen J. Schulhofer, "The Trouble with Trials; The Trouble with Us" (1995) 105 *Yale Law Journal* 825 at 850–51.

28   Dershowitz, *The Abuse Excuse* at 323.

29   *Ibid.* at 340.

30   *Ibid.* at 324.

31   Peter Arenella, "Demystifying the Abuse Excuse: Is There One? (1996) *Harvard Journal of Law and Public Policy* 703 at 707.

32   *Globe and Mail*, 30 September 1997, A16.

33   *Ottawa Citizen*, 3 October 1997, A19.

34   In another three cases she found sufficient evidence of provocation to warrant a review of the sentences imposed. *Self-Defence Review — Final Report.*

35   Martha Shaffer, "The Battered Woman Syndrome Revisited: Some Complicating Thoughts Five Years after *Lavallee*" (1997) 47 *University of Toronto Law Journal* 1 at 15.

36   Since the Shaffer study, Margaret Ann Malott has been convicted of murder for killing her abusive mate. Her mistake was undoubtedly in driving from the scene of his death to his girlfriend's trailer and trying to kill her too: *R. v. Malott* (1998), 121 CCC (3d) 456 (SCC).

37   Shaffer, "The Battered Woman Syndrome Revisited" at 18.

38   *Ibid.*

39   This was the finding of the *Self-Defence Review — Final Report*, 23–24.

40   Shaffer, "The Battered Woman Syndrome Revisited" at 18–19.

41   Dershowitz, *The Abuse Excuse* at 312–13.

42   Pearson, *When She Was Bad* at 62.

43   Neal Hall, "Woman who cut off husband's penis won't go to jail," *Ottawa Citizen*, 7 July 1998, A5.

44   Statistics Canada reports that between 1984 and 1993, an average of 110 victims a year were killed by their spouse, with women representing three-quarters of the victims. In 1994 family homicides involved 40 percent of the killings, with 76 percent of spousal homicide victims being female. In total, during that year, twenty men were killed by a current or separated spouse: Statistics Canada, *Juristat*, vol.15, no.11, *Homicide in Canada — 1994*, Orest Fedorowycz at 11. In the United States, between 1976 and 1985, studies suggest that the overall rate of murdered wives to murdered husbands is much higher. It was found to be 1.3 to 1.0 in a

study by J.A. Mercy and L.E. Saltzman, "Fatal Violence among Spouses in the United States, 1976–85" (1989) 79 (5) *American Journal of Public Health* 595. Dershowitz cites federal Department of Justice Statistics disclosing that for all spousal murders, American women are the defendants in more than 40 percent of the cases: *The Abuse Excuse* at 31. In conducting her study of the convictions of women who kill, Judge Ratushny sent out 236 application packages to women currently under sentence in Canada for homicide. Of those, most had killed their partner: *Self-Defence Review — Final Report* at 15.

45 Speaking of similar killings, a recent report states: "So-called honour crimes remain common in Turkey's religiously conservative Anatolian hinterland." Amberin Zaman, "Attempted 'honour' murder appals Turks," *Ottawa Citizen*, 19 February 1998, A11.

46 *R. v. Hem*, [1989] BCJ No. 1566 (BC Co. Ct.).

47 Don Terry, "Tradition, law collide in new homeland," *Ottawa Citizen*, 2 December 1997, A5, quoting the *New York Times*.

48 Neil Bissoondath, "A Question of Belonging: Multiculturalism and Citizenship" in William Kaplan, ed., *Belonging: The Meaning and Future of Canadian Citizenship* (Montreal and Kingston: McGill-Queen's University Press, 1993) 368 at 380–81.

49 Lisa Fitterman, "Haitian culture induces judge to leniency for rapists," *Ottawa Citizen*, 27 January 1998, A3.

50 "Judge accepts 'spirit defence,' " *Ottawa Citizen*, 30 May 1997, A2.

51 " 'Sorcerers' killed by lynch mobs," *Globe and Mail*, 2 August 1997, A2.

52 See *Tutton v. Tutton*, [1989] 1 SCR 1392, where the sincerely held religious beliefs of the accused that their daughter had been cured by the Virgin Mary were not allowed to influence the assessment of whether they acted negligently in refusing to obtain medical treatment for her.

53 " 'Possessed' Maori spared jail," *Ottawa Citizen*, 24 March 1998, A10.

54 Schulhofer, "The Trouble with Trials" at 852.

CHAPTER 15: **Disordered Minds: Insanity, Automatism, and Intoxication**

1 For a compelling and sometimes moving account of the experiences of Ken and Karen, see June Callwood, *The Sleepwalker* (Toronto: Lester & Orpen Dennys, 1990).

2 The illustration is based on the tragic death of two-and-a-half-month-old Hesham Sayegh, whose mother, Dunia, was holding him as he went over the falls. The Crown initially charged her with murder, but reduced the charges to manslaughter before the preliminary inquiry. The judge

conducting the preliminary inquiry threw the charges out because there was no evidence to support even a manslaughter conviction. Edward L. Greenspan and George Jonas, *Greenspan: The Case for the Defence* (Toronto: Macmillan of Canada, 1987), chapter 1.

3   Summary of the evidence by Justice Galligan, *R. v. Parks* (1990), 56 CCC (3d) 449 at 461 (Ont. CA), affirmed (1992), 75 CCC (3d) 287 (SCC).

4   *R. v. K.* (1971), 3 CCC (3d) 84 at 84 (Ont. HC).

5   Automatism caused by voluntary intoxication has its own special rules, which will be discussed below.

6   George P. Fletcher, *With Justice for Some: Protecting Victims' Rights in Criminal Trials* (Reading, Mass.: Addison-Wesley, 1996) at 23.

7   The following account of the M'Naughton case, sometimes referred to as the McNaughton case, is taken from Nigel Walker, *Crime and Insanity in England* (Edinburgh: Edinburgh University Press, 1968) I at 84–103.

8   *Cooper v. R.* (1980), 51 CCC (2d) 129 at 145 (SCC).

9   *R. v. O.* (1959) 3 *Criminal Law Quarterly* 151, where the charge to the jury is found, and see *R. v. Simpson* (1977), 35 CCC (2d) 337 at 352 (Ont. CA), where the facts are provided.

10 The standard diagnostic manual, *Diagnostic and Statistical Manual of Mental Disorders*, 4th ed. (Washington, DC: American Psychiatric Institute, 1994) [*DSM IV*] at 640–50, lists psychopathy and sociopathy under the mental disorder known as "Antisocial Personality Disorder."

11 *R. v. Chaulk* (1991), 2 CR (4th) 1 at 45 (SCC).

12 *R. v. Oommen* (1994), 30 CR (4th) 195 (SCC).

13 Neil Vidmar, "Generic Prejudice and the Presumption of Guilt in Sex Abuse Trials" (1997) 21 *Law and Human Behaviour* 5 at 22.

14 Patricia Chisholm and Ross Laver, "A Matter of Opinion," *MacLean's*, 18 January 1993, at 55.

15 Walker, *Crime and Insanity in England* at 89. The book is called *Medical Jurisprudence as It Relates to Insanity according to the Law of England* (1817).

16 Mike Blanchfield, "Killer was no Romeo with a crossbow, Crown scoffs," *Ottawa Citizen*, 10 February 1993, B1.

17 Mike Blanchfield, "Killer regained moral values quickly, MD says," *Ottawa Citizen*, 6 February 1993, G4.

18 Mike Blanchfield, "Psychiatrist uncertain McGregor insane when he killed wife," *Ottawa Citizen*, 12 February 1993, B2.

19 *R. v. Oommen* (1994), 30 CR (4th) 195 at 205 (SCC).

20 *R. v. Parks* (1992), 75 CCC (3d) 287 at 310 (SCC).

21 *Ibid.* at 311 (SCC).

22 *D.P.P. v. Beard*, [1920] AC 479 at 502.

23   An alternative but equally sophisticated mental state could suffice. If the accused saw that the complainant may not be consenting but chose to go ahead anyway, he could be convicted, even though it could not be said that he knew she was not consenting.

24   *R. v. Daviault* (1994), 33 CR (4th) 165 at 213–14 (SCC).

25   *R. v. Parks* (1992), 75 CCC (3d) 287 at 311 (SCC).

26   Joseph S. Wilkinson, "The Possibility of Alcoholic Automatism: Some Empirical Evidence" (1997) 2 *Canadian Criminal Law Review* 217.

27   *R. v. Lafleur* (1996), 50 CR (4th) 386 (Que. SC).

CHAPTER 16: **The Sad Truth about Victims' Rights**

1   *R. v. Coelho* (1995), 41 CR (4th) 324 at 330 (BCSC).

2   David Mellinkoff, *The Conscience of a Lawyer* (St. Paul, Minn.: West Publishing Co., 1973) at 42.

3   A.K.R. Kiralfy, *Potter's Historical Introduction to English Law*, 4th ed. (London: Sweet & Maxwell, 1958) at 348.

4   Mellinkoff, *The Conscience of a Lawyer* at 42.

5   *Ibid.*

6   *Ashford v. Thornton*, 1 B & Ald. 421, 106 ER 149 (1818).

7   59 Geor. III, c. 46 (1819).

8   Kiralfy, *Potter's Historical Introduction to English Law* at 348.

9   See H.L. Pohlman, *Oliver Wendell Holmes & Utilitarian Jurisprudence* (Cambridge, Mass.: Harvard University Press, 1984) at 19.

10   Kiralfy, *Potter's Historical Introduction to English Law* at 349.

11   *Ibid.* at 351.

12   See Pohlman, *Oliver Wendell Holmes & Utilitarian Jurisprudence* at 20.

13   Kiralfy, *Potter's Historical Introduction to English Law* at 352.

14   *R. v. Friginette* (1994), 53 BCAC 153 at 155 (BCCA).

15   *Ibid.*

16   Pohlman, *Oliver Wendell Holmes & Utilitarian Jurisprudence* at 19.

17   *Ibid.*

18   YB 21 Hen. VII, T, pl. 5, cited in Kiralfy, *Potter's Historical Introduction to English Law* at 359.

19   *R. v. Levitt* (1629) Carcoar. 538, cited in Kiralfy, *Potter's Historical Introduction to English Law* at 359.

20   Pohlman, *Oliver Wendell Holmes & Utilitarian Jurisprudence* at 18.

21   Ron Stang, "Murder acquittal triggers wrongful death suit," *The Law Times*, 23–29 June 1997 at 1–2.

22   *R. v. Boucher*, [1955] SCR 16 at 23–24.

23   George P. Fletcher, *With Justice for Some: Protecting Victims' Rights in Criminal Trials* (Reading, Mass.: Addison-Wesley, 1996) at 248–50.

24   Stephen J. Schulhofer, "The Trouble with Trials; The Trouble with Us" (1995) 105 *Yale Law Journal* 825 at 840.

25   Lynne Henderson, "Whose Justice? Which Victims'? (1996) 94 *Michigan Law Review* 1596 at 1605.

26   Fletcher, *With Justice for Some* at 248.

27   Schulhofer, "The Trouble with Trials" at 826.

28   Schulhofer, "The Trouble with Trials" at 847.

29   Henderson, "Whose Justice?" at 1607.

30   The law has since been amended. A seventeen-year-old charged with homicide will now be tried in adult court unless he or she establishes that Young Offender court is the suitable forum.

31   See, for example, *An Act Respecting Victims of Crime*, 1995, RSO, c. 6, s. 2(1) (x).

32   "Live or die? It's his call," *Ottawa Citizen*, 30 May 1997, A8.

33   Caroline Davies and Colin Randall, "Mystery shrouds fate of Briton," *ibid.*, 24 September 1997, A9. "Slain nurse's brother demands $2 million," *ibid.*, 25 September 1997, A8.

34   "Nurse convicted of killing to sue victim's brother," *Ottawa Citizen*, 25 May 1998, A9.

35   *R. v. Sweeney* (1992), 11 CR (4th) 1 at 15 (BCCA).

36   Fletcher, *With Justice for Some* at 200–1.

37   See, for example, *Report of the Attorney General's Advisory Committee on Charge Screening, Disclosure, and Resolution Discussions*, The Honourable G. Arthur Martin, chair (Toronto: Queen's Printer of Ontario, 1993) at 100.

38   Lynne N. Henderson, "The Wrongs in Victim's Rights" (1985) 37 *Stanford Law Review* 937 at 953.

39   *R. v. L.(D.O.)*, [1993] 4 SCR 419.

40   *R. v. Levogiannis*, [1993] 4 SCR 475.

41   *R. v. O'Connor* (1995), 44 CR (4th) 1, per L'Heureux-Dubé J, dissenting, with the concurrence of three other Justices, on the scheme adopted by the bare majority of the Court. *R. v. A.(L.L.)* v. *B.(A.)* (1995), 44 CR (4th) 91, with a majority of the Court agreeing in the result.

42   *R. v. Seaboyer*, [1991] 2 SCR 577. The Court spoke of competing interests of a constitutional nature rather than of firm constitutional rights for victims.

43   *R. v. Osolin*, [1993] 4 SCR 595.

44   "Cowboys' accuser pleads guilty to perjury," *Ottawa Citizen*, 16 September 1997, A6.

45   George Jonas, " 'Putting the victim on trial' should happen more often," *ibid.*, 1 August 1997, A15.

CHAPTER 17: **Responding to the Credibility Crisis**

1 Franz Kafka, *The Trial* (Toronto: Alfred A. Knopf, 1992) at 234–35.
2 *Ibid.* at 251.
3 Julian V. Roberts and Loretta J. Stalans, *Public Opinion, Crime and Criminal Justice* (Boulder, Colo.: Westview Press, 1997) at 292.
4 *Crime (Sentences) Act 1997* (UK), 1997, c. 43, s. 2(2):

> The court shall impose a life sentence . . .
> unless the court is of the opinion that there are exceptional circumstances relating to either of the offences or to the offender which justify it not doing so.

5 Walter Schaeffer, "Federalism and State Criminal Procedure" (1956) 70 *Harvard Law Review* 1 at 26.